A Commentary on Daniel

A Commentary on Daniel

by
Leon Wood

ZONDERVAN PUBLISHING HOUSE
A DIVISION OF THE ZONDERVAN CORPORATION
GRAND RAPIDS, MICHIGAN

A COMMENTARY ON DANIEL

Copyright © 1973 by The Zondervan Corporation
Grand Rapids, Michigan

Library of Congress Catalog Card Number 72-83884

Printed in the United States of America

CONTENTS

PREFACE

The book of Daniel stands as a monument to one of the outstanding personalities of the Old Testament. Daniel, an executive in one of the grand courts of ancient time, stood tall in faith and obedience to God, maintaining a brilliant testimony in spite of engulfing pagan wickedness. A study of his experiences provides continual example and challenge to the Christian of any day. God honored Daniel by inspiring him to write the book called by his name, and gave him remarkable information pertaining to the future through a series of visions. Because of this information, the book of Daniel has been called the Old Testament's counterpart to the New Testament's book of Revelation. It provides many of the core truths by which one may understand large portions of predictive prophecy found elsewhere in the Scriptures.

Numerous commentaries on Daniel have been written, but few in recent years. Works principally employed in the writing of this exposition can be found listed in the footnotes and/or bibliography. These fall mainly under four categories. A few are liberal, represented by the monumental volume of James A. Montgomery. Others are conservative but amillennial in eschatology, represented by the fine works of C. F. Keil, Albert Barnes, H. C. Leupold, and E. J. Young. A few are premillennial but more popular in style, represented by the helpful studies of A. C. Gaebelein and H. A. Ironside. One is conservative, premillennial, scholarly, and of recent date: that of John Walvoord. The author wishes this last work had appeared in time for him to make greater use of it.

The intention of the present writing is to provide a grammatico-historical commentary from the premillennial viewpoint, using information recently brought to light by archaeological and linguistic research. Much more is known today regarding historical background to Daniel than only a few years ago. Especially important has been the reading of the Babylonian Chronicles, giving the official history of Babylonia from the point of view of the royal court. A particular attempt is made in the Introduction to correlate this information with the history revealed in Daniel's book.

The author has long favored commentaries which proceed verse by verse and phrase by phrase. A commentary of this kind must deal with every significant question, if only to say very little about it or even to state that no answer is known. He has also liked commentaries which present argumentation, point by point, for views espoused. This procedure has been seen as particularly important with Daniel, since positions in eschatology, which play a major role in one's view of the book, differ markedly. He has likewise appreciated commentaries which spend less time in refuting an opposing writer and give more time to presenting positive evidence for the interpretation favored. Some attention must be given, of course, to opposing writers, for one's own view can best be seen in its distinctiveness when so compared; but still the prime endeavor should be analysis, not refutation. These considerations have provided guidelines in the writing of this commentary.

The translation used is the author's own. Some reference to the original words has been thought unavoidable. The intention, however, has been to give sufficient explanation so that the person lacking a knowledge of the original languages can follow the thought without difficulty. Paragraphing under translated verses carries the following rationale: a new paragraph is begun with each new verse (should more than one be involved); and more than one paragraph is employed for a single verse if the commentary is extended in length. The spelling "Yahweh" is employed, rather than the more common "Jehovah," for the name (tetragrammaton) of God. As explained more fully under 9:2,4, this spelling shows the original pronunciation of the name more accurately. The book of Daniel employs this name for God in chapter nine only.

ABBREVIATIONS

ANET   *Ancient Near Eastern Texts,* James B. Pritchard, ed.

ASV   American Standard Version

BD   Barnes' commentary on Daniel

BDB   *Hebrew Lexicon,* Brown, Driver, Briggs

DLD   *Daniel and the Latter Days,* Robert D. Culver

DM   *Darius the Mede,* John C. Whitcomb

DP   *Daniel the Prophet,* E. B. Pusey

GD   *The Prophet Daniel,* Arno C. Gaebelein

IABD   *In and Around the Book of Daniel,* Charles Boutflower

KDC   Keil and Delitzsch commentaries

KJV   King James Version

LCD   *Lange's Commentary on Daniel,* O. Zockler

LED   *Exposition of Daniel,* Herbert C. Leupold

MICC   *Commentary on the Book of Daniel,* James A. Montgomery

NB   *Nabonidus and Belshazzar,* Raymond P. Dougherty

NIP   *Nations in Prophecy,* John F. Walvoord

SD   *Studies in Daniel,* Robert Dick Wilson

SOTI   *A Survey of Old Testament Introduction,* Gleason L. Archer, Jr.

TTC   *Things To Come,* J. Dwight Pentecost

WD   *Daniel, The Key to Prophetic Revelation,* John F. Walvoord

YPD   *The Prophecy of Daniel,* Edward J. Young

A Commentary on Daniel

INTRODUCTION

A. PLACE IN ISRAEL'S HISTORY

The historical events set forth in the book of Daniel transpired at a difficult time in Israel's existence. This was her day of severe punishment by captivity at the hand of God. When the tribes of Israel had first settled in the Promised Land, God had told them that they would prosper under His blessing, if they remained faithful to Him (Deut. 28:1-14), but that they would suffer grievous punishment, if they did not (Deut. 28:15-68). That which happened was the latter, and punishment at the hands of enemies ensued, already in the days of the judges (Judg. 3-16). The time of David brought temporary reprieve, because of his leadership in faithfulness. But Solomon, after a good beginning, "turned away from the Lord," and problems arose, leading to a complete separation within the kingdom just after his reign. Prophets were used to speak strongly against sin and to sound warnings of continued punishment and even captivity to a foreign land, but to no avail. Captivity did come for the northern division of the kingdom, Israel, in 722 B.C., when Samaria fell to Assyria (2 Kings 17:4-23); and then also for the southern division, Judah, just over one century later, at the hand of the Babylonians.

The main blow to Judah came in 586 B.C. when Jerusalem was destroyed and the country became a province of Babylonia (2 Kings 25:1-21). Eleven years before (597), however, a prior taking into captivity had occurred when Jehoiachin ruled, and some 10,000 leading people were carried to Babylon (2 Kings 24:11-16). Eight years before this still, Daniel, his three friends, and other young Judeans had been forced to go (605). Their captivity in Babylon is the occasion of central interest in the book of Daniel. This occasion is sometimes called the first aspect, in the series of three, of the overall Judean captivity. Thus, Daniel had been in Babylon for eight years when Judeans of the captivity of 597 arrived, and nineteen years when those of 586 came. He continued to live during the full period of the

13

captivity and was able to witness the return to Judah of many of the people in 538/537 B.C.

It is noteworthy that the time of Daniel marks the third of four great periods of miracles in the history of God's working with men. The first period came at the time of Moses and the deliverance of Israel from Egypt; the second, at the time of the outstanding prophets, Elijah and Elisha; and the fourth, at the time of Christ's first advent. All of these times were characterized by significant developments, calling for the demonstration of authenticating credentials. The first and fourth were the occasions of establishing the Old and the New Covenants, respectively; and the first and third, the two times of captivity to, and deliverance from, a foreign power. The second period, when Elijah and Elisha wrought miracles, was the day of beginning for an enlarged prophetic ministry. Prophets had ministered before, though not on a national basis, warning the nation as a whole of impending punishment for sin, if correction was not forthcoming. God was now instituting this form of ministry, and He wanted the people to recognize that Elijah and Elisha, and those who would follow them, were indeed His authorized servants.

Daniel's time especially called for credentials so that the pagans, among whom the Judeans had been forced to live, might have reason to think highly of Israel's God, Yahweh. This was significant because normal factors of evaluation tended to make them think otherwise, a line of reasoning to be explored at greater length presently. Credentials were necessary also in respect to Daniel's own people. They needed to see the sure, miraculous hand of their God working, that they might be encouraged and press on in their faith, under difficult circumstances. It should be noted further that God's presence was made evident, not only in miracles of deed, but also in miracles of word. It was necessary that the people hear from God as well as witness His power. The people about them were saying that God had cast them aside (Jer. 33:24), and they needed to hear that this was not so. They needed to hear, indeed, that God actually had a long, attractive future in mind for them. Through Daniel, the welcome information was revealed and recorded in his book, characterizing the book as containing the most explicit predictions in all the Old Testament.

B. Daniel the Man

Daniel stands as one of the most admirable of God's servants in the Old Testament. His name means either "God is my Judge" or "God is Judge," depending on whether the middle "i" is taken as a first person suffix or merely a connective *(yôd compaginis)*. Little is known of Daniel's early life. His parents are not named, but he was clearly of either royal or noble descent (Dan. 1:3),[1] and his parents must have been devoted people to account for his own remarkable dedication to God. His early home was likely in the capital city, Jerusalem, and from where he had been taken captive to Babylon, along with his three close friends—Hananiah, Mishael, and Azariah. Each probably was not more than fifteen years of age.

The book of Daniel sets forth five outstanding events from Daniel's life in Babylon. The first was the decision he made, along with the three friends, to request food other than that prescribed by King Nebuchadnezzar (ch. 1). This came almost immediately after the arrival of the four in the foreign land. The second, occurring about two years later, concerned Daniel's revealing to the king what the king had dreamed and the interpretation of it (ch. 2). The third had to do with Daniel's interpretation of a second dream of Nebuchadnezzar, which likely came about thirty years after the first. This event concerned Nebuchadnezzar's seven-year period of insanity, which is best taken as having transpired toward the close of his forty-three-year reign (ch. 4). The fourth was his reading of the miraculous writing on the palace wall of Belshazzar. This event occurred the evening prior to Babylon's fall to the Persians (539 B.C.) when Daniel was at least eighty years of age (ch. 5). The fifth, the occasion of his being cast into the den of lions, came probably within three years of Babylon's capture by Cyrus (ch. 6). At this time Daniel had chosen to honor his God rather than obey an improper, foolish decree of King Darius. The Persian ruler had found it necessary to effect the punishment designated in the decree he had signed, even though trickery had been used by enemies of Daniel to persuade him to sign it. One event listed does not concern Daniel, but, rather, his three friends, when they refused to bow to Nebuchadnezzar's image and were cast into a fiery furnace as a result (ch. 3). Thus, all of the first six chapters of the book concern primarily historical events in the life of Daniel and/or the three friends.

Intermixed with these events were four times of revelation, given by God to Daniel. These concerned future events involving God's people. The first two came in the first and third years, respectively, of Belshazzar's reign, when Daniel was about sixty-four and sixty-six years old; and the last two in the first and third years of Cyrus' rule, when the prophet was about eighty-one and eighty-three years old. The first three times of receiving revelations are recorded, respectively, in chapters 7, 8, and 9, and the fourth in chapters 10, 11, and 12. A basic division of the book is suggested by the fact that the first six chapters are principally history, and the last six mainly predictive prophecy.

---

[1] Josephus (*Antiq.* X, 10, 1) says that David and his three friends were all kinsmen of King Zedekiah.

Other than in his own book, Daniel is mentioned five times in Scripture: Ezekiel 14:14, 20; 28:3; Matthew 24:15; and Mark 13:14. In the first two instances, Daniel is named in association with Noah and Job as an outstanding example of righteousness; in the third as a paragon of wisdom, with whom the king of Tyre could not hope to measure himself.[2] The two New Testament references provide evidence regarding the proper interpretation of an aspect of Daniel's predictive revelations; for Jesus there identifies the "abomination of desolation" mentioned by Daniel (9:27; 12:11) with a development falling in the Great Tribulation time.

Ezekiel's three references to Daniel are important for what they say as to the character of Daniel.[3] Daniel's own book presents him as a man of outstanding righteousness and wisdom, and Ezekiel's references significantly reinforce that presentation. To appreciate this reinforcement, it should be noted that Ezekiel was Daniel's contemporary, arriving as a captive in Babylon eight years later. By this time, Daniel would have already held the important position he attained in the government, and Ezekiel, it may be assumed, would have made inquiry, on arrival, regarding the young Judean who had risen to such a height so quickly. He likely thought at first that one would have to cater to pagan ways to do this. But Ezekiel clearly had discovered differently and was sufficiently impressed by what he had found to mention Daniel in parallel with Noah and Job as a great man of righteousness. This fact is still more remarkable when one recognizes that persons who live in a prior generation tend to stand out more brilliantly than contemporaries. Both Noah and Job lived centuries prior to the day when Ezekiel listed Daniel with them.

There is evidence for other fine qualities of Daniel. His three-year education in Babylon, which no doubt followed good training before this in Jerusalem, equipped him well for his life's work. Along with this must have been a natural ability for administration, because once granted a high position at the court, he remained there. Later he achieved a place even as one of three top presidents in the Persian government of Darius. This honor was clearly the result of God's special blessing, but God regularly employs natural means to accomplish His will. Still another quality was his admirable faith in God. While still a youth of about seventeen, he and his three friends had faith to believe that God would reveal to them the dream of King

[2] The view of some scholars that the Daniel mentioned by Ezekiel is to be identified with a semi-mythical person from the epic literature of Ras Shamra, must be rejected. It is unthinkable that Ezekiel would have compared a pagan, Baal-worshiping personage with the two historical stalwarts, Noah and Job, especially on the score of righteousness.

[3] The first two were given six years after Ezekiel arrived in the land (Ezek. 8:1), and the other, eleven years after his arrival (Ezek. 26:1), giving ample time for Ezekiel's inquiry and conclusion.

Nebuchadnezzar, and the four held a prayer meeting to ask God to do so (2:14-23).

In view of the kind of person Daniel was, and the degree to which God was pleased to prosper him in the foreign government, it follows that God desired to accomplish something particular through him. Two areas of work suggest themselves. The first concerns Daniel's being used to maintain the honor of the true God in the pagan land, when natural developments tended to make the Babylonians think of Him dishonorably. Pagans evaluated any foreign deity in terms of the size of the country whose people worshiped him, the degree of prosperity of that country, and the size and success of the army. When Judah had been taken captive by Babylonia, her God did not measure well by any of these standards. To Babylonians, their own deities seemed to be stronger. This was not a pleasing situation to God, and He used Daniel as His special instrument to bring a change.[4] Particularly through the interpretation of two dreams for Nebuchadnezzar, the reading of the miraculous writing on the palace wall for Belshazzar, and the deliverance from the lions' den in the reign of Darius, God used Daniel to prompt adoration from the lips of these foreign rulers (cf. Dan. 2:46-49; 3:28-30 [which concerns God's use also of the three friends]; 4:1-3, 34-37; 5:29; 6:25-27).

The other area of work concerns Daniel's enhancement of the welfare of Judeans, while they were in captivity. One would naturally expect the lot of captives to be a hard and oppressive one, but this was not the case for many, if not the majority, of Judeans in Babylonia. There is evidence that they lived in a good farming area of the land, had their own homes, enjoyed freedom of movement, continued their own institutions of elders, priests, and prophets, experienced employment opportunities, and even carried on correspondence with the homeland.[5] The likely human factor to account for this surprising condition was the influence of Daniel, working from his position in the government. A principal reason for God's permitting him to be taken captive eight years earlier than the captivity involving the large group of Judeans may well have been to allow opportunity for him to achieve such a position. Then Daniel may also have had much to do with effecting the return of the captives to Judah in due time. He still lived at the time of their return and, as has been noted, held the highest post of his life under Darius (6:2, 3). That this was true was most remarkable, especially since a complete change in government had occurred, and he was then more than

---

[4] This was much as He used Joseph and later Moses in Egypt centuries before. The Pharaohs of the day were caused to change their thinking regarding Israel's God (cf. Ex. 5:2) as a result of God's working through these two men.
[5] Cf. L. Wood, *A Survey of Israel's History* (Grand Rapids: Zondervan Publishing House, 1970), pp. 385-87 for discussion.

eighty years of age. God's hand is unmistakable in Daniel's promotion, suggesting that He yet had work for him to do. This work could well have been to bring influence on King Cyrus to issue the decree which would permit the return to Judah.

C. Languages and the Jewish-Gentile Division of the Book

The book of Daniel is unique in the Old Testament in having an extensive section written in Aramaic.[6] The Aramaic extends from 2:4 to 7:28; thus less than half of the book was written in Hebrew. The reason for the use of Aramaic is best seen in terms of the subject matter of the section where it is found. The material deals with matters pertaining to the Gentile world, with little notice of God's people, the Jews; and, apparently, God saw that Aramaic, the language of the Gentile world of the day, was more suitable to record it than was Hebrew, which was distinctly Jewish.

This fact suggests the thought that another division to the book exists, besides that noted earlier. The one noted was that the first six chapters are basically history and the last six prophecy. This division must stand, because the materials presented clearly fall into this literary pattern. But the employment of the two languages points to an equally valid division, which has to do with the identity of the people concerned, rather than with literary criteria. For want of better terms, these two divisions may be called by the names "Jewish" and "Gentile."

The first chapter of the book clearly places itself in the "Jewish" category, because here four young Judeans are taken captive from their native land and placed in a position where they must decide whether to remain faithful to their God or not. The eighth chapter is again of this group, for it concerns oppression of the Jews by the Syrian ruler, Antiochus Epiphanes (called here "little horn"), and these oppressions are made typical of similar actions to be brought by the Antichrist upon them much later, during the time of the Great Tribulation. The ninth chapter belongs to the same group, because it concerns seventy weeks of years in the history of the Jews, extending from the time of Ezra even to that of the Antichrist again (with a considerable time-gap intervening between the sixty-ninth and seventieth weeks). Then the tenth, eleventh, and twelfth chapters must also be so classified, because they set forth oppressions of the Jews, effected first by Antiochus Epiphanes and then by the Antichrist once more.

The intervening seven chapters, however, place matters pertaining to Gentile history in the fore. The second and seventh chapters, which begin and end the section, are parallel in content and show

---

[6] Two other Old Testament books do have shorter sections: Ezra 4:8-6:18; 7:12-26; and Jeremiah 10:11.

this stress by setting forth the overall scope of Gentile history, following the time of Daniel. The second chapter does this through the symbolism of Nebuchadnezzar's dream-image, which predicts the rise and fall of four successive Gentile empires (Babylonian, Medo-Persian, Greek, Roman), and then the destruction of the last one, in a restored form, by the rise of Christ's millennial kingdom. The seventh chapter presents similar information, under the symbolism of four successive animals, depicting the same four Gentile empires, with a climax coming again in Christ's dominant future kingdom.

Between these two chapters, four chapters intervene which picture Gentile power in action, with its definite limitations before almighty God. The four chapters fall into two pairs, in respect to the type of picture they present. The third and sixth chapters set forth Gentile power bringing persecution on the people of God. The former does this in telling of King Nebuchadnezzar forcing Daniel's three friends to bow to his image; and the latter in describing how officials under King Darius attempt to take the life of Daniel by means of a treacherous plot. Both occasions involve unjust punishment being brought upon God's representatives, with corresponding supernatural deliverance being effected in their behalf as a reward for faithfulness. The fourth and fifth chapters tell of supernatural revelations given to Gentile kings and the need in each instance for a man of God to give the interpretations. The former concerns Nebuchadnezzar's second dream, which remains an enigma for him until Daniel comes to give the meaning; and the latter the miraculous writing on the palace wall of Belshazzar, which again calls for interpretation by Daniel, now very aged. The first pair of chapters illustrates the fact that the world has long brought persecution on the people of God and that God in turn has granted gracious protection for those found faithful. The second pair pictures the dependence of the world upon almighty God and the need for the children of God to tell the people of the world about God's truth, if they are to know it.

D. AUTHOR OF THE BOOK

Modern critical scholarship denies Daniel's authorship of this book. It believes that an unknown penman wrote it about 165 B.C. for the purpose of encouraging disheartened Jews who had recently suffered under Antiochus Epiphanes. A main reason for this view is that the book admittedly presents history at least until the time of Antiochus in remarkable detail, and liberal thinking holds that such material could have been written only after the events had occurred. Those who accept the idea of supernatural revelation do not have this problem.

There are several reasons for believing, contrary to this liberal thinking, that Daniel himself was indeed the author of the book.

1. The book directly presents Daniel as the author of at least the

latter half of it, because he is made the recipient repeatedly of the divine revelations given, and he, as author, speaks regularly in the first person in chapters seven to twelve. Also, in 12:4 Daniel is directed to preserve "the book," a reference to at least a substantial portion of the entire book, if not all.

2. That Daniel must have written also the first half follows from the unity of the book, as demonstrated by several considerations. (1) The two halves of the book are interdependent; which is seen, for instance, in a comparison of Daniel's interpretation of Nebuchadnezzar's dream in chapter two and the revelations given directly through him in chapters seven through twelve. (2) Terminology used in 2:28; 4:2, 7, 10 of the first half; is similar to that of 7:1, 2, 15 of the second. (3) Unity exists in the presentation of Daniel as a person throughout the book. (4) All chapters combine in the purpose of showing the supremacy of the God of heaven over all nations and their supposed deities. (5) The literary unity of the book is acknowledged even by leading liberal scholars, such as Charles, Driver, Pfeiffer, and Rowley.

3. The author shows remarkable knowledge of Babylonian and early Persian history, such as would be true of a contemporary like Daniel. In the fourth chapter, Nebuchadnezzar is presented correctly as the creator of the Neo-Babylonian empire.[7] In the fifth chapter, Belshazzar is set forth as co-ruler of Babylon, a fact recently demonstrated by archaeological research. In the sixth chapter, Darius is presented as ruler of Babylon, even though Cyrus was the supreme ruler of Persia; Cyrus is now known to have appointed one Gubaru in this capacity, with whom Darius may well be identified.[8] In the second chapter (cf. vv. 12, 13, 46) Nebuchadnezzar is shown to have been able to change Babylonian laws which he had previously made (such a change is now known to have been possible in Babylonia); whereas in the sixth chapter (cf. vv. 8, 9, 12, 15) Darius is presented as not having been able to do this (such a change is now known to have been impossible in Persia).

4. Manuscript fragments of the book have been found in Cave I and Cave IV of Wadi Qumran, and these date to at least the first century, and probably the second, B.C., which makes the date of 165 B.C. for the writing of the book, as held by liberals, most unlikely.

5. Christ Himself spoke of Daniel as having foretold that the "abomination of desolation" would stand in the holy place (Matt. 24:15; Mk. 13:14), and it is commonly and correctly accepted that He referred to what is stated in Daniel 9:27 and 12:11.

Modern critical scholarship sets forth numerous arguments for its

---

[7] Cf. R. H. Pfeiffer, *Introduction to the Old Testament* (New York: Harper and Brothers, 1941), pp. 758, 59 for his comment, as a liberal.

[8] Cf. J. Whitcomb, *DM,* a work devoted to substantiating this point.

position also; but these may be answered without difficulty when one accepts the basic idea of supernatural revelation.

1. The assertion is made that in 1:21 the writer refers to the date of Daniel's death, and the assumption is that no author could do this of himself. The author declares there, however, only that Daniel lived until Cyrus' first year, without indicating that he then died. In 10:1, in fact, it is made clear that he did not die at that time, but lived at least until the third year of Cyrus.[9]

2. The statement is made that the author avoids using the name "Yahweh" for God, and that this can be expected of a postexilic author, but not of Daniel, who lived before the name ceased to be spoken (as did occur following the Exile). In the ninth chapter, however, the name is used no less than seven times. On the same basis, then, this argues against a postexilic authorship. This reasoning of the liberals overlooks the fact that the employment of names for God in the Old Testament depends on the thought-context, each name carrying a particular connotation suitable to the text.

3. Evidence is presented that the book of Daniel has a literary style like that of the apocryphal books, which do date much later than Daniel. The response may be given that, though similarity does exist, it could well be because these later books copy a style set long before by Daniel. This explanation finds support in the probability that writers of the Maccabean period (from which these books date), having seen the exact correspondence between Daniel's predictions and history recently experienced, would have come to respect the book highly and would have been inclined to pattern their own books after it.

4. Frequent reference is made to a few Persian and Greek words in the book, asserting that these could have been known only by a writer living after the day of Daniel. Daniel himself, however, wrote in early Persian times and would have known Persian vocabulary; and the Greek words are limited to the names of three musical instruments, that may have been imported earlier into Babylon. Archaeological discoveries show that considerable trade and cultural interchange existed by this time between countries of the region, including Greece and Babylonia. It was formerly said also that the Aramaic of Daniel is western and not the type used in Babylon in Daniel's day. Recent discoveries of fifth-century Aramaic documents, however, show that "Daniel was, like Ezra, written in a form of Imperial Aramaic (Reichsaramäisch), an official or literary dialect which had currency in all parts of the Near East."[10]

---

[9] Cf. further discussion in the commentary under 1:21.
[10] Archer, *SOTI,* p. 376. Cf. E. M. Yamauchi, *Greece and Babylon* (Grand Rapids: Baker Book House, 1967), pp. 17-24; also R. D. Wilson, "The Aramaic of Daniel," in *Biblical and Theological Studies,* p. 296, who states that, had Daniel

5. Objection is made to the alleged advanced theology of the book, particularly in respect to angels and the resurrection of the dead. The ideas presented are said to have been developed only by Maccabean times. This argument assumes, however, a type of evolution in theological concept contrary to Scripture. God's people did come to understand such concepts in greater fullness, as God revealed more concerning them; but God had given much information regarding both angels and resurrection even long before Daniel (cf., concerning angels, Gen. 19:1-22; 2 Sam. 24:16, 17; 2 Kings 19:35; Job 1:6; 2:1; Ps. 91:11; Zech. 1:9, 12-14, 19 and, concerning resurrection, Job 14:11-14; 19:25-27; Ps. 16:10; 49:15; Isa. 25:8; 26:19; Hosea 13:14; Heb. 11:17-19).

6. The fact that the book of Daniel appears in the Old Testament wit' :he "writings" of the third section, rather than with the "prophets" of the second, is said to indicate lateness of authorship; assuming that the book would have been included in the second section if written before that section was closed, and noting that the section was not closed until the third century B.C., after which only the third section remained open. Another possible reason for the placement of the book, however, is that Daniel, serving in a secular position as administrator in the palace, was not classified as a prophet occupationally; and only books written by those who were came to be placed in the "prophets" section. Daniel is called a "prophet" by Christ, in Matthew 24:15 (Mk. 13:14), but this is because of the remarkable prediction given through him, not because of his occupation.

7. The fact that the apocryphal writer, Jesus Sirach, in his well-known book *Ecclesiasticus,* chapter forty-four, does not mention Daniel when he does list many other biblical heroes is said to indicate that Daniel was unknown to him. In reply, it may be stated that this writer did not mention certain other well-known biblical figures either, such as none of the judges except Samuel, and not even Ezra, who was actually nearer to him in time than Daniel. Why he omitted Daniel is not known, but that he did does not prove that he did not know of him.

8. An argument built on alleged historical errors in the book is not used with the same frequency today as formerly, because archaeological discoveries have repeatedly demonstrated that such "errors" were not errors at all. For example, a father-son relationship between Nebuchadnezzar and Belshazzar, as indicated in 5:2, 11, 13, 18, was said to be impossible, since the two were of different dynastic families, but the distinct possibility that this was true through the mother of Belshazzar is now recognized. Even if this were not the case, an

lived later, many more Greek words would have appeared in the book than are actually found.

Assyrian text shows that merely a royal successor on a throne could be called a "son" of a predecessor, even if there were no blood relationship.[11] Or, again, an error was alleged in the setting forth of Belshazzar as the concluding king of Babylonia, when secular history showed that Nabonidus was. But Nabonidus is now known to have left his eldest son, named Belshazzar, in charge as king in Babylon, while he himself was away from the capital for extended periods of time, even making his son a co-ruler for this purpose. Other matters of like kind could be added.[12]

E. PURPOSE OF THE BOOK

Four main purposes of the book are revealed by the nature of its contents. First, the book presents challenging illustrations of what true dedication to God means, and shows what God is willing to do through and for those who are committed to Him. Second, the book portrays God's interest in, and care over, His chosen people, even when they are being punished for sin. This is shown in the historical portion by actual events described, and in the predictive portion by the nature of the prophecies, in which Jewish interests are continually placed in the fore. Third, the book, therefore, provided for Jews in that day a solid basis for comfort. Though they were then being punished in a foreign land, they could know that God had not forgotten them and, in fact, had attractive plans for them in future days; these plans including especially the coming of their delivering Messiah. Fourth, the book is quite parallel with the book of Revelation in the New Testament for giving information relative to the last days. Eschatological studies would be greatly impoverished if the Old Testament did not include the book of Daniel.

F. HISTORICAL BACKGROUND OF THE BOOK

The events set forth in the book of Daniel are only a part of a much larger history transpiring in that day, and can be understood only in the light of the fuller story. With the publication in 1956 of D. J. Wiseman's *The Chronicles of Chaldean Kings,* considerably more of this story has become available. Four new texts of official Babylonian records were published in this volume, and these, with texts published previously, cover the years 626-595 and 556-539 B.C.

Nineveh, capital of the preceding Assyrian empire, fell in 612 B.C. to an allied force of Babylonians, Medians, and probably Scythians. The city was devastated, but some Assyrians, apparently under the leadership of the last Assyrian ruler, Assur-uballit, escaped to the

---

[11] King Shalmaneser III, on his Black Obelisk, speaks of Jehu as "son of Omri"; cf. *ANET*, p. 281.

[12] For extensive treatment of historical matters, cf. Pusey, *DP,* 1891; or Wilson, *SD,* 1917. Though both are older works, they are very valuable.

west. In the fall of the same year, this escaped group claimed sovereignty over all of Assyria from a center at Harran, some 250 miles west of Nineveh. The next year, 611 B.C., Nabopolassar, king of Babylonia, leading Babylonian forces only, campaigned in the vicinity of Harran, but without actually doing battle with the Assyrians themselves. The following year, 610, the Babylonians were joined once more by their former allies, with the result that the Assyrians, though now reinforced by Egyptian troops, withdrew from Harran west across the Euphrates, while the allies entered and sacked Harran. In 609, the Assyrians, apparently supported by still more Egyptian troops, recrossed the Euphrates in an attempt to take Harran once again, but failed. Nabopolassar himself lent his main interest that year to campaigning northeast of Harran, suggesting that possibly Assur-uballit, after his failure at Harran, fled in that direction. At least the Chronicle makes no mention of him in further conflict after that time.

At this point, biblical history lends information. Josiah, good king of Judah, attempted to hinder the Egyptian troops, under Pharaoh Necho, from going to the aid of the Assyrians for the 609 B.C. campaign. Josiah took his army to Megiddo to intercept the great power at the strategic Carmel pass, but he was defeated and killed for his effort (2 Kings 23:28-30; 2 Chron. 35:20-24). By this action, the Judean king was apparently courting Babylonian favor, believing that Judah's future lay with the eastern power. Pharaoh Necho continued north, after this defeat of Josiah, to join with the Assyrians in the unsuccessful attack on Harran, just noted.

After 609 B.C., Assyrian forces played no major role in the continuing struggle. Egypt now was the principal opponent of Babylonia, who also contended quite alone from this time on. For three years the two giants were content merely to spar with each other, not engaging once in major battle. Minor skirmishes occurred, with strategic cities located on either side of the Euphrates changing hands more than once; but the main armies did not meet. The Babylonians lent extensive efforts to strengthening their hold in the area of Izalla, to the northeast. It is noteworthy that the crown prince, Nebuchadnezzar, took on prominence in those efforts for the first time, being mentioned as commanding one of the Babyonian forces for the campaign of 607 B.C.

Finally, in 605, the issue was decided in the great battle of Carchemish. The aging Nabopolassar remained at home this year, with the Babylonian forces being led by the young and brilliant Nebuchadnezzar. He led his troops across the Euphrates in the vicinity of Carchemish and engaged the Egyptians in hand-to-hand fighting, apparently both within and without the city. The Egyptians were decisively defeated, and Carchemish was put to the torch by the Babylonians. The Egyptians retreated south to Hamath, but the Babylonians pressed hard and once more routed the force so that "not a man escaped to his own country." The result was that now "Nebuchadnezzar conquered the whole area of Hatti," meaning all Syria and Palestine.[13]

This important victory by Nebuchadnezzar occurred sometime after the beginning of Nabopolassar's twenty-first year, which means after the month Nisan (April), 605 B.C. Then on the 8th of the month Ab (August 15) following, Nabopolassar died, and Nebuchadnezzar found it necessary to return quickly to Babylon, receiving the crown on the first of the month Elul (September 6). After initial activities as king, however, and apparently believing that matters of government were well in hand, he returned to the west that fall and continued his work of subjugating the Syria-Palestinian region, until the month Sebat (February), 604 B.C. At that time, he found it necessary to return to the capital for the annual New Year Festival, held the first of Nisan, but once more marched to the west in the month Sivan (June) for a further six-month effort. The Chronicle says that at this point all "the kings of the Hatti-land came before him and he received their heavy tribute."

G. CAPTIVITY OF DANIEL

Comparing this history and Daniel's story, as recorded in his book, a rather certain conclusion can be made as to when he and his companions were taken captive from Jerusalem. It was during the summer of 605 B.C., sometime between the Carchemish battle and Nebuchadnezzar's return to Babylon to receive the crown. The following is noted in evidence.

1. This occasion could not have preceded the Carchemish victory, because the Babylonian king, who at the time laid siege to Jerusalem (Dan. 1:1), had no access as far west as Jerusalem until after this victory had been achieved.

2. Neither could it have followed Nebuchadnezzar's return to Babylon to receive the crown—for instance, during the ensuing months of 605 B.C., when he did go back to continue subjugating the west—because Daniel 1:1 gives the date as Jehoiakim's third year; and this year could not have extended beyond the month Tishri (October), 605 B.C., as the following shows. From 2 Kings 23:28-37 (2 Chron. 36: 1-5), it is known that Jehoiakim began to rule in the fall of 609 (following the three-month rule of Jehoiahaz, who had immediately succeeded Josiah, killed by Pharaoh Necho at Megiddo, July, 609). This means that his initial year, called the accession year (on the accession-year system then in use), would have ended in the month Tishri (first month of the civil year), 608 B.C., making his official

---

[13] Quotations from the Chronicle, cf. Wiseman, *The Chronicles of Chaldean Kings* (London: Trustees of the British Museum, 1956), pp. 25, 69.

first year to have extended to Tishri, 607, his second to Tishri, 606, and his third to Tishri, 605.

3. Corroborating these two chronological termini is the mention in Jeremiah 46:2 that the Carchemish battle, which had to precede Daniel's captivity as noted, occurred in Jehoiakim's fourth year. The explanation of what appears to be a discrepancy with Daniel's mention of Jehoiakim's third year, shows that the only period which could be correctly designated as both Jehoiakim's third year and his fourth year, was the six months between the months Nisan and Tishri, 605 B.C. The Hebrews maintained two calendars, a religious one beginning with Nisan in the spring and a civil one starting with Tishri in the fall.[14] Thus, an event occurring between Nisan and Tishri would be dated one year differently, depending on which calendar system was employed. Only between the months Nisan and Tishri in 605 B.C. would the date indications of both Daniel 1:1 and Jeremiah 46:2 be correct.

Admittedly, three months (June to August)[15] did not afford Nebuchadnezzar much time to sweep as far south as Jerusalem and make the siege indicated in Daniel 1:1 (cf. 2 Kings 24:1; 2 Chron. 36:6, 7). A few matters may be pointed out, however, which give further evidence that this is indeed what happened. For one thing, the Babylonian Chronicle states that, as a result of the Carchemish victory, "Nebuchadnezzar conquered the whole area of the Hatti-country."[16] This is, no doubt, a reference principally to a titular role, but it follows that Nebuchadnezzar would have wanted to make the conquest actual as soon as possible. It is also clear that the Babylonian king did remain in the west after the victory until called home to receive the crown, and certainly he would have used this time to the best advantage. Further, that he in fact did this is demonstrated by his immediate return to the west for further subjugation after the coronation, both the following fall and the next summer. That he wanted to return so soon shows that he had been interrupted in what he had been doing. Fourthly, that Nebuchadnezzar had, indeed, taken some captives, including Jews, from the newly won West by the time of his father's death, is indicated by a quotation from Berossus;[17] stating that Nebuchadnezzar "committed the captives he had taken from the Jews, and Phoenicians, and Syrians, and of the nations belonging to Egypt, to some of his friends" so that he could hurry the more quickly back to his capital.

[14] Cf. Thiele, *The Mysterious Numbers of the Hebrew Kings,* rev. ed. (Grand Rapids: Wm. B. Eerdmans Pub. Co., 1965), pp. 16f., 165-66.

[15] The battle of Carchemish probably did not occur before May of 605 B.C. and possibly not until early June.

[16] Nebuchadnezzar's own terminology, cf. Thomas, ed., *Documents From Old Testament Times* (New York: Harper & Brothers, 1958), p. 79.

[17] Quoted by Josephus, *Contra Opion,* I, 19; *Antiq.* X, 11, 1.

In view of these considerations, it may be concluded that, after Nebuchadnezzar's rout of the Egyptians at Carchemish and Hamath, he did move south to make actual subjugation of key cities in Syria and Palestine. Likely he pursued Egyptian stragglers for some distance, seeking to bring the fullest destruction possible on the enemy, and then turned to receive the desired submission of the local inhabitants. Jerusalem may well have been one of the first cities approached, since Josiah had attempted to help Babylonia only four years earlier at Megiddo. Though Daniel 1:1 speaks of his laying siege to the city, this likely means only that he demanded its submission. It is noteworthy that no battle is suggested by either Daniel 1:1; 2 Kings 24:1, or 2 Chronicles 36:6, 7. Jehoiakim, then king, whose politics may have differed from those of friendly Josiah, apparently resisted at first, because 2 Chronicles speaks of his being bound; but he must have been later released, for no change of ruler was forced by the Babylonian conqueror. Nebuchadnezzar did take sacred vessels of the Temple, however, as well as numerous captives, among whom principally were choice young men, including Daniel, Hananiah, Mishael, and Azariah.

The purpose for taking these young men seems not to have been the imposition of punishment, however,[18] but to bring those to Babylon from whom in due time prospective governmental personnel might be selected (Dan. 1:4). Nebuchadnezzar was one of the most capable of ancient rulers, and could be expected to have wanted the best talent his new empire could provide in his regime. It could be expected, also, that he would have wanted such young men to be taken from all the cities he approached, and not merely Jerusalem. No doubt, the brevity of time before he was called back to Babylon that first summer did not permit him to assemble many others there, but he would have added to the number on his successive return campaigns. In fact, even Daniel's group apparently did not reach Babylon until after the coronation, if Berossus' account, mentioned above, is correct. Probably Nebuchadnezzar picked them up during his return the following fall; meaning, if so, that Daniel arrived in Babylon at the same time as those taken from other cities, the spring of Nebuchadnezzar's accession year, 604 B.C.

[18] Nebuchadnezzar may have thought of them as hostages, however, serving to warn the people at home against revolt.

CHAPTER 1

The first chapter of Daniel concerns the introduction of Daniel and his three friends to their captive situation in Babylonia. It presents more particularly a critical and difficult choice which confronted them at this introduction, their commendable decision in respect to it, and God's consequent blessing on them.

A. NEBUCHADNEZZAR COMES AGAINST JERUSALEM (vv. 1, 2)

To give the setting for this story, the chapter begins by telling of Nebuchadnezzar's coming against Jerusalem and demanding submission. As noted in the Introduction, this was a part to his overall subjugation of key cities in the west, which had fallen into his titular domain by the victory of Carchemish.

1:1. In the third year of the reign of Jehoiakim, king of Judah, Nebuchadnezzar, king of Babylon, came against Jerusalem and besieged it.

The third year: As observed in the Introduction, the seeming conflict with Jeremiah 46:2, regarding the exact year of Jehoiakim's rule involved, whether the third or fourth, is resolved in terms of Nisan and Tishri reckoning for the Hebrew calendar.[1] Nisan reckoning began the new year on the first day of the spring month, Nisan (April), and Tishri the first of the fall month, Tishri (October). Any event falling in the six-month period between these two months would carry different year-dates, according to which term of reckoning was employed. Nebuchadnezzar's siege of Jerusalem came during that period, the summer of 605 B.C.[2] *Jehoiakim:* Jehoiakim was the seventeenth king of Judah, the eldest son of the godly Josiah. His younger brother Jehoahaz had been crowned at the father's death (609 B.C.), but within three months was dethroned by Pharaoh Necho

[1] Cf. *supra*, p. 26.
[2] Cf. *supra*, pp. 25-27.

of Egypt. Necho had authority to make this change because of his recent defeat of Judah's army under Josiah at Megiddo. For some reason he did not want Jehoahaz to rule and replaced him with the older Eliakim, whose name he then changed to Jehoiakim.[3] Jehoiakim did not prove to be a capable king. Possibly the people had feared this, and therefore had chosen his younger brother earlier to rule instead of him. Jehoiakim was the one, for instance, who foolishly cut and burned Jeremiah's book, apparently thinking that this would in some way offset its dire warnings (Jer. 36:23). He also squandered state funds to build a new palace unnecessarily, and for this, Jeremiah, in disdain, foretold that he would be "buried with the burial of an ass" (Jer. 22:13-19). Jehoiakim ruled for eleven years, the last three of which were in revolt against Babylon; and this prompted Nebuchadnezzar to initiate another attack on Jerusalem in 597 B.C.

Judah: This is the kingdom of Judah, comprised of the two tribes of Judah and Benjamin. Following the kingdom division at the begining of Rehoboam's reign, these two tribes were all that continued faithful to the family of David, holding Jerusalem as capital. Nineteen kings ruled over Judah until its fall to Babylon in 586 B.C.—a total period of 345 years. Eight of the nineteen kings are called good, and eleven wicked. Jehoiakim was one of the latter. *Nebuchadnezzar, king of Babylon:* In Jeremiah and Ezekiel, this name is spelled "Nebuchadrezzar"; in Babylonian it is *Nabu-kudurri-usur.* Son of Nabopolassar, this Babylonian ruler was one of the great kings of ancient time. His reign of 43 years (605-562 B.C.) marked the duration of Babylonian brilliance during the Neo-Babylonian period. He was outstanding as military strategist, statesman, and builder. The phrase "king of Babylon" is here used in a proleptic sense, because he was not yet king at the time of this siege of Jerusalem. He was summoned to the capital on his father's death the same summer and was crowned Sept. 6. *Came against Jerusalem:* This occasion of attack on Jerusalem is mentioned in both 2 Kings 24:1 and 2 Chronicles 36:6, 7. The first passage states that Jehoiakim then became Nebuchadnezzar's servant for three years, before rebelling; the second, that Jehoiakim was at that time bound by fetters for transporting him to Babylon, and also that Nebuchadnezzar carried sacred vessels of the Temple to his home country, as mentioned also in Daniel 1:2. Jehoiakim was not actually taken to Babylon, for he continued to rule in Jerusalem for another seven years. Apparently he was bound and then released, perhaps on acceding to Nebuchadnezzar's demands. Since

---

[3] Eliakim means "God has established," and Jehoiakim, "Yahweh has established." Since the meaning is basically the same, Necho apparently only wanted to show his authority in forcing the change.

no fighting is mentioned, likely only token resistance was made, with the Judeans recognizing the wisdom of peaceful capitulation.[4]

1:2. And the Lord gave into his hand Jehoiakim, king of Judah, and part of the vessels of the house of God, and he brought them to the land of Shinar to the house of his god, and he brought the vessels into the treasure house of his god.

The Lord: This is the Hebrew name *Adonai;* not *Yahweh* (Jehovah), which occurs only in chapter nine. *Adonai* speaks of God as supreme master. The significance of using this name here is to say that, though outward signs did not seem to show it, God was the master of this situation, as Jehoiakim was given into the hand of Nebuchadnezzar. It was not Nebuchadnezzar's strength nor Jehoiakim's weakness that really decided the matter, but God's good pleasure. Kings like to think themselves sufficient as rulers, but they are as much under the supreme control of God as any person. There is comfort in knowing that no governmental authority can go beyond the bounds permitted by God. *Gave into his hand:* As God exercises absolute control, He normally works through natural means. Here, Nebuchadnezzar did all he thought necessary to make Jehoiakim capitulate; and certainly he believed, when Jehoiakim did so, that he, Nebuchadnezzar, had been the one responsible. But the verse says that God gave (root, *naṯan*) Jehoiakim into his hand. Nebuchadnezzar was only the instrument used. *Part of the vessels:* Reference is to the sacred vessels of the Temple, many of which had been made years before by Solomon (1 Kings 7:48-51). Nebuchadnezzar would have desired them, both for their intrinsic value and as a prize showing his power to take even such sacred items as these. Hezekiah had displayed them, along with other treasure, one century earlier (701 B.C.) to Babylonian emissaries (2 Kings 20:13); Isaiah had then predicted that they would be seized one day, even as now they were. That Nebuchadnezzar took only "part" *(miqtsaṯ)* of them is in keeping with his taking more on each of the two later occasions of captivity (2 Kings 24:13; 25: 14-16). Why he did not take all the first time is not revealed. Many were later sent back to Jerusalem by Cyrus, king of Persia, with the returning exiles (Ezra 1:7).

He brought them: It is likely that Nebuchadnezzar took at least some of these vessels to Babylon at the time he returned home to receive the crown, wanting them as representative booty; but since he seems to have left seized captives "with some of his friends" in the west at this time, due to the need for swiftness of travel,[5] he may have left much of this type of plunder as well. If so, it was all brought

[4] Cf. *supra,* Introduction, pp. 23-25, for historical background.
[5] Cf. *supra,* Introduction, pp. 26-27, for discussion.

to the eastern capital at least during the following year. *Land of Shinar:* Reference is to Babylonia. This is sure because, though the explanation of the term is still uncertain, it is used several times in the Old Testament for Babylonia (Gen. 10:10; 11:2; 14:1, 9; Josh. 7:21; Isa. 11:11; Zech. 5:11). Babylonia proper covered only lower Mesopotamia, and this is the region here in view. However, the empire of Babylonia extended entirely across upper Mesopotamia also, and even down the Mediterranean coastline to and including Palestine. *To the house of his god:* Babylon was the main city and capital of Babylonia. It was situated on the Euphrates River, some fifty miles south of modern Baghdad. Within the city were more than fifty temples to various deities, but the main one was to Marduk, located in what was called the sacred area. In this area, entered by the magnificent Ishtar gate, was also a great ziggurat, a sacred tower crowned with a small shrine. The splendid Marduk temple boasted numerous chapels to deities other than Marduk, but his was the principal one, richly decorated with cedar-wood paneling, gold, alabaster, and semiprecious stones. This temple was likely the one to which Nebuchadnezzar brought Judah's sacred vessels.

B. Introduction of Daniel, Hananiah, Mishael, and Azariah (vv. 3-7)

The story now presents the four young Judeans who are the chief characters in the book. Nebuchadnezzar's order that such young men be chosen is first set forth, then the qualifications demanded of them, followed by an indication that they were to be assigned a special menu, and a statement that among these were particularly Daniel, Hananiah, Mishael, and Azariah. The specific time when these young men were chosen is not indicated. It is possible that Nebuchadnezzar took a large number of Judeans captive and then, after the arrival of all of them in Babylon, made selection from among them of the young men he wanted. It is more likely, however, in view of the reason for picking them, that the selection was made already in Jerusalem. The very choicest young men were desired, and greater selection would have been possible if made in the home country. Nothing is suggested in the story, either, that any persons besides the youths were taken. Nebuchadnezzar's interest seems not to have been punishment, but only selection of those who could strengthen his rule.[6]

1:3. Then the king ordered Ashpenaz, chief of his eunuchs, to bring from the children of Israel, even from the seed of the kingdom and from the nobles.

[6] Cf. *supra,* Introduction, p. 27, n. 18.

Ashpenaz, chief of his eunuchs: The meaning of "Ashpenaz"[7] is uncertain. The man was an important official, serving as chief of the eunuchs. "Eunuch" *(saris)* may refer to officers in general, as, for instance, to Potiphar (Gen. 37:36), who was even married. Courts of the day did include many who were truly eunuchs, however. It is not necessary to believe that these imported youths were made eunuchs simply because they had been given into the jurisdiction of this person. He was merely to superintend their selection and care. *To bring:* The word indicates that those selected had no alternative but to go when chosen. Those who met the qualifications were simply taken. Some of the more adventuresome may not have minded very much, but others would have suffered greatly in being wrenched from home ties. All would have found the adjustment difficult after arrival. *From the children of Israel:* "Children of Israel" *(b^enê yisra'el)* was the theocratic name of God's people, Israel, without having reference to either the northern or southern nations, after the kingdom division. Most of the young men chosen would have come from the southern nation, since the northern had been taken captive long before; but some may have been taken from northern tribes, who were still represented in their respective areas by sizable populations. Nebuchadnezzar probably sent messengers to look quite widely, even outside Jerusalem; and some northern families may even have moved to Jerusalem by this time. *Even from the seed of the kingdom and from the nobles:* Some expositors believe that those chosen were from three classes of people: the "children of Israel," meaning the common people; the "seed of the kingdom," meaning royalty; and the "nobles," meaning families ranking just below royalty. "Children of Israel," however, is not an ordinary name for the common people. It is better to take that term as the general indication and the other two in reference to the specific classes. This means that Nebuchadnezzar believed that the families of higher status could best supply the type of young men he wanted. According to Josephus,[8] Daniel and his three friends were members of Zedekiah's royal family, but this remains uncertain.

1:4. Young men in whom was no defect, but pleasing in appearance, characterized by wisdom, possessing knowledge, and understanding science; who had ability to stand in the palace of the king, and who might be taught the literature and language of the Chaldeans.

Young men: "Young men" *(y^elad̲îm)* is not definitive as to age. Daniel could hardly have been older than fifteen years, however, in view of his being able to serve as a president in the Persian kingdom

---

[7] The name is found in texts from Nippur as *'SPNZ*; cf. S. H. Horn, *Seventh Day Adventist Dictionary of the Bible*, p. 83.
[8] Cf. *supra*, Introduction, p. 15, n. 1.

67 years later (538 B.C., cf. 6:1). Plato[9] says that the education of youths in Persia began at fourteen years, and Xenophon[10] speaks of the seventeenth year as the completion. Babylonian custom need not have been the same as later Persian, but an approximate parallel could be expected. It was necessary that the young men be old enough to make the adjustment psychologically and young enough yet to learn easily and come to feel at home in the new cultural surroundings. *No defect, but pleasing in appearance:* The high qualifications set down by Nebuchadnezzar are now listed. This first item refers to physical features. The word for "defect" *(mu'ûm)* speaks primarily of something physical (Lev. 21:17, 18; 2 Sam. 14:25). The men were to be healthy and without physical handicap. They were to have a pleasing appearance, no doubt both in facial presentation and body shape and size. Nebuchadnezzar wanted those who would lend attraction to his court. The argument of some that this requirement prohibits the idea that the young men were made eunuchs may carry weight. *Characterized by wisdom, possessing knowledge, and understanding science:* These items refer to mental ability. Not only were the youths to be physically appealing, but they were also to be (1) intelligent, (2) quick of mind, and (3) able to learn well. The first item refers more specifically to learning capability, the word "wisdom" *(hokmah)* connoting the ability to make distinctions and proper decisions. The second speaks of knowledge attained, the words for "possessing knowledge" *(yode''ê da'at)* meaning literally "knowers of knowledge." The third carries reference to the power of comprehension, the words for "understanding science" *(mebînê madda')* meaning literally "understanders of knowledge." That three phrases are used shows the stress that Nebuchadnezzar placed on intellectual capacity.

Ability to stand in the palace: This refers to personality. The young men were to have a personality which would allow them to live in a royal court without embarrassment. They should have a proper manner, poise, confidence, and knowledge of social proprieties. *The literature and language of the Chaldeans:* Stress here is on the fields of learning for the young men. The Babylonian language was a principal language of the day, but youths of the west would not have known it without special study. They would have to learn it. Babylonian literature was extensive. It was written on clay tablets, using cuneiform (wedge-shaped) impressions made by a wooden stylus. The clay was later baked to retain the impressions. Much of this literature has been found, some dating even to the time of Abraham. It was much more voluminous by the time of Nebuchadnezzar. Thousands of tablets are now extant. The term "Chaldean" is here used in an ethnic sense,[11]

---

9 *Alcibiades* 1:121.
10 *Cyropaedia*, I, 2.
11 For discussion, cf. *infra,* under 2:2.

but probably not with its original reference to a particular people of southern Babylonia. By this time it had come to be used with some frequency for Babylonians generally (cf. Isa. 13:19; 47:1; 48:14) and is best so taken here. The young men would have had to learn this literature of the Babylonians.

1:5. And the king appointed for them a daily portion of the king's own food and wine, and that they should be trained three years, so that at the end of this time they might stand before the king.

The king appointed: Literally, "the king apportioned," the verb used being *manah* ("to divide, apportion"). Nebuchadnezzar designated the menu of the young men. The word suggests, and Ashpenaz' fear as set forth in verse ten confirms, that this appointment by the king constituted a command. The young men did not have a choice in the matter. *A daily portion:* Literally, "the thing of a day in a day" (cf. 1 Chron. 16:37; Jer. 52:34). Nebuchadnezzar's order was sufficiently detailed to assign the amount of food each man should have. In view of the overall purpose, this likely was a substantial portion. *The king's own food:* The word for "own food" *(pat-bag)* is Old Persian *(patibaga),* and means "portion" or "assignment."[12] The phrase translates literally: "from the portion of the king," meaning "from the very food which the king ate." Such food would have been the finest, of course. Without question, the king believed that he was doing the young men a favor. Two reasons for the favor may be noted at this point: first, that the good will of the young men might be solicited; and, second, that a well-rounded menu might be insured, so that the young men might maintain and further develop healthy bodies. A third and more significant reason is noted under verse eight. *And wine:* Literally, "and wine from his drinking," meaning "and wine which the king himself drank." Both food and wine, then, were to be the same as set before Nebuchadnezzar himself. Wine was the common drink of the day, and there were various grades of it. The young men were to have the best. *They should be trained three years:* The Hebrew says "made great" (root, *gadal*) for three years. The word is used in Isaiah 1:2 to mean "making great in physical stature," and in 2 Kings 10:6 "making great in intellectual stature." Likely both ideas are intended here. The type of diet ordered carries implications as to the physical aspect, and the manner of the king's questions at the end of three years (vv. 19, 20) does the same in reference to the intellectual. Besides eating the prescribed food for three years, then, the young men were to be educated. The later Persians are known to have also allowed a period of three years for

---

[12] For discussion, cf. Montgomery, MICC, pp. 127, 28.

this kind of training.[13] *They might stand before the king:* To stand before a king meant *to serve the king* (cf. Deut. 1:38; 1 Kings 10:8; 12:8). Nebuchadnezzar, investing so much time and money in these young foreigners, had more in mind for them than merely to grace his court. They were to be educated so that they might later serve well in important governmental posts. It is reasonable to assume that those who would have done the best in their educational pursuits would have been those to receive the more honored positions.

1:6. Now among these, of the children of Judah, were Daniel, Hananiah, Mishael, and Azariah.

Among these: Reference is to the total number of young men involved. Both verses ten and fifteen indicate further that there were many besides the main four. The next phrase, "of the children of Judah," shows that these four were specifically of that nation. Likely others were of Judah, too, in view of the context; but the implication is that a sizable number were also of other nations. This is only what one would expect, for Nebuchadnezzar would have wanted the best young men available, whether from Syria, Phoenicia, Philistia, or wherever he might look. *Daniel, Hananiah, Mishael, and Azariah:* These are the four men of particular importance in the story. All four of their names are clearly Hebrew in type. "Daniel" and "Mishael" both contain the element *el,* one of the names for God; and "Hananiah" and "Azariah" the element *iah (yah),* an abbreviation found in so many Hebrew names for *Yahweh* (Jehovah). The story reveals that Daniel was the leader, but all were committed Judeans, who had certainly received early training in obedience to God. Jeremiah's denunciations of the Jerusalem populace imply that not many godly homes existed at this time; but surely some did, to account for fine young men like these. Coming from such homes, and with the type of personality demonstrated in the story, each of the four would have found captive conditions difficult to bear. Home and religious ties would have been especially strong for them. The name Daniel means "God is my judge"; Hananiah, "Yahweh is gracious"; Mishael, "Who is what God is?"; Azariah, "Yahweh has helped."

1:7. The prince of the eunuchs gave them names; and he gave to Daniel, Belteshazzar, and to Hananiah, Shadrach, and to Mishael, Meshach, and to Azariah, Abed-nego.

Prince of the eunuchs: This prince presumably is the Ashpenaz of verse three. The term "prince" *(sar),* employed here, may be used

---

[13] In the *Avesta,* it is stated, "How long a time of a year's length shall a student go to a master of spiritual learning? For a period of three springtides (years) he shall gird himself with the holy education"; quoted by Montgomery, MICC, p. 122.

synonymously with "chief" *(rab),* used there. The man not only super-vised the selection and transportation of the chosen youths, but now their change of name. *Gave them names:* The kind of name-change indicated, replacing Hebrew with Babylonian-type names, was not un-common in ancient custom. Joseph was given the Egyptian name Zaph-nath-paaneah (Gen. 41:45) and Esther's Hebrew name was Hadassah (Esth. 2:7). There were reasons for making such changes, however, and here it was certainly to make the young men more Babylonian. If they were eventually to make good governmental personnel, they should become Babylonians in their thinking and manner of life as soon as possible; and Babylonian-type names should help. *Belteshazzar, Shadrach, Meshach, Abed-nego:* The Babylonian meanings of the names remain uncertain. "Belteshazzar" may represent the Babylonian *Balatsu-usur,* meaning "protect his life," with the deity addressed, supposedly Bel, not named. In view of Daniel 4:8, however, it seems better to find it represented in *Belti-shar-usur,* meaning "Belti, protect the king," in which the deity Bel (Belti) is identified. "Shadrach" may be an intentional perversion of *Marduk,* a chief Babylonian deity. "Meshach" has not as yet yielded to any likely analysis. "Abed-nego" means "serv-ant of Nego," in which "Nego" may be an alternative spelling for "Nebo," another well-known Babylonian deity.

C. DANIEL AND HIS COMPANIONS REFUSE THE KING'S FOOD (vv. 8-16)

This portion of the chapter presents the admirable decision of Daniel and his friends concerning the menu appointed by the king; and also their insistence on carrying out their decision in spite of strong opposition.

1:8. But Daniel purposed in his heart not to defile himself with the king's own food and wine, and he made request of the prince of the eunuchs that he might not defile himself.

Daniel purposed in his heart: Literally, "Daniel placed upon his heart." The thought is that Daniel, having made a decision not to eat the king's food, placed this decision on his heart, thus putting himself under full obligation to act according to it. He did not make it to forget it, as is so often done. Though only Daniel is mentioned as making this choice, the overall story makes clear that the three friends were involved in it, as well as he. Daniel was the leader, and this accounts for the fact that only he is mentioned. *Not to defile himself:* The word for "defile himself" (root, *ga'al*) is used in the hithpael (reflexive) and carries the thought of *polluting, staining, defiling* one-self (cf. Isa. 59:3; Zeph. 3:1; Mal. 1:7). This is the first indication that the king's order regarding the menu presented a problem to the four. The thought is clear, however, that they believed their eating the food would mean the defilement of themselves; and accordingly they chose not to do so. The reasons for the defilement, which they saw, would have been basically two: first, that the food would likely include at times meat declared unclean by the law of Moses;[14] and, second, that it would regularly be food first offered to the Babylonian gods. As to the first, to eat the food would have been to disobey God's direct command in the Law; and as to the second, it would have been to give recognition, though in an indirect manner, to the existence of Babylon's false deities. Food first dedicated to gods was thought to insure to the eaters the favor of those gods. Nebuchadnezzar, like other kings, would have insisted that all food coming from the royal kitchen be so dedicated, that his government might be benefited. Everyone eating it, then, would have been considered as also desiring favor and thus giving recognition and obeisance to the Babylonian deities. In fact, the main reason for Nebuchadnezzar's ordering that the imported youths eat this prescribed food may have been thus to elicit this recognition and obeisance. They were first given Babylonian names in the overall desire to make them good Babylonians, and now they were to give this degree of acquiescence to the Babylonian religion. Daniel and his friends clearly saw through these implications and recognized that they had a decision to make.

It is well to note factors which would have made this decision difficult. (1) The king had ordered this menu; therefore the order was a law. Being the kind of young men they were, their first inclination would have been to obey it. The godly homes in which they had been raised may be assumed to have intructed them to be law-abiding. Indeed, in view of other attractions to obey, they could have argued that they really had no alternative. In choosing to disobey, they demonstrated their recognition of the principle laid down in Acts 5:29 that God's law is higher than man's. (2) To disobey could incur punishment. Kings of the day were known for their severe punishments, as witnessed, for instance, by the punishment of the fiery furnace Nebuchadnezzar devised for those who would not bow to his great image (chap. 3). These four young men could well have cringed at the thought of what might happen to them if they refused to comply with the royal order. (3) To refuse the food would have seemed a sure way to spoil all chances of advancement toward the goal of a fine governmental position, at the close of the training period. Each of the four would have desired to make good marks during this period, that a better position might be his at the close. To go against this first order of the king could well have seemed the worst they could do to make this a reality. (4) The quality of the food ordered by the king would have been very attractive. Coming

[14] Cf. Lev. 11; Deut. 14:3-20.

from the king's own kitchen, it would have been the finest. No doubt, the king, his servants, and the other youths thought that high favor was being extended to the young men. Such food would have been hard to turn down. This would have been the more difficult in view of the food they would get in its place: vegetables and water (v. 12). To have only vegetables and water, for no less than three years, when they might have the best the land could offer, would indeed not have been attractive. (5) The four were a long way from home, and parents and relatives would never know if they chose wrongly. It is possible, that their parents had also been brought captive, but not likely; and, if not, the fact that they would not have to give account to them for their actions might have been an enticing factor in their thinking. (6) It would have been natural to argue that, since God had not protected them from this captivity, they did not have to be careful in obeying His demands. Too many Christians do this in comparable situations, rationalizing that if God has not been "fair" with them, they do not have to be good Christians themselves. The young men might have become sour and bitter of spirit because of having been taken from home; but, if they had, they never would have been able to make the fine decision they did.

He made request: The decision of the four was firm enough to do what was necessary to carry it out. Request was made to the proper authority, the prince of the eunuchs (Ashpenaz), to be relieved of obeying the king's order. It is one thing to make a decision; but another to effect it, especially if difficulty is encountered in doing so. These men did carry out their decision, and this in spite of meeting with difficulty, as the following verses indicate. Also, they could not have helped but realize that their supervisors would think them very foolish in their request, turning down such an attractive menu; indeed, even ungrateful for the favor being shown. But none of this deterred them. *That he might not defile himself:* The inclusion of these words suggests that Daniel explained the reason to Ashpenaz for the request; namely, that he and his friends would be defiled if they ate the king's food. This would have involved explaining the nature of the defilement, the explanation, in turn, giving witness to the true religion to which they held. It is evident that Daniel was not ashamed of his faith, even in pagan Babylon. If Ashpenaz was not impressed by the reasoning of Daniel, he must have been impressed by his devotion to the God he served. He could not have helped but admire one who did what he thought was right, in spite of great attraction to do otherwise.

1:9. Then God made Daniel to find kindness and favor before the prince of the eunuchs.

Then God: Daniel's life repeatedly portrays what God will do for the person who is faithful in obedience to His will. Daniel had just determined to do what was right, when it would have been easy to do wrong; and now God intervened to help. God is always faithful. The Bible is filled with promises of what God will do for those who please Him. *Made Daniel to find kindness and favor:* The word for "kindness" *(ḥeseḏ)* is used often to indicate God's *unfailing love* for His people (Ps. 5:7; 36:5), and may be understood here to indicate unusual *good will* on the part of Ashpenaz toward these four. The word for "favor" *(raḥᵃmîm)* is a plural of intensity of a word meaning, literally, "the bowels." Here, and more commonly, it means the "love" and "compassion" that have their seat in the "bowels." The implication is that this remarkable attitude of Ashpenaz toward the four Judeans was demonstrated in response to the request. It is stated that God effected it; but God regularly uses means. The means here was the prior good behavior of the four. Had they not conducted themselves well before this, they would not have enjoyed this favor now. It pays to build good reputations. Because of this favor, Ashpenaz was willing to listen seriously to Daniel; if he had not been so inclined, he doubtless would have dimissed the request quite abruptly.

1:10. The prince of the eunuchs replied to Daniel, I fear my lord the king, who has designated your food and your drink, lest he should find your faces worse looking than the youths of your own age and you should endanger my head to the king.

I fear my lord the king: Even feeling favorable, Ashpenaz was reluctant to fill the request. It presented a problem for him. He wanted to favor the young men; but he was first an officer of Nebuchadnezzar, who had given the young men an order. For them to disobey could endanger not only them but him also, and he feared what Nebuchadnezzar might do. Besides, he no doubt had difficulty in appreciating the reason behind their requests. It may have seemed that they should be able on some basis to eat the food, in spite of their religious commitment. *Find your faces worse looking:* The word for "worse looking" (root, *za'ap,* "to be sad") is a participle meaning, literally, "something saddened" (cf. Gen. 40:6). Ashpenaz feared that a variation in menu might bring a poorer condition of health to the four, which would show in a saddened facial appearance. From this fear, further evidence may be taken that the menu prescribed was a good one; well-balanced for health, as well as appetizing. It follows, too, that the king expected all the young men to portray good health as a result. *Youths of your own age:* Reference is to the other young captives. Ashpenaz feared that the others, eating the prescribed food, would appear more healthy than the four. The manner of reference adds evidence that all were of about the same age. *Endanger my head to the king:* The word for "endanger" (root, *ḥûḇ,* "to be made liable to penalty") may carry only the thought of "putting (responsibility) on my head," but most expositors find capital punishment being indicated. Ashpenaz showed his human nature in thinking first of his own welfare before that of the four friends: if he should accede to their request, he might lose not only his fine position but his very life. It is to his credit, however, that he at least considered the request when he did have this fear for himself. This gives added stress to the high standing they held with him.

1:11. Then Daniel said to the melzar, whom the prince of the eunuchs had appointed over Daniel, Hananiah, Mishael, and Azariah.

The melzar: The article is employed with this word, favoring the explanation that it is an appellative, rather than a person's name. The derivation is uncertain, but reference is best taken to a steward or guard.[15] *Had appointed:* Ashpenaz had appointed this man as his subordinate to oversee the training of the young men. No doubt, Ashpenaz had many other tasks to supervise and needed assistants. Daniel had taken the request directly to him as head authority at first, but now worked with the assistant. In view of the type of petition Daniel now brought, it appears that Ashpenaz had chosen to decline the request as first presented. But Daniel was not to be deterred, and began working to prove that the four would not suffer physically from the alternative diet. There is further reason in this for giving commendation to Daniel. Now that he had properly asked for relief from the order and been refused, he had a ready-made excuse for desisting in his decision. Most would have been glad to use it. But Daniel clearly was not looking for an excuse—only a way to carry out his well-made choice.

1:12, 13. Try your servants ten days, I beseech you, and let them give us vegetables to eat and water to drink; and let our countenance and the countenance of the youths who eat the king's own food be compared by you, and, as you see, do with your servants.

Try your servants ten days: Daniel proposed a ten-day trial period. The period seems extremely short, but likely Daniel wanted one which the melzar could not reasonably turn down. It shows remarkable faith on Daniel's part to believe that in ten days God would so improve their appearance that this man would be convinced of the propriety of the menu. *Let them give us:* Reference is to those who would actually bring the food. It was necessary that the melzar be persuaded to give others the order for this special diet to be prepared and brought. It is easy to imagine that, as such servants carried out the order, they would have dropped remarks to the four which would

[15] For discussion, cf. E. Young, YPD, pp. 45-46; J. Montgomery, MICC, pp. 131, 134.

have shown their surprise and wonder at this foolishness. Why turn down the king's food for only vegetables and water? They could wish that they themselves would have had such a choice. *Vegetables to eat:* The word for "vegetables" *(zero'îm)* is from the root *zara'* "to sow seed" and means "that which grows from sown seed." This includes vegetables and grains. Daniel was asking that the new menu be vegetarian, free from meat. Such a bill of fare would have been healthful, but to most people not nearly as appealing as the king's food. *Water to drink:* The literal reading of the verse is of interest: "Let them give to us from the vegetables and we will eat, and water and we will drink." Daniel's refusal of the wine suggests that, like the food, it was dedicated to the gods. He and his friends would drink water instead.

Countenance: Literally, "appearance" *(mar'eh,* from the root, *ra'ah* "to see"), that which one sees as he looks upon another. *Be compared by you:* Literally, "be seen by you," using the niphal (passive) form of *ra'ah.* The context makes clear that a comparative type of seeing is in mind. The two groups of youths were to be compared at the end of the ten days. Apparently, the melzar himself was to make the decision. *As you see, do:* Daniel wanted the man to act after making his choice. If he decided that the four friends did look healthier than the others, he should do what was necessary to maintain the substitute menu. Daniel was placing the fate of the four in this man's hand. He apparently had confidence that he would judge objectively. Probably the youths' good conduct had elicited the melzar's good will, as well as that of Ashpenaz, and Daniel had this in mind.

1:14-16. Then he listened to them in this matter and tried them ten days; and at the end of ten days their countenance was seen to be better and fatter of flesh than all the youths who had eaten the king's own food. The melzar, therefore, continued to take away their appointed food and wine for drinking, and to give them vegetables.

He listened to them: What Daniel proposed evidently made sense to the man, and he listened. Commendation is due Daniel for devising a plan that would have this appeal. Daniel recognized the melzar's problem, saw the matter from his point of view, and made a proposal which he could understand and accept.

At the end of ten days: The decision was made by this man at the end of the designated ten days, likely after he had kept close watch all during the period. He may often have brought the food to them personally, to keep check on how they were faring. *Better and fatter of flesh:* The word for "better" is the comparative degree of the adjective "good" *(tôḇ),* and that for "fatter" is the adjective "fat" *(barî')* in the construct state with "flesh." Together they indicate that the four showed a definite advantage in healthful characteristics over the others. Rather than suffering from the substitute food, they were actually benefiting. Probably the skin showed better color, their eyes more alertness, and their body some additional weight. God's direct intervention would have been necessary to effect this manner of observable change in so short a period—truly a demonstration of God's faithfulness to those who do His will.

Continued to take away: Continuation of action is indicated by the use of an active participle (*nose'* "one taking away"). For the previous ten days, the melzar had not required them to eat the king's food, and he now continued this. It should be noted that he is not said to have done this for the three years. The context indicates that he actually did, but he may not have promised to continue for that length of time at the start. He may have chosen to proceed only on a day-to-day basis. Had he noticed any change for the worse in the men's appearance, he no doubt would have desisted immediately. *To give them:* A parallel participle is used here (*noten* "one giving"). Not only did the melzar continue to take away the king's food, but he continued to give the vegetables and water. It is reasonable to assume that, at this point, the melzar notified his superior, Ashpenaz, concerning the ten-day test and his resulting decision; inquiring whether he had Ashpenaz' approval for the continuance. He probably made it a point to add that he could change the menu at any time, as a safeguard. Ashpenaz evidently gave the approval. It would have been at this stage in the developments that the favor of Ashpenaz toward the youths, as noted in verse nine, would have carried its greatest significance.

D. GOD'S BLESSING ON THE FOUR YOUTHS (vv. 17-21)

The last five verses of the chapter indicate the result of the fine choice made by the young men. This result was that, rather than suffering punishment at the hands of an angry king, or experiencing any loss in their competition with the other young captives, they actually were advanced in position above the others.

1:17. As for these four youths, God gave them knowledge and understanding in all literature and wisdom: and Daniel had insight regarding every vision and dream.

As for these four youths: This formal phrase appears at first to be out of keeping with the movement of the story. Its purpose, however, is to show the beginning of this new section, and to stress that God's favor was on these four in distinction from the other young captives. *God gave them:* The credit for the advance of these young men is properly given to God. He gave the benefits now listed. To God must be given the praise for all life's attainments, for in truth they are His gracious gifts. God, however, regularly uses means to accomplish

His purpose, and we may be sure that He did here. The "knowledge and understanding" that God bestowed on the four were not given apart from their own diligent effort. God gave them this intellectual advance only through the natural manner of their own study programs. From their point of view, the outcome lay with them to do their very best, especially since they had not been able to cooperate as to the menu designated. From God's point of view, the result was entirely in His hands for granting them the desire and learning capacity for this attainment. *Knowledge and understanding:* The word for "knowledge" *(mada'),* translated "science" in verse four, coming from the root "to know" *(yada'),* means "that which is known." The word for "understanding" *(haskîl)* refers to mental activity involving this knowledge, so that one is able to explain its nature and significance. The two concepts nicely complement each other, and both are necessary for true education. *All literature and wisdom:* "All" stresses the extent of the youth's intellectual attainments. "Literature," literally "book" *(seper),* refers to the area of their mental mastery; namely, the Babylonian books. "Wisdom" *(hokmah)* depicts the nature of the books: books of wisdom, the products of trained minds. Babylon was the center of knowledge of the day. The various areas of science appear to have been more advanced there than anywhere else in the world. Babylonians had the benefit of extensive literature from earlier days, especially through the remarkable library left by the Assyrian emperor, Ashurbanipal (669-626 B.C.),[16] as well as advanced studies by contemporary scholars. Many of these writings have been found and are known today.

Daniel had insight: In addition to what the others received, Daniel was given special interpretative ability as to visions and dreams. In contrast to the gifts of "knowledge and understanding," in the attainment of which the human instruments had a part, this gift was entirely of God. Daniel could not learn the technique of true vision and dream interpretation. There is point to noting this here, for the Babylonians believed one could do so. In fact, much of the literature in which the young men would have had to become proficient concerned such techniques. Methods of divination for determining the will of the gods had been devised, and serious attention was given to these methods by specialists. The four Judeans would have had to reject all such thinking, as they recognized that true revelation could come only from God, and as He pleased. One reason for including the statement concerning Daniel's special gift is likely to make clear that he, with the others, did reject the Babylonian way and that God replaced this methodology with His own enabling gift. Another reason is more obvious; namely, to prepare the reader for Daniel's activity in the

[16] Cf. "Asurbanipal, Library of," *The Biblical World, A Dictionary of Biblical Archaeology,* pp. 101, 102.

following chapters, where he is repeatedly depicted in the role of interpreter of God's revelations. *Regarding every vision and dream:* "Vision" *(ḥazôn)* and "dream" *(ḥᵃlomôt,* plural here) are listed only, for they were the more normal forms of revelation used by God, but they represent other possible forms, such as that employed in the writing on Belshazzar's palace wall (chap. 5). "Every" *(kol)* must be understood in the sense that only those visions and dreams are in view as specially given by God for revelation. While Daniel lived, he was the one gifted by God, and accordingly the only one used, to give the interpretation of them. The pagans believed that dreams regularly carried significance, and they even induced dreams for this reason. Certain priests were considered experts in dream interpretation. Scripture teaches, however, that only certain dreams are revelatory: namely, those which God gives for that purpose. Daniel's gift was that he was specially endowed for receiving God's interpretations of such occasions of divine communication. It may be noted further that when God gave His revelations to Nebuchadnezzar, He used only the dream type of communication, never the vision, whereas He did use the vision with Daniel. In fact, the Scripture shows God regularly employing the dream when giving a revelation to pagans. The reason seems to be that, with the dream, the human personality is neutralized and made a passive instrument for the occasion. With the vision, however, the person himself is often a participant and must be constituted to respond and react in a proper manner, something true only of a child of God. Though the revelation to Belshazzar (chap. 5) was not a dream, it was still of a type entirely objective to himself, in which he played no part. Daniel was necessary for its interpretation, just as he had been with Nebuchadnezzar's dreams.

1:18, 19. At the end of the days that the king had designated to bring them in, the prince of the eunuchs did bring them before Nebuchadnezzar. And the king spoke with them, and among them all was none found like Daniel, Hananiah, Mishael, and Azariah; therefore they stood before the king.

At the end of the days: The subject now turns to what occurred at the close of the trial period. The days here in view are those of the three-year time. During this period, Daniel and his companions continued to eat the special menu, in distinction from the others. All of the young men engaged in the study of the Babylonian language and books. *The prince:* This "prince" was Ashpenaz, the one placed over the young men and their training program. The presentation of the young men before Nebuchadnezzar was as important for him as for them. The appearance and abilities they would show would demonstrate how well his program of training had been planned and effected. *Did bring them before Nebuchadnezzar:* "Them" refers to all the young men involved, whether Judeans or others, Daniel and his friends being among them. Ashpenaz brought them before Nebuchadnezzar, for the king desired to make his own selection of those who would fill the various court positions.

The king spoke with them: The king examined the young men by conversing with them, probably individually, or at least in small enough groups to make individual judgments. He may have had trained subordinates with him to help in noting strengths and weaknesses, and to lend advice. Some of the factors considered would have been fluency in the Babylonian language, extent of knowledge gained, personality characteristics, and personal appearance. The interviews provided tense moments for the young men, for the outcome would determine their future standing in the court. *None found like Daniel:* The day was particularly crucial for Daniel and his friends, because it was the time when any possible health deficiency due to their special diet would appear; with consequent dire results for both them and their supervisors—Ashpenaz and the melzar. But they had nothing to fear, as they well knew, being quite aware of their own excellent health. When Nebuchadnezzar evaluated them, he found them the most outstanding of all, not only in respect to physical appearance, but also in personality and intelligence, which were even more important (cf. v. 20). One may assume that all four had applied themselves well to their studies—probably extra well, because they had asked for the special dispensation regarding food. *They stood before the king:* The meaning is not merely that they stood before the king for examination, because all the young men did that; but that they were selected for important posts of government (cf. v. 5 for discussion of the phrase). Probably many others were also selected, which means that this special notation indicates that the four were given the higher positions. What these positions were is not stated here, but is set forth in 2:48, 49. This is one of the fine illustrations in Scripture of how God takes care of those who put His will first in their lives (cf. Matt. 6:33).

1:20. Then in every matter of wisdom of understanding which the king sought from them, he found them ten times better than all the magicians and enchanters who were in all his kingdom.

In every matter: The degree of superiority of the four is now presented, stressing the intellectual aspect. The verse is best understood to refer to time following the occasion of the king's decision and their appointment to positions. This is evidenced as follows: first, that verse nineteen above concerns that examination time and its result, so that this verse need not speak of it further; second, that Daniel and his friends are compared here with "magicians and enchanters," terms designating classes of wise men and hardly appropriate for young men just completing their education; and, third, that these "magicians and enchanters" are said to have been from *all* the kingdom, a statement which would not have been true regarding the young trainees. The thought is that, following the time of appointments, these four were found to be superior to others with whom they worked "in all matters." *Wisdom of understanding:* Some versions read "wisdom and understanding," but the more unusual reading, here used, must be preferred; in which "wisdom" is in construct with "understanding," making the two words one unit of thought. The basic idea of each word may be seen from verses four and seventeen, where the one *(ḥokmah)* is translated "wisdom" the two times it is used, and the other *(bînah)* is used in its verbal form, once as "understanding" and once as "had insight." The context of this verse calls for "wisdom" to refer to the general area of subject matter concerned at any given time, and "understanding" to the intellectual capacity required for dealing with it properly. The thought might be paraphrased: "area of wisdom calling for understanding to deal with it properly." Since the four young men are compared with "magicians and enchanters," whose main work involved counseling, it is likely that the principal matters in view concerned those in which they were asked to give counsel. This gives the full thought: "In respect to every subject area (whether scientific, governmental, military, etc.) in which counseling was requested and which required keen understanding for giving the best advice, the young men were found. . . ."

The king sought: Other people besides kings sought counsel from wise men, but when kings did so, which was often, the occasion was more important. Nebuchadnezzar used wise men frequently, as witnessed particularly in chapters two and four following. When he did, he found Daniel and his friends more capable than the others. *Ten times better:* An indication is now given as to how much better he found them. "Times" is literally "hands" *(yaḏôt).* The thought is that they were the equal of ten hands, meaning ten persons. Occasionally the number "ten" is used indefinitely in the sense of "several," which may be the case here (cf. Zech. 8:23). *Magicians and enchanters:* These two terms indicate the groups of men among whom Daniel and his friends worked and probably were classified. The name "magicians" *(ḥartummîm)* may be related to the word "stylus" *(ḥeret),* meaning, basically, those who use the stylus; in other words, sacred writers. The name "enchanters" *('ashshapîm)* is a designation for the Ashupu priests of Babylonian texts. Neither term, however, appears to be used in its restricted sense; but broadly, referring to all wise men, no matter their distinctive type.[17] Wise men of the day, of whatever

---

[17] For instances of the word "magicians" *(ḥartummîm)* being used in such a general sense, cf. Genesis 41:8, 24 and Exodus 7:11, 22 in reference to Egyptian religious personnel.

branch, were thought to be skilled in giving counsel, both out of their own broad knowledge as educated men and as a result of alleged ability to contact the realm of deity.

1:21. Daniel continued until the first year of Cyrus the king.

Daniel continued: This verse tells of still a third aspect in God's blessings on Daniel. He lived and continued as a valuable member of the court until old age. He not only was rewarded with a fine position on his graduation from training (v. 19), and later served more capably in that position than any other (v. 20), but he also continued in that capacity until the "first year of Cyrus." As Daniel so wrote, he must have thrilled at what it meant that God had blessed him with such a long life and long service. Through all the plots and intrigues that regularly exist in oriental courts; through all the jealousy and envy that could only be expected toward a foreign captive in high office; through a series of four rapid successions of Babylonian kings, two of which had suffered assassination; and through the fall of Babylon itself to the genius of Cyrus, the Medo-Persian, he, Daniel, had lived and still served in high office! *First year of Cyrus:* Babylon fell to Cyrus in October, 539 B.C. This was 66 years after Daniel's captivity, making him at the time about 81 years of age. From 10:1, it is known that Daniel actually lived at least until Cyrus' third year. There may have been two reasons why he did not mention the later date here. One is that he merely wanted to make the point that he had continued throughout the entire Babylonian period, even until the conquest of Cyrus. The other is that the time of his writing this chapter may have been in Cyrus' first year, when he could not have known concerning any later years.

CHAPTER **2**

Chapter two concerns the first dream of Nebuchadnezzar. The date of the dream falls early in Daniel's experience in Babylon. The dream is significant for picturing history through four successive Gentile empires, the last of which, in a reconstituted form, continues even into last days. The dream then pictures the rise of Christ's millennial kingdom and its complete destruction of the restored authority.

A. NEBUCHADNEZZAR'S DISTURBING DREAM (vv. 1-13)

The first dream of Nebuchadnezzar was used by him as a way of testing the authenticity of Babylon's wise men. The king was disturbed by the dream, recognized it to be unusually significant, and wanted it interpreted. According to custom, he called for the wise men to do this; but then, not according to custom, he insisted that they tell him also the nature of the dream itself, as a way of proving the accuracy of the interpretation they might give. Their inability to meet this requirement gave opportunity to Daniel to present God's true interpretation. This interpretation is the principal interest of the chapter.

2:1. In the second year of the reign of Nebuchadnezzar, Nebuchadnezzar dreamed dreams, so that his spirit was troubled and his sleep left him.

In the second year: Nebuchadnezzar's dream and Daniel's exaltation to high office, received as a result of interpreting the dream, occurred in the king's second year. Comparing this with the notation of 1:5 that the trial period of the youths lasted three years, a question regarding chronological relationship arises. Did Nebuchadnezzar's dream occur within the three-year period, or after? Some expositors

48

believe that it came after, arguing that otherwise Daniel would have received his appointment to office before the close of the test period. They resolve the resulting conflict in chronology by explaining the three-year length of the trial period as including only one full year plus some part of the preceding and succeeding years. They point out that the first (partial) year of the three-year period could have been Nebuchadnezzar's accession year, the second (full) year his first official year of rule, and the third (partial) year his second official year. Thus, within the king's second year, the three-year trial period could have been finished and adequate time still left for Nebuchadnezzar's dream and Daniel's exaltation to high office. This explanation deserves careful attention and is possible.

The view that sees Nebuchadnezzar's dream occurring within the three-year trial period, however, appears to carry greater probability; as several considerations show. (1) Although, as the above explanation implies, certain situations presented in the Bible do permit a three-year designation to mean something less than three full years, this one regarding the education of young men does not seem to do so. A period of education would have called for a definite length of time, not one loosely designated as only some parts of three successive years. Also, there is evidence that a parallel training period of the later Persians[1] did cover three full years. (2) Applying this full three-year period to the case of Daniel and his friends, who likely arrived in Babylon in the spring of Nebuchadnezzar's accession year,[2] the completion of the third year would have been in the spring of the king's third year, not the second. (3) The assumption of the opposing view, that Daniel could not have received his exaltation to high office prior to the close of the three-year trial period, is not necessarily correct. The account in 1:18, 19, where the examination of the youths is set forth, does not require Daniel to have been among the others who were then tested. Probably the three friends were there, but Daniel may well have already been established in the position that he received as a reward for the interpretation. The comparison indicated there, that none of the other youths came up to the measure of Daniel and the friends, would still have been appropriate. (4) The opposing view further asserts that Daniel and his friends must have already received appointments as ordinary wise men prior to Nebuchadnezzar's dream, because they were included in the resulting order that all wise men be killed (2:13). This receives answer, however, in the probability that the four were classified as trainees for this specific type of work, which automatically included them in the blanket order. (5) As positive evidence that they were only trainees at the time, the fact may be noted

---

[1] Cf. Montgomery, MICC, p. 122, for references.
[2] Cf. *supra,* Introduction, pp. 25-27.

that Daniel was not summoned by Nebuchadnezzar when the regular wise men were (2:2), and also that Daniel clearly dissociated himself from the wise men, as indicated in 2:27.

Dreamed dreams: The plural "dreams" is used, whereas the following verses refer to Nebuchadnezzar's dream in the singular, and Daniel's later recall of the dream indicates singularity. Possibly Nebuchadnezzer dreamed the same dream more than once, or it may be a reference to the various aspects of the dream. Some believe the plural form may indicate a dream state, in which the God-sent dream was given. *His spirit was troubled:* Literally, "his spirit smote itself." The verb *pa'am* "to strike" is used in the hithpael (reflexive). The significance is that Nebuchadnezzar was highly agitated on awaking. This means that he recognized the dream to be significant and a cause of concern, prompting him to desire that an interpretation be given immediately. *His sleep left him:* Literally, "his sleep had happened upon him," meaning that his sleep was finished. He could sleep no more.

2:2. Then the king commanded to call the magicians, the enchanters, the sorcerers, and the Chaldeans to make known to the king his dreams. So they came and stood before the king.

The king commanded: The hour was likely still early when the king gave the order to attendants that interpreters be summoned. Those summoned would not have hesitated, no matter how inconvenient the hour. *Magicians, enchanters:* These terms are the same as used in 1:20 (which see). *Sorcerers:* The word is *mᵉkashshᵉpîm* and likely refers to the religious group known from Akkadian texts as *kashshapu*. This group used herbs, charms, and various potions, and was considered to be in league with evil forces. Sorcery (also called witchcraft) of this kind was widespread in ancient time and is strongly condemned in the Old Testament (cf. Ex. 22:18; Deut. 18:10; Isa. 47:9, 12; Jer. 27:9). This type of person, as well as the magician, had been employed by the Pharaoh to compete with Moses (Ex. 7:11). In the New Testament, Simon of Samaria, who made a false profession of salvation, was a sorcerer (Acts 8:9-24). *Chaldeans:* This term *(kasdîm)* carries two different meanings in the book of Daniel. One is ethnic, designating a group of people who had migrated into Babylonia, and who had by this time even succeeded in placing a family on the throne. Nebuchadnezzar himself was a Chaldean. The other is descriptive, designating a class of priests or wise men,[3] which is the use here. Neither this, nor the other three terms, however, should be pressed as to their technical distinctions, as was noted to be the case also in respect to two of them in 1:20. In fact, the book of Daniel

---

[3] For a discussion of Chaldeans in Daniel, cf. Young, YPD, appendix III, pp. 271-73, where he points out that Herodotus (1:181) uses the term to designate "priests of this god (Bel)."

refers to classes of wise men numerous times (cf. 2:10, 27; 4:7; 5:7, 11, 15), using a total of six different terms for them, and in none of the instances should the distinctions be pressed. Reference is regularly to the overall group of wise men. The use of as many as four terms here is to say that Nebuchadnezzar wanted all present who could possibly contribute to the information he wanted. *They came and stood:* In an appropriate room, likely designated in the king's order, the wise men assembled, probably with haste.

2:3, 4.   The king said to them, I have dreamed a dream, and my spirit is troubled to know the dream. Then the Chaldeans responded to the king (in Aramaic) O king, live forever; tell your servants the dream, and we will show its interpretation.

The king said: Properly, the king began the word interchange; stating that he had dreamed, was disturbed as a result, and wanted to know what the dream meant.

The Chaldeans: Whether this term is used specifically or generally is difficult to know. It may refer to all the wise men thus cited, as answering as a total group; or, it may refer to only the Chaldeans in the group, answering on behalf of all. If the latter is true, this group must have been considered the more important. *(In Aramaic):* This phrase is placed in parentheses because it is best taken as Daniel's indication to the reader that the Aramaic language was from that point on to be used in the book.[4] This means that the phrase is not a part of the story proper; that is, not saying particularly that these Chaldeans spoke at this time in Aramaic. They probably did, and that they did may have been the reason for Daniel's beginning to use Aramaic at this point in the story; but the main import of the phrase is to say that from here on (until 7:28) Daniel's account is written in Aramaic.[5] *O king, live forever:* This manner of address to monarchs was customary for the day (cf. 3:9; 5:10; 6:6, 21). *We will show:* This was a well-meant promise on the part of these men. Extant religious texts show that interpretation of dreams was an art in which wise men were believed to be skilled. They had manuals to state what the various factors which might appear in a dream signified. All they had to know was the nature of the dream so that their rules could be applied. Such an interpretation would not have been a true one, but it would have satisfied ignorant people.

[4] Cf. *supra,* Introduction, pp. 18, 19 for discussion of the reason.
[5] The Aramaic language was known by both Assyrians and some Israelites as early as 701 B.C. (2 Kings 18:26; Isa. 36:11). It was the official language of the Persian Empire (550-450 B.C.). Many business documents in Aramaic have been found dating from the eighth to the fifth centuries, which, with the Aramaic papyri of Elephantine in Egypt, show that Aramaic became actually the *lingua franca* of all southwest Asia.

2:5, 6. The king answered and said to the Chaldeans, The order from me is sure, that if you do not tell me the dream and its interpretation, you shall be cut in pieces and your houses made a dunghill. But if you tell the dream and its interpretation, you will receive gifts, a present, and high honor from me; therefore, show the dream and its interpretation.

Order from me is sure: The word for "sure" *('azda')* is a noun. It occurs in the Old Testament only here and in verse eight. The Greek and Latin versions give it a verbal sense, "has gone from me," apparently taking it as a derivative of the root *'azal* "to go away or depart." This derivation is not likely, however, for it requires the substitution of a "d" for an "l." It is better taken as a Persian loan word[6] meaning "sure." It is not probable that Nebuchadnezzar spoke of having forgotten the dream, then, as the translation of KJV indicates (influenced by the Greek and Latin), but of his warning regarding punishment of the wise men that it was sure and unchangeable (cf. 6:12). This means that Nebuchadnezzar, in requiring the men to tell the dream, was testing them. They should prove the accuracy of the interpretation by revealing the contents of the dream. He had no criterion by which to judge their interpretation, but he did as to the dream itself. The fact that he had not forgotten the dream is further indicated by both the degree of emotional disturbance he experienced as a result of the dream and the continual insistence of the wise men that he not require them to tell it. They clearly did not believe that he had forgotten it. *Cut in pieces:* This punishment was to dismember the body, something terribly abhorrent but apparently practiced with some frequency in ancient times (cf. 3:29; 1 Sam. 15:33). *Made a dunghill:* The word for "dunghill" *(neʷwalî)* is dubious in meaning. It may mean "dunghill" as usually translated here, but rather good evidence is adduced from the Akkadian that it means simply "ruin." Support for this is taken from Ezra 6:11, where it appears again, the text there speaking of a house being pulled down, resulting in a "ruin." At any rate, both meanings speak of a tragic end to a house, and both are possible so far as practices of the day are concerned.

But if: The king next listed benefits for compliance with his order, thus providing both negative and positive incentives for the wise men. In this the king demonstrated further his keen desire that the dream be interpreted. *Gifts, a present, and high honor:* The first two items appear to refer to material benefits and the third to an aspect of public recognition. The word for "present" *(neʷbizbah)* is also uncertain in meaning, but it appears to be in the singular, making it a reference to a particular present, no doubt known then though not today. Nebu-

[6] Cf. Montgomery, MICC, pp. 147, 48.

chadnezzar could be expected to give valuable gifts, and certainly any public honor would have been very attractive. The positive incentives were as desirable as the negative were fearful.

2:7-9. They answered a second time and said, Let the king tell his servants the dream, and we will tell the interpretation. The king replied and said, I know with certainty that you are trying to gain time, because you see that the order from me is sure that if you do not tell me the dream there is but one sentence for you. You have agreed to speak lying and corrupt words before me until the time be changed; therefore, tell me the dream so that I can know that you can declare its interpretation.

They answered a second time: The double incentives made no difference; the wise men were unable to add anything to their first response. They could give an interpretation, according to their rule books, but they could not tell the dream itself. They recognized their limitation and apparently hoped that the king would become more "reasonable" in his demand.

To gain time: Literally, "to buy time," meaning to put off the fatal moment when their inability would be found out. In these and the following words, Nebuchadnezzar gave additional evidence that he was testing the men. In fact, the words show the purpose for the test to be a confirmation of his suspicions of them. He may have been suspicious of them because of past interpretations, for he was quick to charge them with lack of integrity. This was most unusual for a king of that time when most leaders acceded to the declarations of their diviners without question, for fear of supernatural reprisal if they did not. Nebuchadnezzar, however, was an unusual king. *The order from me is sure:* See the comments on verse five for a discussion of the word "sure."

But one sentence: Reference is to the sentence set forth in verse five, that the men would be cut in pieces and their houses be made dunghills. The phrase stresses the idea of no alternative to this severe punishment. *Lying and corrupt words:* "Lying" and "corrupt" should be taken together, to mean "wicked lies." This is the second charge the king made against the men. Not only were they trying "to gain time," but they were doing so by employing "lying and corrupt words" on which they had agreed. The lying words to which he referred must be the promise of the men to give the interpretation if only the king would tell the content of the dream. It seems clear that Nebuchadnezzar did not believe they could do this. *Until the time be changed:* The word for "time" *('iddana')* is significantly the same as in verse eight. Nebuchadnezzar charged them with employing deceit until success might come in gaining the time they needed. He perceived their thoughts—that if they could be given more time, they could somehow maneuver out of their perilous situation. Nebuchadnezzar seems to have revealed by these words his evaluation of their performance on previous occasions. It is quite clear that he had been less than satisfied. *So that I can know:* With these words, the king stated directly that the ability of the men to tell the dream would be proof of their ability to give the interpretation.

2:10, 11. The Chaldeans answered before the king and said, There is not a man upon the earth who is able to tell the king's matter; for no great and mighty king has ever asked a matter like this of any magician, enchanter, or Chaldean. The thing which the king asks is difficult, and there is not another that can tell it before the king except the gods, whose dwelling is not with flesh.

Not a man: In reply to the king, the wise men openly admitted their inability to tell the king's dream. They tried to temper the confession by asserting that no one else could tell it either. In other words, the king was simply unreasonable to require it. They were correct in stating that "not a man upon the earth" could do this, but what they did not realize was that a man was at hand who could receive the information from heaven. Their admission nicely set the stage for Daniel's entry to bring God's interpretation. Nebuchadnezzar's impression of him would be the greater as a result. *Great and mighty king:* "Great" *(rab)* and "mighty" *(shallît)* are better taken as adjectives modifying "king," than as nouns ("lord" and "ruler") as in KJV. The thought is that no king, even though great and mighty (as Nebuchadnezzar was), had ever asked such a thing. By this the wise men wished to stress the degree of difficulty involved in meeting the request. It should be noted also that they were quite critical of Nebuchadnezzar in this statement, implying that he was wrong in making the demand. This was hardly a wise action, since his displeasure with them was already marked.

Difficult: The word for "difficult" *(yaqqîrah)* is from a root meaning "heavy." The wise men thus enlarged on the reason why they could not comply with the king's demand. *Not another:* This repeats their statement of verse ten, indicating their desire to emphasize the point. *Except the gods:* This element was implied in the previous verse, but here it is stated directly. Only superintelligence, belonging to deity, could reveal this kind of information. Actually, this was a major confession on the part of these men—admitting that they could not do what they were supposed to do. Their business was to make contact with the divine realm and find out such information. This confession further paved the way for Daniel's entry. *Not with flesh:* That is, "not with man." The men thus showed their thinking regarding the distinction between the natural and supernatural realms: gods lived above men, not with them. Pagan concepts of the day did not view gods as infinite, however, but merely more capable than men.

2:12, 13. Therefore the king was indignant and very angry, and commanded to destroy all the wise men of Babylon. Then the decree went forth, so that wise men were being slain, and they sought Daniel and his companions to slay them.

Therefore: The phrase for "therefore" *(kol-qᵉbel d nah)* shows a causal relationship between the king's anger and what has gone before. Three contributing factors may be distinguished as constituting this cause: the king's disappointment in not receiving satisfactory information relative to this matter of extreme concern to him; the confirmation of his suspicion that these men could not do what they had been purporting to do, which meant that previous interpretations likely had been wrong and he could not expect anything better in the future; and the audacity of these men, incapable and deceiving as they were, in now daring to criticize him for testing them in this manner. *Indignant and very angry:* The words for "indignant" *(bᵉnas)* and for "angry" *(qᵉtsap)* are verbs and close synonyms, with the second modified by the adverb. Together they indicate intense anger on the king's part. Nebuchadnezzar had numerous virtues, but self-control was not one of them (cf. 3:19-22). *Commanded to destroy:* This was an order for violence. The number of all the wise men would have been large, but all were to be killed. Apparently, the king reasoned—with what reason remained to him in his fury—that if these men could not do their job, they might as well be done away with. *Babylon:* Since in 2:49 and 3:1 the full phrase "province of Babylon" is used for designating the entire country, Nebuchadnezzar may have had in mind here only the city of Babylon. If so, the number to be killed would not have been quite as many, though likely most did live in the capital city.

Decree went forth: Having pronounced the sentence to the wise men before him, Nebuchadnezzar issued the order publicly, so that his executioners might begin the gruesome task. Certainly, the people would have been deeply stirred at such an order against men highly honored. *Were being slain:* The word used is a participle *(mitqattᵉlîn)* and is best taken to signify that the slaying was already being done by the time word came to Daniel and his companions. This is supported by the fact that when the informers came to Daniel and his friends, they did so, not only to state the decree, but to take their lives. *They sought Daniel:* That Daniel and his friends were sought as a result of the decree makes the fact clear that they were classified as wise men. That they did not know of the decree, however, until the informers arrived at their room implies that they were not full members, but only trainees, as noted under verse one above.

B. THE DREAM REVEALED TO DANIEL (vv. 14-30)

The story now tells of God revealing the contents of the dream to Daniel, so that he might convey the information to the king.

2:14, 15. Then Daniel answered with wisdom and discretion to Arioch, the captain of the king's guard, who had gone forth to kill the wise men of Babylon. He answered and said to Arioch, high-officer of the king, Why is the decree from the king so harsh? Then Arioch made the matter known to Daniel.

Then Daniel: Daniel is now introduced into the story. His strength and quality as a person became evident immediately. He was suddenly confronted by men who had been sent to take the life of himself and friends for no crime at all, and he was able to respond in the remarkable manner indicated. He evidenced no panic, no despair, no frustration, but only spoke wise words in response. People live and act in the moment of crisis as they have prepared themselves through previous experiences. Daniel demonstrated his sterling character, developed through prior days of trusting God. *Wisdom and discretion:* The word for "wisdom" *('eta')* comes from a root word meaning "to counsel," and means that which is the cause or product of good counsel. The word for "discretion" *(te'em)* literally means "taste," and speaks of *appropriateness, suitability*. Daniel replied wisely and in good taste, in keeping with the occasion and importance of the visitors. To be able to speak in this manner, under these conditions, says so much in regard to character, temperament, and ability. *Arioch, the captain of the king's guard:* The word for "guard" is from a root *(tᵉbah)* meaning "to slay," giving literally here the meaning of "king's executioners"—a designation, however, used for a king's bodyguard. Arioch, being "captain" *(rab* "chief") of this group, was an important person, and likely the one given the main responsibility to carry out the general order. That this leader was with those who came to Daniel's door was by God's providence, because it required such a person to make the necessary arrangements for Daniel to see the king. At the same time, being the head man, his appearance before Daniel and his friends would have been authoritarian and fearful. His words to them would have been brief and rough, bidding them to come with him without delay.

High officer: This word *(shallîta')* is not the same as in verse fourteen *(rab)*. It is used in verse ten to mean "mighty." It reinforces the indication just given that this man was important, saying that he was one of the king's "mighty" ones. *Harsh:* This word comes from a root *(hᵃtsap)* meaning "to be sharp." Daniel wondered why the king's word was so sharp or harsh. In the light of what follows, Daniel apparently was asking for information. If the king had issued an order of this severity, a major reason must exist. *Then Arioch:* This high official may have been quite surprised that the four did not know about the general order. Why they did not is not indicated, but perhaps they had kept much to themselves, being God-fearing Judeans and maintaining distinctness in their menu. Whatever the reason, Arioch now took time to inform them. For this he must be commended, for many rough men would have cared little whether their intended victims knew the reasons for their being killed or not. No doubt, Daniel's own controlled manner had a beneficial effect on him. All of this, of course, was under God's blessing and control.

2:16. Then Daniel went in and asked of the king that he would give him time, and the interpretation he would tell the king.

Then Daniel: The story is abbreviated at this point. It may be assumed that, following Arioch's statement of the dire situation for Babylon's wise men, Daniel asked to see the king, promising to do what this verse says he did. Then apparently Arioch, remarkably, made arrangements for him to do so. He might have dismissed the request lightly, thinking the young man to be only a brash upstart. After all, Daniel and his friends were only foreign trainees; and he, Arioch, was the king's high-officer, with much work to do. That he reacted as he did was due, of course, to God's gracious intervention, so that Daniel might be brought before Nebuchadnezzar. The high courage and faith of Daniel and his friends in this request must not be overlooked. They were telling this high-officer that, if he would make arrangements for Daniel to see the king, Daniel would be able to do what all the other wise men could not do! *Give him time:* The promise was given, not only to the king's officer, but then also to Nebuchadnezzar himself. Arioch, being important as he was, could and did arrange for the interview, and Daniel made his appearance before the greatest king of the day. The thrust of his words was that if the king would give him time, he would tell the king what he wanted to know. By this he admitted that he did not know then; but, at the same time, asserted that he would in due course. Probably a limit to the time allotted was established; but clearly the king did accede to the young man's proposition. Implied is the fact that the execution of wise men ceased until that time should come. All the wise men who yet lived owed an enormous debt of gratitude to Daniel that memorable day. *The interpretation:* Though this word normally refers only to the interpretation of a dream, and not its contents, it must stand for both elements here, because the king would not have been satisfied with anything less from Daniel than he had demanded of the other wise men. The record in these verses is intentionally brief.

2:17. Then Daniel returned to his house and told the matter to Hananiah, Mishael, and Azariah his companions:

Returned to his house: With the agreement made, Daniel left the palace and returned to his place of residence. His "house" *(bayit)* was probably a room in one of the residence halls, used for the young training foreigners. As Daniel made his way back there, mixed thoughts must have whirled through his head. He had just been in the very presence of Nebuchadnezzar, high and mighty as he was, and he had told him that he, Daniel, young as he was, would reveal to him what mature wise men had not been able to tell. Furthermore, at that moment he had no idea of what this information was. He did not know what the king had dreamed. Would God really honor him so much as to tell him? He had never experienced this kind of miraculous contact with God before. Would it really happen now? *Told the matter:* When Daniel reached his room, the three young men, his friends, were no doubt eagerly awaiting a report. The scene must have been a stirring one as he told them of the interview—what the king had said, and what he in turn had promised. Surely, they listened eagerly, not wanting to miss any word or implication; and they must have flooded him with questions, wanting to know every detail. *His companions:* This is the first indication of what has been assumed in the commentary; namely, that Daniel's friends were involved in this situation. Verse thirteen states that the order affected them, but they are not said above to have been present when Arioch spoke with Daniel. That Daniel returned to them, however, implies rather clearly that they had been present then; and, moreover, gives reason to believe that the four roomed together. Certainly they would have wanted to do so, and, with their special menu, it is more than likely that Ashpenaz would have wanted it this way also.

2:18. That they would seek mercies from the God of heaven concerning this secret, so that Daniel and his companions might not perish with the rest of the wise men of Babylon.

That they would: This verse continues Daniel's words to his companions as he urged them now to seek mercies from God. In other words, each was to pray that God would be gracious and give them the necessary information. The thought may have been to pray separately, but, since the concern was common to all, likely it was to pray together in a prayer meeting. What a fine picture: four young men, still in their teens, bowed in prayer before God! *Seek mercies:* The word for "mercies" *(raḥ^amîn)* is a plural of intensity, corresponding in meaning to the Hebrew equivalent used in 1:9 (which see). Notice should be made that Daniel wanted them to ask for "mercies," not directly for the needed information. The object in view was the information, of course, but apparently Daniel recognized that something preceded it in importance. This was the merciful attitude of God, which would permit Him to reveal it. This, in turn, required a humbling of their hearts before God, so that He might be thus merciful. *God of heaven:* This designation for God appears to have been employed especially about the time of the Exile (cf. Dan. 2:19, 44; Ezra 1:2; 6:10; 7:12, 21; Neh. 1:5; 2:4). It was particularly significant when used in a country foreign to Israel, for it carried the thought that God was over the sun, moon, and stars, which were worshiped by the pagans. *This secret:* God's mercies were to be sought in reference to the king's dream, now hidden and "secret" from them. Great faith was necessary to ask God to reveal this information which was not known at the time. *Might not perish:* The young men certainly had incentive for praying earnestly: their lives were at stake. The reality of this had been impressed upon them, too, by the actual coming of Arioch to take them off for execution at his first appearance. They prayed earnestly. No doubt, a major reason for little answer to prayer among Christians generally is lack of true earnestness in praying—doing so only as a matter of routine, using repeated, often empty phrases. *Rest of the wise men:* This does not mean that all other wise men did die. Very likely, some already had been killed; but it is safe to believe that executions ceased during Daniel's allotted time to tell the dream. There is no reason, either, to believe that they were resumed when the dream had been revealed. At the time, however, Daniel had no way of knowing what might eventuate in this regard.

2:19. Then the secret was revealed to Daniel in a vision at night, and Daniel blessed the God of heaven.

The secret was revealed: The contents of the dream were revealed to Daniel. The exact events which preceded the revelation itself would be interesting to know, but are not indicated. Since the information came "at night," it is likely that the prayer time of the four closed and that they went to bed, still not having heard from heaven. But during the night, the information came. God revealed it to Daniel. *Vision at night:* God's way of revealing it was by a vision. Visions could be given in the daytime also (Dan. 8:1-3), but God brought this one at night. It was a tremendous experience for a young man. It meant not only that Daniel could fulfill his promise to Nebuchadnezzar, and so save his own life and the lives of many others, but also that God had actually revealed something, supernaturally, to him! Since the information came to Daniel alone, he would have had to share it with the three friends; and, very likely, he did so yet that night, waking them from sleep. The thrill would have been great for them as well. *Daniel blessed:* Daniel not only received from

God, but he also blessed God. "To bless" (root, b^erak), in the sense here intended, is "to wish pleasure towards" and "to praise." Daniel is to be commended for not neglecting this response to God's gracious favor. The content of his blessing follows.

2:20-22. Daniel answered and said, Blessed be the name of God forever and ever, because wisdom and power are his. He changes times and seasons; he removes kings and sets up kings; he gives wisdom to the wise and knowledge to those who know understanding. He reveals the deep and hidden things, he knows what is in the darkness, and light dwells with him.

Name of God: God's name stands for God Himself and all that is gloriously true of Him, particularly as manifested to His creatures. *Wisdom and power:* With these two words, Daniel began to list reasons why God's name should be blessed. The word for "wisdom" $(hokm^eta')$ speaks of knowledge and capacity for proper decision. The word for "power" $(g^eb\hat{u}r^eta')$ refers to ability to effect a decison. God has both.

He changes: The use of the personal pronoun serves to stress God, in distinction from any other, as the One who does the things listed. The word for "changes" (root, sh^ena') is a participle, showing continuedness of action. *Times and seasons:* These two words *('iddanayya'* and *zimmayya'*) are used synonymously; referring not to seasons of the year, but to events of history. God controls historical events, either actively or permissively. Daniel had just been impressed with this truth in the revelation of Nebuchadnezzar's dream and its interpretation; the dream outlining the course of gentile history to come. *Removes kings:* A significant way in which God controls history is by removing and establishing kings. The dream depicted this being done, as empires were symbolized successively falling and being replaced by others. *He gives wisdom . . . and knowledge:* The words for "wisdom" *(hokm^eta')* and "knowledge" *(mand^e'a')* are the equivalents in meaning to the Hebrew words used in 1:4, 17 (which see). The thought is that all the wisdom and knowledge that man has comes from God. Daniel's knowledge of the king's dream had just come directly from God. *Who know understanding:* The word for "understanding" *(bînah)* is the noun form of the verb (root, $bîn$) translated (from its corresponding Hebrew root) "understanding" in 1:4 and "had insight" in 1:17. The phrase means simply, "who possess understanding."

Deep and hidden: The word for "deep" *('ammîqata')* refers to something inaccessible or unsearchable (Ps. 92:6), and the word for "hidden" *(m^esatt^erata')* to something excluded from knowledge (Judges 3:19). The words complement each other in stressing God's ability to disclose information so characterized. *Darkness:* This word *(h^ashôka')* parallels the former two, speaking of that type of information on which the light of understanding does not shine. The three words are closely related: the second showing how the first is "unsearchable," and the third how the second is "hidden." *Light dwells:* "Light" *(nᵉhîra')* symbolizes *knowledge.* Because light dwells with God, He can dispel the darkness of the deep and hidden. The word for "dwells" *(shᵉre')* means first "to loose," and then "to dwell," the latter being derived from the former with the idea of *loosening·* girths or loads of the pack animal for the purpose of encamping. To say that light thus dwells with God means that He has it constantly. The overall thought of the verse is suggested to Daniel by God's revelation, just given, bringing "light" on the "darkness" of the "deep and hidden" dream of the king. Since Christ is particularly "the Light" of God (John 1:4-8), numerous expositors see an intended secondary reference to Him, as the One who dispels the darkness of sin; and Christ does indeed dwell with the Father.

2:23. I thank and praise thee, O God of my fathers, that thou hast given me wisdom and power, and now thou hast caused me to know what we desired from thee, even the matter of the king thou hast caused us to know.

Thank and praise: These two words (roots, *yᵉda'* and *shᵉbah*) are used synonymously to stress Daniel's thanksgiving. With these words, he came to speak particularly of the current revelation; the former words of the prayer having blessed God for wisdom and power in general. Daniel is relieved and delighted that God has so favored him. Notice should be made that "thee" comes first in the Hebrew sentence, giving stress on God as the One to whom the praise is given. God is pleased when His children praise Him (Luke 17:16-18). *God of my fathers:* This designation for God carries a historical connotation. Daniel thus links himself with his forebears in rendering this praise. *Wisdom and power:* The same words are used as in verse twenty. Daniel says that God, who has true wisdom and power, has granted the same to him. His reference appears to be to wisdom and power which he, Daniel, continues to enjoy regularly, and not merely to the fresh insight given regarding the dream. This follows from the fact that the latter is the subject of the following statement. *Caused me to know:* Reference now is to the specific matter of the dream. God had caused Daniel to know this information. As a way of stressing the importance of the information, Daniel referred to it in two ways: first, as that for which the young men had asked in their prayer meeting; and, second, as that which concerned the king. Note that Daniel gave credit and place to his three friends, twice employing the first plural pronoun.

2:24. Therefore, Daniel went to Arioch, whom the king had appointed to destroy the wise men of Babylon. He went and spoke thus to him:

Do not kill the wise men of Babylon; bring me to the king, and I will tell the interpretation to the king.

Went to Arioch: People do not go to kings directly. Daniel was courageous to go even to Arioch, high official that he was. But Arioch was the logical one to approach, because he knew of the earlier meeting between Daniel and Nebuchadnezzar; and Daniel could be sure that he would listen to him, since he had listened to him before and Daniel now had the all-important information concerning the dream. *Do not kill:* It is significant that the first matter of which Daniel spoke was for Arioch not to kill more wise men. This shows his concern for their lives, though he may have had little previous contact with them. He was not so occupied with his own importance (even though he had just received knowledge concerning the dream) that he did not think of others. Because Arioch likely had not been killing wise men since Daniel's agreement with Nebuchadnezzar the previous day, the thrust of Daniel's words was that he not begin to do so again. *I will tell:* Daniel now stated the reason why Arioch need not begin killing again; he, Daniel, would meet the king's condition by telling him what he wanted to know. Whatever Arioch had thought concerning Daniel before—and it must have been good, since he had arranged for even the first meeting with the king—he would have come to think of him more highly now. This young man had apparently experienced a contact with the supernatural realm which had eluded all the other wise men.

2:25, 26. **Then Arioch quickly brought Daniel before the king, and spoke thus to him, I have found a man of the captives of Judah, who will tell the king the interpretation. The king answered and said to Daniel, whose name was Belteshazzar, Are you able to tell me the dream I have seen and its interpretation?**

Arioch quickly brought: The word for "quickly" is an infinitive construct, from the root *bᵉhal,* which means "to be alarmed" and "to hasten." The word connotes emotional involvement on the part of Arioch, as he quickly responded to Daniel's words, made necessary arrangements, and brought the young man to the king. Apparently he wanted to associate himself more closely with Daniel in this second meeting than the first, being now more sure of the outcome. *I have found:* He also sought credit for himself this time, claiming to have found Daniel. He did have some credit coming, at least in that he had not dismissed Daniel's request, either the first or second time, as many would have done. But he had not found Daniel; rather, Daniel had pressed himself on him. Human nature is prone to seek all the credit possible, whether deserved or not. *A man of the captives:* This manner of announcing Daniel sounds very formal, since Daniel had just seen the king shortly before. Indeed, if a set time had then been established for a return meeting, which is likely, the king would have been expecting Daniel, or at least a report from him. Arioch's formality may have been due to his not having been present the first time, and so not knowing of such prior arrangements. Customary court decorum may also have been a factor. Furthermore, Nebuchadnezzar may not have known very much about Daniel at the first meeting, and Arioch was using this second occasion to supply some information. *Who will tell:* These were the crucial words the king wanted to hear. The young man had said he would return with the information, but Nebuchadnezzar would have had serious doubts that he could. Now Arioch was saying that he had done so.

Whose name was Belteshazzar: Daniel had been given this Babylonian name when he first arrived in Babylon (cf. 1:7). It has not been mentioned in the story since the time it was given, but now Nebuchadnezzar used it in addressing Daniel. Its use here likely indicates that Nebuchadnezzar intentionally thought of Daniel, along with the other trainees, as a Babylonian, properly bearing a Babylonian name. *Are you able:* Nebuchadnezzar's interest was in the one matter of the dream and its interpretation, and he asked directly concerning Daniel's ability in regard to it. It should be noted, also, that he mentioned specifically both "the dream" and "its interpretation." He had wanted the first told by the wise men as proof that they could give the second; and he demanded the same from Daniel.

2:27, 28. Daniel answered before the king and said, The secret which the king asks, the wise men, enchanters, magicians, and soothsayers cannot tell the king. But there is a God in heaven who reveals secrets and makes known to King Nebuchadnezzar what shall be in the latter days. Your dream and the visions of your head on your bed are as follows.

Daniel answered: Daniel got his opportunity to tell the king the all-important information. This was a thrilling moment for him. Note, however, that he did not begin with the information itself, but with making clear to the king to whom the credit for it was due. It was not to him, but to God in heaven. In fact, Daniel's entire opening statement, through verse thirty, is to stress that fact. Such an attitude of humility pleases God. For Daniel to show it, was in direct contrast to what Arioch, in his paganism, had just displayed. *Soothsayers:* This term appears here for the first time, the other two employed having been used in 1:20 and 2:2 (which see). The term *gaz^{e}rîn* comes from the root *g^{e}zar,* which means first "to cut" and then "to decide," making this noun form to mean "deciders" or "fate determiners." These three terms are best taken to be appositional with the general first term "wise men." *Cannot tell:* Daniel began by agreeing with the earlier statement of the wise men themselves, that they, mere men, were incapable of telling the king's secret. The observation was made to stress, in contrast, that only God was able to reveal it.

But there is: Daniel proceeded to call Nebuchadnezzar's attention to the true God in heaven. Where the gods of Babylon, through their representatives, had not been able to aid the king, Daniel's God in heaven could do so. Note in Daniel's statement that, whereas Arioch has just directed attention to Daniel himself, Daniel moves that attention on to God. He makes a direct point of telling the king that the information he was about to relate was due to his God and not to himself. *God in heaven:* By this phrase, Daniel distinguished the true God, the God who has revealed the vital information, from Nebuchadnezzar's Babylonian deities. The phrase is nearly the same as in 2:18, 19, but there it is not used in speaking to a pagan. For Daniel to make the sharp distinction and accordingly imply definite superiority for this God over those in which Nebuchadnezzar believed, took remarkable courage. But this was an opportunity to witness to the truth before even this great monarch, and Daniel dared to use it. *King Nebuchadnezzar:* This proper term of address should be noted. In using the term "king" in addition to the name, Daniel was indicating that, though he may have seemed brash in speaking in this manner, he did not intend to be and that he did humbly recognize the high position of the person before him. Humility and courtesy are always appropriate. *The latter days:* This phrase *('aḥᵃrît yômayya')* is used fourteen times in the Old Testament and regularly refers to the closing portion of a time period then in the mind of the speaker or writer (cf. Gen. 49:1). From the nature of the dream, the time period in view here is Gentile history, brought to a close by Christ's millennial kingdom (cf. vv. 44, 45). This Old Testament phrase is paralleled in the New Testament (cf. 1 Tim. 4:1; 2 Tim. 3:1; 1 Pet. 1:5; 2 Pet. 3:3; Jude 18). *Visions:* This plural is best taken as parallel in significance to that of "dreams" in 2:1 (which see). A similar use of the plural occurs with the dream of chapter four (vv. 5, 10, 13).

2:29, 30. You, O king, had thoughts on your bed concerning what should happen after this, and the Revealer of secrets has told you what will be. This secret has been revealed to me, not because of wisdom in me more than others who live, but that the interpretation might be told to the king and that you may know the thoughts of your heart.

Had thoughts: This is not likely a reference to the dream itself, but to thoughts which passed through the king's mind before he fell asleep on the night of the dream. He had been wondering how matters would work out for his vast empire. What did the future hold?

After this: This phrase does not carry the same meaning as "latter days" of the preceding verse. It refers only to days which Nebuchadnezzar could expect to occur within his own lifetime. *Revealer of secrets:* This is a reference to God. The use of the singular carries the thought that He alone can reveal secrets. Daniel meant to say that Nebuchadnezzar's questions that night had been answered by this supreme God in the form of the all-important dream.

To me: This element appears first in the Hebrew sentence, carrying an evident parallel force with the "You" (also coming first) of the preceding verse. "You" (Nebuchadnezzar) and "me" (Daniel) were the two principals involved, and Daniel thus spoke of the relative place of each. *Not because:* Daniel once more disclaimed any credit for his knowledge of the dream. He was himself no wiser than the men who had failed earlier. The difference lay solely with the source of his information. *But that:* Daniel indicated a two-fold reason why he had been given this information: first, that the interpretation which the king wanted might be told to him; and, second, that the questions which the king had wondered about the evening before might be answered. In other words, the king's questions had been proper; God accordingly had answered them through the dream, and now God had revealed the meaning of the dream to Daniel so that Nebuchadnezzar might know those answers. Daniel thus gave God the highest honor, as the One who had given the revelation; assigned Nebuchadnezzar the second place of importance, as central in God's thinking for giving the revelation; and left himself the third place, as merely the one through whom God has given the interpretation. Daniel's commendable humility is once more evident.

C. THE DREAM AND ITS INTERPRETATION (vv. 31-45)

With these preliminary clarifications made, Daniel began to tell the contents of the dream and its interpretation. In respect to significance for the entire book, it is this portion of the chapter which carries the greatest importance. After Daniel told the contents of the dream, as evidence of the authenticity of the interpretation to follow, he gave the interpretation. What he said outlines the centuries of Gentile history following Daniel, and this outline is closely paralleled in Daniel's later personal vision described in chapter seven.

2:31-33. You, O king, were looking, and, lo, a great image—this image was large and its brightness surpassing—stood before you and its appearance was awesome. The head of this image was of fine gold, its chest and arms of silver, its abdomen and thighs of brass, its legs of iron, its feet partly of iron and partly of baked clay.

Were looking: Daniel said that the king saw himself in his dream looking about, when his eyes lighted upon a great image. *A great image:* The image was not an idol for worship, but a statue to be viewed. It stood before the king where he could easily survey it. *This image was large and its brightness surpassing:* These two descriptive items tell how the image was "great." The first is that it was large in size *(rab),* though how large is not indicated, as was the image of chapter three, which was ninety feet high. The second is that it had a bright luster, no doubt because of its metallic construction. *Awesome:* This word is a passive participle from a root verb *(dᵉhal),* meaning "to fear." The image was of a kind to instill fear in the king's heart, apparently because of its size, brightness, and features now to be set forth.

The head of this image: Literally, "It—the image—its head." The entire image, then, is stressed first, with the head being mentioned as the chief of the parts. The importance of the head as chief is symbolized not only by being the head, but by being made of gold. It is also a unified whole, in distinction from the other parts. Three other main divisions are to be distinguished, according to Daniel's following interpretation. *Its chest and arms:* This is the second division, next lowest in the human anatomy. It was made of silver, closer in value to gold than were the various other metals represented. *Its abdomen and thighs:* This is the third division, made of brass, again next in value. *Its legs of iron, its feet:* This is the fourth division, the legs made of iron, and the feet of iron mixed with baked clay, once more materials lesser in value. *Baked clay:* The word used *(ḥaᵃsap)* means clay that has been baked, as a piece of pottery. The mixture of which the feet were made, then, was of hard durable iron and hard brittle clay.

2:34, 35. You continued to look until a stone was cut out without hands, and it struck the image at its feet of iron and clay, and crushed them. Indeed, the iron, the clay, the brass, the silver, and the gold were crushed together, and became like chaff from summer threshing floors, so that the wind carried them away, with no place being found for them. Then the stone which struck the image became a great mountain and filled all the earth.

Continued to look: The use of the participle *(ḥazeh)* is to depict the king continuing to observe the image. *Without hands:* After watching for a time, he saw a stone, apparently large, cut out from a mountain (v. 45) without human hands being involved, signifying supernatural activity. *Struck the image:* He saw the stone move toward the image, presumably at great speed, and strike it at the feet, crushing them.

Were crushed together: Not only the feet, but the entire image, composed of the brass, silver, and gold, as well as the iron and clay, was crushed. *Became like chaff:* The figure is taken from the well-known threshing operation of the day. When the wind blew, the flailed grain was tossed into the air so that the worthless chaff might blow away. The various metals of the image are thus symbolized as worthless and scattered without trace. *Became a great mountain:* In contrast, the destroying stone thereupon became all-important, growing to mountain-size, filling all the earth.

2:36-38. This is the dream, and now we shall set forth its interpretation before the king. You, O king—being king of kings, to whom the God of heaven has given a kingdom, strength, power, and honor, so that wherever sons of men, beasts of the field, or birds of the heavens dwell, he has given them into your hand and caused you to rule over them—are the head of gold.

We shall: The first plural form of the verb is used, designating Daniel plus someone else. No hint otherwise is given that his friends were with him, therefore this other one is God.

God of heaven: This is Daniel's characteristic way of referring to the true God (cf. v. 28), used here to indicate that Nebuchadnezzar, worshiper of Babylon's false gods, was dependent on this God for the fine things now to be listed. This must have sounded strange to the king, here in the midst of Daniel's message to him, but he did not interrupt the speaker, likely because he was so interested in what he was yet to say. *A kingdom:* The first item listed is Nebuchadnezzar's very kingdom. The "strength, power, and honor," listed next were his because of the kingdom.

So that wherever: The matter introduced by these words illustrates the extent of this "strength, power, and honor." Universality for Nebuchadnezzar's rule is thus implied. His kingdom did spread over the more important portion of the world of the day, extending from Egypt to the Persian Gulf. The titles of his rule claimed full universality for his domain. Beasts and birds are mentioned as falling under his control as a way of emphasizing the degree of his authority. He had been constituted truly "king of kings." *Head of gold:* Symbolized as the head of the image and made of gold, Nebuchadnezzar was designated the leading ruler of all represented. Since the items just listed are all given parenthetically, within the main statement, they are the items which particularly constituted him as this "head of gold." It should be noted that Nebuchadnezzar is himself identified as the head; while subsequent kingdoms, not kings, are identified with the other parts of the image. The significance is that, in respect to the kingdom of Babylonia, Nebuchadnezzar was uniquely responsible for its attaining and maintaining empire status. After him, its power diminished rapidly. It was far more his kingdom, than he was its king. The same was not true of any ruler of the succeeding empires.

2:39. After you shall stand another kingdom lower than you; and afterwards a third kingdom of brass, which shall rule over all the earth.

Another kingdom: Very little is said of either the second kingdom or the third, perhaps for the reason that each is described at greater length in Daniel's later visions. Since the third is identified with the brass portion of the image, the second must be with the silver, though this is not stated. The second can only be Medo-Persia, because it succeeded Babylonia in history; and the twofold division of the two arms suggests the twofold division of Media and Persia. *Lower than you:* This notice of inferiority regarding the second is in keeping with the progressive inferiority of the metals and also the lessening importance of the body parts concerned. The same notice is not given for the other two kingdoms, but is implied by the same factors. The aspect in which these kingdoms were inferior did not concern size, because the last three were all larger than the first. It can have referred only to quality of government. This was outstanding in respect to Nebuchadnezzar, but less so for the others. Also, Babylonian rule was truly unified, whereas divisions existed in the others. *A third kingdom:* This kingdom can only be Greece, which succeeded Medo-Persia in history. It is characterized as ruling "over all the earth." The empire fashioned by the genius of Alexander the Great did extend farther than the other three—even all the way from Egypt and Europe eastward to India.

2:40. Then there shall be a fourth kingdom, strong, like iron—for iron breaks and smashes everything—and, as iron breaks in pieces, so it will crush and break all these.

A fourth kingdom: This fourth kingdom must be Rome, for it succeeded Greece. Conservative expositors agree on this identification, but liberals do not. The latter believe it must be Greece, with the second and third kingdoms being Media and Persia, respectively (thus separating the two, rather than taking them together). Their main reason is their denial of true predictive prophecy. Believing that the book was written in the late Grecian period, they can explain the symbolism in history that far, in their naturalistic manner, but not as far as Rome. The descriptive items listed for symbolism from the part of the image concerned, however, do not fit Greece, but Rome; and the parallel symbolism of the animals in Daniel's vision of chapter seven is equally convincing. The four countries in view, then, are Babylonia, Medo-Persia, Greece, and Rome—each distinct from the other as the respective parts of the image are distinct. At the same time, the fact that all are symbolized by one unified image should not be overlooked. This signifies a unity in the distinctness, probably referring to the unity of mankind running through the distinct kingdoms. Before God, history is a whole, made up of variations of the same basic aspirations and activities of mankind involved. *Strong, like iron:* In this fourth aspect of the image, the metal involved is made symbolic of intrinsic quality as well as relative value. The stress regarding this kingdom is on strength. Rome was strong, so that no power could dislodge her as world leader for more than half a millennium, far longer than the other kingdoms.[7] *Smashes everything:* The word for "smashes" *(hashel)* is a participle and means *one which breaks by a hammer,* connoting continuedness of action. *All these:* This is a reference to the preceding kingdoms. The Roman kingdom would break the three earlier ones. The thought is not that Babylonia and Medo-Persia would still exist at the time Greece was overrun by Rome. History indicates that each was destroyed by its predecessor in turn, which is implied also in this passage (vs. 39) by the use of "after" *(batrak,* literally, "in your place") and in 8:3-8, where Medo-Persia and Greece are each represented as destroying its predecessors. The thought is that the two kingdoms preceding Greece would be broken representatively, in that the elements of each would have been respectively caught up and reduplicated in its successor.

2:41. Also, as the feet and toes were partly of potter's clay and partly of iron, as you witnessed, so the kingdom will be composite; and some of the firmness of iron shall be in it, inasmuch as you saw iron mixed with brittle baked clay.

Feet and toes: The toes of the image are mentioned here for the first time. When Daniel set forth the contents of the dream, he mentioned only legs and feet. Here, however, the idea of compositeness, which characterized the feet only (legs solidly iron), is developed as the interpretation reveals the dream in greater detail. *Composite:* The word used *(pᵉligah)* means basically "divided." In this instance, however, the division is not of one part from another, but rather of a dissolution within, as the last phrase makes clear. *Firmness of iron:* The word for "firmness" *(nitsbᵉtah),* from the verbal root *(yᵉtsab)* meaning "to be firm," carries the idea of *resistance to outside influence.* Rome was able to maintain her identity for centuries. Her government was solidly organized, her armies well drilled and disciplined, her policies with subjugated territories well defined and not overly oppressive. *Brittle baked clay:* The word for "baked clay" (vv. 33, 34) is here modified by *tina',* meaning simply "clay." The intent is to stress the clay-type characteristics of hard baked clay, thus signifying the true brittle nature of it, in contrast to the strong iron. Because the mixture of baked clay and iron is found only in the feet and toes, and not in the legs, it follows that this element of brittleness would be true of the Roman empire only in its later period, rather than in its former. Some expositors hold that the symbolism in view carries reference

---

[7] Babylonia lasted 66 years (605-539 B.C.); Medo-Persia 208 years (539-331); Greece 185 years (331-146, though a specific date for the fall of Greece is difficult to assign).

to the East-West divisions of the Roman rule, but this cannot be, since, as noticed, the divisions are intermixed. The weakness of Rome, which led to its fall and which did come to existence especially in its later period, was a deterioration of moral fiber among the people. Idleness, luxurious living, and dissipation of character found their way into, and intermixed with, the still firmly structured aspects of government.

2:42, 43. Indeed, as the toes of the feet were partly iron and partly baked clay, part of the kingdom shall be strong and part of it fragile. Further, as you saw iron mingled with brittle baked clay, they shall mingle themselves with the seed of men, but they shall not cleave one to another, even as iron does not mix with baked clay.

Indeed: This is a translation merely of the waw conjunction which is not usually so translated. Emphasis is called for here, however, because a long gap of time is intended to be distinguished between what is said in verse forty-one and what is said in verse forty-two— a gap falling historically between the demise of the original Roman empire and a restoration of it at a time still future. Several considerations point to this conclusion. (1) A time-gap must fall somewhere in these verses, because verse forty-four speaks of Christ's millennial kingdom (cf. v. 44 for discussion) being established in the days of "these kings," and His kingdom is yet future. The words "these kings" obviously refer back to the immediately preceding verses, making at least some part of them refer to a time contemporary with that future kingdom. (2) If that gap is seen between verse forty-one and verse forty-two, a reason is supplied for the repetition in verse forty-two regarding the intermingling of iron and clay, something strange otherwise, verse forty-one speaking of the intermingling existent during the original empire, and verse forty-two speaking of it during the restored time. (3) The existence of an intended time-gap here would give a reason for only the toes of the feet being mentioned in verse forty-two as being intermixed, whereas both feet and toes are so mentioned in verse forty-one: that reason being that the toes, and the toes only, carry reference to the millennial kingdom, signifying that it will have ten contemporary kings. The existence of these ten contemporary kings is symbolized also by the ten horns of Daniel's first vision (cf. 7:7, 24). (4) This interpretation finds a close and meaningful antecedent for "these kings" of verse forty-four, namely the ten toes just mentioned, as symbolic of ten kings. No other logical antecedent exists in the preceding verses. (5) The general idea of a time-gap of this kind finds support from pertinent aspects of all four of Daniel's visions in the last six chapters of the book, as will be seen. These reasons, taken together, mean that the subject matter of verses forty-two and forty-three concerns restored Rome, which, as the verses indicate, will be characterized by a condition similar to that of original

Rome: partly strong and partly weak. *Fragile:* The word used *(t^ebîrah)* comes from a verbal root *(t^ebar)* meaning "to break," and carries the thought of *something breakable,* a characteristic of baked clay in distinction from iron.

They shall mingle themselves: The activity to which this phrase makes reference will be undertaken for the purpose of offsetting the conflicting elements of strength and weakness, symbolized by the iron and clay. The nature of the activity is difficult to determine, however. The word used is a hithpael participle from the root *"rab,* meaning "to mix," and refers to something which "mixes itself." The idea of intermarriage is held by some, and Ezra 9:2 does use the same participle in reference to intermarriage, but this idea does not fit the context. It is better to think in terms of a general intermingling of people, the strong with the weak. The reference may be either to intermingling strong people from strong countries with weaker people of weaker countries, or else strong people within a given country with weaker people of that country, to provide greater overall strength. The Antichrist, called "little horn" in 7:8, 24-26, the leading king of the restored empire (cf. discussion, chap. 7), will doubtless lead in this activity. *They shall not cleave:* The effort at gaining overall strength in this way will fail. As baked clay and iron will not mix, so also these diverse elements will not mix. This means that the empire of the Antichrist will have its internal problems, making for weakness.

2:44. Then in the days of these kings the God of heaven will set up a kingdom which will not be destroyed for an age, neither will the kingdom be left to other people. It will crush and bring all these kingdoms to an end, but it will stand for an age.

These kings: The text does not supply a clear antecedent for "these kings." That is, no kings as such are mentioned in the prior context. Some expositors (many amillennialists)[8] find the antecedent in the "kingdoms" of the last of the verse, which are the four kingdoms symbolized earlier in the chapter by the various parts of the image. Adherents of the view explain the verse as meaning that God will set up a kingdom (the spiritual kingdom established by Christ at His first advent) in the days of these four kingdoms; noting that the fourth of the kingdoms (Rome) was indeed in existence at Christ's first coming. Against this view, however, is the fact that the word translated here (properly) "kings" *(malkayya')* is not the same as the word translated (properly) "kingdoms" *(malk^ewata')* at the close of the verse. Also, one would expect that reference would have been made only to the last of the four kingdoms, rather than to "kingdoms" taken together, if the intention were to designate the beginning point

---

[8] For instance, Young, YPD, p. 78; Barnes, BD, I, p. 173.

of Christ's spiritual kingdom. The language is better satisfied when the antecedent is found in the ten "toes," symbolizing ten contemporary kings, as noted above. *Will set up a kingdom:* Reference is to Christ's millennial kingdom, established through God's power. Christ will be God's true world Ruler (Ps. 2:6-9), crowned to rule in perfect righteousness (Isa. 11:2-5), over a world enjoying blissful peace at last (Isa. 11:6-9). He will reign in contrast to Satan's counterfeit, the Antichrist, who will have made his try in the earlier years of the restored Roman empire (Rev. 13:1-10; 17:8-14), but who will have been destroyed by the establishment of Christ's reign (indicated at the close of this verse). Evidence of this is seen in the following considerations.[9]

(1) This kingdom is established by God, rather than by men, as signified by the symbolic destroying stone being "cut out of the mountain without hands." This is in contrast to the fact that the image is implied to have been made by man. The great ancient kingdoms were indeed made through human efforts, but Christ's kingdom of the future will be established directly by the activity of God. (2) The fact that the text presents this kingdom as parallel with the earlier kingdoms argues that it will be earthly and physical in character, as they were. If this kingdom is identified with the spiritual rule established by Christ at His first coming, which is done commonly by amillennialist expositors, this parallel is not observed. (3) The text makes clear that this kingdom of Christ is established while the fourth empire still exists, with its division of ten subkingdoms, because the stone smites the image on its feet when it has the ten toes. But, historically, the original Roman empire knew no time when ten contemporaneous subkings ruled; therefore, the time in view here, when this condition will be met, must be still future. Furthermore, even if such a time during the original Roman era could be found (attempts have been made, but unsuccessfully),[10] all times which have presented any possibility are located in history well after the time of Christ and His beginning of the spiritual kingdom. (4) The text presents the rise of this new kingdom as being sudden and with a decisive blow, in which the immediately preceding fourth kingdom is obliterated; but nothing like this happened with the beginning of Christ's spiritual kingdom. To the contrary, not only was Rome not destroyed at the time, but it came to its greatest strength well after Christ died; and, though Christianity did affect the Roman power extensively later on, still the impact was never sudden or crushing in force so as to bring total destruction, as pictured by the stone crushing the image. This will be true, however, when Christ comes in power to the Mount of Olives

[9] For still other considerations, cf. *infra,* under 7:27.
[10] Cf. discussion and references in Barnes, BD, II, pp. 83-92.

(Zech. 14:4) to establish His millennial rule, for He will then destroy the last Roman king, the Antichrist, in a moment of time (Rev. 19:11-19) and set up a rule with Rome no longer a power (Zech. 14:9; Rev. 20:1-6). (5) The new kingdom is pictured as growing continually, after this crushing event, until it fills all the earth. Christ's spiritual kingdom, inaugurated at the first coming, has never become dominant to this degree. In fact, today people continue to be born faster than they are being won to Christ. Ground actually is being lost, rather than gained. But Christ's millennial kingdom will indeed come to fill all the earth. The capital will be established in Jerusalem; Israel will be the special kingdom in the world community; and all the world will be under the supreme rule of the perfect King.

For an age: The word for "age" *('lma'),* equivalent to the Hebrew *'olam,* can mean either "eternity" or "age." According to Revelation 20:3, the millennial kingdom lasts 1000 years, the duration of time intended here.[11] *To other people:* In contrast to the kingdoms depicted by the head, breast, etc., of the image, this kingdom will not be defeated by some enemy country, and thus left "to other people." This kingdom will last as long as the King desires, since He will always be in command and control. *It will crush:* As the great stone (cf. next verse) struck and crushed the entire image by hitting only the feet of the image (cf. v. 35), so Christ's kingdom will destroy all prior kingdoms by smiting only the Roman kingdom. The thought is parallel to that set forth under verse forty, where the Roman kingdom is said to have destroyed all three previous kingdoms in Greece. The elements of each preceding kingdom are conceived of as caught up and reduplicated in its successor, so that, when the successor is destroyed, the predecessor is destroyed as well.

2:45. Inasmuch as the stone was cut out from the mountain without hands and crushed the iron, the brass, the baked clay, the silver and the gold, the great God has revealed to the king what will be after this; and the dream is sure and its interpretation certain.

Inasmuch as: The force of this expression is causal. The overall thought of the verse is that, because God has so favored the king as to give him this dream, the king can be sure that the information symbolized is true. Daniel's point is to impress the king with the certainty of the revelation and also with the fact that God has been very gracious to him in granting him this revelation. *Stone was cut out:* The fact that Daniel mentioned only this portion of the dream in this concluding statement, shows that emphasis is to be placed upon it.

---

[11] It is true, as some expositors argue, that Christ reigns for all eternity, but not in the earthly sense of the millennial rule—something basically in mind here in the light of the obvious comparison with the previous periods of earthly rule. (Cf. *infra,* chap. 7, p. 194)

It was important for Nebuchadnezzar to know of the kingdoms which would follow his, but greater significance lay in the fact that God would one day set up His own kingdom, which would crush all these. Daniel apparently wanted the king to recognize through this the final supremacy of God and His program over mankind, and accordingly he brought to a place of humility before this mighty One who had so graciously revealed these things to him. *From the mountain:* This descriptive element was omitted in verse thirty-four. The king saw a mountain in the dream, from which the large stone was suddenly separated without benefit of human hands. *After this:* Because this verse concerns the time when the millennial kingdom will be brought to reality, these words must refer primarily to the closing period of the future and be roughly equivalent to the phrase "latter days" of verse twenty-eight. *Dream is sure:* The closing line is added to reiterate that the king may be certain of the truth of all that has been told to him. The king had been rightfully skeptical of what the other wise men might tell him, and Daniel wanted to assure him again that his own words were completely reliable.

D. Daniel Honored (vv. 46-49)

The concluding section of the chapter concerns Nebuchadnezzar's response to Daniel's words. He highly honors the young man who has now revealed convincingly all that Nebuchadnezzar has wanted to know and praises the God to whom Daniel has given all credit. Nebuchadnezzar's willingness to bestow such honor on a non-Babylonian who denied Babylon's gods is a mark in his favor, showing unusual objectivity and fairness in judgment.

2:46. Then King Nebuchadnezzar fell upon his face, bowed down to Daniel, and commanded that an oblation and incense be offered to him.

Fell upon his face: This is a remarkable statement; indeed, so remarkable that liberal expositors deny its truth. Kings just do not bow before mere captives, no matter what the situation might otherwise lead one to expect. But this is a part of God's Word, and it is true. The action is highly noteworthy, however. That Nebuchadnezzar did bow before Daniel indicates his complete acceptance of all that Daniel had said; his great appreciation for an interpretation he could trust, showing further how much he had wanted it; and his willingness to humble himself before the God of Daniel. *Bowed down to Daniel:* To bow down before another was a mark of deep respect (1 Sam. 20:41; 2 Sam. 14:4). More than mere respect was intended in this instance, however, for the word employed *(sᵉgid)* is used elsewhere only of the worship of deity (cf. Daniel 3:5, 6, 7, 10, 11, 12, 14, 28; or its corresponding Hebrew form, Isa. 44:15, 17, 19). Nebuchadnez-

head *worship*

zar was worshiping, though probably not really Daniel but the God to whom Daniel gave all credit (cf. Acts 10:25; 14:13). He knew of this God only through Daniel, and it seemed appropriate to worship Him through the human instrument. At the same time, the act demonstrated the high respect he felt also for the man. *Oblation:* The word used *(minhah)* can mean either a "gift" or "bloodless offering." It is likely that the latter is intended in this instance, because the idea of *gifts* is expressed in verse forty-eight, and also the general subject of this verse concerns worship. *Incense:* The word used *(nîhohîn)* means literally "restful odors." It normally refers to incense odors, and carries the thought here that incense was to be offered to Daniel and his God, in keeping with the king's attitude of worship.

2:47. The king answered Daniel and said, Truly, your God is God of gods and Lord of kings and a revealer of secrets, for you have been able to reveal this secret.

The king answered: Having shown his new-found respect for Daniel and the God of heaven, Nebuchadnezzar acknowledged it by words. *God of gods:* By this phrase, Nebuchadnezzer appears to give recognition to the supremacy of Daniel's God over all other gods, including the Babylonian deities. He had seen a work which was convincing to him, and he was honest enough to admit it. The degree of his sincerity, however, becomes a bit suspect in view of his actions in the following chapter. If fully sincere at this time, he must have lost this respect later on. *Lord of kings:* This phrase is significant to show his acknowledgment that the God of heaven was Lord of earthly kings, including himself. This was quite an admission for one in his position. *Revealer of secrets:* This was the matter that was so convincing to Nebuchadnezzar. Both dream and interpretation had been revealed by this God. It is evident that Daniel's stress on God as the One to receive all credit had made its point. The king was giving due praise to Daniel's God. He was the One who had revealed the secret to Daniel, which had now been passed along to him.

2:48. Then the king made Daniel great and gave him many fine presents, and made him ruler over all the province of Babylon and head supervisor over all the wise men of Babylon.

Great: This is a reference to the greatness defined in the last half of the verse. *Presents:* In verse six the king promised the wise men "gifts," using the same word as here *(matt^enan)*. That promise was now kept with Daniel. Two qualifying adjectives are used with the noun, indicating that the presents were both numerous and valuable. Daniel must have been substantially enriched by them. *Made him ruler:* Daniel was given not only presents, but also two positions of power. The first is called "ruler over all the province of Babylon."

The Babylonian empire was divided into provinces, each with a head, called in 3:2 a "satrap" *('ᵃhashdarpᵉnayya').*[12] Daniel apparently was made "satrap" over the province of Babylon proper, a position of high responsibility for one not yet having reached his twentieth year. *Head supervisor:* Daniel's second position of power was as head *(rab signîn,* "chief overseer") over all the wise men. He had just shown himself superior to all of them, and the king suited his future role to this superiority. Because he became their head does not mean, as some have suggested, that he began to practice their divination techniques. Surely Daniel would not have wanted to do so; and the king would not have pressured him to this end, since Daniel's "technique" had already demonstrated its value. In these two roles, especially the latter, Daniel's influence in Babylonian affairs was very significant. Wise men were consulted by many people, including leaders, and people normally followed whatever advice was given, because they believed it came from the deity. As chief of wise men, Daniel's counsel would have been sought in the more important cases and by the more influential people. Having these positions prior to the captivity of his fellow Judeans,[13] Daniel was situated so that he might work to their best welfare when they arrived.[14] The bestowal of these positions must have been most gratifying to Daniel, in view of the crucial decision he and his friends had made two years before, regarding the king's menu. Their choice then to refuse the menu had seemed to preclude their ever obtaining a fine position at the close of the training period, but now Daniel had been given not only one, but two, and both very fine positions indeed.

2:49. Daniel made request of the king and he appointed Shadrach, Meshach, and Abed-nego over the affairs of the province of Babylon. But Daniel was in the gate of the king.

Made request: Daniel asked the king that his three friends be appointed to serve as his assistants. He no doubt wanted them to receive appointments both because he had confidence in their ability and trustworthiness and because he desired them to receive high positions as well as he. He was not about to forget those with whom he had been through so much. Sometimes people do forget friends when they are themselves elevated. *Affairs of the province:* Nebuchadnezzar was ready to oblige Daniel, to whom he felt indebted, and the request was granted. Shadrach, Meshach, and Abed-nego were assigned positions described as being set "over the affairs (*'ᵃbidta',*

---

[12] In Babylonian texts, the term used for this person is *shakkanaku;* cf. Montgomery, MICC, who refers to Meissner I, 121. The term for "satrap" is a Persian loan word; cf. *infra,* under 3:2.

[13] Cf. *supra,* Introduction, pp. 13, 14.

[14] Cf. *supra,* Introduction, pp. 17, 18.

meaning service, work) of the province." Since Daniel was the satrap of the province, these three were made assistants to him as he served in this capacity. Because Daniel had the position also of chief of the wise men, he may have left most of the work in respect to the government of the province to the three friends. Their classification as wise men may have ceased when they were given these administrative duties. *Gate of the king:* Ancient gates were considered appropriate places for judges and other key officers to conduct their business (cf. Deut. 16:18; Esth. 3:2; Ruth 4:1-12). Because gates were used in this way, they came in time to give their name to the royal offices of the king, the chancellery, which is likely the meaning here. If so, Daniel was given his place of authority at the very palace; whereas, apparently the three friends served in some lesser office building.

CHAPTER 3

Chapter three concerns the remarkable courage and faith that Daniel's three friends—Shadrach, Meshach, and Abed-nego—displayed by their refusal to bow to an image made by Nebuchadnezzar, in spite of an announced penalty of death in a flaming furnace for disobedience. There is no explanation for the fact that Daniel himself does not appear in the story. He may have been out of the empire on business for the king, or he may have been ill. The three friends are called upon to show their own sterling quality, and they do so in a most commendable manner. A marked significance of the chapter is the revelation of the character of the young men: they had a personal integrity and were strong not only when led by another such as Daniel. In the first two stories of the book, they appear only as friends of Daniel, and, in the remaining stories, they do not appear at all. But here they are the main characters and portray their own excellent qualities.

No indication is given as to the year of Nebuchadnezzar's reign at the time of this event. The incident certainly followed the time of the king's dream of the second chapter, because Shadrach, Meshach, and Abed-nego are presented as already "set over the affairs of the province" (v. 12), a status given at the close of that occasion. It is likely, too, that it preceded the king's dream of the fourth chapter, because events involved with its interpretation point to the general end-time of Nebuchadnezzar's rule. Many years intervened between these two terminal points, however. The Septuagint version places the date at Nebuchadnezzar's eighteenth year, but probably only because of associating the erection of the statue with the time of Jerusalem's fall to Babylon (Jer. 52:29), the thought being that Nebuchadnezzar thus celebrated that conquest. This thinking assigns too much importance to the fall of Jerusalem, however, for many other great cities were also taken by the great king. A helpful clue may come from a more likely reason for making the statue. This is that the king wanted to assure himself of the allegiance of his official family to the Babylonian religion, especially those members from the young foreign trainees who had now been appointed to office. In respect to these recent additions, he had earlier solicited their allegiance indirectly by insisting that they eat food which had first been dedicated to the Babylonian gods (cf. 1:4, 8), and he could have now desired to force their direct submission by demanding that they openly bow to the image. He may have reasoned that to have them do so in the company of older officers, should provide the proper example for them to follow, and it would also afford evidence of the continued allegiance of those of longer standing. If this was Nebuchadnezzar's thinking, then the occasion likely came soon after the graduation of the young trainees, being thus designed to give the king satisfaction regarding both young and old early in his reign. The young men, then, may have been only about twenty years old, the king having ruled but four or five years. If this seems too soon after the fine statements of Nebuchadnezzar regarding Daniel's god, it should be remembered that he was a Babylonian and still believed fully in the Babylonian gods. Two or three intervening years could have sufficed for him to issue this contrasting order.

A. NEBUCHADNEZZAR'S ORDER (vv. 1-7)

The chapter begins with the indication that Nebuchadnezzar made the great image and gave the command for all of his official family to bow before it, making clear the penalty involved for disobedience. The command brought a second crucial time of decision for Shadrach, Meshach, and Abed-nego, perhaps even more challenging than the first, concerning the king's menu.

3:1. Nebuchadnezzar the king made an image of gold, whose height was sixty cubits and breadth six cubits. He erected it on the plain of Dura in the province of Babylon.

The king made: Nebuchadnezzar's decision to make a great image was not unique to him. Many ancient rulers made statues, often of themselves; as symbols of their dominion. Frequently such statues were inscribed with stories of the ruler's own conquests and other accomplishments. *An image:* The word used *(ts⁻elem)* normally means an image in human form, rather than merely a shaped pillar. This does not mean, however, that the form necessarily depicted Nebuchadnezzar himself. It may have been so intended, since, as just observed, kings often did symbolize their own figures; also, the idea for the image may have been suggested to Nebuchadnezzar by his earlier dream, in which he was represented by the head of gold. On the other hand, people were commanded to worship this image, which means that it was related in the king's thinking to the Babylonian religious system. To him, clearly, it somehow stood for that system, and all who would bow before it would be giving their allegiance and worship according-ly. *Of gold:* The material from which the image was made may have been suggested by the dream statue, the head of which was of gold. This image was extremely costly, for it was very large. Probably the king wished in this way to impress all attending with the importance of both it and the order regarding it. Some have objected that the cost would have been prohibitive, even for a king of Nebuchadnezzar's stature. The image certainly was not solid, however; for if it had been, its weight would have been prohibitive also. It was likely over-laid with gold plates, something not unusual for the day (cf. Isa. 40: 19:41:7). The view of such an image, dazzling in the sunlight, would have been quite overpowering.

Its height was sixty cubits: The image was imposing not only in value and glitter, but also in size. It was sixty cubits (ninety feet) high, comparable to the Colossus of Rhodes at seventy feet—a height calculated further to impress the worshipers. It should be noted that the figures "sixty" and "six" suggest that the sexagesimal system was in use, rather than the decimal; these numbers, then, provide a mark of authenticity, because Babylon employed the sexagesimal system. *Breadth of six cubits:* The height of the image was ten times the breadth, a proportion which has been called incredible. Such a figure, it is pointed out, would be terribly grotesque; for normal proportions of images show the height as only four or five times the width. The image may have had a high base, however, taking up a third or more of the height. Also, the image may intentionally have been made some-what grotesque, for much of Babylonian sculpture was so character-ized. In any case, the oddity of the figures does not argue for the unreliability of the account, for no writer, whether contemporary or of a later date (as critics hold), would have had any reason to use odd figures unless they were accurate. *Plain of Dura:* The word "Dura" means a "walled place," or an "enclosing wall." The designation here may have been of a flat plain, enclosed by surrounding mountains. The name has been found in extant texts, used in reference to several different localities, making exact identification uncertain. It might be Tell Der, sixteen miles southwest of modern Baghdad, or, perhaps more likely, Tolul Dura ("mounds of Dura"), twelve miles south-southeast of Hillah. Near the latter place runs the river Dura, which empties into the Euphrates some six miles south of ancient Babylon. The archaeologist Julius Oppert[1] states that he found on one of these mounds a large brick square, forty-five feet on a side and twenty feet high, which he believes was the foundation for this very image. What-ever the location, the fact that the name "Dura" has been found to fit well into the nomenclature of the day argues further against this

[1] *Expedition scientifique en Mesopotamie,* I, pp. 238f.

story being merely a legend, as set forth by some liberal scholars. *Province of Babylon:* Some of the places known today as Dura are outside the region identified as the province of Babylon, which makes this added notation a help in limiting the possibilities. It is likely, too, that Nebuchadnezzar would have chosen a locality for the image near to the capital city. Tolul Dura qualifies as the most probable.

3:2. Then King Nebuchadnezzar sent to assemble the satraps, prefects and governors, judges, treasurers, lawyers, sheriffs, and all the officials of the provinces to come to the dedication of the image, which King Nebuchadnezzar had erected.

Sent: Since the official people named came from all the provinces of the empire, the king had to send for them, no doubt, by established lines of communication. Some time would have been required for the communication to go and the invited persons to come to Babylon. Those invited were official personnel, not common people. Nebuchadnezzar wished to dedicate the image, and the occasion called for an assembly of persons of the highest standing. The officers are listed, apparently in descending order of rank, though the exact office designated is not always clear. *Satraps:* This office is quite clear; it was the leading one in the various provinces of the empire. The word for "satrap" *('ahashdarpᵉnayya')* is a Persian loan word, meaning "protector of the realm." The main divisions of the later Persian empire were called "satrapies." Because the word is Persian, liberal scholars find evidence from it for an author later than Daniel. This conclusion is not necessary, however, because such terms could have been used in the Babylonian period through Persian influence.[2] The explanation is also possible that Daniel, likely writing this record after the fall of Babylon to Persia, may simply have used Persian terms to make his language more understandable to contemporary readers. *Prefects and governors:* These two terms are joined by the conjunction, though it is commonly accepted that they refer to two different offices. Both terms are Semitic. The first *(sᵉgan)* means a "superintendent" or "prefect." This is the word used earlier in 2:48 to designate Daniel's position as "supervisor" of Babylon's wise men. The second *(peḥah)* is best taken to mean a "governor," one who rules over an assigned region, perhaps here a subdivision of the province. The relation between the two offices is not known. Possibly the conjunction between the terms signifies that they were parallel in rank. *Judges:* Keil believes that this word *('adargazar)* also is Semitic, meaning "chief arbi-

---

[2] A Persian inscription dates as early as 610-580 B.C.; cf. Young YPD, p. 86. K. Kitchen, *Notes on Some Problems in the Book of Daniel,* p. 43, points to the uncertainty displayed in the Septuagint regarding these offices, and then states that the Maccabean age, no more than a century earlier, could not be expected to remember these terms much better. Their employment calls for a contemporary author, like Daniel.

trator." Perhaps judges of the day, serving in the provinces, are in mind. *Treasurers:* Keil believes that this word (g*ʳdabʳrayya'*) is of Aryan origin and means "masters of the treasury." *Lawyers:* This word (d*ʳtabar*) is again better known, being old Persian for a "guardian of the law." *Sheriffs:* This word (*tiptaye'*) may be Semitic again, meaning "ones who give a just sentence," and is usually taken to be a minor judicial title.

All the officials: This phrase seems to refer to all other officials not listed separately in the above designations. The king apparently wanted all his official family, including those of lower levels, to be present. Some expositors have objected that such a sweeping order would have necessitated the suspension of all government operations. For the comparatively brief time involved, however, subordinates (who did the actual work anyway) would have been able to carry on. *Of the provinces:* This phrase makes clear that these officials were indeed from all the divisions of the empire, and not just the city or province of Babylon. *To the dedication:* The announced purpose of the occasion was the dedication of the grand image. Such dedicatory rites are known to have been observed with some frequency in the Near East of the day; as witnessed, for instance, by Solomon's dedication of the Jerusalem Temple.

3:3. Then the satraps, prefects and governors, judges, treasurers, lawyers, sheriffs, and all the officials of the province were gathered together to the dedication of the image, which King Nebuchadnezzar had erected; and they stood before the image which Nebuchadnezzar had erected.

Were gathered together: On the day appointed by the king, all the officers named were in attendance as commanded. The designations of officers in this verse are identical with those of the previous listing. The repetition is typical of the Semitic style of writing. *They stood before the image:* All assembled before the image, as it rose tall and awesome before them. Likely the number was large; probably several hundred officers were present. It may be assumed that all were dressed in their finest uniforms, designating the respective provinces and ranks of each. Among them, no doubt also appropriately dressed, were Shadrach, Meshach, and Abed-nego. Whether or not they had any foreknowledge regarding the impending order to bow before the image is not stated. Any apprehension they felt regarding the matter would not have been helped by the sight of the fiery furnace, which apparently was placed conveniently and ominously near at hand, where it might be seen.

3:4-6. And a herald called in a loud voice, To you it is commanded, peoples, nations, and languages, that, at the time you hear the sound

of the horn, flute, harp, trigon, psaltery, bagpipe, and all kinds of music, you fall down and worship the image of gold that King Nebuchadnezzar has erected; and whoever does not fall down and worship will the same hour be cast into the midst of a burning fiery furnace.

A herald called: This person was likely an official herald of the king, used now to give Nebuchadnezzar's command to the large assembly. He did so "in a loud voice" *(behayil);* literally, "in strength." *Peoples, nations, and languages:* The first two terms are close in meaning, but the third refers to languages which such peoples or nations spoke. That different languages were represented is not surprising, because the empire had come to include many different countries. The three terms together were used apparently as a common formula of address for a conglomerate assembly of the day (cf. 3:7, 29; 4:1; 6:25).

At the time: Nebuchadnezzar wanted precision in the demanded obedience of the people. All were to bow at the same moment, which would be indicated by the beginning of music played by an assembled orchestra. This was probably an official royal orchestra. In keeping with the grandeur of the occasion, the members likely were dressed in colorful costume and seated on a raised decorated stage. *Horn:* This name *(qarna')* is Semitic and refers to a wind instrument. Its Hebrew equivalent refers often to the curved ram's horn (cf. Josh. 6:5). *Flute:* This name *(mashrôqîta')* is also Semitic, the root word meaning "to hiss," or "to whistle." *Harp:* This word *(qayteros)* is normally taken a Greek name, meaning "harp" or "lyre." *Trigon:* This word *(sabeka')* is another Greek name, referring to a triangular instrument of four strings, playing high notes. Greek writers speak of it as being of Syrian origin. *Psaltery:* This word *(pesanterîn)* is a third Greek[3] name and refers to another triangular instrument, which had its strings beneath the sounding board, in distinction from the harp. *Bagpipe:* This word *(sûmponyah)* is of uncertain origin, and some argue against the idea of a "bagpipe," but it remains the most likely. The name appears in Greek as *symphonia,* from which the modern "symphony" comes. Polybius[4] speaks of Antiochus Epiphanes either playing or dancing to this instrument. *All kinds of music:* This is probably a reference to other instruments, not listed specifically. Any orchestra which Nebuchadnezzar would have employed on this important day would have included all the accepted instruments of the time. *Fall down and worship:* These words were the crucial ones for Shadrach, Meshach, and Abed-nego, for they confirmed the fears the three men may have had. Nebuchadnezzar was insisting that all bow and worship this

[3] Because these three Greek names appear here, it has been argued that the author must have lived later, after Grecian culture had spread; but cf. *supra,* Introduction, p. 00 for response.
[4] Cf. Montgomery, MICC, p. 203, who refers to Polybius xxvi, 10 and xxxi, 4.

image. This would mean a recognition of the false god(s) it represented, and they knew that they could not give this. From Nebuchadnezzar's point of view, as indicated in the introduction to this chapter. the order in part likely constituted his way of bringing the young expatriates to the place of giving full allegiance to the Babylonian gods.

Burning fiery furnace: Literally, "furnace of burning fire." The little evidence that exists as to the type of furnace this was suggests that it was upright in form, with a large opening at the top in which material might be placed and a smaller opening at the bottom from which it could be removed. When the furnace was well heated, flames likely could be seen leaping from the top opening. The story implies that the furnace was located close to the scene of action, which suggests that it had been constructed purposely for the occasion and probably was visible to all those called to worship. That Nebuchadnezzar saw fit to insist on such a terrifying form of punishment for any who might be disobedient to his order and that he included a direct reference to it in the general announcement by the herald indicates that he suspected some might not wish to comply. This thought fits further the motivation he had for the occasion just noted. He wanted to give plenty of incentive for all, including especially the foreign young men, to demonstrate their allegiance.

3:7. Therefore, at the time when all the people heard the sound of the horn, flute, harp, trigon, psaltery, and all kinds of music, all the peoples, nations, and languages fell down and worshiped the image of gold that King Nebuchadnezzar had erected.

Fell down and worshiped: The repetition of the formula for the entire assembly (cf. v. 4) is to indicate the inclusiveness of the number who bowed. Nebuchadnezzar had little to fear from most of the people. They did bow, making a sea of bending backs before the great image. Because all others bowed, the fact that three did not was very conspicuous. Shadrach, Meshach, and Abed-nego must have felt terribly alone as they looked about and saw that all others obeyed the order. In the repetition of the instruments, the same are listed as before, except that the "bagpipe" is omitted. No reason or significance for the omission is indicated.

B. THE COURAGE OF SHADRACH, MESHACH, AND ABED-NEGO (vv. 8-18)

With the setting laid, the significant point of the story—that the three did not bow along with the others—is related. The three may have hoped that at least some of their fellow Judeans would stand with them, but none did. The three stood alone, thus providing one of the great examples in Scripture of obedience to God in the most trying of circumstances.

3:8-11. Because of this, at that time certain Chaldeans drew near and accused the Jews. They answered and said to King Nebuchadnezzar, O King, live forever. You, O King, have made a decree that every man who hears the sound of the horn, flute, harp, trigon, psaltery, and bagpipe, and all kinds of music shall fall down and worship the image of gold; and that anyone, who does not fall down and worship, will be cast into the midst of a burning fiery furnace.

Because of this: The specific cause to which reference is made is not stated directly; namely, the refusal of the three to bow to the image. The story implies the fact clearly, however. No indication is given as to when the three actually made their decision, whether at the moment when the music began to play, or beforehand; but, whenever it was, the pressure to acquiesce must have been great. Several factors would have contributed to that pressure. One is that the three did not have Daniel's leadership in this instance, but had to decide for themselves. Daniel had been the leader in the fine earlier choice regarding the king's assigned menu (chap. 1), and he had likely continued to be this all through the months of training; but he was not present now. A second is that a terrible, horrifying punishment awaited them if they did not bow: that of being thrown into the fiery furnace. A third is that the attraction of wanting to move ahead in life's status would not have lessened from earlier days. They had already been granted fine posts in the province of Babylon, but these could easily be lost; and, even if this did not happen, they could at least be kept from making any further advancement. Still a fourth is that, by not bowing, they would be playing into the hands of men who they probably knew were jealous of them; and the natural desire would have been to avoid doing any such thing. Those who now reported them may well have been among those so characterized, only looking for an opportunity to hurt them, like the rivals of Daniel, later on, who plotted his death in the lion's den. *Chaldeans:* The term is used here in its ethnic sense, rather than occupational, as before. They were men of Chaldean extraction, in contrast to the Jews, whom they were accusing. Nebuchadnezzar, being of Chaldean stock himself, may have listened to them with greater attentiveness as a result. *Accused:* Literally, "they ate the pieces of," a vivid idiomatic expression, meaning "calumniate," "denounce." *The Jews:* The accusers refer to the three as "Jews" (cf. v. 12). The implication is that the nationality of the three was held against them. They wanted the king to be aware that those who had dared to disobey were Jews. This suggests that Daniel and his frineds—and possibly other Judeans—had been the cause more than once of prompting jealousy on the part of these Chaldeans, perhaps because they had achieved higher academic honors, or, at least, had obtained high positions after graduation.

They answered: Possibly a question from the king was voiced on the approach of the men, which called for their *answering.* In giving answer, the accusers first set the background by restating the king's decree. This was not to remind the king of what had been said, but only to observe accepted decorum of the day. Their restatement involved giving the list of musical instruments for the third time; and this time the "bagpipe" is mentioned again.

3:12. There are certain Jews whom you have appointed over the affairs of the province of Babylon—Shadrach, Meshach, and Abed-nego: these men pay no regard to you, O King; your gods they do not serve, and the image of gold which you erected they do not worship.

Certain Jews: Again the ethnical identification is made, stressing this to the king. They also included the names of the three this time, however, showing that they did know them personally, and not merely as of a certain nationality. *You have appointed:* Now the accusers relate the three recalcitrants to Nebuchadnezzar himself. He had appointed them to their fine offices. This manner of mention, not called-for otherwise, suggests that they were bitter in reference to these appointments that Nebuchadnezzar had made. Perhaps their own appointments had been at lower rank, and they showed their envy. They demonstrated poor judgment, however, in implying indiscretion on the part of the king. That they did so shows the more clearly the strong nature of their personal feelings. *Pay no regard:* The Chaldeans became particular in their accusation, listing three infractions by the accused. Only the last concerns the specific infraction of the moment, but from this one they evidently inferred the other two, listing them first. The first is that the accused "pay no regard" to Nebuchadnezzar. This one of the three was not true. From attitudes and actions of Daniel depicted in the first two chapters, which the three friends without question followed, it is clear that they did pay high regard to the king. *Your gods they do not serve:* This second accusation was true, a fact which had just been demonstrated by the action of the three and which these accusers had probably seen portrayed in various ways and on several occasions before. These three and Daniel—and perhaps on some occasions other Judeans—had likely gained a reputation for nonconformity to the Babylonian religious system. *They do not worship:* This third accusation was also true, of course, and constituted the prime charge. To these accusers, the fact that the three Jews had not bowed may have seemed incredible. How could anyone put principle so high that he would risk death in a blazing furnace? But the fact that they had gave the accusers the blameworthy charge for which they had hoped, and they were quite ready to use it.

3:13-15. Then Nebuchadnezzar, in rage and fury, commanded to bring Shadrach, Meshach, and Abed-nego; and these men were brought before the king. Nebuchadnezzar spoke and said to them, Is it true, Shadrach, Meshach, and Abed-nego, that my gods you will not serve, and the image of gold that I erected you will not worship? Now if you are ready so that, at the time when you hear the sound of the horn, flute, harp, trigon, psaltery, and bagpipe, and all kinds of music, you will fall down and worship the image that I have made—; but if you do not worship you will be cast the same hour into the midst of a burning fiery furnace, and what god is there who can deliver you out of my hands?

Rage and fury: The two words used *(rᵉgaz* and *hᵃmah)* are close in meaning and emphasize the thought by the repetition. Nebuchadnezzar was intensely angry at being defied in this way. He had put forth great effort that this would not happen. The penalty had been made severe and the order clear. He had wanted to insure compliance by all his officers, but these three had dared to disobey. They had to be punished summarily. *These men were brought:* The king's order was voiced likely to members of his nearby guard, and response was immediate in apprehending Shadrach, Meshach, and Abed-nego. The assumption may be made that the three fearfully expected this to happen, though at the same time hoping that it would not. But, watching developments in the vicinity of the king, who likely was on a raised platform visible to all, they could have seen the men making the accusation and then the quickly summoned guards began to make their way in their direction. The three must have been handled roughly in being pushed along quickly to stand before the angry king.

Is it true: The meaning of the word used *(hatsda')* is known today, the word having been found in a clear context on an Aramaic ostrakon.[5] Before this discovery, many expositors took it to mean, "Is it of purpose?" Nebuchadnezzar was giving the three friends an opportunity to deny the charge if they wished. *That my gods:* It should be noted that Nebuchadnezzar did not repeat the first accusation of the Chaldeans, which was an untrue charge. He mentioned only their nonservice to his gods and nonworship of his image. This may be a clue that he recognized the three as being Daniel's friends and knew from past experience that they did honor him. If so, past experience would have told him also that they did not serve his gods.

Now if: A protasis is here introduced, calling for an apodosis, which is omitted. Nebuchadnezzar seems to give the three another opportunity to bow before the image, as he says, in essence: "If you are yet ready to bow before the image at the sound of the music, then all will be

[5] Cf. Young, YPD, p. 89.

well with you, but, if not, then the terrible punishment will result." The implied apodical element, "all will be well," is sustained by the nature of the contrasting apodosis stated in the following protasis-apodosis construction. Apparently the music was continuing to play at periodic intervals, and Nebuchadnezzar was referring to the next period in this renewal of opportunity to bow. *What god is there:* There is the possibility that if Nebuchadnezzar had not been so controlled by his excessive anger, he would not have added this unwise question. For he had learned earlier, from Daniel, what God it was who could do far more than the Babylonian deities. Perhaps the very calmness, instead of terror, which likely characterized the demeanor of the three, tended to infuriate him the more. Their evident trust in their God sealed his determination to make them realize that no god existed who could deliver from his hand.

3:16-18. Shadrach, Meshach, and Abed-nego answered and said to the king, O Nebuchadnezzar, we have no need to answer you in this matter. If our God whom we serve is able to deliver us from the burning fiery furnace and from your hand, O King, he will deliver. But if not, be it known to you, O King, that we will not serve your gods or worship the image of gold that you have erected.

We have no need: This was not an answer of arrogance, as one might think. The thought is that the three were admitting their "guilt." They had "no need" of answering, because they had nothing to say in the way of denial. They had not bowed to the image.

If our God: The translation used could be taken to mean that the men were not sure regarding God's ability to deliver them. Therefore, other translations have been suggested by expositors; such as, "If it be so (that you will cast us into the furnace), our God is able" (*KJV, ASV*); or, "For behold our God is able" (Jerome). But to reflect an intended parallelism with the following verse, the translation given is to be preferred. When properly understood, the difficulty is removed. The young men were not voicing any uncertainty as to God's ability, but only as to His willingness. They were not sure that He would choose to deliver them. A paraphrase makes the thought clear: "If our God can find it possible to deliver us in terms of what He sees best, then he will deliver." The overall story makes clear the fullness of their faith in God's power. The courage displayed in this statement should not be missed. Nebuchadnezzar had just declared that no god could deliver them out of his hands, and now they were replying stoutly that their God could do so. They were ready to risk all in their earnestness to give a proper witness to their God. This same desire to give a proper witness had no doubt been a major factor in their earlier refusal to bow before the image. To bow would have been to destroy the value of all their prior statements to others regarding the supremacy of their God. Knowing that actions speak louder than words, they had remained standing, without wavering. If one today has difficulty in remaining true to his faith in God, let him remember three Judeans in foreign Babylon, standing tall, first before a golden image and then before a mighty ruler, knowing that a blazing furnace awaited them, and having the courage to speak such words as these.

But if not: The words that now follow are perhaps even more commendable, if that is possible. The preceding words frame a true, significant statement of faith; but these present a unique, challenging statement of submission. If there is anything more rare than faith, it is submission. The thought of the words is this: "Even if our God does not find it best to deliver us, we will still not serve the Babylonian gods or worship the image." Two matters stand out for notice. First, the young men recognized that God's will might be different from what they would find pleasant, and they were willing to have it so, without complaining. Too often Christians are not willing to have God's will different from their own, and then do complain most vigorously when it proves to be that way. Second, they did not make their own obedience contingent upon God's doing that which was pleasant to them. They were ready to obey, whether God chose to deliver them from the furnace or not. In other words, they found their object of affection in God Himself, not in what God did for them. What an example for God's people of any day!

C. The Miraculous Deliverance (vv. 19-27)

The story now tells of God's gracious deliverance of these who shared this manner of submission to God. They were thrown into the furnace, but God delivered them from being harmed. As a result, Nebuchadnezzar was brought once again to confess the superiority of the God of heaven.

3:19, 20. Then Nebuchadnezzar was filled with anger and the fashion of his countenance was changed toward Shadrach, Meshach, and Abed-nego. He spoke and gave an order to heat the furnace seven times beyond what was normal. And he commanded certain strong men of his army to bind Shadrach, Meshach, and Abed-nego and to cast them into the burning fiery furnace.

Filled with anger: Nebuchadnezzar had been extremely angry when he first summoned the three friends (v. 13). This phrase, however, indicates that now his anger was increased to a still higher pitch. He had been able to think quite rationally, until he heard this reply of the young men; even having given them opportunity to defend themselves. But at this point his orders became quite irrational. A point of weakness for this great king clearly was his inability to control

anger. The seeming insolence of the three, daring to defy him in placing their trust completely in their God, apparently was what triggered
this violent reaction. Recognition must be given to the fact, too, that
he had expended enormous sums of money and energy to make this
occasion resplendent, and now these three seemingly were spoiling it.
Countenance was changed: Most people reflect their feelings on their
faces. Nebuchadnezzar did here, indicating further the intensification of
his anger. Prior to that moment, he had displayed a face apparently
of interest, ready to pardon these men, if they could present a proper
defense; but now he reddened in his wrath. High emotion may be
imagined flashing from his eyes, as he thundered horrifying orders,
now to be noted. *Gave an order:* This first order would have been
directed to nearby servants, who, it may be supposed, hastened to
obey; especially with the king displaying this degree of anger. *Seven
times beyond:* Literally, "one times seven beyond." The furnace had
a normal heat level, and the force of Nebuchadnezzar's words was
that this level should be raised by a factor of seven. The number
"seven" may have been used symbolically by him to mean "extremely."
Probably the servants sought to comply by adding much more fuel
to the fire and providing more draft.

Strong men: As Nebuchadnezzar's anger dictated first an extreme
measure with the fire, now it called for strong men to seize the three
friends. The king was a man of superlatives. The image he made had
to be the tallest and the most valuable; the people he assembled had
to be his officials, and all of them; the penalty for disobedience had to
be the most terrifying he could devise; the furnace, for those who
had now dared to disobey, should be heated seven times hotter than
normal; and the men, who would bind them, should be the "strong
men of his army." A principal reason for the last two measures, of
course, was the king's desire to forestall any possible fulfillment of
the trust these three had just expressed in their God. These measures
should insure that no god could deliver them out of Nebuchadnezzar's
hand. The men designated were likely men serving at the time as
personal bodyguard to the king. *To bind:* The order to bind the three
friends was in keeping with the first two directives. The men would
thus be rendered helpless to effect any escape.

**3:21. Then these men were bound in their coats, their trousers, their
hats, and their other garments and were cast into the midst of the
burning fiery furnace.**

Their coats, their trousers, their hats: The word for "their hats"
(karbᵉlathôn) has been well identified as referring to a headdress of
some kind. The word for "their coats" *(sarbalêhôn)* probably refers
to the main garment, the *robe* or the *coat.* It alone is mentioned in
verse twenty-seven as representative of the other garments. The word

for "their trousers" *(patt^eshêhôn)* is quite unknown, though there is some indication for the idea of *leggings* or *trousers.*[6] The addition of "other garments" shows that those mentioned were only the most distinctive. The force of mentioning the garments at all is to say that the men were well dressed, probably in their official uniforms, having come properly dressed for the grand ceremony. That the fine clothes were not removed implies haste, a sense of urgency at the command of the king, and probably roughness on the part of the strong men in handling the three. *Were cast:* Having bound the young men, the soldiers carried them to the furnace and cast them in, likely through the top opening. Though the three friends had bravely asserted their willingness to die in this way, rather than bow to Nebuchadnezzar's image, still the actual experience of being bound and carried to the furnace would have been horrible. In making their earlier statement, well meant as it was, they no doubt hoped that God would bring the deliverance. But God apparently was not doing so. They would have to suffer the terrifying experience of the furnace. Two factors were quite obviously in God's purpose for letting matters go this far, before effecting deliverance. One was that the impression on Nebuchadnezzar and other Babylonians, when the deliverance had been carried out, would be the greater as a result. The other was that, even for the three, the blessing of being saved through the fire rather than from it would be more wonderful. When all was over, they would be glad that God had arranged the overall occasion just as He had. With this said, however, what a sensation they must have experienced on being actually tossed into such flames, expecting only the hot searing pain of the inferno. Perhaps they remembered the comforting words of Isaiah 43:2: "When thou walkest through the fire, thou shalt not be burned; neither shall the flame kindle upon thee."

3:22. Therefore, because the king's command was sharp and the furnace exceedingly hot, the flame of the fire killed those men that took up Shadrach, Meshach, and Abed-nego.

Sharp: The king had spoken urgently and harshly, shown by his changed countenance and probably the tone of his voice. The strong men had recognized that he wanted immediate and full obedience. *Exceedingly hot:* By the time the soldiers arrived at the furnace, with their three bound men, the work of the servants first dispatched had taken effect. The added fuel had caught fire and the furnace was exceedingly hot, with flames possibly leaping from the top opening. One must give the soldiers credit for pressing on near enough to complete their assignment; though, no doubt, if they had not, they would have been killed for lack of obedience. *Killed those men:* The

---

[6] Cf. Montgomery, MICC, p. 212.

men did succeed in reaching the mouth of the furnace and in casting Shadrach, Meshach, and Abed-nego inside, but they themselves were killed in doing so. The heat was too great, their flesh was burned, their breath was taken from them. Great and strong as they were, they dropped in their tracks, perhaps becoming human torches. Nebuchadnezzar's rage thus worked to his own detriment in the loss of capable men.

3:23. And these three men, Shadrach, Meshach, and Abed-nego, fell down bound into the midst of the burning fiery furnace.

And these: This verse completes the picture in view of which to appreciate the remarkable event now to transpire. While the strong soldiers were falling in death outside the furnace, the three friends were falling down inside into the midst of the flaming fire. Paradoxical as it was, the soldiers who fell outside, where there was no fire, died because of the fire; while those who fell inside, where the fire raged, continued to live without harm. *Bound:* This is repetitious, having been stated in verse twenty-one, but it is significant. The men were still bound, in all their fine clothes, as they fell among the flames; and were accordingly incapable of helping themselves. At this point the Septuagint version inserts extra information, which is commonly and correctly taken to be apocryphal. Included first is a prayer of one of the young men, Azariah, covering twenty-two verses, which expresses praise to God and requests deliverance from, and punishment upon, Israel's enemies. Then follow six verses of description which tell of the special heating of the furnace and the descent of the Angel of the Lord, who "smote the flame of the fire out of the oven, and made the midst of the furnace as though a wind of dew had gone hissing through it." Finally a song rendered by the three from the furnace occupies forty verses. This is a song of praise for the deliverance effected by the Angel.

3:24. Then King Nebuchadnezzar was startled and, rising hurriedly and beginning to speak, said to his counselors, Did we not cast three men into the midst of the fire bound? They answered and said to the king, True, O King.

Was startled: The king now experienced something totally unexpected. Apparently he had walked with the soldiers to the furnace and seated himself in a position where he could see inside; evidently wanting to be a firsthand witness to his triumph over the God in whom these men had placed their trust. But what he saw did not constitute a triumph. First had come the death of his fine soldiers, and now, far more remarkable, the miraculous survival of the three friends. They had been cast in, bound, but now, as the next verse indicates, they were bound no longer. They were actually walking about within the furnace, and most amazing of all, they were in the company of a fourth being. *Rising hurriedly:* What he saw prompted the king to rise quickly and excitedly from where he was seated. The counselors were likely not far away, but still he arose to address them. *Counselors:* The exact meaning of the word used *(haddabᵉrôhî)* remains questionable. Probably it refers to high government officials, because it is used again in verse twenty-seven (cf. 4:36; 6:7) in parallel with terms which are known to designate important positions. Since those in mind were particularly addressed by Nebuchadnezzar, they likely were ministers whose work included giving counsel to the king. *Did we not:* Nebuchadnezzar had been startled at several matters, but the chief one was the addition of the fourth member to the group walking in the furnace. He wanted confirmation as to the number that had been thrown in. Could a fourth have somehow been included, without his knowing it? The response of the counselors was that indeed the number had been only three.

3:25. He replied and said, Indeed, I see four men loose, walking in the midst of the fire; they are not hurt, and the appearance of the fourth is like that of a son of the gods.

Indeed: Nebuchadnezzar replied with the use of an interjection to stress that what he was about to say was actually true. *Walking:* If four men were walking, the bonds of the three men had been removed, apparently having been consumed by the fire. This is all that had been burned, however, as indicated by verse twenty-seven following. God had permitted the fire to bring only benefit to His servants. That the men were walking implies also that the furnace was large, with room for four to move about within it. *Not hurt:* Nebuchadnezzar could see no sign that the men had been hurt. Apparently no pain was etched on their faces; they were not limping; nor were they clutching some part of their body as though suffering. The story deals only with the reaction of the king, outside of the furnace, but how thrilling must have been the experience of the three inside! They had expected only pain and death, but now were enjoying perfect comfort. They had been bound so that they could not move, but now they were free to walk about as they wished. What a contrast, and what an experience to be walking in the hottest of flame, and feel no hurt! *A son of the gods:* These words must be understood in the light of the speaker's being a pagan. They express the thought "a son of deity"; that is, a divine being. That Nebuchadnezzar calls this being an "angel" (v. 28) does not argue against an identification of deity on Nebuchadnezzar's part, for in Aramaic the word "angel" may stand for deity. Why the king immediately came to this conclusion is not indicated; but he probably did so because of the miraculous element involved, which alone could make such an appearance possible. There are two possibilities concerning the actual identity of this one: he is either an angel sent by God or the second person of the Godhead in a preincarnate appearance. No certain answer is possible, but the likelihood lies with the second suggestion. Christ, in similar form had appeared as the Angel of Yahweh to Abraham at Mamre (Gen. 18), later to Joshua as the "captain of the host of Yahweh" (Josh. 5:13-6:5), and at various times to others. This story affords one of the most meaningful illustrations in the Bible of God's tender care for His children. God might have effected deliverance for Shadrach, Meshach, and Abed-nego without sending such a personal messenger, and this would have been wonderful of itself. But He did more. He effected the deliverance by a special emissary who tangibly demonstrated God's presence with them in the trying hour. God had permitted the men to be cast into the horrifying furnace, but in doing so He had literally gone in with them. What a great blessing this was for the men; what a wonderful comfort it was at the time; and what a precious memory it must have provided for all the rest of their lives! Daniel may have had a similar experience when later he was cast into the den of lions, for he then told King Darius that God had sent "his angel" to shut the lions' mouths (6:22). Years before, Elijah had been similarly honored by having God's Angel sent personally to serve him food, at a time when he was terribly discouraged (1 Kings 19:5-7).

3:26. Then Nebuchadnezzar, drawing near to the opening of the burning fiery furnace, spoke and said, Shadrach, Meshach, and Abed-nego, servants of the Most High God, come out and come here. So Shadrach, Meshach, and Abed-nego came out from the midst of the fire.

Drawing near: Nebuchadnezzar then returned to the furnace, probably where he had been seated, and called for the three young men to come out. *Spoke:* That the king was minded to speak to the three indicates further his complete persuasion that they were truly alive and able to communicate as before with the outside world. Likely his voice was well raised for them to hear above the roaring of the flames. Contrary to the apocryphal addition, noted above, the fire was still very real within the furnace, as both verses twenty-five and twenty-six make clear. *Most High God:* This fine reference to God shows a marked change on the king's part from what he had manifested earlier. He had seen an amazing demonstration of the power of this God and he had been convinced of His supremacy. In admitting that He was "Most High God," Nebuchadnezzar was saying about the same thing that he did earlier to Daniel when he used the phrase "God of gods" (2:47). His admission here was probably aided by his memory of the former occasion. *Come out:* With this call for the men to come out from the furnace, the king was admitting complete defeat. He had taken special measures to bring about their deaths, but the measures had been ineffective; and therefore the men should come forth. These measures, employed out of anger at the time had actually worked to his detriment, not only in bringing death to his strong soldiers, but in making his humiliation the greater. The careful and extreme effort that had been made to destroy the men made the miracle wrought in the furnace still more remarkable in the eyes of the king's counselors and others standing by. *Came out:* Since it is not likely that the three made their exit by the upper opening, through which they had been thrown, they must have been able to use a lower one. It should be noted that nothing is said regarding the fourth Person coming forth. It is understandable that He would have remained with the three only as long as they needed His comfort within the furnace.

3:27. Gathered together were the satraps, prefects and governors, and counselors of the king, and they took note that the fire had effected no harm to their bodies, that the hair of their head had not been singed, that their garments remained unchanged, and that the smell of fire had not come upon them.

Gathered together: These words give the setting as the three friends emerged from the flames. Not only was the king present, but the four classes of officials named were also there. These men, all high in government and responsible, saw, and could later give united witness to, what occurred. Note that the first three of the groups are the same as the first three in the listings of verses two and three. The fourth is the counseling group to whom the king directed his question in verse twenty-four. The king had wanted the most influential men of his realm present when he punished the three recalcitrants; but now they served as the most authoritative witnesses to this miracle of God. *Took note:* The word used (root, $h^a zah$) normally means simply "to see," but here, in view of the context, this "seeing" was in the sense of noting unusual matters. These officials were very much interested in observing all details relative to the young men. Four matters are cited as having drawn particular attention. *Effected no harm:* Literally, "had no power." The fire had not been able to hurt the men's bodies. They showed no burned skin nor even any red mark giving evidence of excessive heat. *The hair:* The men's hair was not singed. Hair normally suffers the effect of fire more quickly than skin areas. *Their garments:* The spectators then considered the fine garments of the men, but these, too, were whole. The text says that they were "unchanged" *(la' sh^e nô),* which significantly indicates that not only were they not burned, but did not show even a black mark, as from smoke or soot. *Smell of fire:* The climaxing matter was the remarkable absence of even the smell of fire. Fire smell clings persistently to objects burned, but the young men did not even have this. The only object that had suffered harm, was the king's own rope, with which they had been bound. This had been consumed to give the men freedom. What a testimony these men were to the power and supremacy of their God, standing there unhurt and with their fine clothes still ready to wear to another occasion.

D. The Commendable Reaction of Nebuchadnezzar (vv. 28-30)

Nebuchadnezzar and his officers witnessed undeniable evidence of the supremacy of the Judean God that day. They could not claim the use of trickery, for they had all observed everything that had transpired. Their minds had to accept the fact that the God of these men had done something which they had never seen Babylonian gods do. It would be pleasing to think that some of them turned to personal trust in this God. Nothing is indicated regarding the others, but of Nebuchadnezzar, at least, it is stated that he did make some tangible acknowledgments. He had been directly involved with the first miracle when Daniel had revealed to him his dream, and perhaps he could be expected to be more greatly affected now by this second demonstration.

3:28. Nebuchadnezzar spoke and said, Blessed be the God of Shadrach, Meshach, and Abed-nego, who has sent his angel and delivered his servants who trusted in him. They have frustrated the king's word by devoting their bodies so that they would not serve or worship any god except their God.

Spoke: Nebuchadnezzar, being a man of action, spoke the words of verses twenty-eight and twenty-nine, apparently while all the dignitaries were yet present. This was a significant group before whom to make these statements, for likely they represented many parts of the empire on this day of dedication. *Blessed be:* This expression shows an attitude of reverence, awe, and approval on Nebuchadnezzar's part. He used the same expression years later after his recovery from the period of insanity (4:34), both times indicating a depth of feeling in respect to God. *God of Shadrach:* The pagan idea of deity did not deny the existence of gods of other nations. Nebuchadnezzar had not denied the existence of this Judean God at any time. Thus, on this occasion, he naturally spoke of God as being the God of these three Judeans. This would not preclude the possibility, however, that he was thinking, even if ever so slightly, regarding his own relation to this God. *Sent his angel:* This is a reference to the fourth Person in the furnace, showing that Nebuchadnezzar recognized that He had been sent to effect the deliverance witnessed. *Who trusted:* He recognized also that the trust in God of the three had been related to this deliverance. Their words of trust, when spoken to Nebuchadnezzar, had angered him; but his subsequent remarks show that he had been impressed by them all the time. One never knows what the impact of a faithful witness for God will be on those who hear. *Frustrated:* Literally, "have changed" *(shannîw).* The thought is that, through this turn of events, these men had changed the results which the king had anticipated by his words. He had expected them to die, but they had escaped completely unharmed. *Devoting:* Literally, "have given" *(yᵉhabû).* The thought is that the three had so devoted their bodies to God that even suffering had not brought them to serve or worship any other deity. The three had told the king that this was their commitment when they were first brought before him, and he showed now that he had understood them and was ready to commend them for it. A word of commendation is due also for Nebuchadnezzar. Just after he had been severely humiliated by these men, he owned up to his defeat and even gave them credit for their stand. Few kings would have done as much.

3:29. Therefore I make a decree that every people, nation, and language that speaks anything amiss against the God of Shadrach, Meshach, and Abed-nego shall be cut in pieces and their houses made a dunghill; because there is no other god who is able to deliver in this manner.

Therefore: Reference is to the convincing deliverance. Because God had so demonstrated His power, Nebuchadnezzar desired to issue the decree now related. *I make a decree:* The word for "decree" *(tᵉ'ēm)* means an official edict of government. The word is so used more than twenty times in the Aramaic portions of Daniel and Ezra; thus, decrees were issued with some frequency, though always regarding matters of importance. That Nebuchadnezzar put this announcement in the form of a decree made it more significant to the people, and it shows the importance that he placed on it. That the king would issue such an official word regarding a foreign deity must have been a topic of conversation for some time. *People, nation, and language:* These are the same words of reference to all people of the realm, used earlier in 3:4, 7; though here each word is in the singular, a change for which no significance is apparent. That Nebuchadnezzar used them shows that he wanted this decree heard by all in his empire. *Shall speak anything amiss:* The word for "anything amiss" *(shaluh)* means "erroneous," from a root meaning "to wander, to sin." The king was forbidding anyone in all his realm to say anything "erroneous" concerning the Judean God; that is, anything that would be to His detraction. The king had just done this himself so shortly before, but now he was forbidding anyone else to do so. *Cut in pieces:* This is the same phrase that is used in 2:5 (which see). It is noteworthy that the king added this strong deterrent to his decree. He showed that he meant what he said and was not merely going through a formality which the occasion seemed to require. *No other god:* Nebuchadnezzar here gave the reason for the directive: this foreign deity was greater than any other. This admission had been implied by his earlier use of the term, "Most High God" (v. 26), but now he was making it directly and in a public decree. People everywhere, including the Babylonian priests, would read the decree, and what would they think? Was not the king being disloyal, not only to his own religious system, but to the very country? Certainly Nebuchadnezzar, capable as he was, realized the serious nature of his words, which raises the question of why he issued them. The answer must be that he was personally very much affected by what had just happened. The evidence was too convincing to pass off lightly. Expositors have noted that he did not go so far as to command people to worship the Judean God, nor promise to do so even himself. This is true. He was too much of a Babylonian to commit himself this far. There is no doubt, however, that he was doing some serious thinking that could lead later in that direction.

3:30. Then the king caused Shadrach, Meshach, and Abed-nego to prosper in the province of Babylon.

Then the king: After this event Nebuchadnezzar honored the three young men by causing them to prosper. What this meant specifically is not indicated. They may have been promoted to higher positions; their financial income may have been increased; they may have been given gifts; or their housing situation, likely already good, may have been improved. Possibly they experienced all of these. Whatever was included, the honor that was shown must have been highly gratifying. When the three had stood before Nebuchadnezzar's image, with the announcement requiring them to bow ringing in their ears, it had seemed that they might lose all; but God had worked matters out so that they were actually receiving much more. How good their God was, and how wonderful that they had chosen to obey Him, no matter how great the cost!

CHAPTER 4

Chapter four presents Nebuchadnezzar's second dream. In the dream the king saw a great spreading tree and then a messenger come down from heaven to command that the tree be cut down. Daniel interpreted the dream for the king, stating that the tree represented Nebuchadnezzar himself and that its fall symbolized a seven-year period of insanity that he would experience. The chapter concludes by telling of this condition coming on the great man and the resulting honor he ascribed to the God of heaven following his restoration to normal mental health.

The time of these events in Nebuchadnezzar's reign is not indicated, but clues which exist point toward the close of his forty-three-year rule. His extensive building operations in Babylon seem to have been concluded by the time (4:30), and possible references to Nebuchadnezzar's illness from both Abydenus and Berosus (cf. under 4:33) make it late in his life. The dream cannot be placed later than his thirty-fifth year of rule, however, for the insanity lasted seven years, and he was back on his throne for at least a short time after the recovery. These factors together place the time of the dream likely between the thirtieth and thirty-fifth year of Nebuchadnezzar's reign, when Daniel was between forty-five and fifty years old, and when twenty-five to thirty years had elapsed since the deliverance of the three friends from the fiery furnace.

The chapter records the third miraculous contact of God with this heathen ruler. Daniel's narration and interpretation of the king's first dream had come in his second year, the miraculous deliverance of the three friends in perhaps his fifth year, and now this in about his thirty-fifth year. Nebuchadnezzar had been significantly impressed by each of the first two contacts, especially the second when he had made the public decree regarding the greatness of the Judeans' God as a result. But he was still more impressed with this third occasion and may even have come to place personal trust in the true God of heaven, as will be pointed out.

The form of chapter four is unique in the book, because it is presented as Nebuchadnezzar's own account. It begins with the king's address to "all peoples, nations, and languages," and employs the first person manner of presentation for most of the chapter. It is probable that Nebuchadnezzar himself wrote it and that Daniel then included the writing in the book. Some scholars deny this and believe that Daniel was the original author, simply employing this different style for the one chapter. They find evidence in the fact that the first person presentation is not observed throughout (vv. 19 and 28-33) and that some included expressions sound too "biblical" to have been penned by a pagan king (especially vv. 3 and 34). In response to the first factor, however, it may be pointed out that the use of the third person in the verses designated is likely due to the different subject matter there in view; and in respect to the second that the biblical nature of the expressions may well be due to Daniel's influence on Nebuchadnezzar and could be a further indication (in addition to others to be noted in the commentary) that this able man did come to place personal faith in the true God. Furthermore, other expressions in the chapter (particularly in vv. 8, 9, 13, 17, 18) suit better the type of language Nebuchadnezzar, rather than Daniel, might have used.

The rationale of Nebuchadnezzar's desire to write this information is not difficult to see. Such a report would have clarified to his people the nature and significance of what had occurred during his years of absence from the throne, and also provided further opportunity to give testimony to his own appreciation of the Judean God. Some have argued that it is absurd to think that a king would tell of his own insanity. However, the purpose was not found in this but to speak of God's power, justice, and grace, in connection with which the insanity only played an impotrant role. With Nebuchadnezzar choosing to write the document, it follows that he would have assured it appropriate circulation. Daniel may well have assisted him in its writing. Later David saw fit, under the direction of God, to include it in his book.

A. The Significant Introduction (vv. 1-3)

The first three verses of the account constitutes a unique, significant introduction. After giving an appropriate greeting in verse one, the king explained why he chose to issue the document. He stated that he wanted to tell of the miracles that God had performed in respect to him, so that all might know that God's kingdom is eternal. Nebuchadnezzar's thinking, as revealed in this statement, is not difficult to recognize. He had just been removed from, though later restored to, his throne, and would, like other kings, soon be removed permanently in death; but, in contrast, God would never be removed from His throne, and was rightfully supreme over all earthly kingdoms. The chapter division of the Aramaic rendition places these verses at the conclusion of chapter three, as if they are a part of the story regarding the three friends and the fiery furnace. The verses belong here, however, where the English translation has them, for Nebuchadnezzar's reference in them to miracles wrought in his behalf fits his experiences as set forth in the fourth chapter better than those in the third.

4:1. Nebuchadnezzar the king to all peoples, nations, and languages that dwell on all the earth: Peace be multiplied to you.

Nebuchadnezzar: The king employed a proper, formal beginning for this proclamation. Some versions insert a verb, either "wrote" or "sent," which has the force of presenting what follows as having been written by Daniel. The abrupt style without such a verb, however, fits the form of a royal proclamation, which is in keeping with the manner of presentation in the chapter generally. The Septuagint version inserts a historical statement at this point, saying that Nebuchadnezzar "wrote an encyclical epistle to" many nations. This too, however, is clearly an addition to the original. *Peoples, nations, and languages:* This is the same form of general address employed several times in chapter two (cf. 2:4). *All the earth:* Both the Assyrian and the Babylonian kings thought of themselves as rulers over all the earth, so describing themselves in their inscriptions. Actual dominion extended only from the Zagros mountains to Egypt, but this was the known world of the day. It is not likely that Nebuchadnezzar thought this proclamation would be circulated any farther than the boundaries of his own kingdom (cf. Jer. 25:26; 27:5, 6). *Peace be multiplied:* The same phrase is used later by the Persian, Darius (6:25), in a similar context. Apparently it was a common form of salutation (cf. Gen. 43:23; 1 Sam. 25:6; Luke 10:5; 1 Pet. 1:2). Still today in the Middle East, whether by Jew or Arab, the word "peace" *(shalom* or *salam)* constitutes the common greeting.

4:2, 3. It seemed good to me to show the signs and wonders that God Most High has wrought for me. How great are His signs and how mighty His wonders! His kingdom is an everlasting kingdom, and His rule is from generation to generation.

Seemed good to me: Literally, "was beautiful before me." Nebuchadnezzar looked upon the issuance of this proclamation as something fine to do. This means that he was neither coerced nor reluctant, but engaged in the matter readily. *The signs and wonders:* The word for "signs" *('at)* means something which points out. When used of God's "signs," it regularly means something pointing out His existence and power, that is, something supernatural, miraculous. The word for "wonder" *(t⁼mah)* means that which produces surprise, astonishment, admiration. When used with the word "sign," it refers to the response which God's signs solicit on the part of witnesses. The two words together commonly designate miracles of God (cf. Ex. 7:3; Deut. 4:34; 13:1; 34:11; Isa. 8:18, Jer. 32:20). *God Most High:* This is the same phrase as in 3:26 (which see). *For me:* Literally, "with me" *('immi).* The primary reference is to God's miracle involving Nebuchadnezzar's insanity; thus having to do *with* him, while at the same time being *for* his benefit.

How great . . . how mighty: The two adjectives used *(rabrᵉbîn* and *taqqîpîn)* are close in meaning and serve to reinforce each other in stressing the greatness of God's miracles. *An everlasting kingdom:* The word for "everlasting" *('alam)* carries reference here to all eternity. Nebuchadnezzar was comparing God's rule with his own, so recently taken from him by illness. God was not subject to interruptions of this kind. His rule was stable, unchanging, eternal. *From generation to generation:* In contrast to human kingdoms, which change in rule even between generations, God's kingdom was perpetual. No assassinations or usurpations could bring a halt to it. The same authority, the same set of rules, the same equity in judgment, the same rewards and punishments continued in His kingdom without variation. Nebuchadnezzar had enjoyed a long and brilliant reign of his own, but he was here admitting that it was little in comparison with God's. The words of verse three constitute one of the portions in the chapter said to be too "biblical" to have been written by a pagan king. It sounds much like Psalm 145:13. In the light of the general setting, however, as now set forth, it may be fairly said that its factors all fit well into what one might expect the king to have said. When one views the words as a part to his praise to God, resulting from God's miracle just experienced, any difficulty vanishes.

B. Nebuchadnezzar's Second Dream (vv. 4-8)

With the introduction completed, Nebuchadnezzar began to tell of his dream. He spoke first of having the dream and then of summoning his counselors to interpret it for him. Daniel, who was still head of the counselors, did not come with the main group, but only later when the others had again shown themselves incapable of meeting the king's demand.

4:4, 5. I Nebuchadnezzar was at rest in my house and prospering in my palace. I had a dream which made me afraid; and the thoughts upon my bed and the visions of my head terrified me.

I Nebuchadnezzar: Beginning the account proper, Nebuchadnezzar gave his own name again, along with the personal pronoun. This provided a touch of formality appropriate to such a proclamation, and at the same time made clear to all that he was indeed the one giving the account. The Septuagint version prefaces the verse with the words, "In the eighteenth year of his reign Nebuchadnezzar said." Textual evidence indicates, however, that these are not from the original. As noted, the time was likely after Nebuchadnezzar's thirtieth year. *At rest in my house:* The word for "at rest" *(sh^eleh)* means "to be free from apprehension or fear." Nebuchadnezzar designates the place where he was so characterized as his "house" *(bayit).* This means his place of residence, where he lived as family head. Together, the words signify that the king was experiencing no serious problems at home when the dream was given to him. *Prospering:* Literally, "growing green" *(ra'^enan).* In Psalm 52:8, the word is used in its Hebrew form regarding a flourishing tree. Nebuchadnezzar's vast empire was being controlled with a minimum of disturbance. No outside powers were seriously challenging him. His country was prosperous. *In my palace:* The word for "palace" *(hêkal)* means an important building, usually a palace or temple. Here it refers to Nebuchadnezzar's official palace. Used here in parallel with "house," it speaks of his place of business as over against his place of residence. The overall thought suggested is that he was "at rest" in his private life and prosperous in his official capacity as king.

I had a dream: It was in this fine setting that God visited the king with this dream of warning. *Made me afraid:* As with the first dream, Nebuchadnezzar recognized that this one too was unusual, signifying a message to him. God, having sent the dream, would have imparted this recognition as well. The result was that Nebuchadnezzar was afraid, for the nature of the dream portended an undesirable interpretation. *Thoughts ... visions:* The word for "thoughts" is from the root verb *harher* "to think," and the word for "visions" from *h^azah* "to see." The likely relation of the two ideas is that the thoughts of his mind were prompted by what he saw in the dream. Whether these thoughts were a part of the dream, or whether they came to the king later as he reflected while still on his bed, is not made clear. The word for "thoughts" has been found in other literature to mean "dream phantasies,"[1] a fact which could argue for the first possibility. *Terrified me:* The word used is expressive of greater emotional disturbance than the word for "made me afraid." The "thoughts," then, whether a part of the dream or of later reflection, were very real and troubled him deeply.

4:6, 7. **Therefore, I made a decree to assemble all the wise men of Babylon before me, that they might make known to me the interpretation of the dream. Then the magicians, the enchanters, the Chaldeans, and the soothsayers came in; and I told them the dream. but they did not make known its interpretation to me.**

[1] Cf. Montgomery, MICC, pp. 226, 27.

I made a decree: The exact same phrase is used here as in 3:29. Nebuchadnezzar's employment of it shows the urgency he felt in having the dream interpreted. *All the wise men:* Once again, those summoned to give the interpretation were the wise men, as in the case of the first dream (2:2). *The interpretation:* No mention is made this time that Nebuchadnezzar wanted the content of the dream stated to him, but only that the interpretation be given. What may have prompted a seemingly greater confidence in the wise men this time is not revealed.

Magicians, enchanters, Chaldeans, soothsayers: All four of these terms are used in either 2:2 or 2:27 (which see). Once again, as in those verses, the intention is to designate those persons who were supposed to be experts in interpreting omens, including the omens of dreams. Certainly time had changed the thinking of Nebuchadnezzar regarding these men from what it was when he had ordered the death of all. During the intervening thirty years they probably had been called on many times, and apparently had performed to his satisfaction. *I told them the dream:* The statement is now made directly that he told them the contents of what he had dreamed. *They did not make known:* With the dream told, however, the men still did not reveal its interpretation. The question arises as to why they did not. As noted regarding the first dream (cf. 2:4), they had rule books for giving such interpretations. The interpretation they would have given would not have been the true one, but they would have thought it was. The answer likely is that they did not want to give it, rather than that they could not. Significantly, the text does not say that they could not give it, but only that they did not: stating, literally, "They were not ones making known *(mᵉhôdᵉ'în,* pl. act. participle from the root *yᵉda',* to know) the interpretation to me." The reason why they would not have wished to give it was due to the nature of the dream. It was a dream which meant humiliation and tragedy for the king, which their rules would very likely also have indicated, and they simply would not have wanted to convey this kind of information to the great Nebuchadnezzar.

4:8. Until at last Daniel came in before me, whose name is Belteshazzar, according to the name of my god, and in whom is the spirit of the Holy God; and I told him the dream.

Until at last Daniel came: Numerous reasons have been suggested as to why Daniel did not come with the main group of wise men. One is that the king simply had forgotten him and his remarkable interpretation of some thirty years before. This hardly seems likely, however, both because of the great significance of that occasion for the king and also because of the glad manner with which Nebuchadnezzar greeted him when he did come. Another is that Nebuchadnezzar himself suspected the ominous meaning of his dream and hoped that it might prove to be less unpleasant if it came from the lips of wise men other than Daniel. But certainly the king was too wise a man to fall into unrealistic and wishful thinking of this kind. A third suggested reason is that the custom of the day forbade that the chief of the wise men (Daniel's position) be summoned first; but there is no evidence of this, and such a custom does not present itself as having been likely. A fourth is that Daniel was considered more an officer of the state (being head of the province of Babylon, 2:48) than chief of the wise men, and accordingly was not called first. When Daniel appeared, however, the king readily called him "master of the magicians," as though he did so think of him.

A more likely answer is suggested by the text itself. It does not say that "at last Nebuchadnezzar called Daniel," but "at last Daniel came in." It is quite possible that Daniel's lateness was of his own choosing, not the king's. When Nebuchadnezzar's word calling for the wise men was received, Daniel may simply have intentionally stayed behind, possibly because of an undisclosed revelation from God to that end. The reason could have been that such a delayed appearance of Daniel would give time for the deficiency of the other wise men to show itself once more, which in turn would make his true interpretation all the more impressive. Fitting into this explanation is the usage of the word "until" *('ad),* coming at the beginning of the verse. It suggests that Daniel's arrival was timed at a point when the wise men had been deliberating a long time, with the king having become quite impatient. This explanation would account for Nebuchadnezzar's not becoming angry with the wise men, as he had thirty years earlier, for they would not yet have had to tell him that they would not, or could not, give the interpretation. Also it would suit the joyful attitude displayed by the king when Daniel did come at last. He would have looked for him at the first, and wondered why he was absent. His arrival at the crucial point of the proceedings would have relieved the king of his anxiety that the interpretation he wanted was not to be forthcoming.

Belteshazzar: This is the Babylonian name given to Daniel as stated in 1:7 (which see). Nebuchadnezzar used it throughout his report (cf. vv. 9, 18, 19), as might be expected, and this fact shows further that this report is truly his. His employment of both names, Daniel and Belteshazzar, in this verse and in verse nineteen, may be due to his writing for many people. The use of both the Hebrew and Babylonian names could make more people certain of the person so identified. *Name of my god:* In adding this phrase of explanation, the king probably had more in mind than merely to tell the significance of the name, which any Babylonian would have known. He probably was seeking to give at least some credit to the Babylonian god Bel for the interpretation given. He was saying that Daniel, who had given the interpretation, was at least named after Bel (cf. name significance, under 1:7), whom he identifies as his own god by the possessive pronoun "my." That Nebuchadnezzar did still speak of Bel as his god shows that, along with whatever degree of allegiance he had now given to the God of heaven, he was continuing to hold also, though possibly for public show, to the Babylonian deities. *Spirit of the Holy God:* Some expositors argue that Nebuchadnezzar used this phrase here in respect to gods generally. Keil, for instance, states that Nebuchadnezzar could be expected to have been speaking out of the usual pagan concepts of the day, and Keil finds evidence also in the use of the plural "gods" *('ᵉlahîn)* here. A similar mention by Pharaoh in connection with Joseph, years earlier, is taken as parallel in significance (Gen. 41:38).[2] There are several reasons, however, for taking the phrase as a direct reference to Daniel's God in particular. (1) The plural "gods" can be used in reference to a single deity in the Aramaic language as well as in Hebrew.[3] (2) Nebuchadnezzar had already experienced, on two different occasions, the supremacy of Daniel's God (in contrast to Pharaoh with Joseph). He could not have forgotten these occasions, especially since this was another dream situation like the first; hence, he had ample reason to refer to the God of heaven. (3) In verses nine and eighteen Nebuchadnezzar's continued use of this same phrase in a context telling why Daniel would be able to reveal the interpretation is more meaningful if Daniel's God is particularly in mind. (4) Nebuchadnezzar's attitude on seeing Daniel was clearly one of gladness, relief, and expectancy, indicating that he was seeing him as the one who had met his need a prior time—the time when Daniel had revealed the first dream and had explicitly identified the God of heaven as the one to receive all the credit. The word "spirit" *(ruaḥ),* as used here by a person of pagan background, is not a reference to the Holy Spirit, but it is the king's way of identifying the point of contact within Daniel by which this holy God could make the necessary revelation. Nebuchadnezzar was only saying that Daniel had that within him which made possible the impartation, by the Holy God, of such information as here desired. *I told him the dream:* As the king had not required that the other wise men tell him the content of the dream this time, so he did not require it of Daniel. That he did repeat it for Daniel shows further that Daniel was not present at the first. The other wise men may still have been within hearing as the details were once again set forth.

[2] KDC on Daniel, p. 147.
[3] Cf. Montgomery, MICC, pp. 225, 26.

C. Content of the Dream (vv. 9-18)

Nebuchadnezzar's report now presents the content of the dream, as told to Daniel.

4:9. O Belteshazzar, chief of the magicians, I know that the spirit of the Holy God is in you and that no mystery troubles you: declare the interpretation of the visions of my dream that I have seen.

Chief of the magicians: This was the position granted to Daniel by Nebuchadnezzar many years earlier, according to 2:48. Apparently, he still retained it, and the king addressed him accordingly. He employed the term "magicians" (cf. 1:20) representatively of the other terms, which together designated all the wise men. The term "magicians" is regularly listed first when several of the terms are grouped, suggesting that those so called may have been considered leaders. *Spirit of the Holy God:* This is the second occurrence of the phrase in the chapter (cf. v. 8); again it is used as the basis of Daniel's qualification for giving the interpretation. *No mystery troubles you:* The word for "mystery" *(raz)* is the same as that translated "secret" in 2:18, 19, 27-30. It means that which is hidden in meaning, with reference here to the interpretation of the dream. The word for "troubles" *('anes)* means basically "to oppress, burden." No *secret* was a *burden* to Daniel because he could reveal it. *Declare the interpretation of the visions:* This is a rather free translation of a difficult part of the verse. The translation which is most natural makes Nebuchadnezzar to be asking Daniel to give both the content of the dream and its interpretation (cf. KJV, ASV, etc.), but this is not in keeping with the fact that Nebuchadnezzar actually told the dream himself, expecting Daniel to give only the interpretation. Montgomery[4] seeks to solve the problem by taking *hezwê* (visions) as *h^azî*, meaning "behold," thus giving the translation "Behold, my dream that I have seen: declare its interpretation." He believes this change can be philologically defended. Without making such a change, however, the following and preferable translation is possible: "The visions of my dream that I have seen, even its interpretation declare." The free translation used above simply expresses this thought in more acceptable English.

4:10-12. Thus were the visions of my head upon my bed: I was looking and, indeed, a tree in the midst of the earth, and its height was great. The tree grew and became strong, and its height reached to the heavens, so that it was visible to the end of all the earth. Its leaves were fair and its fruit abundant, and in it was food for all. Under it the beasts of the field found shade, in its branches the birds of the heavens nestled, and from it all flesh took nourishment.

[4] MICC, p. 228.

Thus were the visions: This first phrase serves as a title for the entire description following. *I was looking:* Literally, "looking, I was looking." The force is to say that Nebuchadnezzar was engrossed in his looking; hence, looking carefully. Apparently, he wanted to assure Daniel that he had taken good note of what he saw, giving reason for Daniel to depend on his narration as being accurate. Accuracy respecting the dream itself, obviously, was essential to accuracy in interpretation. *A tree:* The center of the dream was a tree. That it stood "in the midst of the earth" suggests that it stood alone and that it was important to all the earth.

The tree grew and became strong: The thought is best taken to be that the tree continued to grow even beyond the great height already attained, as noted in verse ten. Nebuchadnezzar watched it grow yet higher and stronger, achieving a massive trunk and large extending branches, until its height finally "reached to the heavens." This made it visible at a great distance. The phrase "to the end of all the earth" is hyperbolic, like the descriptive terms which Babylonian kings were accustomed to use regarding the extent of their dominion. Nebuchadnezzar likely suspected that the tree represented himself, both because of its importance in the dream and because trees were frequently used in ancient time to symbolize great rulers: (cf. Ezek. 17:22; 19:10ff; 31:3ff.; Amos 2:9). Herodotus wrote regarding a dream of the Persian king, Xerxes, in which Xerxes saw himself crowned with an olive shoot, which had branches that reached to the end of the earth.[5]

Its leaves were fair: Not only was the tree large, but it was healthy, with beautiful foliage and abundant fruit. This suggests prosperity for the one symbolized. The degree of this prosperity is indicated by the statement that "in it was food for all."

4:13. I kept looking in the visions of my head upon my bed, and, indeed, a watcher, a holy one, came down from heaven.

I kept looking: This phrase is identical to that used in verse ten, indicating continued intense observation. The reason for the repetition is probably that Nebuchadnezzar was beginning a new aspect of the dream. *A watcher, a holy one:* Into the static scene suddenly entered an active participant. He was clearly one person only, because all verbs employed regarding him are singular, but he is described with the two qualifiers "watcher" and "holy." The first one (*'îr*) is from the root verb *'ûr*, meaning "to watch," with vigilance implied. The second one (*qadîsh*) is the well-known adjective "holy," here used with the *waw*, signifying "even." The participant to which reference is made must be an angel, but it should be noted that only in this

---

[5] For similar references to the tree, cf. O. Zockler, *LCD*, p. 111, who refers to Havernick.

chapter is this way of referring to an angel used. It is possible that Nebuchadnezzar, the speaker, may have been influenced in this manner of reference by concepts characteristic of the East of his day. Barnes[6] gives evidence that the expression used was of the East, quoting, for instance, from the Bun-Dehesh, a commentary on the Zendavesta of the Zoroastrians: "Ormuzd has set four *watchers* in the four parts of the heavens, to keep their eye upon the host of the stars." Whatever Nebuchadnezzar's own thinking, however, the two qualities, watchfulness and holiness, fit well as descriptive of God's angels; and were, accordingly, admissible into the sacred text. *Came down from heaven:* This angel, seen apparently in tangible form, descended from heaven into the scene, and Nebuchadnezzar, observing, heard him begin to speak.

4:14, 15a. He cried aloud and said, Hew down the tree and cut off its branches, shake off its leaves and scatter its fruit; let the beasts flee from under it and the birds from its branches. But leave the stump of its roots in the earth, even with a band of iron and bronze, in the grass of the field.

Cried aloud: Literally, "cried in strength." Nebuchadnezzar heard him cry with a loud, firm voice, thus lending importance to what he had to say. *Hew down the tree:* The angel's words constituted orders to be carried out in connection with the tree, but gave no indication regarding the one to effect them. Because a plural form of the verb is employed, the implication is that more than one would be involved. The first order concerned the destruction of the tree, cutting it down, lopping off its branches, stripping it of leaves, and scattering its fruit. It was to be completely removed from its place of influence, with even its fruit scattered so that none would be available as a benefit to any being. No doubt, it was this aspect of the dream which contributed mainly to the king's fear. If the tree symbolized himself, its being cut down must mean that he was to suffer a similar kind of fate. *Beasts . . . birds:* From the tree itself, the angel's attention moves to the animals and birds mentioned earlier, who were benefiting from the tree. Both would now have to flee from it, so that no longer could they enjoy its comfort and protection. The symbolism was that Nebuchadnezzar's subjects no longer would receive the same from him.

Stump of its roots: The word for "stump" (*'iqqar*) carries the connotation of something alive, not dead. The word could easily be translated "root" here, were it not that the normal word for "root" (*shoresh*) follows. It is best to take it, then, as that which grows from the root, which in this instance, with the tree having been cut down, could

[6] BD, pp. 251, 52.

only have been the stump. That this stump was alive, with life-giving roots still attached, is important in the dream, because it signifies that Nebuchadnezzar would continue to live, after being removed from his throne, and that there would be the prospect of his being restored some day. *Band of iron and bronze:* The stump was to have a band of iron and bronze around it. Expositors differ on the symbolism of this band. Some see it as representing Nebuchadnezzar's state of insanity, when he would be bound by its terrible grip. This view, however, requires the subject in mind to have already changed from the stump itself to Nebuchadnezzar. The subject does change in the next sentence, and one might argue that it does already here; but this is not likely and there are reasons in favor of another view; that is, that the subject is still the stump and the band is for the purpose of preserving it. This preservation could have been effected either by a band encompassing the top of the stump, thus keeping it from splitting and rotting; or by an enclosing railing or fence surrounding the stump, to keep animals or people from bringing injury. Two reasons favor the general idea of preservation. First, this idea fits the rationale for the mention of the stump at all. Nebuchadnezzar was not to be uprooted entirely, but only cut down, with the promise (signified as certain of fulfillment by the preserving band or fence) of being restored in due time. This thought of certainty in preservation is brought out also in Daniel's later interpretation in verse twenty-six. Second, the phrase concerning the metal band or fence falls at the middle of that part of the verse which deals with the continuing stump. The Aramaic word order places the phrase "even with a band of iron and bronze" immediately after "leave the stump of its roots in the earth." This order has the force of relating the idea of *band* or *fence* closely to the idea of a *preserved stump*. Then, favoring the *fence* explanation, in respect to the manner of preservation intended, over that of the *band,* is the good rationale for this explanation: the protective fence could symbolize the care given by assigned guards as they would watch over Nebuchadnezzar, while allowing him to live in the open with animals (cf. v. 33 following). *In the grass of the field:* The stump was to be left untouched, out in the open, in the grass of the field, where the forces of nature would come upon it. The symbolism is that Nebuchadnezzar would experience his days of insanity similarly in the open, where the forces of nature would come upon him.

4:15b, 16. Let him be wet with the dew of heaven, and let him share the herbage of the earth with the beasts. Let his heart be changed from a man's, and let the heart of a beast be given to him; and let seven times pass over him.

Let him be wet . . . let him share: That the subject in view from this point on has changed to the person, Nebuchadnezzar, is self-evident. Only a person, not a stump, can share food, or have his heart changed, etc. The symbolism in respect to Nebuchanezzar is not difficult. As the stump was to remain in the field, so Nebuchadnezzar would dwell in a similar situation, where he would be wet by the dew and find his nourishment in herbage much as the beasts.

Let his heart be changed: The context calls for "heart" (*l^eḇaḇ*) to mean the "seat of reason." Nebuchadnezzar would be changed so that he would reason like an animal. This is noted to explain why he would share food with the animals. The thought suggests the nature of the mental affliction predicted for Nebuchadnezzar; namely lycanthropy (cf. under v. 33 following). A person with this illness thinks of himself as some kind of animal and lives accordingly. The disease is known today, and numerous historical cases are on record. *Let seven times pass over him:* This phrase is included to indicate the length of time through which Nebuchadnezzar would suffer this condition, as made clear further by Daniel's later interpretation (vv. 25, 26). There is a question, however, regarding the meaning of "seven times." The word for "times" (*'iddanîn*) has appeared three times in the book (2:8; 3:5, 15), but none of these are parallel in type so as to lend help here. In 7:25, however, a parallel employment does exist, in the words "they shall be given into his hand until a time, and times, and a dividing of time." The meaning of "time" there, as will then be argued, is "one year." This suggests that the meaning here should be the same; making "seven times" to signify "seven years." This meaning fits other considerations also. For one thing, it suits for the likely duration of Nebuchadnezzar's illness; because to speak of seven days, or weeks, or even months appears to be too short in view of the overall story. Also, it is reasonable to use the word "times" on this basis: the full cycle of seasons, with all the changes in types of weather involved, would pass over the king seven times.

4:17. By the decree of the watchers is the command, and by the word of the holy ones the demand; to the intent that the living may know that the Most High rules over the kingdom of men and gives it to whomever He will, and sets over it the lowly of men.

Decree of the watchers . . . holy ones: The words for "watchers" and "holy ones" are plurals of the singulars used in verse thirteen. This means that reference is to a group of angels, one of whom came down to give the announcement of these verses. The words "command" and "demand" quite obviously refer to this same message. The force of the verse is to say that the thoughts conveyed in the announcement were by the "decree" or "word" of this group. One may not conclude from this, however, that angels are themselves formulators of decisions; because, among other reasons, Daniel makes clear later (v.

24) that this decree was by the Most High. The thought intended must be only that angels concur with, and then convey, such decrees as are here in view. Some expositors have suggested that, since the Scriptures occasionally refer to councils held in heaven (cf. 1 Kings 22:19-22; Job 1:6-12; 2:1-6), the angelic realm does play some part in making divine decisions; but this cannot be, for it would imply an impairment of the sovereignty of God, who alone is capable of making any decision in the final sense. Others have suggested that these terms were used in accommodation to the pagan background of Nebuchadnezzar, since eastern religions of the day did include the idea of planetary deities keeping watch in a sort of council over the affairs of men.[7] The response must be given, however, that, if any accommodation was intended, it was limited by the teaching of Scripture elsewhere, which makes plain that God is sovereign and angels are merely His helpers. *To the intent that:* Literally, "unto the matter that." This decree had a purpose, something to be accomplished, and now to be stated. *The living:* The reference here seems to be both general and specific. The general reference is to all living humans, and the specific to Nebuchadnezzar. God had a lesson in the decree for all to learn, and one specifically for Nebuchadnezzar.

Most High rules: The lesson consisted in learning that there is one higher than humans, who rules supremely in the world. He is the Most High God of heaven. He rules "over the kingdom of men," which means over the realm of mankind. He carries final authority and is judge in the affairs of men. Nebuchadnezzar was a proud man. In his might as great king of his day, he lost sight of his dependence; and he needed to be humbled. God was about to humble him in the manner symbolized by the fallen tree. *Gives it to whomever He will:* One aspect of God's sovereignty in the world, particularly pertinent in reference to Nebuchadnezzar, is His superintendence over the election and appointments of national rulers. God permits only those to be placed in office whom, for some reason, He desires (cf. Rom. 13:1). This does not mean that He approves of all they do or of the kind of people they are. Certainly He disapproves strongly on both counts concerning most rulers. But He reserves control so that no person is allowed into office whom He rejects, in view of the circumstances then existing. From the words here given, Nebuchadnezzar should know that he held his particular office only because God had permitted it. *The lowly of men:* In superintending royal appointments, God gives precedence to those who are lowly and humble. The word for "lowly" *(sheᵖal)* does not mean base, vile, or incapable; but humble and unassuming. This is but a particularization of the general biblical truth that "God resisteth the proud, but giveth grace

---

[7] Cf. Montgomery, MICC, pp. 231, 32 for discussion.

to the humble" (James 4:6; cf. 1 Sam. 2:7, 8; Luke 1:52; 1 Cor. 1:26ff.). The point for Nebuchadnezzar to notice was that, because he was not thus characterized, he was in line for the punishment symbolized in the dream.

4:18. This dream I, King Nebuchadnezzar, have seen; now you, O Belteshazzar, declare the interpretation, because all of the wise men of my kingdom are unable to make known to me the interpretation; but you are able, because the spirit of the Holy God is in you.

This dream I: Nebuchadnezzar thus signified his conclusion of the dream. The significance of doing so in this tautological manner was apparently to assure Daniel that the report was accurate, exactly as the dream had been given to him. The inclusion of his own name lends a note of authenticity. *Are unable:* The wise men had been told the same story earlier, but had not responded by giving the interpretation. This meant to the king that they were unable to give it at that time, just as in the former instance thirty years before. This need not be taken as evidence that they actually had not been able to make an interpretation, which would be contrary to the conclusion reached under verse seven, but only that the king believed they had not. *Spirit of the Holy God:* This is the third time the king used this reference, each time with the recognition that Daniel's qualification for dream interpretation was based on this fact.

D. Interpretation of the Dream (vv. 19-27)

As Nebuchadnezzar recited the story, he did not mention Daniel as speaking a word, until the dream was told. The king gave Daniel's words of interpretation, which continue through verse twenty-seven. First, however, he said that Daniel hesitated in starting to speak because he was troubled at the meaning of the dream.

4:19. Then Daniel, whose name was Belteshazzar, was dumbfounded for a short time, because his thoughts troubled him. And the king spoke and said, Let not the dream and its interpretation trouble you. Belteshazzar answered and said, My Lord, may the dream be for those who hate you and its interpretation for your enemies.

Daniel . . . Belteshazzar: This is the second use of both names in one context, likely for the purpose of clarification (cf. v. 8). *Was dumbfounded:* After the king finished speaking, Daniel simply remained silent, apparently with a perplexed look on his face. This silence continued for a "short time" *(sha'ah).* The derivation of *sha'ah* is unknown, but it is commonly related to an Arabic root, which can mean either an "hour" or a "moment." Though the former meaning seems best in respect to four other times the word is used in the book (3:6, 15; 4:33; 5:5), here the latter is preferable, not in the sense of specifically a minute of sixty seconds, but simply as a short period of time. The next phrase gives the reason for the silence: Daniel was troubled concerning the dream, not because he was uncertain of its meaning, but because he was distressed regarding what it portended for the king. *The king spoke:* The silence was broken, not by Daniel, but once again by the king. He noted Daniel's appearance of anxiety and desired to extend encouragement. He may have been momentarily worried that Daniel was unable to give the interpretation this time; or he may have recognized Daniel's true problem and wanted him to know that he, Nebuchadnezzar, stood ready to receive the interpretation, good or bad as it might be.

Those who hate you . . . your enemies: The king's reassurance was followed by a response from Daniel. He expressed the wish that the meaning of this dream could be for the king's enemies, rather than for the king himself, stressing the thought by a parallelism. These words indicated several items of information to the king: first, that Daniel's hesitancy was not due to any perplexity as to the meaning of the dream, but only to anxiety for Nebuchadnezzar; second, that the interpretation did portend unpleasant developments for the king, as no doubt he had feared; third, that Daniel himself had Nebuchadnezzar's interests in mind, wishing that these developments could be for someone other than the king; and fourth, by implication, that the king could count on Daniel's support and further assistance, as it might be needed, through the difficult time forewarned. Recognition of these matters would have enhanced the king's favor toward Daniel. Daniel's words, further, showed that he held the king in high respect. This does not mean that he was blind to Nebuchadnezzar's deficiencies, particularly as to anger and pride, but something regarding the mighty ruler had commended itself to him. It may have been simply Nebuchadnezzar's ability to rule his great empire. Daniel, in his two important positions, had no doubt enjoyed considerable opportunity to observe the man in action. Also, Daniel's desire that Nebuchadnezzar come to place faith in the true God would have helped to enlarge any affection for him. The king had shown real interest thirty years before, and Daniel would have hoped that this second dream might stir that interest again. He may have recognized, too, that for him to display this affection could help in persuading the great man to exercise real trust in the God of heaven.

4:20-22. **The tree that you saw, which grew and became strong, and its height reached to the heavens, so that it was visible to all the earth, whose leaves were fair and its fruit abundant, and in it was food for all; under which the beasts of the field dwelt, and in whose branches the birds of the heavens lodged: it is you, O King, who have grown and become strong, and your greatness has increased**

and reached the heavens, and your dominion to the end of the earth.

The tree that you saw: These words begin Daniel's restatement of the king's earlier description, which is repeated almost exactly. The few changes he makes are of no significance, with the possible exception of his additional use of the word "dominion" *(shaltan),* which gives the symbolism of the tree being visible at long range. By this repetition, Daniel showed Nebuchadnezzar that he had heard well and would be able to give the right interpretation accordingly.

It is you, O King: With these words, the interpretation proper began. The words are direct, in the vein of Nathan's words to David years before: "You are the man" (2 Sam. 12:7). With them, Daniel settled the basic question in the king's mind. Yes, the tree did signify him. The king had probably feared so, but now he heard it stated by this trusted interpreter. *Who have grown and become strong:* These words from Daniel may have helped to relieve the staggering blow a little for Nebuchadnezzar, reminding him that he had indeed become great and his dominion very extensive.

4:23-26. **And that the king saw a watcher, a holy one, come down from heaven and say, Hew down the tree and destroy it, but leave the stump of its roots in the earth, even with a band of iron and bronze, in the grass of the field; and let him be wet with the dew of heaven, and let him share with the beasts of the field, until seven times pass over him; this is the interpretation, O King: it is the decree of the Most High which has come upon my lord the king, that you will be driven from among men, and your dwelling will be with the beasts of the field; you will be made to eat herbage like oxen, you will be wet with the dew of heaven, and seven times will pass over you, until you know that the Most High rules over the kingdom of men and gives it to whomever He will. And that it was commanded to leave the stump of the roots of the tree, your kingdom is assured to you from the time that you come to know that heaven rules.**

The king saw a watcher: These and the following words of verse twenty-three continue the same careful repetition from the record of the dream proper, with two main exceptions: the use of the simple "destroy it," in place of detailed phrases regarding the shaking off of leaves, scattering of fruit, etc.; and the complete omission regarding the change of heart from a man's to a beast's. This omission is understandable because Nebuchadnezzar's statement to Daniel was already an aspect of interpretation.

Decree of the Most High: Here "Most High" is substituted for "watchers" of Nebuchadnezzar's statement (v. 17). No conflict exists, as noted already regarding verse seventeen, for Daniel simply made clear that this decree, like all decrees, belonged in the last analysis to God.

You will be driven from among men . . . with the beasts: With these words, Daniel indicated the symbolism of the tree being cut down and destroyed. Nebuchadnezzar was to be driven from dwelling with men to live with animals. This brought the second great shock to the king, the first being that he was the tree. This second statement, too, he likely had feared beforehand, but the directness of the statement made it so much more real. Again, as with the narration of the dream, no indication is given as to who would effect these changes for the king. The Aramaic employs impersonal active plurals, here translated somewhat freely as passives. *Made to eat herbage:* This phrase and the next are included to show what Nebuchadnezzar's manner of life was to be while living with the animals. He would not merely live *where* they lived, but *as* they lived. He would eat "herbage" like oxen. "Herbage" (*ᵃseḇ*) is a broader term than "grass" (*deṭe'*), used in the phrase "in the grass of the field" (vv. 15, 23), for "herbage" includes also the vegetable realm. The likelihood is, then, that Nebuchadnezzar's menu would include, if not consist principally of, vegetables, rather than merely grass, on which oxen feed. The phrase "like oxen" probably refers mainly to the manner of eating, rather than content. The next phrase, that he would "be wet with the dew of heaven," means that he would live in the open, with a minimum of shelter, like animals. *Seven times . . . until you know:* Nebuchadnezzar would experience this manner of life for seven years (cf. discussion of "times," v. 16), at the end of which he would have learned the intended lesson concerning the supremacy of the Most High. In verse seventeen, the general designation "that the living may know" is used, but here Daniel was more specific in referring only to Nebuchadnezzar. Otherwise, his repetition is exact once more, except that he omitted the closing phrase given in verse seventeen.

Your kingdom is assured: In this closing observation, Daniel gave a hopeful note to the king. He would assuredly receive his kingdom again. This was the significance of the stump's being left in the ground, protected by the band of iron and bronze (cf. discussion under v. 15). *Heaven:* This is an unusual employment for "heaven," here meaning "God." Daniel likely used it because a basic distinction between the true God and Babylonian deities concerned their respective places of abode: heaven versus earth. To employ it provided a short way of referring unmistakably to the Judean God.

4:27. Therefore, O King, let my counsel be acceptable to you: break with your sins by acting righteously and your iniquities by showing mercy to the afflicted; perhaps there may be a lengthening of your prosperity.

Therefore: Daniel had completed the interpretation, but desired yet to add a word of counsel, something called for by the grave significance of the dream. In this way, Daniel again showed his concern for the king's welfare. At the same time, for him to give such counsel, when he had been asked only to give the dream's interpretaton, was a calculated risk and therefore a courageous thing to do. That which prompted him to take the risk was his desire to solicit Nebuchadnezzar's recognition of, and proper response to, God. *Be acceptable to you:* Literally, "be pleasing upon you" *(yishpar ʿᵃ layk)*. Nebuchadnezzar would have recognized this form of expression as indicating urgency on Daniel's part. Daniel strongly wished that the king would comply with his counsel. *Break with your sins:* The word for "break with" *(pᵉruq)* means "tear away, break off." Its corresponding Hebrew form *(paraq)* is used, for instance, in Exodus 32:2: "Break off the golden earrings" (cf. Gen. 27:40; Ex. 32:3, 24; 1 Kings 19:11; Ezek. 19:12; Zech. 11:16). Those who use this text as evidence for a doctrine of salvation by works take the word to mean "redeem," translating the phrase, "redeem your sins by well-doing." It is true that the meaning "redeem" is used in the Septuagint and Vulgate versions, but this meaning seems to have arisen only later, in post-Old Testament time. The meaning in Daniel's day clearly was "break with." Nebuchadnezzar was to cease from committing sin. The story shows that a principal area of sin in view concerned Nebuchadnezzar's acts of pride. Verses which follow in the text indicate that a continued display of pride, after Daniel's interpretation and counsel, was what particularly prompted the fulfillment of the dream's warning.

Acting righteously: The word used is *tsidqah,* meaning "to act righteously." Such translations as "well-doing" or "almsgiving" (Jerome) are not satisfactory. Again, post-Old Testament writings carry this secondary meaning,[8] but in the time of the Old Testament, the corresponding Hebrew word was used definitely for the concept "righteousness," so basic in conservative theology. Daniel was telling the king to correct his sinful life by conducting himself righteously. The passage cannot be used to defend the teaching that the soul can be redeemed or sins expiated by acts of charity. *Showing mercy to the afflicted:* With this phrase, Daniel refers to a specific wrong of the king. He should show greater mercy to the afflicted. Nebuchadnezzar was a noted builder. Often kings showed little consideration to those who did the work on building projects, with hundreds dying of extreme heat and difficult conditions. Nebuchadnezzar was probably guilty of this lack of concern, like others. In his pride, he may also have taken little notice of injustices meted out by judges and other officials, as well as by the rich of his kingdom. Daniel's counsel was that

---

[8] For instance, Tobit 12:9 and 14:11 show a near equation between "righteousness" and "almsgiving."

all this should be corrected. *Lengthening of your prosperity:* Daniel suggested that, if the king would comply, a benefit might result. He did not promise it, significantly using the conjunctive *hen,* meaning "if" or "perhaps." The benefit is a "lengthening" *('arkah)* of "prosperity" *(sheᵉlewah).* This is commonly taken to mean an averting of the threatened judgment. Young,[9] however, believes that it means only a lengthening of the king's tranquil period, either before or after, the judgment time. He argues persuasively that the period of insanity had a purpose that needed to be served, whether the king repented or not; that purpose being to bring him to a knowledge of the Most High (v. 25).

E. INSANITY OF NEBUCHADNEZZAR (vv. 28-33)

The following six verses tell of the fulfillment of the dream's prediction. Nebuchadnezzar experienced the seven years of insanity, but this state did not come on him immediately. God permitted twelve months to elapse first, apparently giving the king opportunity to follow Daniel's advice, if he would. God's grace and patience were thus demonstrated.

4:28, 29. All this came on King Nebuchadnezzar. At the end of twelve months, he was walking upon the royal palace of Babylon.

All this came: Nebuchadnezzar introduced this part of his account with the general indication of the dream's fulfillment. The clause constitutes a type of caption for what follows. *King Nebuchadnezzar:* Beginning with this reference, and continuing through verse thirty-three, the account speaks of Nebuchadnezzar in the third person. This occurs also in verse nineteen earlier. Since the first person is employed otherwise, some expositors believe that these verses were written by someone other than Nebuchadnezzar. This is not likely, however, since these verses fall between first person sections and the information they contain is so much a part of the overall story. The change of person is more likely due to the type of subject matter concerned. As the king spoke of himself suffering insanity, he could simply have preferred to do this as if he were an outside spectator. The reason for the change in verse nineteen could be that he there recognized Daniel to be the prime subject and considered a third person manner of reference to himself as only appropriate.

End of twelve months: The twelve months referred to apparently intervened between the time of the king's dream and the day presented here, when the insanity came upon him. That an exact number of months is specified suggests that this period was intentionally given to the king as a time when he might profit from Daniel's counsel. He

9 YPD, p. 108.

had not profited, however, as the following story makes clear. He may have intended to, for he did respect Daniel highly; but good intentions somehow had been lost, as days had slipped by and old patterns had been hard to change. *Was walking upon:* The preposition "upon" (*'al*) suggests that the king was walking on the roof of his palace, which likely was flat, like that of David's house (2 Sam. 11:2). From the roof he probably could see much of his splendid city and the fine structures that he had built. The word for "was walking" (root, *hᵃlaḵ*) is a participle, picturing the king in the act of walking back and forth, while he voiced the proud statements of the next verse. The implication is that he often did this, taking personal satisfaction in his accomplishments. *Of Babylon:* Some expositors believe that this mention of Babylon gives evidence that the account was written elsewhere than in Babylon, probably in Palestine by a writer long after Daniel's time. Nebuchadnezzar could have included it, however, if only because he knew the account would be read by strangers in other parts of the world, who would find the identification of location helpful.

4:30. The king spoke and said, Is not this great Babylon that I have built as a royal residence, by the might of my power and for the glory of my majesty?

Great Babylon: Similar expressions occur in Revelation 14:8 and 18:2. In the time of Nebuchadnezzar, the city of Babylon was at its height of glory, being one of the largest and finest cities of the world. It was surrounded by a system of double walls, the outer one of which was seventeen miles long and wide enough for chariots to pass on its top. Of the cities' eight gates, the most celebrated was the Ishtar Gate. It gave access from the north to the sacred processional way, which led to the citadel of Esagila, where was the grand temple of Marduk and the imposing ziggurat Enemenanki. The processional street was about 1000 yards long, and it was decorated on either side by enameled bricks, showing 120 lions (Ishtar symbol) and 575 dragons and bulls (Marduk and Bel symbols). More than fifty temples crowded within the city walls at the time. The Greeks considered the "hanging gardens" within the city one of the seven wonders of the world. These were elevated gardens, high enough to be seen beyond the city walls. They boasted many different kinds of plants and palm trees. Ingenious hoists had been contrived by which to raise water to the high terraces from the Euphrates River. It is believed that the gardens were made by the king especially for the enjoyment of his wife, who had been raised in the mountins of Media. *I have built:* Statements of Berosus[10] and cuneiform inscriptions combine in their testimony

---

[10] As quoted by Josephus, *Antiq.* X, 11, 1.

that Nebuchadnezzar majored in building operations. The Grotefend Cylinder gives Nebuchadnezzar's own words: "Then built I the palace, the seat of my royalty, the bond of the race of men, the dwelling of joy and rejoicing."[11] From the East India House Inscriptions come these words from him: "In Babylon, my dear city, which I love, was the palace, the house of wonder of the people, the bond of the land, the brilliant place, the abode of majesty in Babylon."[12] Besides building his own palace, he reconstructed two temples to Marduk in Babylon and one to Nebo in Borsippa; he also restored fifteen other temples in the capital city and erected the two great outer walls. The "hanging gardens" were his product as well. That Nebuchadnezzar built Babylon means only that he enlarged it. The city had been founded centuries earlier, as related in Genesis 11:5-9. *Glory of my majesty:* The thought is that the palace was considered of sufficient grandeur to be suitable for someone of his high position. The whole verse speaks loudly of Nebuchadnezzar's pride.

4:31, 32. While the word was in the mouth of the king, a voice fell from heaven, To you it is declared, O King Nebuchadnezzar; the kingdom is taken from you; you will be driven from among men, and your dwelling will be with the beasts of the field; you will be made to eat herbage like oxen, and seven times will pass over you, until you know that the Most High rules over the kingdom of men and gives it to whomever He will.

While: The revelation from heaven now stated came while the king walked and mused in his pride on the palace roof. The moment was opportune, because the king could not miss the obvious relation of the message to his proud words just spoken. The punishment predicted twelve months before would have come back to his mind, especially with the words now declared being so similar to those of Daniel at that time. *A voice fell from heaven:* The meaning apparently is that this message came by a supernatural voice, with no human instrument involved. To be addressed in such a manner would have added measurably to the impression made on the king. *To you it is declared:* This element appears first in the Aramaic word order, thus indicating stress on it. Nebuchadnezzar was accustomed to giving words of doom to others, but this one was coming to him. The word for "it is declared" *('am^{e}rîn)* is literally, "they do declare." This is the use of the impersonal third person plural, however, as in 3:4, which is best translated passively. *Kingdom is taken from you:* This again is a general caption, elaborated in what follows. Nebuchadnezzar was to lose his kingdom. This was to be in the sense of his not being able any longer to fill the office of head ruler because of mental in-

[11] Montgomery, MICC, p. 243.
[12] *Ibid.,* p. 244.

capacity. The perfect state of the verb indicates that in God's mind it had already been taken from him.

You will be driven from among men: From this point, the Voice repeated the words of Daniel (v. 25), with the omission of the element concerning being wet with the dew of heaven. This repetition no doubt made the king realize that what was about to happen was that which Daniel had predicted.

4:33. That very hour the matter was fulfilled concerning Nebuchadnezzar: he was driven from men, did eat herbage like oxen, and his body was wet with the dew of heaven, until his hair was grown like eagles' feathers and his nails as the claws of a bird.

That very hour: This is the same expression as in 3:6 (cf. 4:19). The thought is that the mental illness struck him, probably while he still remained on the roof. He may have been given time to reflect on what had been said, so that the significance might register in his mind properly. *He was driven from men:* Not only was the king removed from office, but put away from men. He was not allowed to live in society. The actual effecting of so much must have taken some time. There was the first recognition that the king had become ill, probably by attendants who had stood by or had soon come to inquire as to what delayed the king; then there was likely the assembly of proper officers and their deliberation of the best course of action; and this was followed by the effecting of the decision made. The form of Nebuchadnezzar's illness seems to have been that he imagined himself to be an animal and, at least in part, acted like one. This type of disease is not unknown. Pusey states that one of the earliest records comes from a Greek medical writer of the 4th century.[13] The most common form is lycanthropy, in which the person imagines himself to be a wolf. From the description given of Nebuchadnezzar, however, he thought of himself as an ox; which makes the disease more specifically to have been boanthropy. The disease is curable and, as Pusey points out, is known to allow the victim sufficient consciousness of self and God to make intelligent prayer possible.

Asserting that ancient writers make no mention of this sickness in regard to Nebuchadnezzar, liberal expositors hold that the record cannot be historical. To this it may be replied, for one thing, that such an omission in official records is only to be expected. Kings wrote of matters pleasant to them, not of the unpleasant. Also, the statement that no early writers mention the illness may not be correct. Eusebius quotes the following from Abydenus, a Greek historian of 268 B.C.:

And afterwards, the Chaldeans say, he went up to his palace,

13 *DP*, pp. 360-66.

and being possessed by some god or other uttered the following speech: "O men of Babylon, I Nebuchadnezzar here foretell to you the coming calamity, which neither Belus my ancestor, nor Queen Peltis are able to persuade the fates to avert. There will come a Persian mule (presumably Cyrus), aided by the alliance of your deities, and will bring you into slavery. And the joint author of this will be a Mede, in whom the Assyrians glory. O would that before he gave up my citizens some Charybdis or sea might swallow him up utterly out of sight; or that, turning in other directions, he might be carried across the desert, where there are neither cities nor foot of man, but where wild beasts have pasture and birds their haunts, that he might wander alone among rocks and ravines; and that, before he took such thoughts into his mind, I myself had found a better end." He after uttering this prediction had immediately disappeared.[14]

Some noteworthy items from this quotation are the following: first, both the phrase "the Chaldeans say" and the element concerning the fate desired for the "Persian mule" suggest that the statement, attributed to Nebuchadnezzar, was actually composed by a later writer, who then could have taken the ideas expressed from aspects in Nebuchadnezzar's own experience of insanity; second, Nebuchadnezzar is said here to have been "possessed by some god," which is the likely way people of the day would have referred to mental illness; third, the king was on the palace roof both in this experience and that of the account in Daniel; fourth, the closing notice concerning the king's sudden disappearance could well be a reference to his forced exile among animals; and fifth, all this took place, according to both accounts, at the close of the king's reign. Then, a statement from the ancient historian, Berosus,[15] also deserves notice: "After beginning the wall of which I have spoken, Nabuchodonosor fell sick and died, after a reign of forty-three years."[16] The sickness to which reference is made could well have been major in kind, since Berosus mentioned it in this manner, for death is commonly preceded by a sickness of some kind.

Argument is also made that an absence from the throne for seven years would have brought serious disruption to the country's governmental operations, if not revolution. Admittedly, matters would not have been normal, but it should be remembered that one of Nebuchadnezzar's strong points was the staffing of government posts

---

[14] Eusebius, *Praeparatio Evangelica,* IX, 41 (Gifford's translation), as quoted by Young, YPD, pp. 110, 11.

[15] Berosus was a Chaldean priest of the time of Alexander the Great. He learned the Greek language and went to Greece, where he opened a school and had Abydenus, quoted above, as one of his pupils. Berosus wrote three books on Chaldean history, and fragments are preserved in Josephus and Eusebius. Abydenus later wrote his history of Babylonia and Assyria, and only portions of this are today extant in Eusebius, Cyrill, and Syncellus; cf. Barnes, BD, I, pp. 234-37.

[16] Josephus, *Contra Apion,* I, 20 (Thackery's translation), as quoted in Young, YPD, p. 111.

by able personnel. Capable hands in key positions could have maintained the rule and kept subordinates working in their customary patterns.

His hair was grown . . . and his nails: The last two elements are literally "until his hair was grown like eagles' and his nails as birds'." The words "feathers" and "claws" are not in the text, but are implied. Neither of the two elements *in toto* are included in either Daniel's earlier words of interpretation (v. 25) or the supernatural announcement from heaven (v. 32), but both follow logically from what is said. The king apparently was allowed to live in the woods with animals, where he would have taken on the type of unkempt appearance prophesied. In his madness, he may have resisted anyone trying to cut his hair or trim his nails. This does not necessarily mean that he was placed in a forest at large, where he would have been a public spectacle. It is more likely that, wanting to keep his condition unknown as far as possible, officials would have placed him in a royal woods, private and secluded, where he could be under constant supervision and care. In such a locality, conditions could have been maintained in keeping both with the king's true identity and his temporary insane insistence on the way he wanted to live. There probably was constant hope for recovery, which did come finally after the seven years had elapsed.

F. NEBUCHADNEZZAR HONORS THE MOST HIGH (vv. 34-37)

When the predicted seven years had elapsed, Nebuchadnezzar was restored to his normal faculties and then he gave appropriate honor to God. He had learned God's intended lesson and was ready to ascribe praise to the Most High. The remaining verses of the chapter tell of this praise.

4:34. At the end of the days, I Nebuchadnezzar lifted up my eyes to heaven and my understanding returned to me. Then I blessed the Most High and I praised and glorified Him who lives forever; because his dominion is an everlasting dominion and his kingdom is from generation to generation.

End of the days: This is a reference to the end of the predicted period of seven years (cf. v. 16). *Lifted up my eyes:* The phrase order shows that Nebuchadnezzar first lifted up his eyes to heaven and then experienced the return of his understanding. If this chronological sequence was not intended, one would expect the two phrases to have been reversed in order. The lifting up of Nebuchadnezzar's eyes likely constituted the initial phase of the return of his understanding, but the full return did not come until after that had been done, signifying that the humility and sense of dependence thus symbolized was necessary before restoration could be granted. The insanity had been sent especially because the king had been proud; and now, before the illness could be entirely removed, there had to be the indication that pride had been taken away. The fact, as stated above, that the person suffering from boanthropy can still have a sense of self and God is probably what made this gesture possible, prior to the full return of Nebuchadnezzar's understanding. *My understanding returned:* With the display of submission to God, Nebuchadnezzar's mind was made to work normally again. Likely a part of raising his eyes to heaven lay in asking God to restore his reason. God did so, apparently returning to him all the keen ability he had enjoyed before. The shock must have been severe as the great man, restored to normal rationality, saw his long hair and unkempt nails, and thus was made to realize something of the kind of life he had been living. *Blessed . . . praised . . . glorified:* These three verbs are used synonymously. They indicate that Nebuchadnezzar now engaged in praising God; and they show on his part a sense of awe and respect for God, a recognition of God's greatness, a feeling of his own thankfulness, an admission of personal dependency, and a spirit of humble admiration. That Nebuchadnezzar employed three verbs indicates that he wished to stress the overall thought. He was truly repentant and submissive now before the great God of heaven. *Who lives forever:* The word for "forever" *('alam),* used here in reference to God, refers to all eternity. That Nebuchadnezzar spoke of God as the one "who lives forever" as well as the "Most High" (his common reference) suggests that he was thinking of Him here especially as the eternal Being. In contrast to himself, who would someday die, God would never experience an end.

Because: The word used *(dî)* can be taken either as the causal conjunction "because" or the possessive relative pronoun "whose." If the causal "because" is employed, the notice concerning God's dominion being eternal shows the reason for Nebuchadnezzar's glorification of God; and, if the relative pronoun "whose" is used, the notice indicates a further attribute of God for which this praise was being given. Either thought fits the context well, but the first is preferred, because the attribute of God already stated (that He lives forever) has been mentioned without use of the *dî,* which makes this employment of *dî* more likely as being used to introduce another type of construction. *An everlasting dominion:* The cause cited concerns the nonending of God's dominion, which, in Nebuchadnezzar's mind, contrasted so much with his own rule. God not only lives forever, but He maintains universal control forever. This fact, more than any other, apparently impressed the king and brought him to the full submission displayed. This implied, in turn, that the king had indeed come to recognize that God rules over the affairs of men—which recognition was the purpose of the imposed insanity, as Daniel had indicated at the first (v. 25). *From generation to generation:* This second expression of the same general truth is added here, as it is in verse three (which see). That it is shows further the depth of the impression this truth had made on Nebuchadnezzar's mind.

4:35. All the inhabitants of the earth are accounted as nothing, and He does as He will with the army of heaven and the inhabitants of earth; and none can stay his hand or say to Him, What are you doing?

All the inhabitants: Nebuchadnezzar in these words expressed the implied corollary of God's greatness, just stated. Man on earth is nothing in comparison to God. When he said, "all the inhabitants," he apparently included himself, thus further showing the humility that at last characterized him. *He does as He will:* The king reiterated God's authority. Because God has the dominion, He has the right to do with others as He will. Nebuchadnezzar had just experienced that himself in the imposed insanity, but he included in this subjection also the "army" *(hayil)* of heaven. The word *hayil* means basically "strength" or "might," and then comes to mean an "army," which possesses this quality. The word is used in 3:20 to mean Nebuchadnezzar's army; therefore its meaning here is probably similar. The army of heaven consists of all heaven's inhabitants who do His will. The king had seen one representative in the fiery furnace thirty years before, and apparently believed others existed. *Stay his hand:* Literally, "strike (root, m^eha') his hand." The thought is of striking God's hand with the intention of altering its operation. Keil believes that the expression comes from the "custom of striking children on the hand in chastising them."[17] The Targums use the expression to mean "to restrain" or "to hinder." Nebuchadnezzar is saying that no person can hinder God in what He desires to do. *What are you doing?* Not only can no inhabitant of heaven or earth hinder God, but none can question what He does. If God does something, it is right, if only because He is the one who does it. Man is not to judge. This was a remarkable thing for the king to say, for he had just experienced severe punishment. He was admitting that this punishment had been proper and that he, Nebuchadnezzar, had no place in questioning the action.

4:36. At the same time that my understanding returned to me, my glory and splendor returned to me for the honor of my kingdom; indeed, my counselors and lords sought me and I was established over my kingdom, and surpassing greatness was added to me.

At the same time: Nebuchadnezzar made clear that the return of his kingdom rule came coincidentally with the restoration of his

---

[17] KDC on Daniel, pp. 160, 61.

mental powers. *My glory and splendor:* The word for "glory" *(hᵃdar)* refers to whatever makes for attraction and admiration in respect to a person or thing. The word for "splendor" *(ziw)* means "brightness," used, for instance, in 2:31 to refer to the shining of the image in Nebuchadnezzar's dream. Together, the words speak of a "shining attraction." This is a reference to the shining attraction of Babylon's restored monarch. *For the honor of my kingdom:* In the Aramaic word order, this element precedes that just noticed regarding Nebuchadnezzar's glory and splendor, signifying stress upon it. The *lamed̲* prefix to "honor" signifies purpose. This means that the reason for the return of Nebuchadnezzar's rule was that the honor of the kingdom might be furthered. No doubt, kingdom business and prosperity had suffered during Nebuchadnezzar's absence, and now they could be expected to improve. *My counselors and lords:* The first term is used in 3:24, 27 (which see); the second *(rabrᵉban)* means "great ones," and is probably not the name of a particular office, but a designation of the importance of those involved in the activity indicated. A free translation would be, "counselors and other officials of importance." Likely these were the ones who had been responsible for the continued functioning of the kingdom during Nebuchadnezzar's absence. *Sought me:* These persons came to where he had been confined and they returned him to his former position. The significance is that Nebuchadnezzar did not have to seek the throne again by political maneuvering or actual fighting. This must have been gratifying to him. That this was true testifies both to his own excellent qualities as a ruler during prior years and also to God's gracious superintendence so that conditions would be maintained to this end. God may have directed Daniel to tell certain key persons that the insanity of the king would last only seven years and so have given them reason to wait and anticipate Nebuchadnezzar's return after that time. *I was established:* Nebuchadnezzar was thus made sovereign over Babylonia once more. *Surpassing greatness was added to me:* The word for "surpassing" *(yattîr)* is from a root verb corresponding to the Hebrew *yatar,* meaning "to remain over, be in excess." The thought is that Nebuchadnezzar's greatness on his return exceeded what it had been before. The word for "added" *(yᵉsap̲)* amplifies the idea.

4:37. Now I Nebuchadnezzar praise, extol, and glorify the king of heaven, for all his works are righteous and his ways just, and those who walk in pride he is able to abase.

Now I Nebuchadnezzar: This is the king's concluding statement to his account. It, along with his statements in the first three verses, summarizes his thinking concerning God at the time of composing the report. The question is debated as to whether he may have come to the place of true conversion. It is important to notice carefully what he says in these verses in making a judgment. *Praise, extol, and glorify:* These words are used synonymously, like the three of verse thirty-four. Two of these are the same as used there. The overall thought is that of giving honor, lauding, telling fine things about, becoming emotionally lifted with admiration for, worshiping. It is noteworthy that these words, in distinction from those of verse thirty-four, are active participles, indicating continuedness of action. Nebuchadnezzar was continuing in his activity of giving such praise to God, something apparently different from what had followed both his first dream and the deliverance of the three friends from the fiery furnace. His praise at those two times had been temporary. *For:* This is the word *dî* and is best taken in its causal sense; signifying that Nebuchadnezzar's exaltation of God was prompted by matters now to be stated. *His works are righteous:* The word for "righteous" *(qᵉshot)* carries the idea of "truthfulness." The meaning is that God's actions correspond truly to His own standard of righteousness, and are in keeping with situations as they truly are. God does not have to guess as to the nature of any situation, but He knows it truly and deals with it truly. *His ways just:* The word for "way" *('orah)* refers to method of doing things. The way in which God responds to situations is just. So, then, what God does and the way in which He does it correspond to that which is truthful and equitable. The significance of Nebuchadnezzar's stating this is that he was thereby admitting God's justice in the seven-year insanity he had recently experienced. *Those who walk in pride:* Nebuchadnezzar closed with a particularization of the general truths just expressed. One way in which God works truthfully and justly is in humbling proud men. The idea of *truthfulness* would apply here in respect to the knowledge of who it is that are proud and the extent of their pride, and *justice* in respect to the employment of the best and most equitable method of bringing discipline. By this the king once more admitted that he had been proud and he asserted that God's method of bringing the needed humiliation had been proper.

What now may be said as to the status of the king's own heart before God? In summary, what he said both in this verse and in verses one to three amounts to the following: the God of Daniel is supreme in power to do miracles, has full dominion over all men forever, is fully honest and equitable in all His works and ways with men, which includes matters of discipline, and that for this reason he, Nebuchadnezzar, was now giving himself regularly to praise of Him. Because no element of recognizing God's mercy is included, Calvin, Keil, and others believe that the king fell short of true conversion. This may be true; but, on the other hand, what he does say, in view of his pagan background, is most remarkable. His sincerity in these statements is borne out by the fact that he wrote this extensive record, which God, through Daniel, was pleased to include in the Scriptures. Young believes that all this is too significant to deny that "his faith was saving faith."[18] No doubt, Nebuchadnezzar's knowledge of God at this point was meager, but it seems that what he had he held sincerely and that he did experience a change of heart.

There is no way of knowing how long Nebuchadnezzar continued to rule after his restoration. He died in 562 B.C., forty-three years after his inauguration; but how many of these forty-three years were left after the seven years of illness is unknown. They were enough for him to speak of them as being even "greater" years than before his exile, but two or three would be sufficient for this. When he died, Babylonia's brilliance passed with him.

18 YPD, pp. 113, 14.

CHAPTER **5**

In chapter five, the words of Daniel himself are again found. He did not quote the report of another, as in chapter four, but told the happenings as he had come to know them. The story concerns the dramatic time when Belshazzar, then king of Babylonia, witnessed supernatural writing on the palace wall and understood its meaning only after Daniel had been summoned to give the interpretation.

This story transpired many years after the events of chapter four. Nebuchadnezzar died in 562 B.C., after forty-three years of reign, which included his seven years of insanity. None of his successors could match his achievements, and Babylonia's glory soon began to fade. His son, Amel-marduk, succeeded him but ruled only two years (562-560 B.C.). The Bible mentions him (by the name of Evil-merodach) as the one who released Jehoiachin from prison and gave the deposed Judean ruler a place of privilege at the Babylonian court (2 Kings 25:27-30; Jer. 52:31-34). Amel-marduk was murdered by his brother-in-law, Neriglissar (Nergal-shar-usur), who was then enthroned in August, 560 B.C. The identity of this man with the Nergal-sharezer of Jeremiah 39:3, 13, who as the official *(rab mag)* under Nebuchadnezzar had played a part in releasing Jeremiah from prison in 586 B.C., is generally accepted. As king, he is known mainly for his building activity and a major military venture across the Taurus Mountains. He died in 556 B.C. and was succeeded by his young son, Labashi-marduk, who was assassinated that same year by a group of courtiers, including Nabonidus, who then seized the throne.

Nabonidus (556-539 B.C.) was probably the most capable ruler following Nebuchadnezzar. Of priestly lineage, he was deeply religious and rebuilt the temple of the god Sin in Haran, excavated temple sites in Babylonia, and restored long-abandoned rites. He differed from other rulers in choosing to be absent from his capital for extended periods of time. It is well evidenced that he even maintained a separate royal residence at Tema in Arabia, southeast of Edom, and for one period of fourteen years did not so much as visit his capital city.

Belshazzar, the one and only king mentioned in chapter five, was for years declared unhistorical by liberal writers. Since Nabonidus was known to be the last ruler of Babylonia before its fall to the Persians, it was asserted that no time existed when this Belshazzar could have ruled. There is now ample evidence, however, that Belshazzar, as Nabonidus' eldest son, was made coregent by his father, apparently to serve as king while the father was away for those long periods of time. An important text so indicating is *A Persian Verse Account of Nabonidus,* which reads: "He freed his hand; he entrusted the kingship to him. Then he himself undertook a distant campaign."[1] The first year of rule in which he gave this trust was his third, but then he continued the coregency until the fall of Babylon.[2] The fact that Belshazzar was a coregent makes understandable his action of making Daniel a "Triumvir" (third ruler) in the kingdom (5:29).

Information relative to the manner of Babylon's fall to the Persians is available from several sources. These do not agree in all points, but they do make possible a general knowledge of the events concerned. Herodotus states that the Babylonians first moved north to meet Cyrus' oncoming forces, but, when initially defeated, they retreated to the protection of Babylon's walls. He adds that when the enemy reached the city, Cyrus diverted the Euphrates River from its normal bed under those walls, so that he might use the riverbed for entering and capturing the city.[3] Xenophon agrees that Cyrus diverted the river so that "the bed of the river, where it traverses the city, became passable for men," and states further that entrance to the city was made while the Babylonians were feasting in a time of drunken revelry. He includes a notice also that one "Gobryas," commander under Cyrus, led men into the very palace, where they found the king "already risen with his dagger in his hand," and that they then overpowered him along with his attendants.[4]

Of two helpful cuneiform inscriptions, one from Nabonidus,[5] called the Nabonidus Chronicle, is the more complete. It tells of Cyrus' approach to Babylon, of his defeating one city after another as he came, and of Nabonidus' flight from before him at Sippar on the 14th of the month Tishri (Oct. 10, 539 B.C.). Cyrus' commander,

---

[1] Cf. Sidney Smith, *Babylonian Historical Texts, Relating to the Downfall of Babylon* (London: Mathuen & Co., Ltd., 1924), quoted in YPD, p. 116.
[2] Cf. Dougherty, *NB,* for full discussion.
[3] Herodotus, I, pp. 190, 191.
[4] Cyropaedia, VII, 5:7-34.
[5] The other is from Cyrus. Cf. *ANET,* p. 306, for the Nabonidus text, and p. 316 for Cyrus. For discussion of texts from both Nabonidus and Xenophon, cf. Whitcomb, *DM,* pp. 10-24, 73, 75-79.

Ugbaru,[6] is said to have then entered "Babylon without a battle" on the sixteenth of the same month. Noticeably absent in this account is any reference to the river's being diverted. The text says further that on the third of the month Marchesvan (Oct. 29, 539 B.C.) Cyrus himself entered Babylon and was welcomed with "green twigs" spread before him; and that later the same month the "wife(?) of the king died." The text is damaged at this point, and some scholars believe that "son" is a better reading than "wife." If so, it could be a reference to Belshazzar, as son of Nabonidus. If the correct reading is "wife," this one could have been the queen-mother, Nitocris, mother of Belshazzar.[7]

From these reports, the following summary of the story is possible. Babylon fell to the Persians easily and quickly. A contributing factor may have been the diverting of the Euphrates River, as both Herodotus and Xenophon testify. The commander of the Persian army at the time was not Cyrus himself, but an officer, Ugbaru, indicated by both the Nabonidus Chronicle and Xenophon. Drunken feasting was in progress within the city at the time, according to Xenophon. The king who was within the city when it fell was Belshazzar, not Nabonidus, who had fled earlier from Sippar and was arrested only later when he came to Babylon following its fall—all indicated by the Nabonidus Chronicle. This story fits the account in Daniel very well, particularly in respect to the suddenness of the city's capture, the drunken feasting at the time, and the fact that Belshazzar was himself in charge within the city. The fact is clear that the city was in imminent danger of falling to the Persians at the time when Belshazzar held the grand feast set forth in this chapter.

A. An Impious Feast (vv. 1-4)

The first four verses of the chapter give the setting of the scene when miraculous handwriting appeared on the palace wall. A great feast of Belshazzar, climaxed by drinking and revelry, was in progress.

5:1. King Belshazzar made a great feast for a thousand of his lords, and he drank wine in the presence of the thousand.

King Belshazzar: For the identity of this man and a revision of Babylon's history since the events of chapter four, see the introduction to this chapter. The time of the invasion of Babylon was about thirty years after Nebuchadnezzar's period of insanity, and Daniel had become an old man of about eighty-one years. *A great feast:* The word for "feast" *(leḥem)* means "bread," but it is used here to indicate the full feast, which clearly was sumptuous, having been put on by the

---

[6] Often called Gobryas, but cf. discussion on name distinctions, *infra,* chap. 6, p. 154.

[7] Cf. *infra,* p. 133.

king for his official family. The occasion for such a gathering is not easy to determine, since it was known that the Persian army was outside Babylon's walls (cf. introduction to this chapter). It may have been designed to build morale. At least, morale was at low ebb and needed rebuilding. Babylonians had become provoked at their own king, Nabonidus, even before the approach of the Persians, because of his extended absences and also because he had shown disregard for some of the established religious practices. He had returned to the city only shortly before the Persian attack and then had fled from the enemy forces already when they had only reached Sippar to the north. Now the enemy was outside the very walls of Babylon itself. With the outlook so bleak, Belshazzar may have reasoned that a feast of this kind would constitute a gesture of confidence on his part that could alleviate some of the anxiety his people felt. He may have intended, also, to give some words of instruction following the feast; if so, those words were never uttered. *Thousand of his lords:* The word for "lords" *(rabrᵉban)* is used in 4:36 (which see). Belshazzar had assembled his leading men for this event. The number indicated is large, but royal feasts of the day were normally sizable. Montgomery quotes Havernick, as follows: "According to Ctesias (in Athenaeus, *Deipn.,* iv, 10) the Persian king fed 15,000 men daily from his table; there was the brilliant international marriage festival celebrated by Alexander, when 10,000 guests were present (Niese, *Griech. Geshch.,* I, 165f.); and a similar instance is cited for the last Ptolemy (Pliny, *H.N.,* xxxiii, 47)"[8] (cf. Esth. 1:1-4). If in this instance, Belshazzar's purpose was to build morale, he would have wanted a maximum number of his influential people present. *He drank wine:* Oriental custom for such feasts called for the king to sit at a separate table, where he could be seen by the others.[9] That Belshazzar drank wine in the presence of the others signifies that he intentionally set the tone of the feast as one of carefree hilarity, marked by drinking, perhaps in an effort to free their minds from tense concern.

5:2. Belshazzar, while tasting the wine, commanded to bring the vessels of gold and silver, which Nebuchadnezzar his father had taken out of the Temple that is in Jerusalem, that the king and his lords, his wives and his concubines might drink from them.

While tasting the wine: The word "tasting" seems to carry reference, not only to sensing the flavor of the wine, but also feeling its inebriating effects. Implied is a causal connection between this "tasting" and Belshazzar's command, which is next noted. Through the wine, the king lost his better sense of judgment and ordered the gold and

[8] Montgomery, MICC, p. 250.
[9] Cf. Zockler, *LCD,* p. 125, for discussion.

silver vessels from Jerusalem to be brought. Strong drink quickly blurs one's sense of propriety. History is replete with costly mistakes made while men were under the influence of liquor (cf. Prov. 20:1; Acts 2:13). *The vessels of gold and silver:* These vessels had been brought from the Temple in Jerusalem by Nebuchadnezzar nearly fifty years before,[10] as indicated in 1:2 (which see). The implication, from the manner of reference to them here, is that they had not been used by any previous Babylonian king. Nebuchadnezzar had placed them in "the house of his god" (1:2) and apparently had left them there unused, in keeping with accepted proprieties. Belshazzar, however, in what Montgomery calls a loss of a "sense of decency,"[11] ordered them brought forth to be used for the drinking, which he was personally instituting. Two reasons likely motivated him. First, they would add luster to his feast, in view of their beauty and value. Second, and more important, he desired to bring reproach on the religion and God of the Judeans. This second reason is made clear by statements of verses three and four, from Daniel's direct words that Belshazzar desired to bring this reproach (v. 23), and from God's employment of this occasion to warn and punish the king, showing that Belshazzar had indeed been acting in a way deserving this manner of divine response. It seems that Belshazzar, knowing of Nebuchadnezzar's earlier humiliation before the Judean God (v. 22), had reacted by resolving not to be intimidated as a result, and even here by showing open defiance. It could be that, in God's providence, a recent reminder of Nebuchadnezzar's experience had come his way, and that this prompted the provocative order at this time.

Nebuchadnezzar his father: Since Nebuchadnezzar was not the immediate father of Belshazzar,[12] this statement (cf. vv. 11, 13, 18, 22) has often been challenged for its accuracy. As noted in the Introduction,[13] however, Belshazzar could well have been the grandson of Nebuchadnezzar, through his mother; and, as Pusey points out, the same word would have been used in the text, whether referring to "son" or "grandson."[14] His mother would then have been Nitocris, wife of Nabonidus and daughter of Nebuchadnezzar.[15] Besides this, as also noted in the Introduction, evidence has been found on the Black Obelisk of Shalmaneser III that simply a successor on a royal throne could be called "son" of the predecessor, when no blood relation existed. R. D. Wilson, in fact, lists seven ways in which the term "father" was used in the time of Nebuchadnezzar and twelve ways in which "son" was used, giving ample evidence that the terms cannot

---

[10] Taken in 586 B.C., and it was now 539 B.C.
[11] MICC, p. 251.
[12] Cf. *supra*, pp. 129, 30.
[13] *Supra*, pp. 22, 23.
[14] Pusey, *DP*, p. 346.
[15] For discussion, cf. Dougherty, *NB*.

be pressed here to convey any inaccuracy.[16] *His wives and his con-cubines:* Royal harems of the day were commonly divided into two classes: women with the status of wives, who carried higher privileges; and women with the status of concubines (cf. 1 Kings 11:3). Belshaz-zar's harem, apparently, was so divided, and he wanted both groups present at this time. Since no women are mentioned as being present for the feasting proper, it is likely that they were summoned, sig-nificantly, only for the drinking portion (note their mention similarly in verses three and twenty-three; cf. also Esther 1:9-11).

5:3, 4. Then they brought the vessels of gold, which had been taken out of the Temple of the house of God that is in Jerusalem; and the king and his lords, his wives and his concubines drank from them. They drank wine and praised the gods of gold and silver, bronze, iron, wood, and stone.

Then they brought: Servants moved quickly to carry out the king's order. Though only gold vessels are mentioned here, no doubt the silver ones were included, according to the command. The total num-ber of vessels is not indicated, but it must have been large to provide for so many people. *Temple of the house of God:* Likely "temple" designates only the Temple proper, in distinction from the whole sacred area, here called the "house of God." The significance of in-cluding this item of description is probably to point up the serious-ness of the sinful act of Belshazzar. These vessels, so to be desecrated, were from the very holiest place in Jerusalem, the Temple proper.

They drank wine and praised the gods: The two verbs used are intentionally placed in close proximity to say that the drinking and the praising went together. The more the people drank, the more they praised the false gods of Babylon. This praising would have been mainly in the form of songs to these deities. With wine flowing freely and the women present, the scene no doubt degenerated into a drunken orgy. An inebriated person sings with wild abandon. Loud talking and hollow laughter must have added to the din, with gold and silver vessels spilling wine as they clattered to the floor. It was serious enough to bring these vessels to the feast at all, but to use them in this manner was the height of desecration. *Gold and silver, bronze, iron, wood, and stone:* Through all the wicked hilarity, Bel-shazzar apparently was able to keep the action directed in the re-ligious vein he desired. He was not interested merely in a "morale-building" time of so-called fun, but in a time of insulting the Judean God. The Babylonians made their images of all the types of material here listed, and the listing is apparently given to point up the empti-ness and vanity found in the gods so constructed. This action by Bel-

[16] *SD,* pp. 117, 18.

shazzar was in bold defiance of God, as if to dare Him to strike him as he had Nebuchadnezzar. How foolish he was.

B.   THE MIRACULOUS WRITING (vv. 5-9)

At a divinely-chosen point in the drunken revelry, fingers, as of a human hand, suddenly appeared, writing words on a well-lighted portion of the wall of the banquet room. The king quickly recognized the phenomenon as a visit from the supernatural realm, and his bold face changed to one of stark terror. He cried immediately for the wise men to come and tell him the meaning, but when they came, they were no more successful than they had been in respect to Nebuchadnezzar's dreams. The scene was thus set advantageously once more for an entrance of Daniel.

5:5.   In the same hour the fingers of a man's hand appeared near the lampstand, writing upon the plaster of the palace wall of the king, and the king saw the extremity of the hand that wrote.

In the same hour: This is the same phrase as that used in 3:6, 15 (which see). The thought conveyed is that this miracle occurred while the revelry was being carried on, likely at its height. *Fingers of a man's hand:* That which was seen doing the writing was only the fingers (*'etsbe'an*) of a man's hand, not even the whole hand. The word for "extremity" *(pas)* at the close of the verse suggests the same conclusion, for *pas* (root, *p'sas,* "to cease, come to an end," cf. Ps. 12:2) refers to that part of the hand where it ends, that is, the fingers. Fingers only were needed to grip whatever device was employed to mark the wall. No instrument is mentioned, but it is implied. *Appeared:* Literally, "came out" *(n'paq).* The implication is that, to the spectators, the fingers seemed to "come out" of the wall. The manner of appearance itself would have told all that they were witnessing something supernatural. One can imagine each person quickly looking about, to note whether others seemed to see what they saw, wanting to be sure that they were not deceived. Drinking and singing, of course, ceased immediately. Loud defiant mouths spoke no more. The room which had been drowned in noise now became deathly silent, with fear gripping all. Those who knew from where the drinking vessels had come and had noted the act of defiance against the Judean God may have suspected from the first the reason for the strange writing. *Near the lampstand:* Literally, "before" *(laq°bel)* the lampstand. Since good illumination was necessary if all were to see, the meaning clearly is that the fingers appeared where the lampstand shed this kind of light. The king himself would likely have been seated where the light was brightest, which suggests that the writing took place near him.

The plaster of the palace wall: The word for "plaster" *(gîr)* is used also in the Hebrew, meaning "chalk" or "lime" (e.g., Isa. 27:9). The surface on which the writing appeared was apparently of lime plaster. The archaeologist Koldeway, who excavated Babylon, says that the largest room he found in the palace complex was 55 feet wide by 169 feet long, and had plastered walls. He tells also of a niche in one of the long walls, opposite the entrance, in which he suggests the king may have been seated during such times of feasting.[17] Against a white plastered surface, any dark object would have stood out distinctly. *The king saw:* Though everyone present saw the writing, the king was the most important and the fact is noted accordingly. He is the one who had called for the sacred vessels and led in the defiance of the Judean God. For him, especially, the fingers wrote. The reason that God used this method of revealing to Belshazzar, when he had employed the dream with Nebuchadnezzar, may be fourfold. First, a dream would have been private, for Belshazzar alone; and there was need for a public anouncement, one witnessed by all those present, for all were deserving of rebuke. Although Belshazzar had been centrally important, these others had also shared in the God-defying activities. Second, the writing no doubt remained on the wall to be seen during all the following hours of the evening, thus serving more fully to impress the spectators, who would look at it again and again. Evidence that the writing did remain visible for some time is seen in the fact that it was still there for Daniel to read after he arrived, which would have been substantially later than the time it first appeared. Third, this manner of revelation was fully objective to the king—like a dream in this respect—so that his pagan way of thinking could not change or distort the information conveyed. Fourth, like the dream also, it called for an interpreter, thus making possible and necessary the entrance of God's representative, Daniel.

5:6, 7. Then the king's color changed and his thoughts troubled him, so that the joints of his loins were loosened and his knees knocked one against the other. The king called in earnest to assemble the enchanters, the Chaldeans, and the soothsayers. He spoke and said to the wise men of Babylon: Whoever will read this writing and make known its interpretation will be clothed in purple, with a necklace of gold about his neck, and shall rule as Triumvir in the kingdom.

Then the king's color changed: Literally, "Then, as for the king, his brightness changed." The word for "color" *(zîw)* means more precisely "brightness, splendor," used, for instance, in 4:36 to refer to the splendor Nebuchadnezzar received again after his period of insanity. Before the writing appeared, the king's face may have been flushed with drink and emotion; but this now left him, as great fear made him ashen white. *His thoughts troubled him:* Thoughts flooded through Belshazzar's mind, which brought this fear and change of color. These thoughts probably concerned the distinct possibility that the Judean God was now to retaliate against him, as a result of the bold defiance he, Belshazzar, had just been manifesting—possibly a retaliation in the pattern of Nebuchadnezzar's experience years before. His thoughts also would have concerned the Persian enemy just outside the city. Did this writing mean that the city was now surely to fall to Cyrus? These two thoughts may have conjoined to cause the king to fear that God's retaliation was taking the form of Babylon's fall into Persian hands. When one is excited, he is not in control of his thoughts, but simply is witness as they race, quite uncontrolled, through his mind. The result is often extreme fright. *Joints of his loins:* The word for "joints" *(qᵉtar)* literally means "knots." As used here, the word means "joints" in the sense that the joints of the body resemble "knots" in fastening bones together. The word "loins" in Scripture refers to that part of the body around which the girdle is tied, just above the hips. Loins are mentioned often as the seat of strength (Job 40:16; Ps. 66:11; Prov. 31:17), making understandable the thought that to be weak in the loins is to be weak all over. Belshazzar, who felt so strong earlier in the evening, now felt all his strength leave him. *His knees knocked:* This expression is used also in Nahum 2:10. It is still used today as a symbol of fear. Both of these symbolic physical effects are said to have resulted from Belshazzar's troubled thoughts. *Called in earnest:* The word for "in earnest" *(bᵉhayil)* is used similarly in 3:4 and 4:14. Belshazzar responded in his fear by giving an urgent call for those who might help him in reading the writing. For him, this meant Babylon's wise men, just as with Nebuchadnezzar.

Enchanters, Chaldeans, soothsayers: All three terms have appeared in prior contexts: the first two already in the initial list of 1:20 and the third for the first time in 2:27 (which see). Since the term for "magicians" is omitted in this instance, and Daniel is expressly called the "master of the magicians" in 4:9, some expositors suggest that Belshazzar may have intentionally omitted calling this group to avoid including Daniel. This does not seem likely, however. The king was desperately interested in having the writing interpreted and would not intentionally have omitted one entire division of wise men. Furthermore, verse eight specifically states that "all the wise men" came before the king. Still further, the term "magicians" in 4:9 likely stands for all the wise men, because Daniel was originally appointed to head them all (2:48). As noted before, these terms for the wise men were not used technically by Daniel, so that different terms could be used to refer to the entire group. *This writing . . . its interpretation:*

The king wanted two matters accomplished: the writing read and its interpretation given. The problem was quite different from that regarding Nebuchadnezzar's dreams. Interpretation of dreams called for giving explanation of symbolic scenes and/or events. Here the need was to interpret written words, after first deciphering them. It may be assumed that these wise men had never before encountered this type of problem. *Will be clothed in purple:* Like Nebuchadnezzar before him (cf. 2:5, 6), Belshazzar gave incentives for compliance with his order. The incentives this time are identified, no doubt because of their remarkable nature. The first is that the man who would do what the king asked would be clothed with purple, meaning a purple robe. Purple was the royal color, worn by those who had the rank of royalty (Esth. 8:15).[18] This in itself indicated that the man would be raised to this high standing. *A necklace of gold:* The second gift, a gold necklace, was not given exclusively to royalty, but was a type of gift which royalty would bestow on those they desired to honor highly. Joseph received such a necklace (Gen. 41: 42). Under later Persian rule, only persons of rank could wear one, and only when presented by the king.[19] *Triumvir in the kingdom:* The word for "Triumvir" is *taltî*, the meaning of which has caused much discussion. At one time, it was commonly believed to be the equivalent of *t^elîtay,* meaning "third" and is so used in 2:39. Accordingly, KJV and other versions show "the third ruler," which implies third in rank. Montgomery argues strongly and quite convincingly, however, that it is the equivalent of the old Akkadian *shalsû,* which was a high official title, the equivalent of "Triumvir."[20] What Belshazzar was probably offering, then, was not merely to be third in rank, but equal in rank with two others, a member of a Triumvirate—a high honor, indeed.

5:8, 9. So all the wise men of the king came in, but they were not able to read the writing or make known the interpretation to the king. As a result King Belshazzar was exceedingly troubled, and his color was changed, and his lords were perplexed.

The wise men of the king came in: This indication of the wise men coming in before the king seems strange, when verse seven has implied that they were already present. More than one explanation is possible. One is that some of the wise men were present when the king gave the words of verse seven, but that later others kept arriving. Evidence is taken from the participial form of the verb, meaning literally, "ones coming in," indicating such a continuance of action.

---

[18] In respect to Persia, cf. Xenophon, *Anabasis,* I, 5, 8; to Media, *Anabasis,* I, 3, 2; II, 4, 6; to Greece, 1 Maccabees 10:20; 14:23.
[19] Cf. *Anabasis,* I, 5, 8; I, 8, 29.
[20] MICC, p. 254.

Another is that Belshazzar's words of verse seven were sent along with those who summoned the wise men, as a message of incentive before they arrived. Still a third, and perhaps the best, is that this is a normal type of Semitic repetition, not so much to say again that the wise men arrived, as to make preparation for the statement following that, having arrived, they could not do what the king desired. *Not able to read . . . or make known:* Not being able to read the words, the wise men, of course, could not give the interpretation. But why could they not at least do the reading? The language employed, as shown by Daniel's later reading, was Aramaic, and Aramaic was known at this time in Babylon. The answer most often given, and probably correct, is that the characters of the words were unusual in shape. It has been suggested, for instance, that their shape was of old Phoenician writing, which Daniel, being a Hebrew, would have known, but which these Babylonians, knowing only the shape used in eastern Aramaic,[21] would not. Keil, among others, however, objects to this particular possibility on the ground that Babylonian wise men would likely have known both forms of Aramaic writing.[22] It may be that God simply employed shapes of letters that even Daniel would not have known apart from special revelation at the time. There was reason to use a form of writing which the wise men could not read, because this would point up the significance of Daniel's being able to do so in due time.

As a result: The word used (*'ᵉdayin*) is normally translated "then," implying a temporal sequence (cf. vs. 8, et al.), but here it shows logical sequence. The king had been frightened only by the writing before the wise men had come, but now he was frightened further by their inability to read it. If they could not decipher it, the significance of it must be worse than he had thought! *Exceedingly troubled . . . color was changed:* The same word for "troubled" (*bᵉhal*) is used here as in verse six, but two factors indicate an increase now in anxiety. First, the word this time is in the form of a participle, indicating continuation of action; and second, the word "exceedingly" (*sagî'*) is added. The phrase for "color was changed" is basically the same as in verse six. Apparently, color[23] had returned to Belshazzar's face during the time of waiting for the wise men, but now, with their failure, it once more drained away. *His lords were perplexed:* The word for "were perplexed" is an Hithpael participle, and in this form "not only comprehends the idea of alarm, but also that of confusion and excited movement."[24] Not only the king was

---

[21] Represented, for instance, in the Syro-Palmyrenian inscriptions.
[22] KDC on Daniel, p. 185.
[23] This is the same word for "brightness" as used in verse six, but can hardly carry the idea of being *flushed* this time, as was possible then.
[24] Quoted from Hitzig, as quoted in turn by Zöckler, *LCD,* p. 129.

alarmed, but the guests were also. One can easily imagine them suddenly moving about, talking and gesturing quite wildly, as they came to realize the inability of the wise men. If these men, experts of the day in such matters, could not read the writing, who could? What evil portent might this writing signify, especially when the troops of Persia were just outside the city's walls?

C. DANIEL SUMMONED (vv. 10-16)

The developments just noted provided a most advantageous preparation for Daniel's arrival. Just as Daniel was not present initially regarding either Nebuchadnezzar's first or second dream, so he was not present when the miraculous writing first appeared at Belshazzar's banquet. But now events transpired by which Daniel was introduced. The queen (or better, queen-mother) entered to remind Belshazzar of Daniel's availability, and the king called for him. When he arrived, the king told him of the failure of the wise men to read the writing and promised him the same rewards if he would do what they could not.

5:10. Because of the words of the king and his lords, the queen had come into the banquet hall. The queen spoke and said: O King, live forever; let not your thoughts trouble you, and let not the color of your face be changed.

Because of the words: Literally, "in the presence" *(laqᵒbel)* of the words, as in 5:1, 5, etc. The queen is pictured as confronted by the words, and therefore taking the action that she did. The word for "words" is the construct form of *millah,* which means "things" as well as "words." Here it likely has reference to both the actions and words of the king and these lords. Because of their anxiety, so indicated, she made her entrance and spoke the message now given. Evidently, someone had gone to tell her so that she knew what had occurred. *The queen:* Two matters suggest that this person was not the queen proper, the wife of Belshazzar, but the queen-mother, possibly Nitocris, mentioned under verse two as the daughter of Nebuchadnezzar and wife of Nabonidus. One is that verse three states that the king's wives were already present, and this person arrived only after the writing appeared. The other is that this person showed firsthand acquaintance with the affairs of Nebuchadnezzar, as if she had lived during his time, telling of times when Daniel had helped this great predecessor of Belshazzar. It is known that queen-mothers of the day did hold honored positions,[25] such as implied here regarding this person, as she is pictured walking into the disturbed scene and addressing the king with confidence and freedom. *The queen spoke and said:* The queen-mother likely first assessed the situation in the room

[25] For numerous references, cf. Montgomery, MICC, p. 258.

on her arrival, but then without great delay began to speak to the king. She started by urging him not to let himself be disturbed, implying that she had helpful information.

5:11, 12. **There is a man in whom is the spirit of the holy God; and in the days of your father, enlightenment and understanding and wisdom like the wisdom of God were found in him; and King Nebuchadnezzar, your father, appointed him as chief of the magicians, enchanters, Chaldeans, and soothsayers, even your father, O King. Because an excellent spirit and knowledge and understanding, interpretation of dreams and solving riddles and answering knotty problems were found in this Daniel, whom the king named Belteshazzar, now let Daniel be called and he will declare the interpretation.**

There is a man: The manner of the queen-mother in referring to Daniel implies that he no longer held his position as head of the wise men and that the king was not well acquainted with him. The likely situation was that all Nebuchadnezzar's wise men had been replaced seventeen years earlier, when Nabonidus had seized the throne and begun a new dynasty.[26] From 8:27 (cf. 8:1), however, it is clear that Daniel did retain some governmental post, which may have been his governorship of the province of Babylon, also granted by Nebuchadnezzar (2:49). Belshazzar's first question to Daniel, when later he came before him (v. 13, which see), shows some knowledge of the aged man, but this may have been by reputation only, as established under the great Nebuchadnezzar. Daniel's kind of reputation, too, would have stayed in Belshazzar's memory, though unwanted, for it would have shown him to represent the religion and God that Belshazzar so opposed, as just demonstrated in the feast. Because of this, the king likely found it difficult now to extend the summons to Daniel which the queen-mother urged. That he did, obviously, was due to his extreme desire to have the writing interpreted. The courage of the queen-mother in speaking as she did, since the king felt this way, should not be missed. *Spirit of the holy God:* The queen-mother used the same phrase as did Nebuchadnezzar in 4:8, 9, 18, (cf. 4:8 for discussion), which may be evidence of the great king's influence upon her. In view of this, plus her general knowledge of Nebuchadnezzar's relation to Daniel and her willingness to speak so courageously of Daniel before the unsympathetic Belshazzar, the possibility presents itself that she had been converted to a true faith in the Judean God, even as her father may have been (cf. under 4:37).

Enlightenment and understanding and wisdom: These three nouns designate characteristics of Daniel for which the queen-mother be-

[26] It is known regarding Persian history that such a sweeping change was customary on the part of a usurping ruler.

lieved Nebuchadnezzar had appointed him chief of the wise men. The first means literally "light," which suggests the thought of keen insight. The other two speak more of mental reflection and discernment. The queen-mother exhibited her high evaluation of Daniel's wisdom, when she compared it to that of God. She may have meant by this that she believed it came from God, as Daniel himself had explicitly stated to Nebuchadnezzar (2:28-30). *Appointed him:* The queen-mother tied Daniel's qualifications and Nebuchadnezzar's appointment of him together. The force of her words is that if Nebuchadnezzar evaluated this man so highly as to make him chief of his wise men, then Belshazzar should at least summon him to interpret the writing. Belshazzar may not have known very much himself regarding Nebuchadnezzar's initial appointment of Daniel, some sixty-four years having elapsed since that time, and the queen-mother wanted to make sure that he knew at least that he had been appointed. *Magicians, enchanters, Chaldeans and soothsayers:* All four terms have been used before (cf. 1:20; 2:2, 27; 4:7; 5:7). *Even your father, O King:* Three times, in this one verse, the queen-mother referred to Nebuchadnezzar as Belshazzar's father (cf. v. 2). Apparently she believed that her counsel would be more persuasive if Belshazzar was fully aware that the one who had so honored Daniel before was his own father (grandfather). Such a stress on her part fits the thought, too, that she was herself closely related, as has been suggested: daughter of Nebuchadnezzar and actual mother of Belshazzar. The word for "O King" is good also for "the King"; and some expositors take it in reference to Nebuchadnezzar. Its position, coming last in the verse, however, argues that it is used as an address to Belshazzar.

Because: The queen-mother, surprisingly, listed Daniel's qualifications once again, even adding to them. That she did so indicates further both the extent of her desire that the king be persuaded and her fear that she might be unsuccessful in effecting that persuasion. *Excellent spirit and knowledge and understanding:* The words for "excellent spirit" do not refer to Daniel's commendable attitude, good as it was, but to his surpassing ability in the area of "knowledge and understanding." The word for "understanding" is a repetition from verse eleven, but "knowledge" is new, signifying the idea of Daniel's mind being filled with information. *Interpretation of dreams and solving riddles and answering knotty problems:* These three items are best taken as information-areas in which Daniel had this spirit of knowledge and understanding. He had demonstrated his capacity as to the first, i.e., interpretation of dreams, before Nebuchadnezzar. Apparently, the queen-mother added the other two, believing that these would better cover the type of problem confronting Belshazzar; though Daniel may have aided Nebuchadnezzar in these aspects also, of which no record was kept. The word for "riddles" *('ᵃḥîḏan)* is used in its equivalent Hebrew form for what Samson propounded to challenge the Philistines (Judg. 14:12). Contests of wit in riddle propounding and solving are known to have been common in that day. The word for "knotty problems" *(qit⁻rîn)* literally means "knots" (same word as for "loins" in v. 6). Life's problems can become tangled, as if tied in knots. Daniel had ability in going to the heart of, and answering, such problems. *In this Daniel:* Literally, "in him, in Daniel." The queen-mother here identified by name the one of whom she had been speaking. In doing so, she used both his Hebrew name, Daniel, and his Babylonian name, Belteshazzar. That she used the Hebrew name as well as the Babylonian—in fact, she used the Hebrew name twice in these closing words—suggests that she thought of him as a Hebrew, not a Babylonian, though by this time he had been in Babylon some 66 years. This means that she knew him well and was sympathetic to him as a Hebrew representing the Hebrew God. These facts lend further evidence to the supposition that she may have been converted to a personal faith in the Judean God.

5:13. Then was Daniel brought in before the king. The king spoke and said to Daniel: Are you that Daniel that is of the children of the captivity of Judah, whom my father, the king, brought from Judah?

Then was Daniel brought in: The queen-mother's counsel was quickly followed. Apparently Belshazzar, in his highly disturbed state, was ready to call anyone who might help, no matter what his loyalties were. Daniel seems to have arrived without prolonged delay, which suggests that the government position he still held kept him in the vicinity of the palace. He was now about eighty-one years of age, much the senior of Belshazzar. If he had not had opportunity before to speak with this ruler, which is quite possible, he must have been pleased with this occasion. The words he spoke in response to the king show that his age in no way had detracted from his readiness to testify for God. *Are you that Daniel:* Belshazzar's opening words are best taken as a question, though the interrogative particle is omitted. The question, however, carried the force of a statement, the king not waiting for an answer. By the question, Belshazzar made clear to Daniel that he knew his background, of having been brought captive from Judah by Nebuchadnezzar, to whom he also referred as his "father." It should be noticed that the queen-mother had not said anything about Daniel as a captive from Judah; therefore, Belshazzar must have known this of himself. He did know of Daniel, then, perhaps better than the queen-mother thought; and this leads to the significant fact that he knew Daniel's home country to be the same as that of the sacred vessels which he and his riotous guests had just been desecrating (cf. v. 2). In this light, it may be assumed that he feared the manner of interpretation that such a man might bring, but, since his regular advisers had failed, he had no alternative but to listen. God has His ways of backing men into corners from which there is no escape, even when those men are mighty kings.

5:14-16. I have heard concerning you that the spirit of God is in you, and enlightenment and understanding and excellent wisdom have been found in you. Now the wise men, the enchanters, were brought before me that they might read this writing and make known to me its interpretation, but they have not been able to show the interpretation of the matter. I have heard concerning you that you are able to declare interpretations and to answer knotty problems. Now, if you are able to read the writing and tell me its interpretation, you will be clothed in purple, with a necklace of gold about your neck, and shall rule as Triumvir in the kingdom.

I have heard: Reference was mainly, if not fully, to the words the queen-mother had just spoken. Belshazzar mentioned particularly two matters: first, that Daniel possessed the "spirit of God," a factor which had been decisive for Nebuchadnezzar (4:8, 9, 18), which still was decisive for the queen-mother (5:11), and apparently also became so for Belshazzar; and, second, that Daniel was said to have "enlightenment and understanding and excellent wisdom," the same list used by the queen-mother, with the addition of the qualifier "excellent" to the third item. The queen-mother used this qualifier in another connection, but he shortened her longer description by combining this one word with the first group of qualifications she gave.

The wise men, the enchanters: In verse seven, the wise men are identified under three terms, but here the king employs only one— "enchanters." This apparently was for the sake of brevity, taking only the first of the three to represent the others.

Declare interpretations ... answer knotty problems: The king referred to two of the detailed items from the queen-mother's speech, omitting the one concerning "solving riddles." Again a desire for brevity is evidenced. The two mentioned apparently seemed best to him for covering the type of problem which confronted him. *Clothed with purple:* Whatever the king thought regarding Daniel, he did not let this stand in the way of promising the same rewards to him that he had to the wise men (cf. v. 7). His repeating the promise to Daniel commends him, and, at the same time, shows still further the intensity of his desire to know the interpretation.

D. THE INTERPRETATION (vv. 17-28)

Daniel waited until the king had finished speaking and then gave his response, which is recorded in the next twelve verses. He began, surprisingly to the king, by refusing the rewards, clearly not wishing to be under any obligation to speak only what the king desired. Then he recalled for Belshazzar that which Nebuchadnezzar had experienced when God wished to humble him. His point in this was to prepare the king for hearing that he himself was about to experience a parallel fate, in the form of defeat and death at the hand of the Persians.

5:17. Then Daniel answered and said before the king, Let your gifts be for yourself and give your rewards to another. Nevertheless, I will read the writing for the king and make known the interpretation to him.

Then Daniel: This was a significant moment for Daniel. He had known of the king, had no doubt wished to testify of God's greatness before him, but probably had not found an occasion before. Now the opportunity had come, arranged clearly by God. *Let your gifts . . . your rewards:* The two nouns are the same as those employed in 2:6 (which see). They are used synonymously to refer to the three benefits promised by the king. That he assigned "gifts" to Belshazzar and "rewards" to someone else, is not significant, for the whole statement is only to say that Daniel refused them. The reason was certainly not that he disdained them, for they were very attractive. Any man would have liked them, even if only to have them for a short time, as Daniel knew the case would be in this instance. The refusal, as already indicated, was to avoid any obligation to the king, so that he might speak freely. Daniel's task was to deliver a message, not to receive gifts. (That he did finally accept them, as verse twenty-nine indicates, likely was because the message had then been given, and no longer could any observer think of him as having been influenced by them. If the king still wished to bestow them after the dire warning had been given, that was his business, and Daniel needed no longer to refuse.) *I will read . . . and make known:* Daniel promised to reveal what the king wanted to know. He would do what the others could not: he would read the writing and give the interpretation. It would be interesting to know whether Daniel could read the writing from his own store of knowledge, or whether he recognized that it would necessitate supernatural revelation. Of course, in either case, it would have taken God's revelation for him to know the interpretation. Whatever the situation, Daniel had complete confidence that he would be able to fulfill the king's desire, for God would meet the need.

5:18, 19. O King, the Most High God gave Nebuchadnezzar your father a kingdom and greatness and honor and glory; and, because of the greatness that He gave him, all peoples, nations, and languages trembled and feared before him. Whom he would, he killed; whom he would, he kept alive; whom he would, he exalted; and whom he would, he put down.

O King: Literally, "Thou King." By this direct address, Daniel brought the king into as close a relationship to the facts concerning Nebuchadnezzar as possible. Further address of this kind does not appear until verse twenty-two, showing that all between was intended by Daniel as a unit idea. *The Most High God gave:* This reference to God is identical to that employed in 3:26; 4:2; etc. (which see). Daniel used it again to identify the true God for this pagan ruler. He wanted to make the point that this God was the One who had given Nebuchadnezzar his kingdom, greatness, etc. Such a declaration would have been most difficult for Belshazzar to accept, since he had just been engaged in trying to humiliate this One. *Nebuchadnezzar your father:* Whether Daniel knew that the queen-mother had stressed this father-son relationship in her earlier speech is not indicated; but, in any case, Daniel referred to it at this time, no doubt for the same reason that she had (cf. vv. 2, 11). He may also have thought that the idea would reinforce the parallel he was about to make: as Nebuchadnezzar had been proud, so was Belshazzar; and as the former had been severely humbled before the true God, so would be the latter. *Kingdom and greatness and honor and glory:* Not only had Nebuchadnezzar's kingdom been given to him by God, but also the honor that went with it. Nebuchadnezzar had been indebted to God for all that he had possessed. "Greatness" seems to refer, particularly, to Nebuchadnezzar's ability to rule his kingdom; "honor," to the recognition he achieved for this ability; and "glory," to the widespread fame that resulted wherever his name became known. As Daniel set forth these desirable features of Nebuchadnezzar's reign, Belshazzar could not have avoided comparing his own rule with it and recognizing that his was much less splendid.

Peoples, nations, and languages: This is the same expression as that used in 3:4, 7, 29 (which see). Likely the reference is primarily to peoples within Belshazzar's realm, but there seems to be no reason to exclude all thought of others outside. Nebuchadnezzar's fame and fear had extended very far. *Whom he would, he killed:* Nebuchadnezzar had held complete control over his subjects. His word was law, whether justice was served or not. The people had no constitution for protection; no court system; no safeguards over the king. Actually this was quite normal for kings of the day, but Daniel seems to make a point of it because Nebuchadnezzar had used this power to pervert justice prior to God's severe reprimand of him (cf. 4:27). This was what had contributed to his downfall, and the same could be true now of Belshazzar. Though Belshazzar was not sole ruler, still he seems to have held equal status with Nabonidus (cf. v. 7), which means that he did hold this same degree of power over his subjects as Nebuchadnezzar had, especially when his father was out of the country.

5:20, 21. But when his heart was lifted up and his spirit grew strong with pride, he was deposed from the throne of his kingdom and his honor was taken from him. Then he was driven away from the sons of men, his heart was made like the beasts', and his dwelling was with the wild asses; they fed him herbage like oxen, and his body was wet with the dew of heaven; until he knew that the Most High God rules over the kingdom of men and that he establishes over it whomever he will.

His spirit grew strong with pride: The word for "spirit" is *ruah,* as in Hebrew. Used here in parallel with "heart," it means more than just "mind," as sometimes translated. The word for "with pride" *(lahᵃzadah)* is an infinitive construct and means literally "to act presumptuously." It says strongly that Nebuchadnezzar was proud. Human evaluation might consider that a person of Nebuchadnezzar's ability had a right to be proud, but Daniel makes clear that even he was humbled by God. Implied is the comparative thought that Belshazzar deserved to be humbled still more. *His honor was taken:* Literally, "they took his honor," but with no antecedent given, the passive translation is permissible.

Sons of men: Most of the following expressions parallel closely those of 4:25, 32 (which see); but here "sons of men" is used in place of "men," though with no apparent difference in meaning. *Wild asses:* In 4:25, 32, "beasts" in general are mentioned, while here "wild asses" are particlularized. The wild ass is mentioned in Job 39:5-8 for its quality of being shy of men and difficult to tame. Apparently Daniel wished to impress Belshazzar with the extent of Nebuchadnezzar's humiliation, living among even this kind of animal.

5:22, 23. And you, his son, O Belshazzar, have not humbled your heart, although you knew all this; but against the Lord of heaven you have exalted yourself; and the vessels of His house have been brought before you, and you and your lords, your wives and your concubines have drunk wine in them, and you have praised the gods of silver and gold, bronze, iron, wood, and stone, which do not see or hear or know; but the God, in whose hand is your breath and to whom are all your ways, you have not honored.

His son: Likely, grandson through Nitocris (cf. v. 2). The term "your father" has been used five times in the chapter (vv. 2, 11, 18) but this is the only instance of "his son." Daniel used it for the same reason as he did "thy father" in verse eighteen. *Although you knew:* History is an excellent source of instruction. Belshazzar should have learned from Nebuchadnezzar's experience, but he had not. "All this" *(kol-dᵉnah)* is inclusive, meaning that Belshazzar knew about all that Daniel had just said, with special reference to Nebuchadnezzar's humiliation before the God of heaven. This means that Belshazzar, in having desecrated the sacred vessels of God, had done so deliberately, in full knowledge of what he was doing, as noted earlier under verse two. In fact, the idiom translated "although" (*kol-qᵒbel dî*), meaning literally "all in front of," may well be taken to mean "because," as in 2:8, 41, 45, etc. If so, Belshazzar had done what he did, not *in spite of* what he knew, but *because of* what he knew; that is, he had purposely desecrated God's vessels to demonstrate that he was not intimidated by this God.

Against the Lord of heaven: Daniel directly stated that Belshazzar's actions had been aimed at the God of heaven. The word for "Lord" *(mare')* could be used also in reference to humans (cf. 4:19, 24), but here it refers to God. It connotes authority, which Daniel wanted to stress in Belshazzar's mind. *The vessels of His house:* With this phrase, Daniel began to list the same features of Belshazzar's feast as are indicated in verses three and four. Somehow Daniel had already learned what had occurred and now he let the king know that he knew. Perhaps the queen-mother had found opportunity to tell him. Daniel's thought in rehearsing these matters, after the pointed notice regarding Belshazzar's exaltation of himself against the true God, is to say that this exaltation had been especially revealed in these wicked actions. *Do not see or hear or know:* This one element is added to the listing from verses three and four. The thought is similar to that of Deuteronomy 4:28; Psalms 115:5-7; 135:16, 17; Isaiah 44:9; Revelation 9:20. This is blunt language on Daniel's part, speaking so derogatorily of Belshazzar's deities; but it was true and the king needed to hear it. What a contrast he was making between the true God, who had so worked with Nebuchadnezzar, and these dumb idols. What courage it took for Daniel to speak so plainly. *In whose hand is your breath:* This is further courageous language. Not only had Nebuchadnezzar been under God's control, but Belshazzar also was. His very breath was drawn from the hand of this One. This is true for all men. Little do people realize that every breath they take is only because of God's grace. *To whom are all your ways:* Belshazzar's manner of life was also under God's supervision. The king had thought himself to be in control as he had defiantly ordered the Jerusalem vessels brought, but all the while God had been superintending, so that the end was never in doubt. Belshazzar was soon to learn the nature of that end. This observation and the former are inserted in the text to emphasize further the contrast between the true God and Babylon's false deities. By implication, these words explain also why the wise men, who served these false gods, had not been able to interpret the miraculous writing, whereas he, Daniel, who worshiped the true God, would be able to do so.

5:24-28. Then was the extremity of a hand sent from Him and this writing was inscribed; and this is the writing that was inscribed: MENE, MENE, TEKEL, UPHARSIN. This is the interpretation of the matter: MENE, God has numbered your kingdom and brought it to an end; TEKEL, you have been weighed in the balances and found lacking; PERES, your kingdom is broken and given to the Medes and Persians.

Then: Both a temporal and a causal sense are involved. Temporally, the writing appeared after Belshazzar had demonstrated his pride in the vessel-desecrating, God-dishonoring festivities; and causally, the writing came because of them. This causal relationship provided the reason for Daniel's considerable explanation before giving the reading and interpretation of the writing proper. Belshazzar could not understand fully the effect without knowing first the cause. *Extremity of a hand:* This is the same expression as that in verse five (which see). The use of the expression, which indicated a rather minor detail in the occasion, must have served to impress the king with the authenticity of Daniel's whole account.

MENE, MENE, TEKEL, UPHARSIN: According to the king's desire, Daniel first read the writing and then gave the interpretation. The inscription apparently still remained on the wall, giving a lasting impression for all present, as noted earlier, and permitting Daniel still to read it directly. The writing was not extensive, composed of only three words, with the first repeated.[27] This brevity no doubt made it more impressionable, as well as subject to easier memory retention. Each of the words is best taken as a passive participle, with the doubling of the first being likely for stress or possibly literary balance. The last one differs from the form employed in verse twenty-eight both by the addition of the prefix "U," which is the conjunction "and," and also by the use of the plural ending. Each of the words seems to carry a double sense, as the interpretation indicates.

MENE: This participle *(m^{e}ne')* means "numbered," coming from the verb *m^{e}nah,* "to number, reckon." Its double significance is that the days of Belshazzar's kingdom had been *numbered* by God and, as a result, *reckoned* as brought to an end. The wise men, even if they had been able to read the writing, could not possibly have given this interpretation, for the inscription itself gave no clue as to what was numbered and reckoned.

TEKEL: This participle *(t^{e}qel)* means "weighed," coming from the verb *t^{e}qal,* to weigh." Keil[28] states that it also "accords with the Niphal of *qalal,* 'to be light, to be found light.' " The double sense exists in

---

[27] Some renditions do not double the first: Septuagint, MANE, THEKEL, PHARES; Vulgate, MANE, THECEL, PHARES; and Josephus (*Antiq.* X, 11, 3), MANEH, THEKEL, PHARES.
[28] KDC, on Daniel, p. 189.

that Belshazzar had been *weighed* in the balance of God and found *too light.* The balance was the normal device used for measuring values of payment in the day. The amount of silver a person paid had to balance a designated, standard weight. The thought here is that Belshazzar was found *too light* in moral and spiritual worth to balance out God's standard of righteousness (cf. 1 Sam. 2:3; Job 31:6; Ps. 62:9; Prov. 16:2).

PERES: This participle *(peres)* means "broken" or "divided," coming from the verb *peras,* "to break, divide." The double sense occurs this time in that Belshazzar's kingdom was about to *be broken* and given to the Medes and *Persians,* the word for Persians *(paras)* being essentially the same as the participle. The sense is not that the kingdom would be divided into two parts, with one part given to the Medes and one to the Persians. Belshazzar's kingdom would be brought to an end and the Medes and Persians would take it over, absorbing it into their still larger domain. That the Medes are mentioned before the Persians (cf. 6:8, 12) provides a telling argument against the liberal view which denies the authorship of the book of Daniel. Only for a time were the Medes given this measure of prominence over the Persians, because Cyrus was himself Persian and the form of reference soon became "Persians and Medes" (cf. Esth. 1:3, 14, 18, 19).[29]

In summary, Daniel's interpretation set forth that Belshazzar's kingdom would be destroyed, for the reason that he had been found lacking in moral and spiritual value, and that the encroaching enemy, the Medes and Persians, would absorb the kingdom into their larger domain. The interpretation said nothing particularly as to Belshazzar's personal death, but the night then at hand was to reveal that this, too, was involved. The effect of Daniel's words on the king and all others present would have been marked. They were given to know that the enemy outside Babylon's walls would indeed take the city. Cyrus' forces would conquer, and Babylonia as a country, for all the glory she had known, would be no more. They, as leaders of the country, could anticipate only the worst for themselves: loss of position, at least, and probably loss of life. Excitement must have been high, some disclaiming the truth of Daniel's interpretation, others agreeing that doubtless it was correct. What a contrast there was between the way this feast began and the way it ended.

E. THE RESULT (vv. 29-31)

The last three verses indicate the results of these surprising developments. Belshazzar retained enough self-control to make good on the promised rewards to Daniel; he was killed that same night,

---

[29] The episodes in the book of Esther transpired only about 60 years later, during the reign of Xerxes (485-465 B.C.).

no doubt as a part of the enemy's conquest; and Darius became ruler in Babylon for the conquering Medes and Persians.

5:29. Then Belshazzar gave instructions, and they clothed Daniel in purple, with a necklace of gold about his neck, and they proclaimed concerning him that he would rule as Triumvir in the kingdom.

Then Belshazzar: Since Belshazzar was to die yet that night, his instructions relative to Daniel's rewards must have been given immediately, probably while all the guests were still present. It is to his credit that he retained sufficient composure to do this. Also, he must not have reacted to Daniel's words in anger, though they were completely contrary to what he would have liked to hear. He apparently accepted them as authoritative, and determined to face what had been predicted as properly as he could. *They clothed Daniel:* For the significance of the three rewards, see under verse seven. For a possible reason why Daniel was willing now to receive them, when earlier he had refused, see comments on verse seventeen. Not only did the king issue his instructions that very night, but clearly they were carried out. Personnel were dispatched to bring the type of robe and necklace designated by the king and suited to Daniel's new status as a Triumvir. Some have objected that so much could not have been done that quickly. A loose flowing robe, however, needed no fitting. Both robe and necklace had only to be brought and put on. *They proclaimed:* The assertion is made, too, that this manner of proclamation would have been impossible in the short time of that night. Likely the only announcement given, however, was issued to the group still in the room, who, after all, were the lords of the kingdom. The intent would have been to give a more formal and public announcement later. Some have commented that Belshazzar's honors were really of little meaning, since he would die yet that night. He did not know this at the time, however; and Daniel himself may not have known that the time would be so brief. In the interpretation of the inscription, Daniel had said nothing as to the exact time of the kingdom's fall.

5:30, 31. In that night was Belshazzar, king of the Chaldeans, killed; and Darius the Mede received the kingdom, being about sixty-two years old.

In that night: For discussion as to the circumstances, cf. the introduction to this chapter. The enemy forces must have been making their way into the city even as the events in the palace room were transpiring. In some manner, the king was found and killed, though not many others of his staff suffered this fate; for, as noted, the accounts are agreed that the conquest of the city was with little loss of life. Daniel was not killed. Quite to the contrary, as the next chapter shows, he was even given a high position in the new regime. But on Belshazzar, arrogant and defiant as he was, God's just vengeance fell. Belshazzar provides an example of warning for all who would think to act similarly.

Darius the Mede: Medo-Persian rule took over, and the new monarch over Babylon was called Darius the Mede. The identification of this man is discussed in the introduction to chapter six. He is said to have been sixty-two years old—an advanced age for a man to serve as king. But he was still some nineteen years younger than Daniel, whom he was to appoint as a chief president. The chapter division of the Hebrew Bible places this verse as the first of chapter six.

CHAPTER **6**

The sixth chapter contains one of the best known stories of the Bible, the episode of Daniel in the den of lions. The jealousy of political subordinates, working through the vanity of King Darius brought about this terrible sentence for Daniel. But God effected a miraculous deliverance for him, even as He had for the three friends whom He delivered from the fiery furnace. Then the king condemned those who had schemed against Daniel, sentencing them to the same punishment, and from it they were not delivered. Politically, the situation was quite different from that of the fifth chapter. The Medo-Persians had gained control, with Daniel serving as one of three chief officers under Darius the Mede. A period of time had elapsed since the fall of Babylon, sufficient for the new rule to have become established and jealousies to have arisen among the new officials—a period hardly less than two years, making Daniel now at least eighty-three years of age.

The identity of the Medo-Persian ruler in the story, Darius the Mede, has long been questioned. No one of this name is known from secular history, and it is well established that Cyrus, who captured Babylon, continued as ruler over the empire until 530/29 B.C., nine years after Babylon's fall. Three principal views are represented among scholars: one is that this man was Cyrus himself, under a different name— favored by Donald J. Wiseman of the British Museum;[1] another is that he was Cambyses, son of Cyrus, who served under his father as ruler over Babylon and later succeeded him as emperor—favored by Charles Boutflower;[2] and the third is that he was Gubaru, appointed governor over Babylon by Cyrus immediately after the fall of the city—favored by John Whitcomb.[3] Of the three, the last finds most in its favor.

---

[1] Cf. "The Last Days of Babylon," *Christianity Today,* II (Nov. 25, 1957), pp. 7-10.
[2] Presented in his volume, *IABD,* pp. 142-67.
[3] Cf. his volume, *DM,* largely devoted to proving this view.

A central feature of Whitcomb's presentation is a distinction which he draws between the Ugbaru, who captured Babylon for Cyrus (cf. the introduction to chap. five), and this Gubaru, whom Cyrus made governor. In the past, these two men, both mentioned in the Nabonidus Chronicle, have been identified and called by the name Gobryas; but Whitcomb shows that Ugbaru died within three weeks of his capture of Babylon, while the latter continued as governor of Babylon for at least fourteen years (539-525 B.C.).[4] Whitcomb also responds to several arguments raised by H. H. Rowley[5] against so identifying Darius, and he finds satisfying answers to them.

A rather full picture of this man emerges when the presentations of both Daniel and secular history are put together. Born in 601 B.C. to one Ahasuerus, a Mede, he was appointed by Cyrus as governor ("made king over the realm of the Chaldeans," 9:1) over Babylon and the "Region beyond the River" (Abarnahara), which means over approximately the same area as formerly constituted the Babylonian empire. He assumed authority as *de facto* king over this large territory when Cyrus himself withdrew from Babylon, which was still within the year of Babylon's fall, and Darius then appointed his own supervisors (120 princes and three presidents) over his domain, holding the power of life and death over them. He must have had a talent for organization to establish his rule after this pattern. He demonstrated both a humanitarian and religious interest in his relation to Daniel. That he could be tricked rather easily into signing a flattering decree gives evidence of marked vanity on his part, but that he, in turn, quickly ordered the death of these perpetrators of crime indicates that he had a commendable sense of justice.

Daniel was given a high position in the new Medo-Persian government as one of three top presidents under Darius (cf. v. 1). The significance of his holding this remarkable office—under a new government and when he was more than eighty years old—has been noted in the Introduction.[6] Apparently God wanted him in a place of influence to encourage and assist in the Jews' return to Judah, just as he had been in a position earlier to contribute to their welfare while in Babylonia. The return of the Jews was made in Cyrus' first year, 538/37 B.C. (2 Chron. 36:22, 23; Ezra 1:1, 2), which means probably only a few months before the episode of Daniel and the lion's den. The edict signed by Cyrus, permitting the return, is most remarkable for the privileges it extended to the Jews, suggesting the possible influence of Daniel. Taking the record of it as given in

---

[4] Demonstrated by a series of inscriptions quoted by Whitcomb, which date through years prior to 525/24 B.C.; cf. *DM;* pp. 10-16.

[5] Cf. his book, *Darius the Mede and the Four World Empires in the Book of Daniel* (Cardiff: University of Wales Press Board, 1935), pp. 21-28.

[6] Cf. *supra,* p. 0.

Ezra 1:2-4 and 6:3-5, the following principal features appear: (1) the Jerusalem Temple was to be rebuilt when the people reached Judah, with the cost defrayed from Cyrus' own treasury; (2) certain specifications were to be met in this rebuilding; (3) all Jews who wished could join in the return to the homeland, with Jews who chose to stay in Babylon being urged to assist financially; and (4) the gold and silver vessels, seized by Nebuchadnezzar, should be taken back to the home city. To account for such favor toward the Jews, it is easy to think of Daniel not only influencing Cyrus to write such a decree, but perhaps even helping to formulate it (cf. Prov. 21:1).

A. The New Government (vv. 1-3)

The chapter first provides background for the story proper, noting Darius' organization of his new government. Those who were jealous of Daniel and perpetrated the scheme to have him cast to the lions were members of this organization, as was Daniel.

6:1, 2. It seemed good to Darius to set over the kingdom one hundred and twenty satraps, who should be throughout the kingdom; and over them three presidents of whom Daniel was one; that these satraps might give account to them, so that the king might suffer no loss.

Darius: For the identity of this man, cf. the preceding introduction. The name "Darius" may be an honorific title, meaning "holder of the scepter." It is not used in Persian inscriptions for the man called Gubaru, but it is for five later Persian rulers. If not a title, it was likely a second name for this person—second names not being uncommon for the day.[7] The indication here is that Darius made his own decision regarding the appointments mentioned, and this has prompted the objection that a subordinate of Cyrus could not have wielded such power. In response, two matters are noteworthy. First, the Nabonidus Chronicle states directly that Gubaru did make appointments of such officials. Second, this and other contemporary inscriptions show that persons with the title *pihatu* (the term used for Gubaru in the Chronicle) did hold authority like kings: having armies, levying taxes, possessing palaces, and doing in general such matters as would be in keeping with making their own appointments.[8] *One hundred and twenty satraps:* Comparison has been made between this number and the number 127 of Esther 1:1 (cf. Esth. 8:9), designating Persian provinces. Since Darius' kingdom was not the whole Medo-Persian empire, however, but only the much smaller area approximating that of the former Babylonian empire (cf. introduction to this chapter), there is no intention to say that the two numbers have reference to the same land divisions. The objection

7 Cf. Wilson, *SD,* pp. 138-41, for discussion.
8 Cf. *ibid.,* pp. 203-208, for discussion.

has been raised that this smaller area would not have warranted 120 divisions (satrapies). Two responses are possible. First, the text does not say that Darius made 120 divisions, but 120 satraps to be "throughout the kingdom," suggesting that the king simply wanted this number of "kingdom-protectors" (the meaning of "satraps") to be scattered over his domain; especially since the kingdom was new and would need additional protection and supervision for a time. Second, even if each satrap was to have his own satrapy, the land area was still extensive enough; for, as Wilson points out,[9] the size of satrapies varied greatly, from small to large. *Throughout the kingdom:* Whether in 120 respective satrapies or not, these officers were to be spread out in the kingdom, covering it entirely.

Over them three presidents: The word for "president" *(sarak),* found only in this chapter, is unknown as to etymology, but from other considerations it clearly means "head" or "chief." The arrangement of having three such heads over satraps finds no parallel in nonbiblical sources. Apparently, Darius conceived the idea for his own situation, possibly guided by the triumvirate arrangement for Babylon at the time of Belshazzar. Likely the satraps were divided into three groups, with each reporting to a respective president. *Daniel was one:* Daniel was given a place as one of these three. What means God may have employed to incline Darius to make this appointment, one can only guess. Perhaps Darius recognized the honor which Belshazzar had bestowed on Daniel that last night before the fall of Babylon. It may be, too, that the king had learned of Daniel's remarkable prediction of that fall and believed that such a man could make a valuable contribution to his new government. Certainly Darius would also have made inquiry into Daniel's record as a Babylonian administrator, before making the appointment; and this would have helped, for Daniel clearly had been capable. In respect to the unusualness of keeping a man in office who had already served under a former, deposed regime, it is pertinent to note that Cyrus instituted a policy of forbearance toward the former officers and institutions of Babylonia. The word for "one" *(had)* can be translated as the ordinal "first," as in 7:1, and so give the reading, "Daniel was first," as in KJV; but the meaning of the following verse seems to be that Darius was only contemplating raising Daniel to the first position, which argues that the better translation here is merely the cardinal "one." *King might suffer no loss:* Cf. Ezra 4:13, 22 for a parallel expression. Officers of any king were supposed to serve to benefit the kingdom, and Darius made his appointments accordingly. Darius is called "king" *(malka'),* as he is throughout the chapter and in 9:1. Wilson speaks of the term

---

[9] Cf. *SD,* pp. 175-78, for discussion.

as being the nearest Aramaic equivalent to the Persian "satrap" or Babylonian *"pihatu."*[10]

6:3. Now this Daniel was distinguishing himself above the presidents and satraps, because an excellent spirit was in him, and the king planned to set him over all the kingdom.

Was distinguishing himself: The Aramaic uses a participle, indicating continuedness of action. Daniel was regularly distinguishing himself over the other two presidents, as well as the 120 satraps. That Daniel had remained in responsible positions during the Babylonian time and now was achieving this sort of record under the Persians shows that God had endowed him with excellent ability. He worked hard and well. *An excellent spirit:* The words for "excellent spirit" are the same as in 5:12 *(rûaḥ yattîra').* Here, as there, the thought is likely more than merely a commendable attitude (which certainly he had), but an ability for his work. *The king planned:* The word for "planned" is *ᵃshît,* meaning "to think, purpose." Darius had been taking note of Daniel's superior work and was therefore planning to elevate him in position. The new position is described as "over all the kingdom," which apparently means over all satraps and the other three presidents. Perhaps another man was to have taken his present post, and he himself given a new title. He alone would have reported directly to the king.

B. A Treacherous Plot (vv. 4-9)

With the organizational setting given, the story moves on to tell of jealousy among these appointed officers, directed against Daniel, who was about to receive the promotion. They gave vent to their feelings by devising a decree for the king to sign that would forbid any person to make a petition of any man or god, except the king, for thirty days, with the penalty of death in the den of lions for disobedience. The decree flattered the unsuspecting king, and he signed, much to his later regret.

6:4. Then the presidents and satraps sought to find an occasion against Daniel regarding the kingdom, but they were not able to find any occasion or fault, because he was trustworthy, and no error or fault was found against him.

The presidents and satraps: Since "presidents" is plural, both of the other two officers of equal rank with Daniel must have entered this plot, and at least some of the satraps, since "satraps" is also plural. Because the satraps were scattered throughout the kingdom, it is not likely that all were involved, but only such as lived in or near the capital city. *Sought to find an occasion:* The word for "occasion"

---

[10] *Princeton Theological Review,* XX (1922), 186, 87.

('illah) means "pretext" or "cause for charges." These men, working closely with Daniel, tried to find some cause for charges against him, so that they might accuse him to the king. Several matters may have prompted their bitterness. The text implies the first, that they were envious of Daniel because of the king's intention to elevate him, of which intention they had somehow learned. Another is that Daniel was old and of the Babylonian regime, whereas they probably were much younger and Persians, and thought themselves, accordingly, more properly candidates for all high offices. Still a third is that they simply disliked Daniel, both for being a Jew (just as years earlier other informers had disliked Shadrach, Meshach, and Abed-nego for the same reason, cf. 3:8, 12) and for being faithful to his God, rather than the Persian gods. *Regarding the kingdom:* They tried first to find their ground for charges in connection with Daniel's official life in the kingdom. Did he do his work well? Was he honest in his dealings? Was he fully loyal to the king? They likely observed, inspected, inquired of secretaries, and asked all who might give any pertinent information. *Not able to find any occasion or fault:* For all this effort, they could uncover nothing amiss. The word for "occasion" is the same as above; the word for "fault" *(sheḥîṭah)* is from the root *sheḥaṭ,* meaning "to corrupt, destroy." They found no evidence of corruption that would give ground for charges. This is remarkable. Because of his position, Daniel must have been responsible in many areas, with many different people working under him. Yet he, and apparently his staff, were found to be free from fault. He must have engaged people of integrity and then inspired them by his own exemplary life and ability so that nothing wrong, either in efficiency or morality, could be found. *Trustworthy:* The word used is from the root *'aman,* meaning "to trust, rely on." The reason why the investigators found no fault was that Daniel could be relied on. His word was good; he was honest and a man of integrity. *No error or fault:* The word for "fault" is as above. The word for "error" *(shalû)* carries the thought of *neglect;* being used, for instance, in Ezra 4:22, "Take heed now that you *fail* not to do this." Daniel was found without guilt both as to the way he did things and in not neglecting matters that should be done.

6:5. As a result, these men said: We shall not find any occasion against this Daniel unless we find it against him concerning the law of his God.

As a result: The negative results of this investigation called for a consultation among the conspirators. They must have been amazed at what they had found, and, at the same time, privately chagrined that their own situations did not compare well with his. Daniel's manner of life certainly was a rebuke to them. Bent on their wrongdoing, however, they planned to entrap him another way. *Concerning the law of his God:* After what may have been considerable discussion of possible ways, they decided to strike at Daniel's religious life. They would make his own high degree of commitment to God work against him. Because this was their decision, two matters are made evident. One is that these men knew about his religious commitment and practice, which means that Daniel had not been a secret worshiper of God. He had not hidden his faith in order to keep his office. The second is that these men believed his degree of commitment to be great enough to keep him from changing even though faced by a penalty of death. It is clear that they were not primarily interested in his changing, but rather in trapping him so that he could be executed. The word for "law" *(dat)* is used in 2:13, 15 to mean "decree" of the king, and in 7:25 to mean God's "law" (also in Ezra 7:12, 14, 21, 26). That this word (rather than "religion" or some similar word) is used in this context suggests that Daniel's regularity in practice, which they took as reflecting the law of his God, was what impressed them in making their decision.

6:6, 7. So these presidents and satraps came in concert to the king and said to him, King Darius, live forever. All the presidents of the kingdom, the prefects and the satraps, the counselors and the governors have taken counsel together that the king should establish a statute and set forth a binding decree that anyone who makes a request of any god or man for thirty days, except from you, O King, shall be cast into the den of lions.

Came in concert: The word used (root, *reģash*) is often translated "came tumultuously," but this thought does not fit the context; and Montgomery[11] demonstrates that it may mean "in concert," with the possible thought of implied conspiracy. In its Hebrew form, it is so used in Psalm 55:14 ("in company," KJV), and in Psalm 64:2 it is paralleled with "secret counsel." It is used also in Daniel 6:11, and there again the context calls for the idea of *meeting in concert.*

Presidents of the kingdom: The same word is used for "presidents" as above, but, since it is followed here by "of the kingdom," it may carry a broader reference this time than merely to the two men who paralleled Daniel. It may be a reference to officials in general, of whom the four groups named would be included. The claim that all these leaders were agreed regarding the decree was a lie. Daniel certainly was not, and it is about as sure that satraps scattered far from Babylon were not either, and possibly not even all those near the capital. The active group may not have included a large number, though these men wished the king to think so. *The Prefects and the satraps, the counselors and the governors:* These terms have all been

[11] MICC, pp. 272, 73.

used in the book before (cf. 3:2, 24). The use of the conjunction "and" (copula *waw*) divides the classes into two groups, probably with the thought that the first group of two was higher in standing than the second. The groups together included more people than merely the "presidents" and "satraps" mentioned in verse four. Whether some of the active conspirators were from this wider number or not is not clear. The claim may have been a pure fabrication. *Establish a statute and set forth a binding decree:* This double statement gives unusual emphasis to the thought: first, because it is double; second, the word for "set forth" *(teqep)* means literally "to grow strong," thus carrying the thought of *setting forth strongly;* and, third, the word for "binding decree" *(esar)* is from an unused root meaning "to bind." These men wanted the king to set forth strongly a decree that would be binding. *A request of any god or man:* The word for "request" *(ba'û),* in view of the context, means a prayer-type request, not just any request among men. Such requests would normally be presented only to deity, but, since the king had to be involved in this instance, "men" are also mentioned. The reason for having the decree remain in force for only thirty days was that this would be long enough to trap Daniel, and these men probably did not wish to be restricted longer themselves. Also, opposition from priests could be encountered if the matter were prolonged. Liberal writers have objected that the whole idea of a Persian king signing such a decree is preposterous. Kings of other countries, however, were looked upon as manifestations of deity, and Darius could have thought it flattering that his officers wished to think of him in this way for a period of time. Vanity is one of man's greatest weaknesses.

Den of lions: The word for "den" *(gob),* related to the Hebrew verb *gûb,* meaning "to dig," carries the thought of a "pit" or "cistern," implying that this den was underground, perhaps a natural cave reshaped for the purpose. This idea fits also the indications that Daniel was "drawn up" from the den, after his night of deliverance, and that the conspirators, later cast in, were eaten before they ever came to "the bottom of the den." An opening was clearly at the top of the den, and likely there was one also as a side entrance, for ventilation and through which the animals might be admitted and fed. The den must have been quite large, with room for numerous lions and space in which to cast many people, according to verse twenty-four. Bertholdt describes dens found in Asia and northwestern Africa as being generally constructed underground from

> caves which had been excavated for the purpose, walled up at the sides, inclosed within a wall through which a door led from the outer wall to the space lying between the walls, within which persons could pass around and contemplate the wild beasts.[12]

12 Quoted by Barnes, BD, I, p. 16.

Keil takes the following description of such dens from G. Host:

> They consist of a large square cavern under the earth, having a partition-wall in the middle of it, which is furnished with a door, which the keeper can open and close from above. By throwing in the food they can entice the lions from one chamber into the other, and then, having shut the door, they enter the vacant space for the purpose of cleaning it. The cavern is open above, its mouth being surrounded by a wall of a yard and a half high, over which one can look down into the den.[13]

Even the suggestion of being cast into such a place filled with hungry lions would make a person shudder with fear. The fiery furnace, faced earlier by Daniel's three friends, and this den of lions, soon to be faced by Daniel himself, were two of the most fearsome forms of punishment of the day.

6:8, 9. Now, O King, establish the binding decree and sign the writing that it be not changed, according to the law of the Medes and Persians, which cannot be altered. Therefore, King Darius signed the writing, even the binding decree.

Establish . . . sign the writing: The double phrase is used for emphasis. The men wanted the king to put this decree in writing to insure that it would be carried out. This stress, no doubt, was calculated to impress the king with their earnestness in wanting to honor him. At the same time, of course, they wanted to be sure that the king would not be able to set the decree aside, should he come to realize the true intention behind it. Their language shows that they feared he might wish to change it, which means that they were willing to risk the displeasure he might show, if he did, in their effort to be rid of Daniel. *Which cannot be altered:* The unchangeableness of Medo-Persian law is reflected also in Esther 1:19; 8:8 and in a quotation from Diodorus concerning the attitude of Darius III of Persia in connection with a death sentence he had passed on one Charidemos: "Immediately he repented and blamed himself, as having greatly erred; but it was not possible to undo what was done by royal authority."[14] The reasoning seems to have been that, to change a decree once given, was to admit that it had been faulty, which was considered improper in reference to the high monarch. It was the unchangeableness of the decree which constituted the basis of the plot contrived by these men.

Signed the writing, even the binding decree: The same nouns are used here as in verse eight. The conjunction "even" (copula *waw*) is preferred over "and," because the king did not sign two documents. If the king had waited until the next day before signing,

---

[13] KDC on Daniel, p. 216.
[14] Cf. Montgomery, MICC, p. 270, in a quote from Bochert, *Hierozoicon,* I, p. 748, who in turn cites Diodorus Siculus, XVII, 30.

he might have seen through the scheme; the request being so out of context for these men, and the nature of the request so unreasonable. Great harm can come from matters done in haste.

C. FAITHFULNESS AND ACCUSATION (vv. 10-15)

One of Scripture's outstanding examples of courageous obedience is now presented. Daniel learned of the king's foolish act and recognized its direct bearing on his custom of praying three times daily. But still he prayed. The conspirators gathered to observe and then went quickly to the king to bring their accusation. The king, realizing his own foolishness, tried to release himself from having to effect the decree, but he was so pressed by the conspirators that he could not.

6:10. Now Daniel, when he knew that the writing had been signed, went up to his house, and, with the windows open in his upper chamber toward Jerusalem, he continued to bow on his knees three times a day and to pray and to praise before his God, as he had done previously.

When he knew: The decree was likely proclaimed publicly, by proper channels. Daniel learned of it and was immediately faced with a major decision. *Went up to his house:* From this it appears that Daniel was away from his residence at the time the decree came to his notice. He may have been at his office. From wherever he was, he went to his house to pray when the usual time came. The choice to do so could not have been easy. Hearing of the decree, he must have guessed who had persuaded the king to issue it, for he no doubt knew of the jealousy and opposition of these colleagues. He had probably been quite aware of their earlier investigation of his life and work. Would he now continue to pray, and so seem to fall into their trap? Or would he be wiser to cease for the thirty days, and so "outwit" them? Would it not be better to make sure of keeping his life for prayer and testimony later on than to continue praying now and risk losing it? Such thoughts must have moved through his mind; but his decision was, properly, to proceed as he was accustomed. *With windows open in his upper chamber:* The word for "upper chamber" (*'illît*) seems to indicate a special room on the second floor, used for guests or as a private place of meditation and prayer (cf. 2 Sam. 18:33; 1 Kings 17:19; 2 Kings 4:10; Acts 1:13; 10:9). The Babylonian climate is warm, and windows can be left open for airiness much of the year. It was to this exposed room—no doubt, the customary place—that Daniel went for his time of prayer. Certainly the thought passed his mind of not praying in this open room. Why not pray, if pray he must, somewhere in secret? Certainly there were other rooms in the house that he might have used. The reason for the . clear statement as to where he prayed is to say that he did not change, but prayed where he was accustomed to pray. The reason is not difficult to see. If he should pray elsewhere, those knowing him and his habits, including especially his hostile colleagues, would think that he had ceased, and this would spoil his testimony before them. He had been an open witness before, both in word and life practice; he must continue now lest all that he had done before to influence others to faith in the true God should be for naught. The existence of a continued testimony was more important than the existence of his life!

Toward Jerusalem: Likely the upper room had windows opening in more directions than one, which makes the force of this notice to be that Daniel prayed looking through those which opened toward the west, the direction of Jerusalem. Solomon had suggested the propriety of facing the Temple in prayer, at the time of his dedication of the Temple (cf. 1 Kings 8:33, 35, 38, 44, 48), and David seems to have practiced the idea in principle even before that time (cf. Ps. 5:7; 28:2). When the people had been taken captive, the gesture, symbolizing the direction of their hearts' desire, was even more significant. It is believed that the practice of Moslems today in facing Mecca when they pray is taken from this earlier custom. *Three times a day:* The word order in the Aramaic places this element before those of bowing, praying, and praising; thus giving it a place of emphasis. It is to be fully realized, then, that Daniel prayed not only once but his usual three times that day, thus not changing his normal pattern in even this respect. The three times were probably at morning, noon, and evening (cf. Ps. 55:17). To have maintained such a demanding schedule as this, even apart from continuing it now in the face of penalty, required great discipline of life. In his position as president, Daniel carried heavy responsibility, with much work to do. Under such demands, the temptation to neglect this sort of prayer-program was no doubt strong, especially since he had to return home each noon for the purpose, while keeping on also with the morning and evening occasions. But Daniel had maintained it, apparently recognizing the priority of this faithful contact with God. He continued the same in the face of the unfair decree. *To bow . . . to pray and to praise:* These three verbs are participles, indicating continuedness of action. Daniel not only prayed three times this one day, but he continued to do so on succeeding days. Even his visit in the den of lions would not have interrupted the practice, because he was there for only one night; and he probably prayed then even more than ordinary. The first participle (root, *bᵉrak,* "to bless, kneel"), followed by "knees," indicates that he kneeled each time he prayed. That he prayed in this position shows that he wished to match the contrite attitude of heart, necessary for true prayer, with an appropriate posture (cf. 1 Kings 8:54; Ezra 9:5; Luke 22:41; Acts 7:60; 9:40). He also thus provided observers with an unmistakable indication of what he was doing. Apparently, he prayed near the open windows so that he might be seen in this position. The second participle (root, *ts^{e}la'*, "to pray") indicates the voicing of requests to God, and the third (root, *y^{e}da'*, "to praise"), the expression of praise. Daniel's requests that first day would likely have been that he might be protected in the face of the new danger, and that God would somehow change the hearts of those who were bitter against him. That he was able to praise in the face of such treachery and danger is especially noteworthy. This is a splendid example of fulfilling the admonition in 1 Thessalonians 5:18.

6:11, 12. Then these men came in concert and found Daniel making petition and imploring favor before his God. So they approached and spoke before the king concerning the binding decree that any man who makes request of any god or man for thirty days, except of you, O King, shall be cast into the den of lions? The king answered and said: the matter is certain, according to the law of the Medes and Persians, which cannot be altered.

Came in concert: This is the same word for "in concert" as in verse six (which see). The conspirators, knowing Daniel's normal time to pray, came purposely to observe. They came as a group, united in their purpose of conspiracy. Since Daniel's prayer-room was on the second floor, they may have arranged to view him from another second floor nearby. *Making petition and imploring favor:* The word for "making petition" is used in verses seven and twelve; but that for "imploring favor" (root, *hanan*, "to show favor") is used here for the first time. In the reflexive form employed it means to seek grace or favor for oneself. Daniel was asking God to be gracious toward him in this hour of trial.

So they approached: There is no indication whether these men in any way made their presence or intention known to Daniel. If they observed him from outside his own residence, which seems likely, he may not have known that they were there, though he could easily have suspected it. The indication is only that they went quickly to the king with their information. Events at the moment were working just as they had planned. *The king answered:* The conspirators first asked the king whether he had not signed the binding decree, using the same words as in verse seven. He responded, in proper manner, that he had; probably wondering why they should ask.

6:13. Then they answered and spoke before the king: Daniel, who is from the children of the captivity of Judah, does not show regard for you, O King, or the binding decree which you have signed, but three times a day he makes his petition.

Then they answered: The conspirators thought that they had everything just as they wanted it. The trap was ready to be sprung. They may have kept their composure, but probably some overeagerness displayed itself as they voiced their charge to the king. Their manner in doing so may have contributed to the king's strong reaction against them, as the following verses portray. *Children of the captivity of Judah:* Certainly the king knew that Daniel was one of the Judean captives. He would not have appointed a man president without knowing his background. That these men mentioned the fact of Daniel's captivity, then, suggests that they held it against him. They wanted to picture him to Darius—just as they doubtless thought of him in their bitter jealousy—as a foreign misfit, who was now showing his true nature by disloyalty to the king. Their thinking was much like that of the accusers of the three friends when they refused to bow to Nebuchadnezzar's image, purposely referring to them as "Jews" (cf. 3:8, 12). Like those accusers, too, they were actually charging the king with improper judgment in selecting Daniel to office in the first place. *Regard for you . . . or the binding decree:* With these words also, the conspirators sought to color their report. The only charge they could make truthfully was the last they mentioned—that Daniel prayed three times daily. But this reference to showing disrespect for the king and his decree was an untrue interpretation of Daniel's action. Daniel was in no way showing disrespect by his praying. *Three times a day:* It is doubtful that these men waited with bringing this accusation until they had seen Daniel pray all three times on one day. The likelihood is that they waited until they had seen him pray only one time and then concluded, on the basis of his usual custom, that he would pray all three times. They would not have wanted to wait any longer than necessary before hurrying to the king; and, besides, they likely reasoned that for Daniel to have prayed once was really as damaging for him in respect to breaking the decree, as praying three times. They were actually complimenting him, then, by saying that he was praying three times a day.

6:14. Then the king, when he heard these words, was very displeased, and set his mind on Daniel to deliver him and strove until sunset to rescue him.

Was very displeased: The translation here given is better than that of KJV, "was sore displeased with himself." The word for "displeased" (*beʾesh*) is used impersonally, and, with the adjective and following prepositional phrase, means literally "there was sore displeasure upon him." This was not the kind of reaction by the king for which the accusers had hoped. They had wanted him to be angered that anyone would dare disregard a decree signed by him. But Darius had known Daniel too long and well to believe any such charge against him, even if brought by his officers. It had not been for nought that the king had been thinking about elevating him in position. His displeasure was probably due principally to two facts: first, that Daniel, whom he respected so highly, was the one being charged with disloyalty; and, second, that he had himself been so shortsighted as to sign a decree that would entrap one with the dedication of Daniel. He may not yet have recognized that these men had perpetrated a plot, and so was not yet sore displeased with them. He would recognize it, however, before the day was over, as the next verse shows. *Set his mind on Daniel:* The verse does not merely say that the king set his mind to deliver Daniel, but that he set his mind on Daniel (as a person), and that this involved delivering him. The Aramaic word order places Daniel first in the sentence, the stressed position, giving this thought, literally: "and as for Daniel, he set his mind to deliver him." This fact corroborates what the overall story shows: that Darius did indeed think highly of this man. If the accusers had realized how highly, they might not have dared to try their plan. *Strove until sunset to rescue him:* All that the king did in his endeavor to deliver Daniel is difficult to say. He probably worked with lawyers to see if there were any possibility for setting the decree aside. Perhaps he argued that the king, who had made the law, ought to be able to set it aside; or he may have asked if there were no past cases where similar decrees had been rescinded; or he may have inquired if a man might be pardoned by the king and still satisfy legal requirements. How much of the day still remained when he began this endeavor is not revealed. If the time of Daniel's praying that was observed by the accusers was the noon occasion—a possibility that fits well into all that is known—he probably had most of an afternoon. He continued his efforts until sundown (literally, "going in of the sun," *me'alê shimsha'*), signifying that he expended considerable time and energy in this endeavor. This is a remarkable example of an absolute monarch being bound by a law still more absolute. Every sense of justice within the king cried out that Daniel should be delivered, but law demanded that he be punished.

6:15. Then these men came in concert to the king and said to the king: Know, O King, that it is a law of the Medes and Persians that no binding decree or statute that the king establishes may be changed.

Came in concert: For the third time this word is used (cf. vv. 6, 11). Its repetition stresses the unitedness of purpose that these men maintained throughout the enactment of their plan. The time of this coming before the king was apparently just after sundown, when the king had finished with his efforts. Perhaps the king himself summoned the men on this occasion. With the day's inquiries not having produced results, he may have thought to examine them further as to their evidence regarding Daniel. Were they sure of what they had seen? Did they know that Daniel had disobeyed the decree? *No binding decree . . . may be changed:* If the king hoped that he would receive any help from the men, however, he was due for more disappointment. Their first words were to remind him of the unchangeableness of his decree; something which very likely had been a prime source of irritation to him all afternoon. He surely was in no mood to be reminded of it again. That they did may well have triggered his recognition of the plot which they were carrying out. Pieces of the overall picture may then have fallen into place. These men had been the ones to persuade him to sign the decree; they had been conveniently on hand to observe Daniel in his praying; and now they were insisting that the decree be carried out. These men, then, had plotted Daniel's death, and had used him, the king, as an instument to bring it about!

D. SENTENCE AND DELIVERANCE (vv. 16-23)

With all possibilities for delivering Daniel exhausted, Darius finally gave the order that he be cast to the lions, expressing to Daniel his personal hope that God would deliver him. The time apparently was still the same evening, because the king afterward went to his palace, where he spent a sleepless night in his concern for Daniel. Daniel, however, was not harmed by the beasts; and the king, on finding this to be true the following morning, ordered him to be immediatey released from the den.

6:16. At last the king commanded and they brought Daniel and cast him into the den of lions. The king spoke and said to Daniel: May your God, whom you serve continually, deliver you.

At last: The word is normally translated "then" *(be'dayin),* but here it is best taken in the sense of "at last"; that is, after all attempts by Darius at deliverance had failed. Keil states, "The execution of the sentence was carried out, according to Oriental custom, on the evening of the day in which the accusation was made.[15] This would explain why the king had labored so diligently all that afternoon. Any way of effecting Daniel's deliverance had to be found before evening. *They brought Daniel:* Many details are omitted. With the order given by the king, personnel were dispatched to apprehend Daniel. Daniel would thus have learned only then of the results of his continuing to pray in spite of the decree. He had been faithful in praying, leaving the matter in God's hands. Now it seemed that God was not to spare him. Many years before, it had seemed the same to Daniel's three friends as they had faced the fiery furnace. Knowing the kind of person Daniel was, however, one can believe that he faced the challenge no less courageously than they. He was marched to the den, which was perhaps at some distance from his home. The king prob-

---

[15] KDC on Daniel, p. 215.

ably was already there. A knowing look may have passed between the two as Daniel arrived, Daniel silently inquiring regarding the thinking of the king, and the king trying to reassure him that he was opposed to what was happening. But law had to have its way, and Daniel was marched to the opening of the den (cf. v. 7 for description). *May your God:* These words from Darius may have been spoken before Daniel was actually cast into the den, even though given in the text in the word order indicated by the translation. Typical Aramaic or Hebrew style of writing would allow for this. The context suggests that the words were voiced as Daniel was brought to the mouth of the den. The verb for "deliver" (root, *shêzib*) is in the imperfect state and may be translated as a wish (jussive), as here, or a prediction, as in KJV.[16] It is not likely, however, that Darius, a pagan, could have had a confidence in God to express a flat prediction. It is remarkable that he could voice even such a wish. That he did so shows that Daniel had been busy in witnessing to him, as he had been years earlier to Nebuchadnezzar and Belshazzar. The significance of his words "whom you serve continually" should not be missed. Darius clearly had been impressed by Daniel's faithfulness in life behavior to his God; no doubt a telling factor in molding the king's own thinking. One's life conduct is so important if his oral testimony is to be effective.

6:17. A stone was brought and placed upon the mouth of the den, and the king sealed it with his own signet and the signet of his lords, that the situation concerning Daniel might not be changed.

A stone was brought: As noted under verse seven, the den likely had both a side and a top opening. The opening covered by this stone was probably at the side. The verse reveals that the stone was placed for reasons of security; and a side entrance, on a level with the inside floor, would have called for this more than one above. This entrance was likely covered normally by some type of grating, with the prepared stone at hand when special security was needed. Ventilation may have been solely through the top opening when the stone was in place. Daniel was probably put into the den through this same side entrance, but the next morning taken out through the top, as will be observed. Later the accusers were apparently cast in from the top. *The king sealed it:* Sealing of this kind was done, not so much to give physical security as to make any breaking or moving of whatever was sealed illegal. This sealing may have been done by means of tied cords, the knot being covered with wax into which a seal was pressed to leave its carved configuration. Or a clay mixture may have been applied at the juncture of the stone and the wall of the den and

---

[16] Cf. Walvoord, WD, p. 140, for evidence for the reading, "He must deliver you," denoting obligation of God to do this.

on this a seal impressed. Either way, the removal of the stone would have broken the impression in the clay, the broken seal giving indication that the stone had been moved, making the one who did it liable to punishment. Since every seal was private to its owner, no one else could break a seal and then place the same imprint on freshly applied clay to avoid detection. *His own signet and the signet of his lords:* The word employed denotes a signet ring, used for impressing its design on wax or clay to make such a seal. Other known forms of seals were stamp seals and cylinder seals. Whatever type was used, each had carved on the imprinting surface a design whose impression remained on the clay when so applied. Kings often used the special signet ring (cf. 1 Kings 21:8; Esth. 3:12; 8:8, 10). In this instance, not only was the king's own seal used, but also that of his lords. Apparently, the king's lords (including perhaps both presidents and satraps), as a body, had an official seal too, used as a mark of authority for documents issued in their name. The employment of both rings in this instance indicated that the approval of both the king and the lords would be needed to remove the stone. *Might not be changed:* These words give the reason for the security measure. Daniel's situation in the den was not to be changed by anyone. The accusers, who likely were present and wanted the lords' signet seal used, would have desired in this way to insure against the possibility of the king himself sending men to rescue Daniel;[17] and the king would have wanted to insure against these accusers' trying to take Daniel's life some other way, if the lions did not.

6:18. Then the king went to his palace, and spent the night fasting, with no diversions being brought before him; and his sleep fled from him.

Spent the night fasting: This phrase and the next make clear that Darius normally spent his evenings with eating and entertainment. But this evening was different. He did not eat. Probably he had eaten nothing since noon, either, because the main oriental meal then, as now, seems to have been scheduled late in the evening. His body may have suffered from lack of nourishment, but apparently he did not notice. His mind was occupied with Daniel. He did not wish to lose a valuable officer; and he felt guilty in the part he had unknowingly played in putting Daniel where he was. He probably also was ashamed at having been tricked so easily through flattery. *No diversions:* The reference here is to entertainment. The word used *(daḥᵃwan)* is not specific as to what kind, and probably this varied from evening to evening. Types which have been suggested by expositors include instruments of music, dancing girls, and concubines. The king was not

---

[17] The king likely had authority to break such a lords' seal, but the lords could have reasoned that he would not violate their authority easily.

interested in any kind of entertainment that night. *His sleep fled from him:* When the king tried to sleep, he could not. The word for "fled" *(naddat)* is used in its equivalent Hebrew form to refer to physical flight, from one place to another (cf. Isa. 21:15; 33:3; Jer. 4:25). Used of sleep, it lays stress on the extreme degree to which it leaves the person: as if it had run away. Apparently, the king rolled and tossed on his bed, his mind going over the plight of Daniel, the fruit- lessness of his efforts to deliver him, the craft of the accusers, his own stupidity in being tricked, and the measures he might take in retaliation against the schemers.

6:19, 20. So the king arose very early in the morning and went in haste to the den of lions. As he drew near to the den, he called to Daniel in a voice of anguish. The king spoke and said to Daniel: O Daniel, servant of the living God, has your God, whom you serve continually, been able to deliver you from the lions?

Arose very early: The word for "very early" *(bish^{e}parpara')* means literally "at dawn." The word for "in the morning" *(b^{e}nag^{e}ha')* means literally "in brightness." The time, then, was just at dawn as the first bright light was shining forth in the east. Since the king could not sleep, he arose early and made his way to the den. He went "in haste," showing eagerness to get there, moving along as quickly as his advanced age (see 5:31) permitted, desirous of learning whether Daniel yet lived. This suggests that he really believed this might be true, showing that he had been serious in his wish to Daniel the night before. This hope could only have been based on Daniel's own faith in his God and on reports the king had no doubt heard con- cerning miracles wrought for Daniel and his friends during Babylonian days.

Voice of anguish: Even before fully reaching the den, Darius began to call out to Daniel, his voice reflecting the grief he felt. The language suggests that he did not take time for the stone to be removed from the side entrance, which means that his voice was heard by Daniel through the top opening. Reaching the opening and peering down into the den from the light above, he could not have seen whether Daniel lived or not, for the den would have been black in darkness. *Servant of the living God:* In expressing his wish of the evening before, Darius had employed the phrase "whom you serve continually," used here again, but he did not then refer to Daniel as a "servant" of God. This time he used both expressions, showing that he thought of Daniel as a faithful servant of God. His use of the word "living" *(ḥay)* is par- ticularly noteworthy. Daniel had no doubt used the qualifier in his times of speaking to Darius regarding God and he would have im- plied by it that God lives, in distinction from other deities who do not. Darius could hardly have intended so much here, for he, a Persian, certainly believed his gods lived also, but he probably used it simply as a matter of course, copying Daniel's language, in his hope that this God of life might have been able to save Daniel's life. *Has your God been able:* It is sometimes stated that Darius asked this question merely as a heathen person, believing only generally that gods do benefit those who please them. Certain matters, however, show that his respect for Daniel's God went beyond this. In the first place, as noted, Darius' actions, initially in expressing his wish of the prior evening, then both coming early to the den and calling down to Daniel to see if he was alive, show that he really believed God might deliver this man. The heathen did not have this kind of faith in their gods, for they never witnessed such miracles on their part. Secondly, when Daniel's response from below indicated that he was alive, Darius is not said to have been amazed, as though not really believing this might happen, but only "very glad" at the good news. Thirdly, he then issued the remarkable decree recorded (vv. 25-27), much like the earlier decree of Nebuchadnezzar, calling on people of his domain to give respect to this God.

6:21, 22. Then Daniel spoke with the king: O King, live forever. My God has sent His angel and shut the mouth of the lions, and they have not harmed me, because I was found innocent before Him; and also before you, O King, I have done no wrong.

Then Daniel spoke: The word for "spoke" *(mᵉlal)* has not been used in the book before, but always the less expressive "say" *(ᵃmar).* The significance seems to be to emphasize that Daniel actually voiced words to the king; that is, that he was really able to do so. The reaction of the king, on hearing the words, after such an emotion-filled night, must have been very marked. *O King, live forever:* This was the proper, formal term of greeting for kings of the day. It is used several times in the book (2:4; 3:9; 5:10; 6:6), but never with as much significance as here. Daniel could be proper in addressing the king, even when in a den of lions. He had recognized the words coming from above as those of his monarch, and he responded with appropriate decorum. He thus displayed his willingness to be subject to this man, even though Darius had been instrumental in his being in the den. Likely the king's manner the evening before, however, had convinced Daniel that he had not been sympathetic to what was done. *My God has sent His angel:* Hearing Daniel's voice was enough to tell the king that he was alive, but Daniel wished to tell him how it had happened. God had sent His angel to effect the deliverance. Daniel's God had done what Darius had hoped, then, through the instrumentality of a supernatural agent. How Darius conceived of such an agent is not clear, but the Scriptures teach that angels are spirit beings, created by God for the purpose of serving Him. One area of service is the protection of people (Ps. 34:7; 91:11; Matt. 18:10; Heb. 1:14). It is even possible that this one was the Angel of Yahweh; as was likely true also regarding the fiery furnace occasion years before (cf. 3:25). Since Daniel knew of this heavenly emissary, it is probable that he was visible to Daniel, something also true for the three friends in the furnace. Perhaps, if Darius could have seen down into the darkness of the dungeon, he would have witnessed him as well, just as Nebuchadnezzar had in the furnace. God had sent His personal representative to accompany and protect the three friends in their hour of trial; and now had done the same for Daniel in the den of lions. Both occasions thus were turned into blessed memories rather than times of horror. *Have not harmed me:* The angel had made the great lions powerless to hurt Daniel. The words, "shut the mouth of the lions" should be taken as figurative for general disablement. If only their mouths had been sealed, they could still have mauled Daniel with their feet. But Daniel had not been harmed in any way. He may even have enjoyed a better night's rest than the king. *I was found innocent:* Literally, "innocence was found to me." The word for "innocence" *(zakû)* comes from a verb which, in its corresponding Hebrew form, means "to be clean, pure," always in a moral sense. Daniel says that he was found pure from moral defilement before God. He was not claiming sinlessness (cf. 9:3), but was saying that he was not guilty of the charge of disloyalty to the king. That he adds *before Him* means that God, who knows the heart, recognized this innocence and accordingly had sent the angel. *Before you I have done no wrong:* This has already been implied in the prior statement, but Daniel wished to make this very clear to the king, lest he miss the implication. Daniel had done no wrong (literally, "hurtful act, crime") to the king. How much Daniel had been told as to the charges made against him by the conspirators is not indicated, but he could have guessed their nature; and he wanted the king to know that he was not guilty of any action detrimental to the king.

6:23. Then the king was very glad, and he commanded to draw up Daniel from the den; and Daniel was drawn up from the den, with no injury being found on him, because he had trusted in his God.

Was very glad: Literally, "it was very good to him." The king's anxious thoughts now had reason for rest. Daniel was alive and well. His reaction was one of gladness. That no mention is made of surprise is noteworthy, as already suggested. Remarkable as it is, he had believed that this really might happen. The king was glad because he still had his trusted president available for service, he was relieved of guilt feelings toward him, and he would not have to live with a memory that the trickery of the accusers had worked. *Draw up*

Daniel ... was drawn up: The word s^eleq is used both times, first actively and then passively. It normally carries the idea of vertical movement (cf. 7:3, 8, 20), rather than horizontal, suggesting the thought that Daniel was now taken from the den through the top opening, probably by ropes. It is quite possible that, since the seal of the lords was on the stone at the side entrance, along with that of the king, only the top opening was available for this removal. The king likely had authority to break the lords' seal, but may well have chosen not to do, for the sake of expediency, since the top opening could be used apparently without great difficulty. *No injury:* The repetition of this thought, expressed in verse twenty-two, suggests that Daniel was examined with care on being brought from the den, for the king would have wanted first aid administered if any injury had occurred, and those attending would have found it incredible that one could spend a night with lions and suffer no harm at all. Certainly all who witnessed the miracle had to be enormously impressed at the discovery that Daniel had suffered no injury whatever. *Because he had trusted:* The mention of Daniel's trust at this point suggests that after their inspection, the examiners came to recognize this trust as having accounted for the miracle. That Daniel had such faith would have been a matter of general knowledge, due to his life and witness. Here now was evidence that this faith was productive of amazing ends, for God alone could effect such a deliverance.

E. Two Significant Results (vv. 24-28)

With such a demonstration of the reality and power of Daniel's God, significant results should have followed in the lives of all those present. The degree to which this may have been true in the lives of the king's attendants is not revealed, but two tangible matters in the life of the king are shown. First, he had Daniel's accusers thrown into the same den from which Daniel had just been released; and, second, he issued a decree, much in the pattern of those made years earlier by Nebuchadnezzar, honoring the God of Daniel.

6:24. And the king commanded and they brought those men who had slandered Daniel, and they cast them, their children, and their wives into the den of lions; and they did not reach the bottom of the den before the lions overpowered them and broke all their bones.

The king commanded: The implication is that the king lost no time in bringing retribution on Daniel's accusers. He gave command, perhaps even while at the den, and personnel moved to apprehend those designated. These men had wronged not only Daniel, but also the king. They had insulted him by using him through trickery to accomplish their purpose. It is likely that the king would have so punished them even if Daniel had died. One wonders at the intelligence of men who would not have realized this possibility from the first. *Who had slandered:* Literally this reads "Who had eaten the pieces of" (cf. 3:8). It is not necessary to believe that all 122 presidents and satraps were brought, as some have critically suggested. The den did not have to be large enough to contain all these. But, as pointed out earlier, those who accused Daniel likely were only certain of these officers who lived in the region of Babylon. Their number may not have been great, though when their wives and children were added, the company would have taken on some size. *Their children and their wives:* That wives and children were punished, as well as the guilty men, was in accordance with Persian custom. Ammianus Marcellinus[18] states, "The laws among them (the Persians) are formidable . . . by which, on account of the guilt of one, all the kindred perish." What a turn of events thus came for the accusers. From thinking themselves successful in their plot to rid themselves of Daniel, they now had to face the den of lions themselves. No doubt they were informed, too, that Daniel had escaped the lions completely unharmed. *Did not reach the bottom of the den:* These words suggest that once more the top opening of the den was used. The guarding stone at the side entrance probably had not yet been removed by the time the accusers and their families were brought. One by one, perhaps in the order, and at the moment, of their arrival, they were pushed into the darkness below. As they were, they were caught in midair, without reaching the floor of the den, and devoured by the ferocious beasts. The reason for this unpleasant mention is to show how great the miracle of Daniel's preservation was. The lions were not old and without interest in human flesh. They were simply kept from inflicting the same sort of horrifying death on Daniel by the presiding messenger from God.

6:25-27. Then King Darius wrote to all peoples, nations, and languages that dwell in all the earth: May your peace be multiplied. I make a decree that in all the dominion of my kingdom men tremble and fear before the God of Daniel, for He is the living God and endures forever; His kingdom will never be destroyed, and His dominion will be to the end. He rescues and delivers, and He works signs and wonders in heaven and on earth; who delivered Daniel from the power of the lions.

King Darius wrote: Like Nebuchadnezzar, following the deliverance of Daniel's three companions from the fiery furnace (3:29), so Darius now issued a public decree that men everywhere give proper recognition to the God of Daniel. This decree is specifically said to have been

---

[18] Quoted by Barnes, BD, II, p. 28; cf. Young, YPD, p. 133.

written, but this need not imply that others were not. For Darius to have issued such a document means that he was greatly impressed with the power of Daniel's God, even as Nebuchadnezzar had been. *Peoples, nations, and languages:* These are the same words as used in 3:4, 7, 29; 4:1; etc. (which see). The additional phrase *in all the earth* is a hyperbole customary to kings of the day.

The dominion of my kingdom: This further defines the extent of the king's order. He had in mind all territory where he ruled. Most decrees were likely similarly addressed. *Men tremble and fear:* This is the heart of the decree: all men were to "tremble and fear" before God. Both verbs are participles, indicating continuation of action. Men were to continue trembling and fearing God; in other words, to respect Him and recognize that they could be hurt by Him. Darius thus was admitting that this God's power extended far beyond the boundaries of Judah. Expositors have pointed out that the king did not disown the gods of Babylon in the decree, nor speak of himself as rendering worship to Daniel's God. This is true, and accordingly it is not likely that Darius experienced personal conversion, something which may have been true, as noted, with respect to Nebuchadnezzar. *The living God, and endures forever:* The king then gave reasons for the decree. Two are involved in this element: God lives and He continues as God eternally. The language used is like that which Daniel would have written, and likely reflects either his instruction of the king or else his own actual penning of the document at the king's request. *His kingdom will never be destroyed:* Cf. Nebuchadnezzar's similar words in 4:3. Here Darius was admitting that God has a kingdom and that it, in contrast to human kingdoms, is not subject to cessation. No enemy can attack and make conquest of it.

He rescues and delivers: At this point Darius' reasons for calling men to fear God are taken particularly from Daniel's experience in the den of lions. The God of Daniel can deliver, thus being able to work "signs and wonders" (cf. discussion, 4:3), as demonstrated in Daniel's preservation. "Power" of lions is literally, "hand" *(ya_d)* of lions.

6:28. So this Daniel prospered in the reign of Darius and in the reign of Cyrus the Persian.

This Daniel prospered: The demonstrative pronoun "this" is used here, as in verse three. Its force is to say that truly this same Daniel, who had been so unjustly accused and condemned, was now not only alive but prospering in his activities. *Reign of Darius . . . reign of Cyrus:* Since these two rulers were contemporary, the first subordinate to the second (cf. discussion in the introduction to this chapter), the translation of the verse might be "in the reign of Darius, even in the reign of Cyrus." Darius, if he is properly identified with Gubaru (cf.

introduction), ruled through all of Cyrus' time (until 529 B.C.) and the first four years of Cyrus' son and successor, Cambyses. How long Daniel lived is not revealed, though it was at least until Cyrus' third year (10:1), which means 536 B.C., or when Daniel was about 84. He may have been taken by God shortly after this—a man rich in years, faithfulness, and service to his God.

CHAPTER 7

Chapter seven begins the second division of the book. The first six chapters have been mainly historical, with a minimum of prediction; the second division is mainly predictive, with a minimum of history. The predictions made in the coming six chapters concern the sequence of events from Daniel's day to the coming of the Messiah, as to both His first and second advents.

These predictions are given through four separate visions,[1] which occurred at four different times within the historical period covered by the first six chapters. The first vision, found in chapter seven, is the most comprehensive, covering the entire course of these events, whereas the other three visions treat periods or emphasized aspects within the overall time concerned. The four great world empires of Daniel's day and following constitute the main theme. They are the Babylonian, the Medo-Persian, the Grecian, and the Roman, all four of which were symbolized also in Nebuchadnezzar's first dream (chap. 2). Concerning the last empire, an extensive gap in time is symbolized—a gap involving time between the close of the Roman empire of early Christian centuries and a restoration of that empire still to come. That which calls for this time-gap, or rather for the restoration of the empire which makes for the gap, is a need to present the setting of the second advent as well as that of the first advent of Christ. He came the first time during the Roman period of ancient history, and He will come the second time at the climax of the Roman period of the future. The various ways, in all four visions, by which this time-gap is symbolized will be noticed as the visions are analyzed. Because these visions unfold the great panorama of history, the book of Daniel has been correctly likened to the book of Revelation in the New Testament.

The reason for giving such a predictive survey at this point in Old Testament history is as follows. When God's people were taken

---

[1] All four are commonly called "visions," but the last two vary from the normal form of vision, as will be observed.

captive to Babylonia, it seemed from the human perspective that God was through with them (cf. Jer. 33:24). God was not through with them, however, and He desired that they know He was not. An effective way to do this was to reveal the historical future which God had in mind for them. They not only would return from this captivity but would in due time see their Messiah come to deliver them from spiritual bondage to sin and later from physical bondage to a powerful, earthly empire; this latter deliverance to be followed by a grand kingdom-period of their own. God, in His grace and wisdom, saw fit to choose Daniel, a lay executive in the Babylonian court, as the one through whom to impart this important information.

God's timing for the granting of this information calls for notice. The visions were given to Daniel after Nebuchadnezzar had ruled; two in the early years of Belshazzar and two shortly after the beginning of the Persian period. The visions came, then, nicely before the return to Judah, though only after the people had been in Babylonia for most of their time of captivity. God had not left them entirely in the dark on these matters before this, however, for He had revealed basic information already in Nebuchadnezzar's first dream, which came even before the captivity proper of Judah. From this, Daniel and the other Judeans, whom Daniel likely informed, could know even from the first that God had this meaningful future in mind for them.

Symbolism is employed in the visions, as it was in respect to Nebuchadnezzar's dream-image. The interpretation of much of the symbolism is made clear in the text, just as it was for the earlier dream-image, so that one need not guess. It will be noticed that, in respect to the predicted events which have already occurred, the vision finds a literal historical fulfillment; and the same should be anticipated, then, in respect to the events which lie still in the future.

A marked similarity exists between the predictions symbolized in Nebuchadnezzar's dream image and those of this first vision. As noted in chapter two, the dream-image, in its four divisions, symbolized the four great empires—the Babylonian, the Medo-Persian, the Grecian, and the Roman. The same is true in respect to the four beasts seen in the first vision. There are two main differences, however. First, the dream-image, by its nature, pictures the unity of history running through these empires, in that the image is one whole, having related, symbolic parts; whereas the four beasts, being each fully distinct from the other, depict the diversity of history exhibited by the empires. Second, the humanlike dream-image, seen by the pagan Nebuchadnezzar, represented these empires from the viewpoint of man as each having intrinsic value, corresponding to the descending values of the metals of the image; whereas the four beasts, seen by the godly Daniel, show these empires from God's viewpoint, as each being "beastly" in nature and value. The two times of revelations are similar in that both symbolize the fall of these empires and the establishment in their place of Christ's millennial rule: the dream-image, by the figure of the stone cut out of the mountain without hands, smiting and destroying the image and then growing to fill all the earth; and the four beasts, by being judged and destroyed by God, here called the Ancient of Days, who then gives the kingdom to Christ, here called the Son of Man. This vision gives greater detail regarding the overall subject than did Nebuchadnezzar's dream-image and it anticipates and provides overall background for the other three visions to follow.

A. THE GENERAL SETTING (vv. 1-3)

Before describing the symbolic beasts, the general setting of the vision is presented.

7:1. In the first year of Belshazzar, king of Babylon, Daniel saw a dream and visions of his head upon his bed; whereupon he wrote down the dream and told the sum of the matter.

First year of Belshazzar: Since Nabonidus made Belshazzar his co-regent in his third year,[2] this first year of Belshazzar was 553 B.C., when Daniel was about sixty-seven years old. Nebuchadnezzar had been deceased for nine years, and the kingdom had experienced troubled days while three kings (prior to Nabonidus) had ruled. Nabonidus, with his son Belshazzar, finally brought stability once again, and this condition continued until Babylon's fall, 539 B.C. Since the episode of the miraculous writing on the palace wall (chap. 5) came in Belshazzar's final year, it followed the time of this vision by fourteen years. The significance of God's selecting this particular date for the first vision may be that this was a time of marked concern among the Judean captives regarding their future, and God saw fit thus to give reassurance and instruction. Nebuchadnezzar, the great Babylonian, had been dead for these intervening years, and later rulers were proving ineffective to maintain Babylonia in her place of world leadership. What did these developments mean for God's captive people? Did they augur well for their early return to Judah? Or, would policies soon turn for the worse against them under the dominance of inefficient sovereigns? *King of Babylon:* The propriety of this term for Belshazzar has been discussed in the introduction to chapter five. That Daniel should so use it, without mentioning Nabonidus at all, is understandable, since this man was the ruler with whom Daniel had his contact, not Nabonidus. *Saw a dream and visions:* These same phrases are used in reference to Nebuchadnezzar's two dreams (cf.

---

[2] Cf. *supra,* chapter five, p. 130, for discussion.

2:28 and 4:5, 13). The significance seems to be that this vision came to Daniel in the form of a dream while He slept in his bed. *He wrote down the dream and told the sum:* Daniel put the contents of his dream into writing, presumably the following morning. The word for "sum" *(re'sh)* is literally "head" or "chief," here probably carrying the idea of *essence.* The thought is not that he wrote the dream and then orally told its essence, but that he told the essence in the writing. This means that he did not try to give all the details of the dream in the written record, but the essential points, those of significance. No indication is given that Nebuchadnezzar recorded the dreams that God gave him, but Daniel recognized the importance of the one given him and did put it into permanent form. Sometimes God told prophets specifically to write the information He revealed to them (cf. Isa. 30:8; Hab. 2:2).

7:2, 3. Daniel spoke and said: I was looking in my vision by night, and, lo, the four winds of heaven were stirring up the great sea; and four great beasts were ascending from the sea, each different from the other.

Daniel spoke: Two matters suggest that the words Daniel wrote that following morning begin with this verse, and not verse one. First, the words of this verse do not follow easily after those of verse one, indicating that the words of verse one may have been written later by him as a preface. And, second, whereas verse one uses the third person as a manner of reference to Daniel, all other verses employ the first person. *I was looking:* The form of the verb is a participle, indicating continuation of action. The same expression occurs ten times in the chapter. Daniel depicts himself each time in the act of beholding the scene displayed before him. *Four winds of heaven:* Being used in a context of nature, "heaven" is employed in the sense of the atmospheric realm. The "four winds" are winds from the four directions (cf. 8:8; 11:4). The phrase is used similarly in the Babylonian Creation Tablets, IV: 42, 43 (Heidel, p. 28). *Were stirring up the great sea:* If any particular sea is in mind, it is the Mediterranean, best known to people of the Near East and tangent to all four empires depicted. The word for "were stirring up" *(meḡîhan)* is a participle, meaning basically "to burst forth." The winds are depicted in the act of bursting forth against the sea, meaning that they were stirring it up, as in a time of storm. In the symbolism of Scripture, the sea regularly stands for the nations (cf. Isa. 17:12, 13; 27:1; 57:20; Rev. 17:15). The winds stand for various forces which play upon the nations, serving to bring strife and trouble. That they come contrary to nature, from the four directions at the same time indicates the severity and confusion of this strife and world-turmoil. The thought is to picture the nations of the world at any time, as God views them, and not merely the particular times when each of the four empires arose.

Four great beasts: Daniel witnessed four great animals arise out of this sea, not simultaneously but successively. The beasts represent four successive empires, and, since each arose from the sea (nations), they are of human origin and nature. Similar symbolism is found in Revelation 13:1, and even other nations of the day are known to have represented themselves in the figures of various animals[3] (cf. Ps. 74:13, 14; Isa. 27:1; 51:9; Ezek. 29:3; 32:2). The adjective "great" is a reduplicated form, *rabreban,* meaning "very great." Evidently, as each beast appeared, Daniel saw it as immense in size. He states further that all differed from each other.

B.   THE VISION PROPER (vv. 4-14)

Daniel now describes the vision. The first three beasts are dealt with summarily, but greater detail is devoted to the fourth, especially to its horns among which grows a little horn. The scene then changes to one of judgment, as the Ancient of Days is seen pronouncing sentence on the beasts and granting a new, glorious kingdom to the Son of Man.

7:4. The first was like a lion and it had the wings of an eagle. I kept looking until its wings were plucked off, and it was lifted up from the earth and made to stand on two feet like a man, and the heart of a man was given to it.

Like a lion: The first beast, said to be like a lion, is symbolic of the empire in power in Daniel's day, the Babylonian. More specifically, it is symbolic of Nebuchadnezzar, the principal king of the empire. Notice was made that the head of gold of the dream-image also carried this general and specific representation. Several matters give evidence for this symbolism. First, the lion, as king of beasts, and the eagle, as king of birds, correspond for importance to a head of gold, as indicated for the symbolism of Babylon and Nebuchadnezzar in the dream-image. Second, statues of winged lions, which are believed to have been representative of the empire and her great king, have been recovered from the ruins of Babylon.[4] Third, Daniel's contemporary prophets employed the sign of both the lion and eagle for Nebuchadnezzar (for the lion, cf. Jer. 4:7; 49:19; 50:17, 44; for the eagle, cf. Jer. 49:22; Lam. 4:19; Ezek. 17:3; Hab. 1:8). Fourth, the changes which this beast underwent, as indicated in the remainder of the verse, fit very well the experiences of Nebuchad-

---

[3] Cf. Zockler, *LCD,* p. 150.

[4] Cf. Zockler, *LCD,* p. 151 for discussion; also Barnes, *BD,* p. 45 for actual pictures of winged lions from Assyrian sculptures. The Assyrians apparently used the winged lion as a symbol also.

nezzar, as will appear. *Wings of an eagle:* This element is a fitting symbol for Nebuchadnezzar, not only in respect to the eagle's being the king of birds, as noticed, but that wings are suggestive of speed and capacity for effective action (cf. Jer. 4:13; 48:40). Nebuchadnezzar, in establishing his empire, showed these characteristics in his defeat of the Egyptians at Carchemish (605 B.C.), his ensuing occupation of the extensive territory which then fell to his titular domain, and his continuing rule. *I kept looking:* This is the second use of the participial construction noted in verse two and pictures Daniel continuing to look intently at the vision. *Wings were plucked off:* The root of the verb used is *mᵉrat,* meaning "to pluck, pull out," as one would the beard from his face (Isa. 50:6), symbolizing the loss of this speed and capacity for action. The symbolism is best taken in reference to Nebuchadnezzar's humiliation in his time of insanity, when these abilities were entirely removed. *Lifted up ... made to stand:* With the wings plucked, further changes came as the beast was made to stand upright, on two feet, and apparently took on the appearance of a human. The word for "lifted up" *(nᵉtal)* has been rendered by some expositors as "taken away" (from the earth), believing the thought to concern the destruction of the empire. This verb, however, means properly "to raise up, elevate," and also the context calls for the idea of being made to stand in an upright position. The word for "feet" is in the dual form; thus, "two feet." *The heart of a man:* This phrase reveals the significance of the prior change. The lion became a man outwardly and then inwardly; symbolizing that Nebuchadnezzar, following his time of insanity, became "humanized" in his manner of rule. A humanitarian interest came to play a major role in his life, rather than the former "beastly" lust for power.

7:5. And lo, another beast, a second, like to a bear, and it was raised up on one side; and it had three ribs in its mouth between its teeth; and it was told, Arise, devour much flesh.

Another beast, a second, like to a bear: "Another" means one distinct from the first, and "second" refers to the place of sequence in the order of beasts listed. The empire symbolized by this beast is the Medo-Persian, which succeeded the Babylonian in history; and which was symbolized by the silver chest and arms of Nebuchadnezzar's image. Some expositors hold that the Median kingdom only is symbolized, with the next beast representing the Persian. Three facts make this view untenable. First, the Median kingdom did not follow the Babylonian in historical sequence, as the vision here (and also the dream-image) requires, but was contemporary with it, even rising to a period of strength before the Neo-Babylonian period. Second, the Median kingdom never exercised a world position sufficient to warrant its being made a part to this symbolized empire sequence.

Third, the motivation for making this identification is mainly to avoid identifying the fourth beast with an empire as late in history as the Roman (recognizing that this would call for supernatural prediction), but the fourth beast does represent the Roman empire, as will appear. Medo-Persia, like the bear, was known for its strength and fierceness in battle (Isa. 13:17, 18). This second beast, like the other two following, symbolized an empire only, and not an outstanding ruler of the empire, as in the case of the first beast. *Was raised up on one side:* The words of this much-disputed phrase are best translated as given here, indicating that the bear was seen to have its two feet on the same side raised at one time, making that side to be higher than the other. Two points of symbolism should be noted. First, that the animal had one side rise higher than the other points to the greater importance assumed by the Persian division over the Median, in the Medo-Persian empire—a symbolism formed also by the two horns of the ram in Daniel's second vision (8:3), the second being made to grow higher than the first. Second, that the legs were lifted, as if the animal was about to move forward, points to the great Medo-Persian desire for conquest, carried out so dramatically by Cyrus. It may be noted that this manner of symbolism for movement contrasts with that of the "wings" of the leopard (next beast, v. 6); the raised legs suggesting heavy, plodding progress (true of Medo-Persia)[5] and the "wings" light and swift movement (true of Greece). *Three ribs in its mouth:* Bones held in the mouths of beasts of prey may safely be taken as representative of conquests. That this beast held three ribs suggests the conquests of three major enemies, perhaps Lydia, Egypt, and Babylonia—all defeated by the Persians. *Arise, devour much flesh:* The word for the preceding phrase, "it was told," means literally, "thus they said to it," with no indication of the identity of the speakers. That the beast is directed to "arise [and] devour much flesh" means that it should continue to make conquests. The overall stress for this beast is on conquest; and Medo-Persia did take over far more land than any prior kingdom, reaching finally all the way from the Indus River on the east to Egypt and the Aegean on the west.

7:6. After this I kept looking, and, lo, another like a leopard, and it had four wings of a bird on its back; and the beast had four heads; and dominion was given to it.

After this I kept looking: "After this" indicates that these views of the animals came in sequence, one followed by the next. "I kept looking" is the third instance of the participle indicating continuation

[5] The Medo-Persians moved with massive armies, winning by weight of numbers; cf. Pusey, *DP,* pp. 123, 24, who uses Herodotus' numbers, which are exaggerated, but which still give some idea of the vastness of the armies employed.

of careful observation. *Like a leopard:* The word for "leopard" *(n^emar)* means either a "leopard" or "panther" and is often considered related to an Arabic root meaning "to be spotted" (cf: Jer. 13:23). The outstanding characteristics of the leopard are agility, speed (Hab. 1:8), and an insatiable thirst for blood, as a beast of prey. Its symbolism here can only be of Greece, the next empire in history after the Medo-Persian, and one which indeed was characterized by swiftness of conquest and an insatiable lust for victory, even more than Medo-Persia. It may be pointed out that all three animals used in the symbolism—the lion, bear, and leopard—find rather frequent reference in Scripture, often in conjunction with each other (1 Sam. 17:34-36; Prov. 28:15; Jer. 5:6; Hos. 13:7, 8; Amos 5:19). This could be expected, for they were common animals of the day, though carefully selected here for their respective symbolic suitability to the three empires involved. *Four wings of a bird on its back:* The word for "back" *(gab)* may also be translated "side," which, if proper here, would indicate that the animal was more like the winged beasts found at Babylon. The existence of wings suggests the ideas of speed and action, as also with the wings of the lion. A contrast exists between the two cases, however. The wings on the lion are said to be those of an eagle, whereas these are not identified with any bird and are said to have been four in number. The significance is that the eagle is important in the former instance, connoting kingliness, as noted; and the double number of wings in the latter imagery calls for stress, denoting unusual speed and action. The empire of Greece, more than any of the other empires, was characterized by speed and action—even more than Babylonia. Under Alexander the Great, the borders of Greece were enlarged enormously and with remarkable speed.[6]

Four heads: Because these four heads of the beast are mentioned after the wings, it is logical to take their representation for something regarding the empire which happened after the speedy conquest symbolized by the wings. Since "heads" in Scripture normally represent persons or governments, it is logical further to expect this development to concern some form of fourfold division of government; and this is exactly what did occur after Alexander's death. His vast empire came to be divided among four of his generals: Casander being over the home territory of Greece and Macedonia; Lysimachus over Thrace and a large part of Asia Minor; Seleucus over Syria and much of the Middle East; and Ptolemy over Egypt. The last two of these divisions, having Palestine between them, became the most significant for biblical history, and provide subject matter particularly for Daniel's fourth revelation, as will be noted. The view that these heads represent the four directions,[7] for stressing the vastness of Alexander's

[6] For historical details, cf. under 8:6-8.
[7] Held, for instance by Young, YPD, p. 146.

empire, must be rejected, because the term "heads," as noted, regularly refers to instruments of leadership, not directions. The four "heads" here conform to the four "horns" of the next chapter (v. 8). *Dominion was given:* This phrase corresponds in meaning to that of 2:39, "which shall rule over all the earth," used in reference to the third division of Nebuchadnezzar's dream-image. The passive use of the verb "was given" is noteworthy, Alexander's dominion having been granted him under the providence of God. It became his, and then his general's, but only because God in His overall supervision of history, saw fit to give it.

7:7. After this I kept looking in the night visions, and, lo, a fourth beast, dreadful and terrible and exceedingly strong; and it had great iron teeth. It was devouring and breaking in pieces and stamping the residue with its feet, and differed from all the beasts which were before it; and it had ten horns.

In the night visions: This phrase is preceded by the same words as used similarly in verse six (which see). This added phrase might have been used also in verse six, for it depicts these various presentations of animals as separate visions, though together constituting the one overall vision. *A fourth beast:* The fourth beast differs from the others in not being named. Apparently it did not look like any known animal, probably meaning that no animal was known which could adequately symbolize it. The beast described in Revelation 13: 1-10, which is commonly taken to be parallel in significance to this one, is said to have had features resembling all three animals— leopard, bear, and lion. Since these are the same animals as appear in the earlier part of this vision, the implication is that the fourth beast had characteristics of all three. The outstanding feature of this beast, however, is strength, with all described aspects serving to amplify this quality. The empire symbolized can only be the Roman, that which historically followed the Grecian, and which was truly characterized by strength. Rome also reduplicated within itself many of the characteristics which had been especially true earlier of Babylonia, Medo-Persia, and Greece. More description is given of this beast than of the first three, which means that its significance in the vision is greater. In this it corresponds to the emphasis on the fourth part of Nebuchadnezzar's dream-image. *Dreadful and terrible and exceedingly strong:* The first two verbs are close in meaning, speaking of fearfulness. The beast was one to inspire great fear in the spectator. The third verb gives the reason for this fact: the beast displayed enormous strength. Evidently it was of immense size, showing monstrous legs and body. *Great iron teeth:* Another fear-inspiring aspect was its teeth, which apparently could be seen. They were made of iron, the same metal of which the legs of the dream-image were constituted. Iron also depicts strength.

Devouring . . . breaking . . . stamping: The third fear-inspiring feature concerns the beast's actions. The three verbs used to describe these are participles, indicating continuedness of action. Daniel saw the beast continuing to devour with the iron teeth, to break in pieces all that could be found, and then to stamp with its feet on whatever was left, the residue. All this represents extensive conquest involving enormous destruction of people and property. *Differed from all:* This beast was different from the others, a fact stated also in verse twenty-three. This difference apparently pertained especially to these actions just mentioned, for the word "differed" *(mᵉshannᵉyah)* is also a participle, in parallel with the verbs depicting the actions. It suggests that Rome would make her conquests with greater decisiveness, fearfulness, and terror-inspiring tactics than any of the others. This was true of Rome. Conquest was made at wide range and with the greatest strength and ferocity. Her conquests were more permanent, too; for whereas the other empires had been satisfied with only a loose confederation of countries seized, Rome consolidated and organized for lasting control. Dionysius wrote concerning that time: "It, first and alone of all in all recorded time, made East and West bounds of its sway; and the period of its might is not brief, but such as no other city or kingdom ever had."[8]

It had ten horns: Horns commonly signify kings in Scripture, and it is definitely stated that these do here (cf. v. 24). Since this beast had ten horns, which Daniel saw at the same time, the symbolism is that Rome, at the time depicted, would have ten contemporaneous kings, presumably ruling over the same number of subdivisions of the empire. Various explanations have been suggested. Some expositors, who make this fourth beast representative of the Syrian dominion of the Seleucids (in an attempt to avoid identifying the fourth beast with Rome), find the symbolization in the Seleucid kings which preceded Antiochus Epiphanes, whom they then find pictured in the "little horn" of verse eight. Ten different rulers, however, did not precede this man on the Seleucid throne, and the seven who did were not contemporary, but successive.[9] Another view, which does correctly take the fourth beast as Rome, finds the representation in the numerous small kingdoms into which Rome came to be broken after its demise as an empire,[10] and then seeks the identity of the "little horn" in the papal power. This breaks down, however, in that the pope has never been parallel in position to kings, as a "little horn" could be expected to be with other horns, nor did the papacy

---

[8] Quoted by Pusey, *DP*, p. 129.
[9] Cf. Leupold, *LED*, p. 297, for discussion.
[10] Cf. Barnes, *BD*, pp. 83, 84, for discussion.

ever uproot three kings in establishing itself, as true here for the "little horn" (v. 8). It is also significant that the "little horn" follows in time after the ten kings of the vision, whereas the pope preceded the breakup of Rome into the smaller, petty states.

The correct view can only be that there will be a time still future when the Roman empire will be restored, so that these representations can be true in the manner depicted: a time when ten contemporary kings will rule, among whom another will arise, uprooting three in the process, and then move on to become the head of all. This thought was represented in the earlier dream-image by the ten contemporary toes, symbolizing kings in whose days God would set up a kingdom, which should never be destroyed (2:44). This kingdom, as observed in the discussion of the dream-image, will be Christ's millennial kingdom, to be established still in the future. The thought finds a parallel also in the description of the "beast" of Revelation 17, where again ten horns symbolize ten kings (v. 12). These kings had not yet received power in John's day, but would along with the "beast," who also had not yet appeared (v. 11). The time when they and the "beast" would appear is said to be when they would make war with the Lamb, which means when Christ (the Lamb) returns to deliver the Jews from the power of the "beast" and these kings, just prior to the institution of the millennial kingdom.[11] An extensive gap in time, therefore, is implied here, as in chapter two, and will be again in Daniel's other two times of revelation.

7:8. I was looking at the horns when, lo, another little horn came up among them, and three of the first horns were uprooted before it; and, lo, there were eyes like the eyes of a man in this horn and a mouth speaking great things.

I was looking: This is the fifth instance of this participial construction. *Another little horn:* "Another" distinguishes this horn from the other grown horns, and does not imply the existence of other little horns. "Little" indicates only that this horn started small, as it gradually emerged among the grown horns, not that it remained small; for the context, especially verse twenty, shows that it finally became the greatest of all. The word for "among them" (*bênêhewn*) means literally "between them," indicating further that the other horns were all contemporary, not successive. This means that the new horn must symbolize another king, like the others, only emerging later, though while they still rule. Because the description of this ruler, given in this verse and later in verses twenty-four to twenty-six, corresponds to descriptions of the "beast" of Revelation 13:5-8 and 17:11-14, the two are correctly identified. The one so described is commonly

---

[11] For general discussion, cf. *supra,* chapter two, pp. 70-73.

and properly called the Antichrist, who will be Satan's counterfeit world ruler, trying to preempt the place of God's true world Ruler, Jesus Christ, who will later establish His reign during the millennium. *Three of the first horns were uprooted:* As the "little horn" emerged and grew larger, Daniel saw three of the original ten horns uprooted and displaced; thus leaving a total of eight. This must signify that, when this king comes to power, he takes over control of the kingdoms of three of his predecessors. The word for "uprooted" *(ᵃqar)* connotes a gradual process, where new growth pushes out old. The new king will not take control of all three areas at once, then, but over a period of time. Finally he will become the recognized leader of all (v. 20f.). *Like the eyes of a man:* Eyes are symbolic of insight, intelligence, prudence. The significance here is that the Antichrist will be characterized by unusual mental ability. He will be clever, shrewd, knowledgeable—able to solve problems and give advice, which others will find wise. That the eyes are said to be those of a man may be to indicate that this king will not be more than a man, not a supernatural being, which one otherwise might think. He will be a human king, though a remarkable one. *Mouth speaking great things:* This person will be a boaster, especially in speaking against God (cf. vv. 25; 11:36; Rev. 13:5, 6). He will have outstanding ability, but he will know it and boast of it, vaunting himself against God and even claiming to be greater than God (11:36).

7:9. I kept looking until thrones were placed and the Ancient of Days took a seat, whose garment was white as snow and the hair of His head like pure wool. His throne was flames of fire, and its wheels burning fire.

I kept looking: This is the sixth instance of this phrase. *Thrones were placed:* Then Daniel saw thrones being put in place, indicating a change of scene from that involving the beasts. A courtroom was made ready for the dispensing of judgment, as proper seating was arranged. The translation of KJV "to cast down" these thrones, suggesting the destruction of thrones already existent (thrones of the beasts described), misses the point. It is true that the word for "placed" *(rᵉma')* means "to cast," but in the sense of *locating* or *placing,* not destroying. The time in future history when this scene of judgment will be enacted must follow the time of rule by the Antichrist, which means at the close of the Great Tribulation period, though prior to the establishment of Christ's millennial rule (presented in v. 14). *Ancient of Days:* This phrase *('aṭṭîq yômîn)* refers to one who is old in age. It is used only in this chapter (vv. 9, 13, 22). The indication of age is likely a finite representation of eternalness, because the One so presented can only be God Himself, seen here as Judge of the earth, particularly of the empires symbolized in the four beasts (cf.

Ps. 9:5; 29:10; Isa. 28:6). Since the Ancient of Days took no more than one of the thrones placed, question remains as to who took the others. The answer may be that these are angels, the heavenly throng who do the bidding of God (Heb. 1:14). Perhaps they are not mentioned as such since they do not act here except as passive observers. God is alone Judge. *Garment was white ... and the hair:* Whiteness regularly denotes purity and truth (Isa. 1:18; Rev. 3:5; 4:4; 19:8, 11). Both the garment and the hair of the Judge were white. The garment was the long outer robe (Rev. 1:13). The whiteness of the hair was a further indication of the age and maturity of the Judge. Christ, described in Revelation 1:14, is seen similarly. *Throne was flames of fire, and its wheels burning fire:* Daniel saw the throne on which the Judge sat as fiery flames; and he saw wheels, on which apparently the throne was designed to move, suggesting universality of authority, to be the same. Fire is often associated with God (cf. Exod. 3:2; 19:18; Deut. 4:24; 9:3; Ps. 18:8; 50:3; Ezek. 1:4; Heb. 12:29; Rev. 4:5). Here it seems to depict God's majesty and authority in bringing judgment.

7:10. A river of fire was flowing and coming forth from before Him; a thousand thousands served Him and a myriad myriads stood before Him; the court sat and the books were opened.

Was flowing and coming forth: The two verbs used are participles, and they depict a river of fire continuing to flow from before the Ancient of Days as Daniel watches. Not only were the throne and wheels composed of fire, then, but also this river, running from before the Ancient of Days. The significance is to stress further the idea of judgment flowing from God upon wickedness, especially here upon the beast and the little horn. *Thousand thousands ... myriad myriads:* The words for "myriad myriads" are often translated "ten thousand times ten thousand." They come from the root *rᵉbab,* meaning "to be great." From the fact that those referred to by both sets of numbers are engaged in serving and standing before God, their identification with angels is made clear. A similar immense number of angels is mentioned in Revelation 5:11 (cf. Deut. 33:2; Job 25:3; Ps. 68:17; Heb. 12:22). The number of God's angels is vast, then, and they were seen here by Daniel surrounding the throne of God, ready to do His bidding in any detail. Their presence seemed to be calculated to add to the atmosphere of majesty and authority for the judgment to be meted out. *The court sat:* This reads, literally, "the judgment sat." This is simply to say that the situation was ready for the business at hand. *The books were opened:* The Bible speaks frequently of books kept by God in connection with the status of men on earth (cf. Ex. 32:32; Isa. 65:6; Dan. 12:1; Lk. 10:20). The particular thought here concerns books in which deeds are recorded, as in Revelation 20:12; especially the works of the four beasts and the little horn.

7:11-12. I kept looking, then, because of the voice of the great words that the horn was speaking; I kept looking until the beast was killed, and its body was destroyed and given to the burning of fire. As for the rest of the beasts, their dominion was taken away, but a lengthening of life had been given to them for a time and a season.

I kept looking: The seventh and eighth instances of this phrase occur here. The eighth seems to be a repetition of the seventh, the thought intended having been broken by the inserted causal note. *Because of the voice:* The word for "because" is *min,* meaning "from," but here it means "from reason of" or "due to." Some expositors take it to mean "from" in the sense of "from the time of the voice of the great words," thus seeing the verse as indicating the duration of Daniel's looking, namely, from the time that the horn began to speak until the slaying of the beast in judgment. Daniel began observing the vision, however, long before the horn even appeared. The thought, rather, is that, as Daniel was looking, the matter which impressed him especially was the boastful speaking of the horn; and, accordingly, he kept looking to see what manner of judgment the Ancient of Days would mete out to such an one. *Until the beast was killed:* The pronouncement of judgment is implied, though not mentioned directly, because this death of the beast constitutes the execution of the judgment. The books, when opened, revealed that death was deserved, and death was the sentence. The one beast in view here, since the others are in view in the next verse, is the fourth, the Roman empire. More particularly, it is the restored form of the Roman empire, because a major reason for the judgment, implied by the preceding element of the verse, is the boastful speaking of the little horn. Thus, further evidence is supplied that the judgment pictured is that of restored Rome and her last king, the Antichrist, which will transpire at the close of the Great Tribulation (Zech. 14:1-4; Rev. 19:17-21). Some expositors have noted a possible conflict here with passages (such as Matt. 25:31-46; John 5:22; Rev. 19:11-16) which depict Christ, rather than God the Father, as Judge of the Antichrist and his followers. Accordingly, some (Gaebelein, for instance[12]) identify the Ancient of Days in this passage with Christ; but this cannot be, for verse thirteen tells of Christ coming to the Ancient of Days for the reception of the kingdom. The answer to the difficulty is that, though Christ is the immediate Agent in providing the sentences for those judged, God the Father is the One who prescribes the sentence. Either One, then, may be correctly so desig-

[12] GD, p. 77.

nated, and the context (in view of vv. 13, 14) in this instance calls
for the Father to be the One in mind. *Its body was destroyed:* The
antecedent of the pronoun is clearly the fourth beast, and not merely
the little horn. This means that a destruction of the revived empire
will be effected as a result of the Ancient of Day's judgment. Since
the little horn is a part of the beast's body, this includes his destruction also. According to Revelation 19:20 this destruction comes when
he is cast alive into the lake of fire, following Christ's coming in power
to overthrow his army, assembled in the valley of Jehoshaphat (Joel
3:12; Zech. 14:1-4). The final phrase of this verse, "given to the
burning of fire," may indeed be a special reference to this punishment
of him.

As for the rest of the beasts: Attention is now given to the other
three beasts: the lion (Babylon), the bear (Medo-Persia), and the
leopard (Greece). Daniel's vision has revealed their respective characteristics, but not the nature of their end of existence. Now that
the end of the fourth beast has been noted, it is appropriate to tell
of their decease in comparison with his. Because their end is not
related until this late point in the vision, some expositors identify
these beasts with the seven other horns, left after the rise of the
little horn; but this cannot be correct, because the whole fourth beast,
including all his horns, has been destroyed in the preceding verse.
The likely reason why the destruction of the fourth beast is described
prior to that of the first three beasts is to give emphasis to the importance of the fourth beast, and also to provide appropriate contrast between his end and theirs. *Their dominion was taken away:* No
contrast is indicated by this phrase. It says only that each of the earlier
empires has ceased. Some expositors believe that, since this cessation
is not stated until this point in the vision, the three beasts have somehow remained in the vision, only having moved into the background.
This is doubtful, however, for historically the empires did not remain
in existence after being respectively supplanted. *A lengthening of life:*
This is the contrast intended. Whereas the fourth empire and its closing ruler were fully destroyed at the time of this divine judgment, the
other three had been given an extension of time. That is, when each
of the previous three had been brought to an end by the beginning
of its respective successor, it had continued on in some sense that was
not true for the fourth. The sense in which this had been true is
suggested by a comparison with Nebuchadnezzar's dream of the image.
In the dream, the great stone, signifying Christ's kingdom, destroyed
the entire image at one time, and not only its feet and toes which
it specifically struck. As noted in the comments on this aspect of the
dream (cf. 2:44, 45), the empires prior to the Roman continued to
exist in their respective successors, in that their people and culture
were absorbed into them. It is logical, now, to see this same sense of

continuation of empire as the thought conveyed by the present verse. Each of the three previous empires would be continued, by this reduplication of self in people and culture, in their respective successors; but the fourth would not be. This contrast for the fourth is understandable, for the rule succeeding it will be the millennial reign of Christ, which will not absorb Rome's people and culture, with all their deficient, degenerate features, but will be a new, unique rule—perfect, righteous, and equitable in every way (Isa. 11:1-9). *A time and a season:* This phrase provides an indefinite manner by which to refer to the extent of "lengthening of life" given to each of the prior empires, each being different as to this "lengthening" according to its place in history. Each of the two words, "time" *(zᵉman)* and "season" *('iddan),* refers to a period of time; the first normally being the more general of the two, with the second often denoting an appointed time. Here, however, they seem to be used quite synonymously, as also in 2:21.

7:13, 14. I kept looking in the visions of the night, and, lo, One like a son of man was coming with the clouds of heaven; indeed, to the Ancient of Days He came and was presented before Him. Then to Him was given dominion and glory and a kingdom that all peoples, nations, and languages should pay reverence to Him. His dominion is a dominion of a long time that shall not pass away, and His kingdom one that shall not be destroyed.

I kept looking: This is the ninth instance of the expression. *One like a son of man:* With the sentence of death meted out to the world kingdoms, the vision shows the entrance of a new figure, one said to be like "a son of man." The term "son of man" was later often used by Christ as a name for Himself (cf. Matt. 8:20; 9:6;10:23; 11:19; et al.), and especially in eschatological contexts (cf. Matt. 16:27, 28; 19:28; 24:30; 25:31; et al). Because Christ so frequently couched His language in Old Testament terminology, and since this instance is the only time the phrase is used in the Old Testament with possible reference to Christ, the likelihood is that He had this text in mind when He used the term for Himself. He was identifying Himself with this One whom Daniel saw. That He is said here to be *like* a son of man, has a significance parallel to that of the prior kingdoms being said to be *like* beasts. Those kingdoms were "beastly" in character, but His will be "manly"; that is, humanlike, in all noble, proper features. Christ, when He comes to rule, will come in human form, to rule as a human king (though all the while divine), but with all the perfections of humanity as first created by God. An opposing view finds the term "son of man" representing the people of God, Israel; taking support from statements later in the chapter to the effect that "saints of the Most High will take the kingdom" (v. 18, cf.

22 and 27).[13] This must be rejected, however, for several reasons. First, Christ so significantly used the designation "son of man" for Himself, as noted; and also the term is used for Him in Revelation 1:13, when He is seen by John on Patmos. Second, the person called "son of man" here is ascribed the status of deity in being said to come "with the clouds of heaven," terminology used regarding Christ in Matthew 24:30; 26:64; Mark 13:26, and especially Revelation 1:7 where the preposition employed (*meta,* "with") corresponds to that used in the verse here. Third, according to verse forty-one, "all peoples, nations, and languages" pay reverence to this One, making an identification of Him with a further collection of people quite unlikely. Fourth, even Montgomery admits that "the earliest interpretation of 'the Son of Man' is Messianic,"[14] it being so used numerous times in the parable of Enoch (37-71) where dependence on Daniel 7 is quite clear. Fifth, the statements of verses eighteen, twenty-two, and twenty-seven are not given as aspects of the interpretation of the symbolism, but only as explanatory items in connection with interpretative aspects, and therefore should not be taken as determinative of the meaning in verse thirteen. Sixth, the idea of Christ being the King fits the overall picture of the millennial period, as set forth in the parallel aspect of Nebuchadnezzar's dream (2:44, 45) and elsewhere in Scripture (cf. Ps. 2:6; Isa. 9:6, 7; 11:3-5; Mic. 4:1-7; 5:2-5; Zech. 14:9, 16, 17; Luke 1:32, 33). *Was coming with the clouds of heaven:* The word for "was coming" is a participle depicting Christ, as Daniel looked on, moving into the courtroom before the Ancient of Days. The phrase "with the clouds of heaven," is a mark of divine authority and majesty as noted. That the preposition "with" is used, and not "in" or "upon," is of no significance, being merely less definite in nature. *To the Ancient of Days . . . was presented:* This grand Person not only entered the scene, but was presented before the Ancient of Days, apparently by attendants. The distinction between the two Persons is thus made very clear: the one being Christ the Son, and the other God the Father. The Son was presented that He might receive the Father's gift; namely, the worldwide kingdom (cf. Ps. 2:6-9).

Dominion and glory and a kingdom: The gift bestowed is now identified under three aspects, all referring to this kingdom. The first, "dominion" *(shaltan),* refers to His ruling authority; the second, "glory" *(yᵉqar),* speaks of the honor that would accompany that authority; and the third, "kingdom" *(malk̲û),* designates the organized form of His government. Christ is granted all the features of absolute rule, in parallel with that exercised by rulers of the preceding empires. Some expositors explain the manner of Christ's rule in terms

---

[13] This view is held, for instance by Montgomery, who includes an extensive discussion, MICC, pp. 317-24.
[14] MICC, p. 320.

of His spiritual dominion in the hearts of believers, rather than a literal rule on earth. In support of this explanation, the argument is made that, since the whole vision is symbolic in nature, it should not be thought strange to make Christ's reign symbolic. This overlooks the fact, however, that symbolism is employed in connection with the four earlier empires also, but still the empires themselves were literal, earthly periods of rule. It should be recognized that the idea of ruling kingdoms on earth is the central thought of the overall vision. Symbolism, then, should be seen only in matters which describe these kingdoms, and not in respect to the kingdoms themselves. The contrast intended between the preceding empires and that of Christ concerns only the type and efficiency of rule. The four earlier empires all failed in their periods of dominion, but now one would exist which would not fail. The world would at last have a time of perfect rule, unmarred by sin and its blight on the part of the King. *Peoples, nations, and languages:* These are the same formulistic terms that are used in 3:4, 7, 29, etc. (which see). As noted in chapter three, they are used to indicate all the people of whatever domain might be in mind. Here they indicate all the world, for Christ is to rule all the world. The earlier empires were called world empires also, for they included the advanced, significant world of the day. At the time of Christ's rule, however, all the world will have to be included to carry through the same idea. The word for "should pay reverence" *(pᵉlaḥ)* is often translated "should serve." There is good reason, however, for finding its basic meaning to concern *reverence* rather than *service,* taking it to be related to the Hebrew verbs *yare',* meaning "to fear," and *paḥad,* meaning "to be in awe."[15] This more basic meaning fits best here. *Dominion . . . shall not pass away:* The thought is to bring a contrast with the passing, contingent nature of the previous empires. The kingdom given to the Son will not be of this kind, but will be lasting, self-contained. The exact length of Christ's rule on earth is 1000 years (Rev. 20:1-6); evidently the precise duration here in mind. The word for "a long time" is *'alam,* which may mean either "everlasting" or "long time," and is best taken in the latter sense here, since Christ's kingdom is being compared with the previous earthly empires. At the same time, it may be remembered that His millennial rule is continued on a heavenly plane all through eternity, and in this sense is also "everlasting." The main point here, however, is not duration, but strength, self-containment, noncontingency, as noted in the words "shall not be destroyed."[16]

C. THE INTERPRETATION (vv. 15-28)

The vision still continues in the latter part of the chapter, but its

[15] Cf. BDB, p. 1108.
[16] Cf. *supra,* chapter two, p. 73, footnote 11.

intent changes. The latter half gives the interpretation of the former half, as a conversation now transpires between Daniel, who inserts himself into the vision at this point, and an attendant angel.

7:15, 16. As for me, Daniel, my spirit was distressed in the midst of my body, and the visions of my head were troubling me. I approached one of the attendants and asked him concerning the certainty of all this. So he responded to me and made me know the interpretation of the things.

As for me, Daniel: As Daniel came to this point of change in the vision, he wished to call attention to himself in noting his own re-action to it. *My spirit was distressed:* Daniel's reaction was one of distress, not so much because of wonderment—he continued to be troubled even after the meaning had been explained (v. 28)—but because of the momentous events and calamities set forth. The word for "was distressed" *(k^era')* means literally "to abbreviate, contract," designating bitter grief. The word for "body" *(niḏneh)* means literally "sheath," the body being viewed as containing the spirit as a scabbard contains the sword. *Were troubling me:* Daniel's spirit was distressed because the factors of the vision disturbed him. The word for "were troubling" *(b^ehal)* speaks of *alarm.* Daniel was alarmed by what was predicted.

One of the attendants: The word for "attendants" (root, *qûm*) means literally "standers," referring to those standing near the Ancient of Days; that is, angels (v. 10). Daniel saw himself moving personally into the scene to inquire of one of the angels as to the meaning of all these matters. *The certainty of all this:* The word for "certainty" *(yatstsîḇ)* means that which is *sure, true.* Daniel could have guessed as to the meaning of much of the vision, especially in view of what Nebuchadnezzar's dream had meant, but he wanted to know the certain interpretation, complete and authoritative. *The interpretation of the things:* The word for "interpretation" *(p^eshar)* is used here, giving further indication of that concerning which Daniel wanted certainty. The angel apparently was quite willing to oblige Daniel and began readily to give the appropriate explanations, which now follow.

7:17, 18. These four great beasts are four kings, who shall arise from the earth. But the saints of the Most High shall receive the kingdom, and possess the kingdom for an age, even for an age of ages.

These four great beasts: The literal reading of verse seventeen is unusual: "These great beasts, which are four, four kings shall arise from the earth." In paraphrase, it means: "As for the great beasts, which specifically are four in number, they represent four kings which shall arise from the earth." The angel thus began logically with attention to the four beasts. That he said the beasts represent "kings" *(melek)* rather than "kingdoms" *(malkû),* when later (v. 23) he said that the fourth beast represents a "kingdom," shows how interchangeable the two ideas are in the vision. The first beast, the lion, was noted earlier to represent a king, Nebuchadnezzar, whereas the other three beasts were seen to represent kingdoms. With the last kingdom period, the representation was seen to be the King once more, namely Christ, who will be supremely important at that time. *Who shall arise from the earth:* The form of the verb "shall arise" (root, *qûm*) is imperfect, designating incomplete action. Some expositors have objected that this fact makes impossible the idea that the first beast represents Babylon, particularly Nebuchadnezzar, since he was already dead at the time of the vision. The history of the four empires, however, is taken as a unit, which is incomplete until the last empire is destroyed, and the form of the verb can only be imperfect, even though one aspect of the history has begun well before. "From the earth" does not contradict "from the sea" of verse three, but supplements its thought; indicating that, in its symbolic meaning (cf. v. 3), the latter phrase included the overall concept that these kingdoms were of earthly origin.

Saints of the Most High: The word for "saints" *(qaddîshîn)* means *holy ones,* the same term as used in 4:13, 23, though there in reference to an angel. The term has not been used in this vision before, which suggests that those designated have played no part until this point. Now introduced, they are said to receive the kingdom, which must be the kingdom just given to the Son of Man, since an evident contrast is intended with the four kingdoms of the beasts. Because the Son of Man is King of this realm, these must be the subjects. From the rest of Scripture, they may be identified as of two groups: those from the world at large who have been made holy by faith in Christ as Savior, and the God-fearing Jews who will have been refined by suffering at the hands of the Antichrist (cf. Zech. 13:8, 9) and thus made ready to receive Christ as their true Messiah-King at His coming to deliver them. The word for "Most High" is a plural form, in contrast to several employments of the singular (cf. 3:26; 4:2, 17, 24, etc.), but it should be taken as merely a plural of excellence, for the reference is unquestionably to God, just as in the singular instances. *Shall receive the kingdom:* These saints receive the kingdom, not in the sense of kings (true only for the Son of Man), but in being permitted to enter into and enjoy this time of perfect rule. Those who are not saints, according to Matthew 25:31-46, will not be given this privilege. *Possess the kingdom:* The word for "possess" *(hᵉsan)* carries the thought of *authority of ownership.* The kingdom will be owned by the saints. The significant thought is that, rather than the wicked being in places of leadership, with Satan at large to guide and inspire (cf. 2 Cor. 4:4; Eph. 2:2; 1 Pet. 5:8; Rev.

12:9), the saints of God will be in the ascendancy, while "the earth shall be full of the knowledge of the LORD" (Isa. 11:9), and Satan is bound in the "bottomless pit" (Rev. 20:3). Implied is the fact that during the time of the prior kingdoms, the opposite will have been true. *For an age, even for an age of ages:* This combination of the preposition "for" *('ad)* and "age" *('alam)* is unique, not only for the Aramaic portions of the Old Testament, but also for the Hebrew. The thought of the phrase obviously is superlative, and it is accordingly often translated "for ever, even for ever and ever." Since it is here applied to Christ's millennial rule, however, a problem arises for this translation, because that period is of finite duration, though very long. Young, in fact, uses this as an argument against the idea of the kingdom here in view being the future dominion of Christ on earth.[17] That it can be translated as above, however, indicating only a long finite period, is well evidenced by the fact that its nearest Hebrew equivalent, "unto ages of perpetuity" *('ad 'ôlmê 'ad),* is used in reference to God's people Israel in a finite context (Isa. 45:17).[18] The reason for using the superlative form of expression is to stress the length of the saints' kingdom, with no destruction having to be feared, in contrast to that of the wicked during the prior empires.

7:19, 20. Then I desired to know the truth concerning the fourth beast, which was different from all the others, exceedingly dreadful, with teeth of iron and claws of brass, which was devouring, breaking in pieces, and stamping the residue with its feet; and concerning the ten horns which were on its head, and the other one which came up before which three fell, even the horn which had eyes and a mouth speaking great things, whose appearance was sturdier than its fellows.

I desired to know the truth: Literally, "I desired the certainty." Daniel had already (v. 16) asked for "certainty" in general, and the angel had told him concerning the beasts. Daniel apparently had been satisfied, even though the explanation regarding the first three beasts was brief. But here he asked for "certainty" regarding the fourth beast in particular, on which greater stress had fallen and concerning which his interest was more intense. *Claws of brass:* In identifying this beast, Daniel repeats much of the description given earlier, but this one item is now added. It fits well into the general idea of strength possessed by the beast (v. 7), and fills out the overall idea of the beast stamping the residue.

Concerning the ten horns ... and the other one: Daniel asked in particular also in respect to the horns and the little horn that came

---

[17] YPD, p. 157. Cf. *supra,* p. 194 for pertinent discussion.
[18] Another superlative Hebrew equivalent is "from an age, unto an age" *(min-'olam wᵉad-'olam),* and it is used likewise in reference to man in time (Jer. 7:7; 25:5), as well as to eternal matters.

up later. *Sturdier than its fellows:* The phrase for "sturdier than" is the adjective "great" *(rab)* followed by the preposition *min* to express the comparative degree. The meaning is that the "other" or "little" horn looked greater or sturdier than the earlier horns. Though this horn appeared later and was smaller at first, it did not remain inferior in size, but became even more imposing than the other horns. The last king of the restored Roman empire, the Antichrist, will become the leading king of that time, having displaced three kings and gaining leadership thereby over the rest.

7:21, 22. I kept looking and this horn made war with the saints and prevailed over them, until the Ancient of Days came and judgment was given for the saints of the Most High and the time came when the saints possessed the kingdom.

I kept looking: This is the tenth use of the expression. This time, however, it carries a backward reference to that point in the vision when the little horn still ruled (v. 8), prior to his destruction (v. 11). A paraphrase would be: "As I was looking at the little horn in his time of power, I saw him make war with the saints and prevail over them." *Made war with the saints:* For some reason this detail was omitted earlier in the account when the little horn was first introduced (v. 8). There his appearance was set forth, but without indicating much as to his activity. Now the indication is that he makes war with the saints—said as well of the "beast" in Revelation 13 (v. 7), which also represents the Antichrist. The thought is that saints will be opposed by this person so symbolized, and will be made to suffer. Since the Antichrist will oppose especially the Jews in Palestine during the latter half of the Tribulation (Dan. 9:26, 27; Rev. 12:1-6, 13-17), the primary reference must be to them, but because of the kind of person he will be, all saints of God clearly will experience this opposition to some degree. While the Antichrist rules, life will not be easy for those who love God. *Prevailed over them:* The word for "prevailed" (root, y^ekal) carries the basic idea of "capability." The thought is that the little horn will be able to make good in his war with the saints. In respect to the Jews during the Tribulation, he will be able to do away with two-thirds of their number (Zech. 13:8, 9) and to cause Jerusalem to fall to his army (Zech. 14:1, 2). In respect to Gentiles, he will be able to kill many of them also (Rev. 13:7-10) and cause economic hardship (Rev. 13:16, 17).

Until the Ancient of Days came: The little horn had his way and continued to prevail over saints until the appearance of the Ancient of Days, God the Father. *Judgment was given:* As indicated in verses ten to twelve, the Ancient of Days, when He came, pronounced and executed the sentence of death upon the little horn. Judgment was meted out in behalf of those persecuted. The little horn will be assigned to the Lake of Fire (Rev. 19:20). *Saints possessed the kingdom:* In contrast to the horrible end of the Antichrist, the saints will be ushered into the glorious kingdom age (cf. v. 18).

7:23, 24. **Thus he said: The fourth beast will be a fourth kingdom on earth, which will be different from all other kingdoms, and it will devour the whole earth and will stamp upon it and crush it. As for the ten horns, out of this kingdom ten kings will arise, and another will arise after them, and will be different from the former ones; and he will put down three kings.**

Thus he said: The angel spoke again. Daniel's question continued through four verses (19-22) and the angel here gave answer. Only Daniel and this one angel were active in this part of the vision. *Will be a fourth kingdom:* As has been noted, the ideas of "king" and "kingdom" are used interchangeably in the vision. Here "kingdom" is used, whereas "king" was in verse seventeen, in regard to what was symbolized by the beasts. "Kingdom" is the more appropriate term for the fourth kingdom, because Rome did not have any one outstanding ruler, such as Nebuchadnezzar had been for Babylonia. As has been noted, this fourth kingdom was unique in having two periods of existence: the one of early history, and the one of future time. It is well at this point, in view of coming discussion, to show reasons for identifying this kingdom, whether as to its first or second aspects, with that symbolized by the beasts of Revelation 13:1-10 and 17:1-18. First, that the two beasts of Revelation 13 and 17 are the same is argued by the facts that: (a) they both have seven heads and ten horns (13:1; 17:3); (b) they both are violently opposed to God (13:1, 6; 17:14); and (c) they both effect persecution on God's saints (13:7; 17:6). Second, that the kingdom represented in Daniel 7 is the same as the kingdom represented by the beasts of either Revelation 13 or 17 is argued by: (a) that the symbolism of the lion, bear, and leopard is repeated in the beast of Revelation 13 (v. 2), as though this beast, like the fourth of Daniel 7, recapitulated, in some real sense, the Babylonian, Medo-Persian, and Greek empires; (b) that all three are opposed to God, blaspheming His name (Dan. 7:25; Rev. 13:1, 6; 17:3); (c) that all three beasts have ten horns; (d) that both the beast of Revelation 13 (vv. 5, 6) and Daniel 7 (vv. 7, 25) speak great things against God; (e) that all three wear out the saints (Dan. 7:25; Rev. 13:7; 17:6); and (f) that both the beast of Revelation 13 (v. 5) and of Daniel 7 (v. 25) maintain great power for three and one-half years. Because these three beasts all symbolize the same person, inter-reference can be made among them in the following discussions. *Devour the whole earth:* The fourth beast was said in its earlier description to devour (v. 7), but now the extent of this activity is added: "the whole earth." In the time of the first phase of Rome, this was fulfilled in that the significant, culturally-advanced portion of the earth did come under its control, but it will be fulfilled in greater degree in future Rome in that indeed all the world will, in some sense,[19] come under its domination (Rev. 13:8).

Out of this kingdom ten kings shall arise: Now the direct symbolism of the horns is made. They represent ten kings of this Roman kingdom. Since they all grow at the same time, with the little horn emerging from among them, it must be that these kings all rule at the same time and while the Roman empire still exists. This is indicated also by the ten kings of Revelation 17 (v. 12), who rule for one hour with the beast. Since no period from early Rome reveals this to have occurred, it must be that the empire will be restored (cf. v. 7). Young[20] argues against this idea of a restored empire, stating that it is not true to the symbolism of the vision. He says that to symbolize this, the beast should die and be revived, whereas in actual fact the horns grow from the beast's head while he is still alive, not having died. In response, three matters may be noted. First, Young's explanation does not fit the symbolism either. As a matter of fact, no explanation fits in every respect, for the reason that symbolic illustrations normally do not intend to represent all details of the greater truth being symbolized. Young believes that the horns represent countries which develop after the demise of the Roman empire, but the symbolism shows the horns growing from the beast's head while it is still alive, with the beast being finally judged and killed only after the little horn has had his day. Second, though Young's contention that this beast does not experience a restoration himself is correct, the parallel beast of Revelation 17 does, verse eight including the words "the beast that was, and is not, and yet is" (given twice, in fact). The same thought seems to be implied regarding the beast of Revelation 13, for there one of the beast's heads is "wounded to death" and then healed (v. 2). Third, this restoration idea is involved also in the remaining three visions of Daniel, as will appear (cf. especially 8:23; 9:26, 27; 11:36), and, consequently, it should not be thought strange if it is implied in this first one. It was implied as well in Nebuchadnezzar's dream of the image; cf. discussion under 2:42. *Another shall arise . . . and shall be different:* Reference is to the little horn, with the notation that he "shall be different from the former" horns. This difference consists in matters now to be cited, the first of which is included in this verse; namely, that he shall put down three kings on coming to power (cf. v. 8).

7:25. And he shall speak words against the Most High, and shall

[19] The degree of the Antichrist's authority that will be attained throughout the world is not clear. This authority, whatever its degree, will only be achieved after his victories set forth in Dan. 11:40-45.

[20] YPD, pp. 148-50.

wear out the saints of the Most High; and he shall think to change times and law; and they shall be given into his hand for a time, times, and half a time.

Against the Most High: The little horn's differences continue. The word for "against" is literally "at the side of" *(le'tsad)*, indicating that the little horn will seek to raise himself as high as God and make pronouncements accordingly, which implies making them contrary to what God would make (cf. 11:36, 37; 2 Thess. 2:4). The thought is an enlargement of the closing element of verse seven. *Wear out the saints:* The word for "wear out" *(b^ela')* means literally just that, being used in its corresponding Hebrew form in reference to the wearing out of garments (Deut. 8:4), sacks, wineskins, and sandals (Josh. 9:4, 5). To wear out saints means to harass them continually so that life becomes a wretched existence. Injustice, seizure of property, and outright physical persecution could well be some specific measures in view. These saints are the same as those of verses eighteen and twenty-two. *Change times and law:* With no indication to the contrary, it is logical to take the words for "times" *(zimnîn)* and "law" *(dat)* in a general sense, referring to God's laws of the universe, both moral and natural (Gen. 1:14; 17:21; 18:14). A desire to interfere with and change these laws will be one way in which the Antichrist will seek to oppose God. As an illustration of the type of change that might be tried, Leupold points to attempts made, during the time of the French Revolution, to establish a ten-day work week in place of God's seven-day week.[21] Note, however, that the Antichrist will only "think" (root, *s^ebar*) to make this change, indicating that he will not succeed, any more than the men mentioned by Leupold did. It should be added, however, that he will be able, through his helper, the False Prophet (Rev. 13:11-15; 19:20), to perform many other remarkable feats, which will be enough to convince people of his alleged divinity (2 Thess. 2:9-11; Rev. 13:15). The view that these "times" and "law" refer specifically to the Mosaic Law and special time-designations therein must be rejected. That view is normally based on the erroneous assumption that the little horn is to be identified with Antiochus Epiphanes (making the fourth beast to be the Syrian division of Alexander's empire; cf. discussion under verse seven), who did seek to change Mosaic regulations (cf. 8:9-12).

They shall be given . . . for a time, times, and half a time: The antecedent of "they" is best taken to be the saints of the Most High, who, then, will be given into this wicked king's hand for a period called "time, times, and half a time." The duration of this period is much disputed; but several reasons favor the idea of three and one-half years. First, the placing of a singular (time), a plural (times), and a half

---

[21] LED, pp. 324, 25.

(half a time) together makes sense only if these refer to a total of three and one-half of some unit of time (day, week, month, year), a conclusion to which most expositors agree. Second, that this unit of time must be a year follows from a comparison with parallel passages, of which there are several. (1) It has been seen that seven "times" in 4:16 (cf. 4:23, 25) means seven years, and the word for "year" there is the same as here. (2) The Hebrew equivalent of the same phrase, "time, times, and half a time," is used in 12:7 and is best taken to be approximately equal to the 1,290 days of 12:11 and the 1,335 days of 12:12, both of which are just over three and one-half years. (3) The beast of Revelation 13:1-10, which is correctly identified with this fourth beast of Daniel's vision (cf. discussion at v. 23), and particularly with the "little horn" phase of its dominion, is said definitely to have maintained great power for forty-two months (v. 5), which is the same as three and one-half years. (4) The same phrase, "time, and times, and half a time," is used in Revelation 12:14, relative to the "woman" (best understood to symbolize Israel) who was persecuted by the "dragon" (best taken as Satan working through the Antichrist); and the duration of time signified is identified in the chapter (v. 6) as 1,260 days, which again is three and one-half years. (5) The rationale for a period of this length may be taken from Daniel 9:26, 27 (which see), where the Antichrist breaks covenant with Israel at the midpoint of a week of years, which means at the three-and-one-half-year mark, after which he brings severe persecution on the nation for the last half of the week, a period of three and one-half years, called in Matthew 24:21 the Great Tribulation. In summary, the picture of this final ruling king of Rome is as follows: he is a boastful person, who tries to act like God, making himself equal to God as he utters blasphemous words and tries to change God's laws of the universe; he works severe hardship on God's people (especially Jews in Israel, particularly after breaking covenant with them) for a continuing time of three and one-half years, the last half of the Tribulation period.

7:26, 27. Then the court will sit and his dominion will be taken away, to destroy and to consume it forever. And the kingdom and the dominion and the greatness of the kingdoms under all the heaven will be given to the people of the saints of the Most High; whose kingdom is an age-long kingdom, and all dominions will serve and obey them.

The court will sit: This is the same expression as in verse ten, which suggests that the same occasion is in view. The Ancient of Days is Judge, and will be ready to pronounce sentence on the little horn. This means that the "time, times, and half a time" will be finished when the little horn has had his day of power. The Tribulation period thus will have ended and appropriate judgments will be necessary before the glorious millennial age is entered (cf. vv. 9-11). *His dominion:* The antecedent of "his" is the little horn, the subject of verses twenty-four and twenty-five. When the subject of judgment was treated in verse eleven above, the beast was in view, though particularly at the time when the little horn existed. Here, however, the little horn is in view for himself. In his time, the whole beast will be judged, which means that Rome will no longer head an empire, but the little horn will be judged in a special sense. He will lose his dominion and be cast alive into the Lake of Fire (Rev. 19:20). This is significant especially because the Antichrist will have been Satan's substitute king—substitute for God's King, Christ, who is destined to be the true world Ruler. The false will be displaced so that the True can be installed. *To destroy and to consume it:* Because nothing exists in the Aramaic text corresponding to "it," the antecedent of which is "dominion," "dominion" may be thought of either as subject or object of the two infinitives used. If taken as subject, the thought is that the little horn's dominion "to destroy and to consume" will be taken away; which is a suitable idea. Most expositors favor taking it as object, however, and probably correctly, since the thought then fits the idea of the extent of judgment meted out at this time. That is, not only will the little horn's dominion be taken from him, but the dominion itself will be *destroyed* and *consumed,* and that forever, so that no other ruler will ever be able to assume it after the little horn. In other words, the Roman empire as such will fully cease to exist when the little horn is judged. The two words "destroy" *(sh⁽ᵉ⁾mad)* and "consume" *(⁽ᵃ⁾bad,* used here in the aphel, meaning "cause to perish") are close in meaning. They may carry a secondary reference to the end of the little horn himself, just noted.

Kingdom ... dominion ... greatness of the kingdoms: These three expressions identify the nature and vastness of the rule now established by Christ in place of the one destroyed. The first two expressions make the identification proper, namely that the new rule will be a kingdom wielding dominion; and the third indicates the vastness of power exercised, saying that it will be "great," will be composed of "kingdoms" (plural), and will extend "under all the heaven." The plural form used in reference to kingdoms may be only a plural of importance, or it may be an indication that there will be divisions in the overall kingdom. The phrase "under all the heavens" shows that it will be world-wide in scope. Arguments were set forth in the discussion under 2:44 that the kingdom thus established, following the overthrow of Rome, will indeed be Christ's earthly, millennial rule, rather than a spiritual kingdom established at His first coming. To those arguments now others may be added. First, in this vision, as in Nebuchadnezzar's dream of chapter two, it is only after the emergence of the ten-horn

204 A COMMENTARY ON DANIEL

kings, and even of the little horn, that any mention of Christ's contrasting kingdom is made, giving the suggestion that it will not come to existence until after their time. This requires a time well after Christ's first appearance, even if the idea of the restoration of Rome is rejected, for Rome continued for some centuries after Christ's first coming. Second, it is only after the destruction of the little horn, the Antichrist, that Christ's kingdom is mentioned; and it is commonly accepted, even by those who identify this kingdom with Christ's spiritual rule, that the Antichrist is still future.[22] Third, verses thirteen, fourteen, and twenty-seven speak clearly of the inauguration of the kingdom of Christ (not its close, as Keil argues[23]) and the verses show that this kingdom will be a glorious rule in which all peoples will serve Christ—something not yet true today, so far as His spiritual rule is concerned, but which will be true when He comes to set up His earthly reign after the demise of the Antichrist (Ezek. 37:23).

Will be given to the ... saints: This is the same thought as in verse eighteen (which see). The phrase "will be given" is more explicit as to how the kingdom will be "received" (as indicated in v. 18) by the saints. The One who gives it, of course, is the Ancient of Days, God the Father. *Whose kingdom is an age-long kingdom:* The antecedent of "whose" is disputed, whether the "people of the saints" or the "Most High"; but the former is more in keeping with the context, especially verse eighteen, where the saints are said to "possess the kingdom for an age"—an idea in parallel with "age-long kingdom" *(malkût 'alam)* here. *All dominions will serve and obey them:* The antecedent of "them" (literally, "him," but the singular is due to the collective noun "people") must be the same as of "whose." The thought is that during the millennial reign of Christ, saints, whether God-fearing Jews returned to Palestine or saved people in the world at large, will be the leading people. The wicked will not lead, as they did during the reign of the four beasts and as they will especially at the time of the little horn. In view of other Scripture, the following may be said more explicitly. In respect to the God-fearing Jews returned to Palestine, they will have accepted Christ as their Messiah-King by this time (when Christ will have just delivered them from the Antichrist's armies [Zech. 14:2-4; Rev. 19:11-21]) and will then, with Him as King, assume the role of the leading nation of the world (Deut. 28:1-14; Isa. 65:17-25) so that all other nations will literally render due respect and honor to them. In respect to saved people in the world at large, the thought is that they will be given positions of influence throughout the world, and have literal service and obedience rendered to them (2 Tim. 2:12; Rev. 5:10; 20:6). A further

[22] For instance, Young, YPD, p. 163.
[23] KDC on Daniel, pp. 269-73.

reason for rejecting the idea of this kingdom being Christ's spiritual rule may be noted at this point. Certainly in the age now existent one does not see the dominions of the world serving and obeying "saints." Furthermore, if one holds that this becomes true only after Christ comes again, at which time the eternal state begins (held by those who hold to the idea of a spiritual kingdom), there is little meaning for saying that dominions serve and obey saints then. During the eternal state, all wicked will be suffering the torment of hell.

7:28. Unto this point is the end of the matter. As for me, Daniel, my thoughts greatly troubled me and the color of my countenance was changed, but I kept the matter in my heart.

Unto this point is the end of the matter: Probably this statement also was spoken by the angel, whose words began in verse twenty-three. He simply stated that with the words of verse twenty-seven the interpretation was closed. *As for me, Daniel:* Daniel reintroduced himself, wishing to add a brief note as to his own reaction to the interpretation given. *My thoughts greatly troubled me:* His reaction was one of distress, as it was earlier, at the close of the vision proper (v. 15). His "thoughts," meaning his understanding of, and reflection upon, what had just been stated, troubled him. The word for "troubled" *(behal)* is the same as used in verse fifteen (which see). Such momentous events, with all these kingdoms rising, persecutions of saints ensuing, punishments resulting, and ruling by saints following, were simply too much for Daniel to absorb and understand without difficulty. *Color of my countenance was changed:* Literally, "my color changed upon me." The word for "color" is the same as that used in 5:6, 9, 10, where it is said that Belshazzar's color was changed in fright. The thought is that Daniel's normal healthy color drained from his face and he became pale, the common result of shock. *I kept the matter in my heart:* Though distressed by the words, Daniel did not put them from his mind. He continued to reflect upon them. He did not reject them, but accepted them fully. He only found it hard to understand and adjust to them. This would take time, and he gained time by keeping them in his heart. His keeping the matter in his heart may also imply that he did not share the vision with anyone. This could have been because he knew of no others who would accept or appreciate it. If his three friends still lived and had been near enough, they would have; but no mention of them is made after chapter three, and Daniel may have been without their company for some time past.

CHAPTER 8

In chapter eight, Daniel relates the second vision God gave to him. The vision concerns a portion of the overall period of time symbolized in the first vision; namely, regarding Medo-Persia and Greece. Reference is made also to the Antichrist of future time in the interpretation of the vision included in the chapter. Once more, animals are used for symbolism, but in place of the bear and leopard, employed in the first vision for the two kingdoms concerned, a two-horned ram and a one-horned goat are used. In this vision also, a little horn appears; but it cannot represent the Antichrist, because it grows from one of four horns, which in turn have replaced the one notable horn of the goat, and this animal with these horns symbolizes Greece of ancient time. This little horn can represent only Antiochus Epiphanes, who served as one of the kings of the Syrian division of Alexander's empire. He is noted as a "little horn," in parallel with the "little horn" of the first vision, because he brought severe persecution on the Jewish people of Palestine in his day, after the pattern of what the Antichrist will do in his day yet future.

It should be noted also that the language used in this chapter reverts to Hebrew, rather than continuing in the Aramaic which has been used since 2:4.[1]

A. THE GENERAL SETTING (vv. 1, 2)

As with the first vision, this second one also has an introduction, which gives the setting, particularly as to time and place.

8:1, 2. In the third year of the reign of King Belshazzar, a vision appeared to me, even to me Daniel, after the one which had appeared to me at the first. And I saw in the vision, and as I beheld, I was in Shushan the fortress which is in the province of Elam; and I saw in the vision, and I was by the river Ulai.

In the third year: The first vision having come in Belshazzar's first

---

[1] For significance, cf. *supra,* Introduction, pp. 18, 19.

year, this one, in his third, came two years later—in 551 B.C., when
Daniel was about sixty-nine years old. This vision, like the prior
one, was given well before the events recorded in chapter five.[2] *A vision
appeared:* The former vision came at night and was a form of dream-
vision, but this one came in the daytime, with no mention of sleep
or of being in bed. *Even to me Daniel:* These words stress the fact
that Daniel received this vision also, and indicate that he felt himself
honored that he should be given another such time of revelation. He
apparently was surprised and thrilled that God should favor him so
highly.

I saw in the vision: This phrase, appearing twice in the verse, calls
attention to two matters of which Daniel became aware as the vision
began: first, that he was in Shushan, and second, that he was by
the river Ulai. The vision has already begun at this point, but Daniel
still gives background information, of which he became aware after its
beginning. *And as I beheld, I was in Shushan the fortress:* Literally,
"and it was when I saw that I was in Shushan the fortress." The word-
ing favors the idea that Daniel was not actually in Shushan, but that
he saw himself in the vision as being there. Shushan (called Susa by
the Greeks) was a city about 230 miles east of Babylon and 120
miles north of the Persian Gulf. At the time of Daniel's vision, it was
simply an important eastern city, but earlier it had been the capital
of Elam, and after the time of Daniel's vision it was made one of the
royal cities of the Medo-Persian empire by Cyrus (Neh. 1:1; Esth.
1:2). The word for "fortress" *(birah)* may be translated "palace," but
probably here it is used to depict the importance of the city as the
former Elamite capital. It was in this city that the famous code of
Hammurabi was found,[3] and also where the beautiful Persian palace,
constructed by Darius Hystaspes, where Esther served as queen, has
been completely uncovered. *Province of Elam:* The history of Elam is
not sufficiently clear to indicate whether it was a province of Babylon
or of Media at this time. Some evidence exists that it had come under
Median control about 596 B.C. The country of Elam had been a power
to the east of Babylonia since before the time of Abraham. Assyria,
however, had reduced it to the status of a province under her domain,
during the reign of Ashurbanipal about 645 B.C., and it seems now
to have had a similar relationship with either Babylonia or Media. The
possibility exits, too, that it was not formally a province of any country,
but that the term for "province" *(mᵉdinah)* is used only generally,
denoting simply a "district." *By the river Ulai:* The word for "river"
('ûbal) used here is rare in the Old Testament, found only in this
chapter (vv. 2, 3, 6). The Ulai, known classically as the Eulaeus, is

---

[2] About twelve years before, cf. *supra,* under 7:1.
[3] It had been seized and taken from Babylon by the Elamites, probably at their
time of dominion over the Babylonians, during the 13th century B.C.

best identified with an artificial canal, about 900 feet wide, which flowed between the Choaspes and the Coprates Rivers, passing close to Shushan on the northeast.

B. THE VISION PROPER (vv. 3-14)

Though Daniel's vision as a whole continues through verse twenty-six, the vision proper is confined to verses three to fourteen, with verses fifteen to twenty-six being given to interpretation.

8:3, 4. I lifted up my eyes and looked, and, lo, a ram was standing beside the river; and it had two horns and both horns were high, but the one was higher than the other, and the higher came up last. I observed the ram pushing westward and northward and southward, and no beast could stand before him, nor was there one who could deliver from his power; he did as he pleased and became great.

A ram: A ram, the first of the two symbolic animals of this vision, is now introduced. The verse implies that the ram was already present as Daniel first saw himself in vision by the river. Not far from him stood this animal, symbolizing the "kings of Media and Persia," (v. 20). "A ram" is literally "one ram," and the significance of the number is to make clear that what Daniel saw was a single ram, with the two horns now described. Ammianus Marcellinus, a fourth century historian, states that the Persian ruler bore the head of a ram as he stood at the head of his army. *It had two horns:* Rams normally have two horns, but these were unique. As Daniel watched, one began to grow later than the other and then became higher. The symbolism is clear from Medo-Persian history. Before Cyrus came to power, Media was already a major power, having, for instance, helped Babylonia defeat Assyria in 612 B.C. Persia, on the other hand, was a small country at the time, lying to the south, holding less than 50,000 square miles. But Cyrus, on coming to power there, succeeded in gaining control over powerful Media to the north (c. 550 B.C.), and then making Persia the greater of the two. With these combined, he moved on to establish the vast Medo-Persian empire.

Westward and northward and southward: Daniel observed as the ram began to push or butt with his head in three directions: west, north, and south. The symbolism is that Medo-Persia would similarly make conquest primarily in these three directions. The conquests of Cyrus and his successors were mainly to the west (Babylonia, Syria, Asia Minor) the direction noted first, with later expansion northward (Armenia and the Caspian Sea region) and southward (Egypt and Ethiopia). Some conquest to the east was made, but not of the significance of those in the other directions. *No beast could stand:* Apparently Daniel now saw other animals, unnamed and undescribed, enter the vision and seek to hinder the ram, but none were able. The comparative ease with which Cyrus was able to conquer other nations is a matter of history. Having established himself as master of Persia and Media combined, he moved across northern Mesopotamia to Asia Minor almost unopposed. There he defeated the wealthy Croessus and then marched back east and against Babylon, which also was taken easily. All this was predicted through Isaiah (45:1-3) a century and a half earlier, when he stated that God "would make the crooked places straight" before this ruler. *He did as he pleased:* Because no beast could withstand the ram, and there was no one who could help any do this, the ram was able to push quite as he willed. The word for "became great" *(higdîl)* may be translated "did great things," but the thought is still that by so doing he became great in power in the world of his day. Medo-Persia became the greatest empire in amount of territory controlled of all empires until its day.

8:5. Then, as I was continuing to look, lo, a he-goat came from the west across the face of the whole earth, without touching the ground; and the goat had a prominent horn between his eyes.

A he-goat came: The words translated "he-goat" mean literally "buck of the goats" *(tsᵉ pîr ha'izzîm).* This animal, according to verse twenty-one, symbolizes the "king of Greece."[4] No particular king is in mind, for the same verse makes the "prominent horn" symbolic of the first king, Alexander. The goat itself is best taken as a representative of the country, over which a series of kings would rule. Compared with a ram, a he-goat has greater strength and agility, features significant in the symbolism. *From the west:* Greece lay to the west of Medo-Persia, and Alexander came from that direction as he moved into the Medo-Persian realm. The indication that he crossed the face of the whole earth accords with the vast amount of territory which he conquered for Greece, even more than Medo-Persia had controlled. *Without touching the ground:* The thought is that Alexander's conquest was with great speed; cf. the four wings of the leopard in 7:6. *A prominent horn:* This phrase is literally "a horn of vision" *(qeren ḥazût).* Comparing this with the parallel phrase in verse twenty-one, "the great horn" *(haqqeren haggᵉdôlah),* the thought of height, something easily seen, comes to mind, leading to the translation "prominent." As noted, the horn symbolizes Alexander the Great (cf. v. 21). Goats, like rams, normally have two horns; therefore this horn is unusual. The significance is that Alexander would be unusual, one of the great military strategists of history. He was born in 356 B.C., himself the son of a great conqueror, Philip of Macedon. His father had already united Greece with Macedonia and was planning to fight Persia, when

---

[4] Cf. Barnes, BD, II, pp. 103-105, for discussion, with pictures, of a one-horned goat as a symbol for the ancient Macedonians.

he was murdered. Alexander was only twenty when he succeeded his father as king in 336 B.C., having been educated under the instruction of the famed Aristotle. He moved against the Persians a year and a half later, in 334 B.C.

8:6, 7. And he came to the ram that had two horns, which I had seen standing beside the river, and he ran against him in the fury of his power. And I saw him draw near the ram, and he was enraged against him and struck the ram and broke his two horns, and there was no strength in the ram to stand against him; but he cast him to the ground and trampled him, and there was none to deliver the ram from his power.

The ram that had two horns: Daniel observed the goat drawing near to the ram, as both were ready for combat. The words translated "that had two horns" mean literally "the master of the two horns" *(ba'al haqqᵉranayîm),* but in such a phrase *ba'al* is best taken as merely a word of relation.[5] With about 35,000 troops, Alexander crossed the Hellespont, thereby coming immediately into Persian territory. Not far away was the Granicus River, which he found necessary to cross and where a large Persian force awaited him. *The fury of his power:* Daniel watched as the goat encountered the ram in combat. "The fury of his power" *(baḥᵃmat koḥô)* speaks of infuriated strength. The word for "fury" comes from a root meaning "to be hot." Hatred for the Persians had built up within the Greeks since the days of Cyrus, because of constant tension and quarreling. Normal strength becomes heightened when backed by emotional heat. With this, Alexander joined in battle at the Granicus in 334 B.C., and later in two other vital encounters.

No strength in the ram: Daniel watched as the ram was bested by the goat, his two horns broken and his strength made to vanish. The Persian force at Granicus, as in the two later battles, was larger than Alexander's, but the Greeks won. This left the way clear for freeing Grecian cities of Asia Minor from their hated Persian masters, which was the next order of business. The following year witnessed the second of the major encounters, this time at Issus in the Taurus mountains. The Persian king himself, Darius III, had come to take command now, but the result was the same. Next followed the famous siege of Tyre and later the occupation of all Egypt. Alexander then led his troops on an extensive march all the way east to the Tigris, where, near the site of old Nineveh, he met the Persians for the third time, at the battle of Gaugemela (also called after Arbella), in the fall of 331 B.C. The Persians had assembled there a still larger host of troops, but once more to no avail; and this left the entire

[5] Cf. BDB, p. 162.

Medo-Persian holdings open before the young Grecian conqueror. *He cast him . . . and trampled him:* Daniel saw the goat not only knock the ram to the ground, but then trample him with his sharp hooves. Alexander not only defeated the Persians these three times, but moved on to occuy all their land. He captured and sacked Shushan, Ecbatana, and Persepolis in turn, and then marched all the way to the Indus River and even across it, before turning south to the Indian Ocean and finally back to Babylon. The conquest and humiliation of Persia was complete.

8:8. Thus the he-goat became very great; but when he was strong the great horn was broken, and in place of it came up four prominent horns, toward the four winds of heaven.

Became very great: This is the same phrase as used regarding the ram in verse four, except for the addition of "very." It could be translated "did very great things," but the thought would still be that the goat became very great, so as to be able to do them. The addition of the adverb "very" *(m^e'od)* is apparently meant to indicate that the he-goat became greater than the ram. *Great horn was broken:* Daniel does not state what happened in the vision to cause the great horn to be broken, but this detail is not needed to see the intended symbolism. Alexander died when he had just subjected all Medo-Persia to himself. On returning to Babylon from the east, he was taken with a severe fever, and in June, 323 B.C., died at the age of thirty-two. He had left his home country over eleven years before, and apparently never returned. He was taken in death, a young military genius, cut off at the height of achievement and power. *Four prominent horns:* Where the great horn had been, Daniel now saw four take its place. The word for "prominent" is the same as that used in verse five, but it is used here without the preceding construct word "horn." Its use appears to be adverbial, giving the literal translation: "there came up prominently four in its place." This development is symbolic of the dividing of Alexander's vast holdings between four of his generals: Cassander receiving Macedonia and Greece; Lysimachus, Thrace and much of Asia Minor; Seleucus, Syria and vast regions to the east; and Ptolemy, Egypt. For a while a fifth, Antigonus, held territory in Asia Minor, but in 301 B.C. he was overthrown. It should be noted that the imagery employed in the vision does not imply, correctly, that Alexander himself divided the empire. He did not; the fourfold division came rather as a result of extensive fighting among the generals during twenty-two years. *The four winds:* Reference is to the four directions: Cassander to the west, Lysimachus to the north, Seleucus to the east, and Ptolemy to the south.

8:9. Then from one of them emerged a single horn that began small

but became very great, toward the south, and toward the east, and toward the glorious land.

A single horn: All the horns which Daniel saw grow on the he-goat grew contrary to nature: the one horn, then four horns in its place, and afterward another horn apparently growing out of one of the four. The symbolism of this single horn is clear. From one of the divisions would emerge a king of unusual significance, of which Daniel was now to take note. The king symbolized is commonly and correctly identified as Antiochus Epiphanes,[6] who became the eighth ruler over the domain of Seleucus, reigning from 175 to 164 B.C. He is brought into the vision because of his exploits against the Jews in Palestine—exploits which correspond to the symbolic descriptions of this horn in the following verses. *Began small:* Literally, "went out from littleness." The thought is that the horn emerged from a state of being small, then grew larger as Daniel watched. This is the same idea as that which was expressed in 7:8, 24-26 regarding the "little horn" of Daniel's first vision. The Hebrew word used for "littleness" here *(tseʿîrah)* is the same word as the one used in the Aramaic there *(zeʿerah),* though in a different construction.[7] The two kings symbolized are not the same, however, for in the first vision it was the Antichrist, still to appear in the future, and here it is Antiochus Epiphanes of ancient history. The reason for symbolizing both as a little horn is that the one prefigures the other. Antiochus Epiphanes is sometimes called the antichrist of the Old Testament; that is, the one who brought suffering to the Jews in his day, in the pattern of what the real Antichrist will do during the Great Tribulation (compare 7:24-26 and 9:27 with 8:10-13). From what Antiochus did to Jews in his day, therefore, one may know the general pattern of what the Antichrist will do to them in the future. *Became very great:* Antiochus Epiphanes ascended the throne following the murder of his brother, the former king, Seleucus Philopator. The son of Seleucus, named Demetrius, the rightful heir to the throne, still lived, but he was held as hostage in Rome. Antiochus succeeded in obtaining the throne largely through flattery and bribery, as indicated in 11:21 (which see). Thus his beginning was small, since he was not even the rightful heir. When once crowned, however, he assumed the name Epiphanes, meaning "illustrious," by which he sought to attract attention and admiration to himself. Being extremely proud, his own self-estimate always outweighed his accomplishments; but still he did make significant conquests, which were of sufficient importance to warrant the description that he "became very great."

6 Josephus already so believed: *Antiq.,* X, 11, 7.
7 The difference is accountable from the different way the horn is introduced to the reader.

South . . . east . . . glorious land: The conquests of Antiochus were mainly in respect to the areas here indicated. As to the south, he made gains against Egypt;[8] as to the east, he campaigned in Mesopotamia, particularly Armenia;[9] and as to the "glorious land" (Palestine), he came to exercise full domination over the land of the Jews. The word for "the glorious land" means literally "the glory" *(hatstsebî),* but the identification with Palestine is clear both from a comparison with 11:16, 41, where the full term *('erets hatsts^eḇî)* is used, and also from the fact that one could expect this form of designation to refer to God's chosen land. Geographically, Palestine lay between the other two areas of Antiochus' conquests. Palestine had been an object of dispute between the dynasties of Ptolemy and Seleucus since the day of the division, but was now under the rule of the Seleucids. It was taken from the Ptolemies in a series of battles between Antiochus III, father of Antiochus Epiphanes, and Ptolemy V in the years 202-198 B.C. Antiochus Epihanes now sought to force new religious and civic ways upon the Jews.

8:10. And it became great even against the host of heaven, and it caused some of the host and of the stars to fall to the earth, and it trampled upon them.

Against the host of heaven: The manner in which Antiochus became great in respect to Palestine is now presented. The symbolism shows the goat somehow pressing even against the host of heaven, meaning the stars (Jer. 33:22). How this may have been depicted in the vision is not described, but the significance is clear. The host of heaven, or stars, refers to the people of God (cf. 12:3; Gen. 15:5; 22:17; Ex. 12:41), and the symbolism is that Antiochus would oppress God's people, the Jews, in their land (cf. v. 24). *And of the stars to fall to the earth:* Further detail is now given. The goat was seen to cast some of the host down to the earth. "Stars" likely explains the identity of the "host," making "and" to carry the thought of "even." Reference is to the large number of Jews whom Antiochus put to death because of their resistance to his unfair regulations. *Trampled upon them:* Daniel saw the goat now trample the stars with his feet, symbolizing the degree of persecution which Antiochus effected on the Jews. His desire was to force them to become Grecian in their thinking and ways. The Jews resisted and were made to suffer for it. Two passages from 1 Maccabees, where the most detail is given, provide an indication of how Antiochus "trampled" the people.

> And after two years' time the king [Antiochus] sent his chief collector of tribute unto the cities of Judah; and he came unto

[8] Cf. 1 Macc. 1:16-19.
[9] *Ibid.,* 3:21-37.

Jerusalem with a great multitude. And he spake words of peace unto them, in deceit; and they gave him credence. And he fell suddenly upon the city, and smote it very sore, and destroyed much people of Israel. And when he had taken the spoils of the city, he set it on fire, and pulled down the houses and the walls thereof round about. And the women and the children took they captive, and took possession of the cattle (1:29-32).

And many of the people were gathered unto them, every one that forsook the law; and they committed evils in the land, and drove the Israelites into hiding places, wherever they could find a refuge. And on the fifteenth day of the month Chaseleu, in the hundred forty and fifth year, they built an abomination of desolation upon the altar, and built altars in the cities of Judah round about. And they burnt incense at the doors of their houses, and in the streets. And having rent in pieces the books of the law which they found, they burnt them with fire. And where was found with any a book of the covenant, or if any found pleasure in the law, the king's commandment was that they should put him to death. Thus did they according to their might unto the Israelites every month, to as many as were found in the cities. And on the twenty-fifth day of the month they sacrificed upon the altar, which was upon the altar of burnt offering. And, according to the commandment, they put to death women that had caused their children to be circumcised. And they hanged the infants about their necks, and plundered their houses, and slew them that had circumcised them (1:52-61).[10]

8:11. He even magnified himself against the Prince of the host, and by him the regular ceremonial observances were taken away and the place of his sanctuary was cast away.

Even magnified himself against the Prince: Now some specific anti-Jewish matters are cited. The verbal form of "magnified himself" *(higdî)* is the same as in verses four and eight, where it is rendered "became great," but the context calls here for this changed translation. It is true that the word for "even ... against" *('id)* carries the idea of extent, "even to"; but to magnify oneself "even to" the Prince means basically "even against." The subject in mind cannot be the horn, but the person, Antiochus. "The Prince" must be God Himself, and not merely some earthly representative, such as the high priest Onias (as some hold); because verse twenty-five identifies him as "Prince of princes." "The host" refers to the Jews, whose Prince was God. *By him the regular ceremonial observances:* The way in which Antiochus magnified himself is now indicated. "By him" *(mimmennû)*, referring to Antiochus as agent, is preferable to "from him," referring to God as being deprived. It would be strange to speak of

[10] Cf. also 2 Macc. 6:18-31 and 7:1-42 for particular illustrations of suffering on the part of an Eleazar and of seven brothers and their mother.

God as being deprived of sacrifices by a human being. The word for "regular ceremonial observances" *(tamiḏ)* means literally "continuousness," used also in 8:12, 13; 11:31; 12:11. The context in each instance points clearly to the idea of something which was continuous in action involving the Temple; and that could only be the regular ceremonial observances. All such Antiochus ordered brought to an end. Another passage from 1 Maccabees (1:41-50) reveals the fulfillment of this prophetic statement.

> And the king [Antiochus] wrote to his whole kingdom that all should be as one people, and every one should abandon his customs. And all the heathen agreed to the commandment of the king. Yea, many of the Israelites found pleasure in his religion, and sacrificed unto idols, and profaned the sabbath. And the king sent letters by messengers unto Jerusalem and the cities of Judah, that they should follow the foreign customs of the land, and keep burnt offerings, and sacrifices, and drink offerings out of the sanctuary; and that they should profane sabbaths and festival days; and pollute sanctuary and priests; build altars, and groves, and idol temples, and sacrifice swine's flesh, and unclean animals; that they should also leave their sons uncircumcised, make their souls abominable with all manner of uncleanness and profanation: to the end they might forget the law, and change all the ordinances. And whosoever would not do according to the commandment of the king, he should die.[11]

Place of his sanctuary: The word for "place" *(meḵôn),* from the verb *kûn,* meaning "to stand," is used specifically elsewhere of the place (habitation, dwelling) of God (Ex. 15:17; 1 Kings 8:13, 39, 43); and is best so taken here. Though evidence is lacking that Antiochus actually destroyed the Temple as a building, he did desecrate it terribly, as another quotation (1:20-24) shows—a passage which immediately follows a statement regarding his conquest in Egypt.

> And after that Antiochus had smitten Egypt, he returned in the hundred forty and third year; and he went up against Israel, and he went up against Jerusalem with a great multitude. And he entered in arrogance into the sanctuary, and took the golden altar, and the candlestick of light, and all the vessels thereof, and the table of the shewbread, and the pouring vessels, and the vials, and the censers of gold, and the vail, and the crowns, and the golden ornaments that were on the front of the temple; and he scaled the gold off. And he took the silver and the gold, and the precious vessels; and he took the hidden treasures which he found. And having taken all, he departed into his land. And he made a massacre, and spoke very arrogantly.[12]

---

[11] Cf. further 2 Macc. 6:1-11.
[12] Cf. further 1 Macc. 1:39, 40.

8:12. And a host was given up together with the regular ceremonial observances in transgression, and he cast truth to the ground, and he acted and prospered.

A host: The same word *(tsaba')* is used here as in verse eleven, and reference must be to the Jews again. Since, unlike its use in verse eleven, it is used here without the article, this reference may be to only a part of the total nation, whereas then it was to all. Historically, Antiochus did kill many thousands, but not all. *Together with the regular ceremonial observances:* The word for "regular ceremonial observances" is the same as in verse eleven (which see). The word for "together with" is the preposition *'al,* normally meaning "upon." It can also mean "with" in the sense of one thing accompanying another, and is best so taken here. The thought is that, as Antiochus was permitted by God to take away the regular ceremonial observances, as indicated in verse eleven, so he was permitted to take a host of the Jewish people. *In transgression:* The Hebrew phrase can be rendered as here, "in transgression," meaning transgression by Antiochus, or "because of transgression," meaning transgression by the Jews, for which God permitted this carnage. Either makes good sense, but the former must be preferred because the same word for "transgression" *(pesha')* is used in verse thirteen clearly for the actions of Antiochus. What he did, in slaughtering Jews and forcing such changes in the Mosaic ordinances, constituted, indeed, great transgression in the sight of God. *He cast truth to the ground:* Truth always lies in what God says and does. The true religion was found in God's revelation, as set forth particularly in the Mosaic legislation. This revelation Antiochus was casting to the ground, and he attempted to substitute the false religion of Greece. *He acted and prospered:* The thought is that Antiochus really did these shocking things, and still prospered in it. The Jewish people, no doubt, wondered why God should let him continue doing them and apparently prosper.

8:13. Then I heard one holy one speaking and another holy one said to the one who spoke, How long is the vision, the regular ceremonial observances and the transgression which brings desolation, and the giving over of both the sanctuary and host to be trampled?

Then I heard: With these words Daniel returns to describing the vision proper. In verses eleven and twelve, he has described the activities of Antiochus as symbolized in the vision. Daniel heard two beings speaking, who apparently had not been in the vision before. They spoke about the activities of Antiochus, rather than about the horn itself. It may be that the two animals, the ram and goat, had faded from view as Daniel continued to look. The suggestion of some that the main speaker here is Gabriel (v. 16) is probably not correct, since the word for "one" in the phrase "one who spoke" is indefinite in its designation, meaning "a certain one," or even "a so-and-so." *One holy one . . . another holy one:* The two beings are simply called "holy ones." The designation could refer to earthly saints as well as angels, but the latter must be in view here because of the knowledge displayed relative to the vision—knowledge brought certainly from God. The first one is the main speaker, being depicted in the act of speaking when interrupted by the second. He may have been enlarging on the meaning of the vision, particularly as to Antiochus' actions, prior to this point in the vision. *How long is the vision:* A paraphrase of this question reads: "How much time will elapse in the fulfillment of the destruction symbolized by the vision?" This question was probably much in Daniel's mind as well. An indication had been given concerning the duration of the Antichrist's persecution of God's people in the first vision (7:25), and now an opportunity was provided for indicating the same relative to Antiochus' perverted efforts. *The regular ceremonial observances and the transgression:* The word for "regular ceremonial observances" is the same as in verse eleven (which see). In this and the next element, the angel became more specific as to his question. The two parts of this element are to be taken together, with the first set off from the second for the sake of emphasis. Put more fully, the angel asked how long the transgression that brought desolation on the regular ceremonial observances would last. The word for "which brings desolation" *(shomem)* is a participle depicting Antiochus' transgressing activities in progress. *Sanctuary and host to be trampled:* The "sanctuary" is the Temple and the "host" the Jewish people once again. The word for "to be trampled" *(mirmas)* is a derivative of the verb used in verse ten, thus referring to the same basic idea. Antiochus wrought enormous havoc to the Temple and among the people.

8:14. And he said to me, Until two thousand three hundred evening-mornings; then shall the sanctuary be restored.

He said to me: The main versions (Septuagint, Syriac, Vulgate) have "to him," rather than "to me," as in the Hebrew. Since both the second angel and Daniel very likely heard the reply, the question as to which reading is best is relatively unimportant. *Unto two thousand three hundred evening-mornings:* The angel's answer is a definite number of time units called "evening-mornings" *('ere<u>b</u> bo<u>k</u>er)*, literally, "evening morning." Some expositors[13] take the expression to mean 2,300 evenings and mornings totaled together, equaling only 1,150 full days. They find supporting evidence in the mention in the immediate context of regular offerings and the fact that the regular burnt-offerings came every

---

[13] For instance, Zockler, *LCD*, pp. 178-80.

evening and morning, asserting that the true intent is to designate 2,300 occasions of burnt-offerings. The commentary on verse eleven has shown, however, that all ceremonial observances are in view in the context, and not merely the regular offerings. These expositors also find evidence in the three-and-one-half-year figure of 7:25,[14] showing that a period of 1,150 days is approximately that long (actually, 110 days short); but it has already been seen, when discussing Daniel's first vision, that the time period of 7:25 refers to the activities of the Antichrist, whereas here Antiochus Epiphanes is concerned. Moreover, that two half-days are intended by the expression is not likely, in view of the order of mention: evening-morning, rather than morning-evening. The order of evening-morning suggests that part of the twenty-four-hour period at which one full day closes and a new one begins—a part which comes only once every twenty-four hours. Twenty-three hundred of these parts would mean the elapse of 2,300 full days. This manner of designating days is used only here in the Bible, but may have been suggested by the language of Genesis 1, where a similar phrase seems to carry basically the same idea.

How are 2,300 days to be fitted into the history here concerned? The answer is that this amount of time was the duration of Antiochus' period of oppression of the Jews. Historical data available are insufficient for a precise reckoning to the very day, but an approximation is definitely possible. The closing point of this period is indicated in the verse to have been the restoration of the Temple. The date when this was accomplished, under the leadership of Judas Maccabeus, was December 25, 165 B.C., according to Barnes, who refers to Prideaux.[15] Figuring back from this date 2,300 days brings one to September 6, 171 B.C.; which should be, then, the day when an event occurred that was of sufficient significance to mark it as the beginning of Antiochus' anti-Jewish atrocities. Though the nature of that event is not known, what is clear is that the year 171 B.C. did see the beginning of these atrocities, and such an event could easily have occurred on that date. Until 171 B.C., peaceful relations had existed between Antiochus and the Jews. But beginning that year, a series of events transpired, involving particularly the Jewish high priesthood, which prompted severe measures by Antiochus. Earlier, the pious high priest, Onias III, had been removed from office and replaced by his wicked brother, Jason, because Jason had bribed Antiochus for the position. Then, in the year

[14] A similar correlation is attempted with 12:7, 11, 12, but with equally negative results.

[15] BD, II, p. 115. Prideaux, an outstanding eighteenth-century historian, wrote *The Old and New Testaments Connected in the History of the Jews;* cf. vol. III, pp. 265-68). It should be noted that not all anti-Jewish activities of the Syrians ceased on this date. Some continued, in fact, during four more years, well after the death of Antiochus, until the defeat of the Syrian general, Nicanor. These were sporadic, however, and the most likely date for the termination of the 2,300 days is December 25, 165 B.C.

172 B.C., another brother, Menelaus, succeeded in replacing Jason, by promising a still larger bribe. In 171 B.C. Menelaus had murdered the good Onias III, who had rebuked him for giving away and selling many of the gold utensils of the Temple. Menelaus had sought in this way to pay the large promised bribe. As a result, the anger of the Jews was stirred against both Menelaus and his accomplice, an officer of Antiochus, and this in turn prompted Antiochus to bring the reprisals.[16] From this point on, oppression of the Jews and desecration of the Mosaic ordinances by Antiochus became progressively more severe and continued until the climax six years later, when the Temple was restored.

It should be noted further that some expositors hold that the time when Antiochus gave orders for the erection of the idol altar in the Temple, truly desecrating it (on December 15, 168 B.C.), was the beginning point for this 2,300-day period. This view conflicts with the one set forth above and leaves only three years and ten days until the Temple's restoration. Arguing against it, also, is the fact that the vision itself speaks first of Antiochus attacking the "host of heaven" (v. 10), meaning, as observed, the Jewish people themselves, before the taking away of the regular ceremonial observances (v. 11). This makes likely the thought that the 2,300-day period is to be reckoned as having begun at that same point rather than only at the interruption of Temple activities.[17]

Then shall the sanctuary be restored: The word for "sanctuary" *(qodesh)* means something or someone holy. Here it is commonly and correctly taken to refer to the Temple, the holy place, because the Temple was the center of interest for Antiochus' anti-Jewish activities. Its restoration to normalcy would be the most significant indication of a cessation of these activities. The word for "be restored" *(nitsdaq)* means literally "be justified." The thought is that all that the Temple stood for, after the period of sacriligious desecration, would be vindicated as true and right, in contrast to all that Antiochus had been advocating. The indication of such vindication would be the restoration of its Mosaic ceremonies.

C. THE VISION INTERPRETED (vv. 15-27)

In the pattern of chapter seven, the last half of this chapter is given to the interpretation of the vision of the first half. It follows that pattern further in having the interpretation supplied by a heavenly messenger, so that in effect the vision still continues, though with a change of scene.

---

[16] These events are described in 2 Macc. 4:7-50.

[17] It may be noted further that it was on the basis of this 2,300-day period that Seventh Day Adventists, taking a day for a year, arrived at the date of 1884 for the return of Christ. For a discussion of this view, cf. A. Hoekema, *The Four Major Cults* (Grand Rapids: Wm. B. Eerdmans Pub. Co., 1963), pp. 144f.

8:15, 16. Now while I, Daniel, had been beholding the vision, I had been seeking to understand it, and then, lo, before me stood a figure like that of a man. And I heard a man's voice between the banks of the Ulai, and it called and said, Gabriel, make this man know the vision.

While I, Daniel: Again, Daniel draws attention to himself, this time to depict himself, in relation to the participants of the vision, as having been intently watching. The participants had been doing the various things described, and he, Daniel, had also been active in wondering what it all meant. *Seeking to understand it:* This seeking had not been by formal prayer, for Daniel had been occupied with the observation. His own mind had been active in seeking to understand, perhaps making comparisons with both his first vision (two years earlier) and Nebuchadnezzar's first dream (about fifty-two years earlier). *A figure like that of a man:* Daniel was unable to understand of himself, and God sent one to help him. The interjection "lo" suggests surprise on Daniel's part at the appearance of this one. The one sent, while being an angel, even Gabriel (v.16), is given the appearance of a man likely to make Daniel feel more at ease. The word used for "man" is noteworthy. It is *gabor,* a word which connotes a *mighty man,* and is the basic element in the name "Gabriel," which means *mighty one of God.*

I heard a man's voice: Another supernatural participant is now introduced, but only in the capacity of a speaker. Daniel heard a voice coming from "between the banks of the Ulai" River *(ben 'ûlay,* literally "between Ulai"), apparently in the pattern of what happened later with the fourth vision (12:7). Since no particular being is identified or said to have been seen, it is best to think of this voice as coming from God Himself. The significance of inserting this divine command to Gabriel is likely to impress Daniel with the importance and authority of what was to be stated. *Gabriel:* The identity of the figure before Daniel is revealed to be Gabriel (cf. 9:21). He is named also in Luke 1:19 as the announcer of John's birth to Zacharias, and in Luke 1:26 as the announcer of Christ's birth to Mary. The role of Gabriel is regularly that of one who brings important information from God to man. Only one other good angel is named in Scripture, and that is Michael (Dan. 10:13, 21; 12:1; Jude 9; Rev. 12:7), who is called the "archangel" in Jude 9 and is represented as a leader among the angels in Revelation 12:7.

8:17, 18. Then he came near where I stood, and as he came I was terrified and fell upon my face. But he said to me, Understand, O son of man, that the vision pertains to the time of the end. And as he spoke with me, I fainted, upon my face to the ground; but he touched me and caused me to stand upright.

He came near: Apparently Gabriel had been seen by Daniel as standing at some distance until this time; but now, at the divine order, he drew near for easier communication. *I was terrified:* It is normal for human mortals to experience fear in the presence of the supernatural (cf. Judg. 6:22, 23; Job 42:5, 6; Isa. 6:1-5). A sense of personal sinfulness becomes overpowering in the presence of perfect holiness. This was Daniel's reaction before Gabriel, as he fell to his face in apparent acknowledgment of his own unworthiness. *Understand, O son of man:* Gabriel's response was reassuring. He did not speak of any sin on Daniel's part, but only began to carry out the divine order just given. The form of address, "son of man," emphasizes Daniel's own inability, being merely man, to know the nature of such a vision himself. The same form of address is used regarding Ezekiel many times. This employment in Daniel and those regarding Ezekiel differ in significance from the instance in Daniel 7:13, which concerns Christ. *Time of the end:* This phrase provides a general caption for the explanation to follow. Its meaning is essentially repeated in a parallel phrase of verse nineteen and will be discussed there.

I fainted: Gabriel's words were interrupted at this point by Daniel's falling into a faint. It may be that even Gabriel's first words did not register in Daniel's mind, since Gabriel repeated them in essence in verse nineteen. The word for "I fainted" *(nirdamtî)* means normally to "fall into a deep sleep." (A derived word was used even for the sleep brought on Adam when Eve was formed [Gen. 2:21].) It is better taken to mean "I fainted" here, however, for Daniel experienced an abnormal loss of consciousness because of extreme emotional excitement, and the period of time implied for the unconscious state is not long. This "fainting" occurred no doubt for the same reason that he had already fallen on his face. His sense of unworthiness continued, Gabriel's words not having been understood sufficiently to give the reassurance intended. *Upon my face to the ground:* Daniel was already in a fallen position. This faint, then, did not make him fall from an upright stance, but only brought his face in full contact with the ground. He could have been on his knees or even lying prone at the time. *He touched me:* Gabriel was close enough to Daniel so that he needed only to stoop to touch the prostrate form before him, thus returning him to consciousness. Daniel was caused to "stand upright" (literally, "to stand upon my standing"), in the position he had enjoyed before falling. It should be realized that this was all in vision, Daniel seeing himself as thus fainting and being restored in this manner. Daniel was himself in Babylon and not in Shushan at the time (cf. 8:2).

8:19. He then said, Lo, I am to instruct you concerning that which

will be in the latter portion of the indignation, because it pertains to the appointed time of the end.

I am to instruct you: Literally, "I am one causing you to know." *In the latter portion of the indignation . . . appointed time of the end:* As noted at verse seventeen, this verse states approximately the same idea as set forth there. The two verses may be taken together to determine the overall thought. The earlier verse states that the vision pertained "to the time of the end" *(leʿet-qets,* literally, "to time of end"); and this one that Gabriel was to explain regarding "the latter portion of the indignation" *(ʾaḥᵃrit hazzaʿam),* because it pertained "to the appointed time of the end" *(môʿed qets,* literally, "to appointed time of end"). It should be noted that the second element in the latter verse is the same as in the former, except that the time in reference is made more specific by the addition of "appointed." Being repeated, there is reason to believe that this element is basic in the overall thought, suggesting that "the latter portion of the indignation" is another way of referring to the same time. What is this time? For answer, some expositors (mainly amillennial) look only to the historically completed aspects of the vision, which, as noted, pertain mainly to the Seleucid division of the Grecian empire, and more particularly to the anti-Jewish activities of its eighth king, Antiochus Epiphanes.

If one confines his inquiry to these aspects only, however, several puzzling questions arise. For instance, in what sense can the period of oppression by Antiochus be called an "appointed time of end" and "the latter portion of the indignation"? What ended at that time and of what indignation was it the latter portion? The answer of Young[18] is that the total indignation in view included as its earlier portion the Babylonian captivity and its latter this oppression of Antiochus. He also identifies this latter time with the "end," which, he says, was appointed by God as the closing period of His wrath on Israel.[19] But further questions arise regarding this answer. Why speak of this comparatively short period of just over six years as the latter portion of a time of indignation, when over three and one-half centuries had intervened since the close of the earlier portion? Furthermore, why speak of this latter portion as an "end"? What ended? The particular period of Antiochus' oppression ended, true enough, but this did not bring an end to Jewish suffering. No day of blessedness then set in. It would seem that something of unusual significance should then have ceased and something else begun to make reasonable the employment of this concept. Some expositors have suggested that the great

[18] YPD, p. 177.
[19] The identical phrase "time of end" *(ʿet qets)* is used in 12:4 and Young there takes it as the end of time of Christ's second coming. But should not both be taken in the same way?

change connoted came with the appearance and work of Christ in His first coming. But this leaves one with the question of why the period of Antiochus should be called the "end" when Christ was not born for more than a century and a half; and also the question of what great change actually was made for Israel as a people when Christ did come, since they rejected Him so utterly.

An answer is called for which takes into account all of these questions. Such an answer has already been set forth in connection with Nebuchadnezzar's dream of chapter two and Daniel's first vision of chapter seven. It sees the angel Gabriel as now giving the meaning of the vision by showing, not only the significance involving Antiochus of ancient history, but also that of the one whom Antiochus foreshadowed, the Antichrist of future history. That is, Antiochus' oppression is seen to provide a partial fulfillment of the prophetic vision, but that of the Antichrist the complete fulfillment. The following matters give support to this position.

(1) Since truth concerning the Antichrist has already been presented in Nebuchadnezzar's dream and Daniel's first vision, and since it will be again in both Daniel's third and fourth times of revelation, it is in no way strange to find it here. (2) The pertinent phrases of verses seventeen and eighteen do find satisfactory fulfillment in this interpretation. The period of oppression by the Antichrist will be a "time of end," or more specifically an "appointed time of end," because with it the long period known as the times of the Gentiles (when Gentiles are dominant over Palestine, Luke 21:24) will be brought to a conclusion. This period began with the Judean captivity to Babylonia, since which time God's people have never enjoyed a period of true autonomy over their land, and will end only with the Antichrist's dethronement. The important change that comes at the finish of the Antichrist's rule will be both the cessation of this time of oppression and the beginning of Christ's millennial reign, when Israel will again be autonomous in her land and even be the leading nation of the world. Antichrist's time of oppression may be properly described as "the latter portion of the indignation" by taking "latter portion" in the sense of "concluding portion" of God's continuing indignation against Israel all during the time of the Gentiles. (3) A clear similarity exists between the language of 8:23-25, where actions of the person symbolized by the little horn of this chapter are set forth, and that of 7:24-26, where actions of the Antichrist are presented, making likely the thought that the one acting is the same in both instances. If 8:23-25 concerns the Antichrist, then it is logical that his time is concerned in the present verse.

(4) Several matters may be stated in reply to Young's objection to this position (a position which he takes from the Scofield Reference Bible), when he says that the view "is utterly without exegetical

support."[20] For one thing, it may be stated that the above discussion has shown it to have better exegetical support than his own view. For another, it should be noted that he misunderstands the position, as indicated by his statement concerning it, when he speaks of verse nineteen:

> The force of the verse (if Scofield Reference Bible is correct) would be somewhat as follows: "I shall cause thee to know (i.e., by way of explanation of vv. 1-18) what will occur in the last time of the indignation (i.e., the period after the Exile) since at an appointed time the end (of the times of the Gentiles) will come."[21]

He then continues to say that such "an interpretation does not make good sense"; and it doesn't. He could not pass this judgment, however, if he had correctly stated the position as follows:

> I shall cause thee to know (i.e., by way of explanation of vv. 1-18) what will occur in the latter portion of the indignation (i.e., the Great Tribulation), which will have long before been foreshadowed by the oppression of Antiochus Epiphanes (directly predicted by vv. 1-18), this "latter portion" constituting the appointed time of the end of the period of the Gentiles.

Still further, Young says that this position "causes a mingling of the contents of chapters seven and eight that is not justifiable."[22] He points out that the little horn of chapter seven is the Antichrist whereas that of chapter eight is Antiochus (certainly correct) and then says that there is no reason to find in chapter eight "a double reference" by which both persons could be in view, since neither the text nor the analogy of Scripture demands it. In answer, it need only be said that the presentation set forth above shows that this text and the analogy of Scripture do call for it.

8:20-22. The ram which you saw, that had two horns, symbolizes the kings of Media and Persia. The he-goat symbolizes the king of Greece, with the great horn, which was between his eyes, symbolizing the first king. And as for the horn being broken, when four others arose in place of it, this symbolizes four kingdoms that shall arise from the nation, but not with the same strength.

Kings of Media and Persia: The symbolisms of both the ram and goat have been discussed under verses three to five. Though the symbolism is made here with "the kings" of Medo-Persia and Greece, rather than with the countries themselves, no particular kings are in mind (the notable horn [not the goat] signifying Alexander, in respect to the goat). Reference must be either to all the kings of these empires, taken collectively, or else in a figurative sense, to the countries themselves.

King of Greece: Literally translated, this is "king of Javan" *(mele_k yawan).* Javan (Ionian) was the name by which the Hebrews knew the Greeks (cf. Gen. 10:2, 4; Isa. 66:19; Ezek. 27.13). This should be taken as a figurative reference to the country of Greece (cf. v. 5). *The great horn:* The horn of the he-goat is described as the "great" *(hagg^edolah)* horn, whereas in verse five the phrase "horn of vision" was used, as noted. The meaning of "horn of vision" is thus clarified, justifying the translation "prominent" used in verse five. The person symbolized is Alexander the Great.

Four kingdoms: The symbolism was treated under verse eight. The word "nation" following is used in a loose sense, standing for all the vast territory that Alexander conquered. *Not with the same strength:* Literally, "not in its strength." The meaning is that none of the leaders of the resulting four divisions ruled with the same strength as Alexander. This does not necessarily mean that they were weak, but only that they did not measure up to him. He was one of the truly strong leaders of history: keeping an army together during some eleven years, while continually on foreign soil, until he had won the greatest amount of territory ever conquered by one ruler.

8:23. And at the latter time of their rule, when the transgressors have reached their full measure, a king will arise, fierce of countenance and understanding riddles.

Latter time of their rule: The word for "latter time" is the same as in verse nineteen, translated "latter portion." "Their rule" refers to the rule of the four divisions of Alexander's kingdom mentioned in verse twenty-two, which means that the time primarily in view is the close of their period of rule, not long before the rise of Rome. *The transgressors have reached their full measure:* The word for "the transgressors" *(happosh^e'îm)* is a participle, meaning "those who trangress." Some expositors prefer to take it as a noun, and there is some evidence to support their view; but, either way, the meaning is roughly the same. The word for "have reached their full measure" is a hiphil form of the verb *tamam,* "to make full." The general thought may be paraphrased, "when sinful actions have reached a point where God cannot permit them to go further without bringing punishment" (cf. Gen. 15:16; Matt. 23:32; 1 Thess. 2:16). These transgressors are not the heathen oppressors, but the Jews themselves, who, following their return from captivity, will have continued in sin to an extent causing God to permit their experiencing a punishing oppression. *King will arise:* The king of history to which secondary reference is made is clearly Antiochus Epiphanes, identified in verse nine as the little horn. He did arise in the latter time of the divided kingdoms, ruling from 175 to 164 B.C. Rome's dominion over the four divisions came gradually, beginning with the fall of Macedonia in 168 B.C. and extending to the subjugation of Egypt in 30 B.C. As anticipated in the discussion under verses seventeen and nineteen above, however, the primary reference must be seen as being to the Antichrist, foreshadowed by Antiochus, in whom alone some of the following descriptions find complete fulfillment. *Fierce of countenance and understanding riddles:* The word for "fierce" *('az)* means basically "strong, vehement." The word for "riddles" *(hîdôt),* used in its corresponding Aramaic form in 5:12, means "something twisted, involved." The overall thought is that this king would be both fierce in manner and capable of solving difficult problems of the kingdom. Some expositors take the latter aspect to refer to deceiving tactics, which could surely be included in the total thought. It is better, however, to take it basically in the sense used for its corresponding Aramaic form in 5:12, where it refers to Daniel's ability to solve difficult problems. Antiochus was not particularly outstanding in this ability, but the Antichrist will be (cf. 11:36, 39; 2 Thess. 2:9; Rev. 13:7, 8; 17:13). Both persons qualify as practitioners of deceit.

8:24. His power will be great, but not by his own power, and he will cause remarkable destruction, and will prosper and accomplish, and destroy mighty men and holy people.

His power will be great: The descriptive items set forth in this verse and the next were all true of Antiochus in a limited way, but will be true of the Antichrist in a fuller sense. Antiochus did display unusual strength, but probably no more than, if as much as, his father Antiochus III (cf. 11:10-19). Both fought and won in Egypt, as well as in areas to the east of Syria, but both also suffered defeats. In contrast, so long as the Antichrist, the great final ruler of the restored Roman confederacy, continues in power in his day to come, he will subdue all before him and make himself master of much of the world (cf. 11:40-45). *But not by his own power:* Both the Septuagint and Theodotion's translation omit this phrase, taking it as a gloss carried over from verse twenty-two. It belongs here, however, as the Hebrew and most versions have it; and it is particularly significant in reference to the Antichrist. The Antichrist will be Satan's counterfeit world ruler, whom he attempts to place in this supreme position prior to God's introduction of His own world Ruler, Christ. Revelation 13:2 states specifically, "And the dragon (Satan) gave him (the beast, Antichrist) his power, and his seat, and great authority." It is easy to believe that Satan had much to do with the rise and anti-Jewish activities of Antiochus, too, all under the permissive will of God. This is not stated directly of him, however, as it is of the Antichrist. *He will cause remarkable destruction:* Literally, "he will destroy wonderfully." The word for "wonderfully" *(nipla'ôt)* could be taken as a niphal plural participle, meaning "things made wonderfully," but its thought fits the context better if taken adverbially, meaning "wonderfully, remarkably." The idea is that this king will destroy in a manner and extent unique to himself, meaning, no doubt, worse than any other. This was true of Antiochus in reference to Jews of his day; but it will be true in a greater measure of the Antichrist.

Will prosper and accomplish: These two thoughts go together. The king will undertake many things and be successful in them. Antiochus was unusually active in his rule, pressing against Egypt and countries to the east, as well as against Palestine, with success being achieved frequently. The Antichrist, however, will achieve much more: seizing control of the Roman confederacy (cf. 7:8, 23; Rev. 17:12, 13); defeating a combined army of the "king of the north" and "king of the south," probably in a struggle over Palestine (cf. under 11:40); and effecting a complete subjugation of the Jews, even destroying two-thirds of them in doing so (Zech. 13:8, 9; 14:1, 2). *Destroy mighty men and holy people:* Antiochus killed many "holy people," i.e., God's people, the Jews, but history does not record that very many who could be called "mighty men" were among his victims. Some expositors point to certain rival claimants to the Syrian throne, whom he killed, but these were not outstanding persons. The Antichrist, on the other hand, does destroy "mighty men" as well as "holy people." The first vision, for instance, has already depicted him uprooting three who were kings before him, as he propels himself to power (7:8, 20), as well as "wearing out" the saints (7:25). It is easy to believe that many more leading people will be disposed of as he forces his will finally over all the world.

8:25. By his cunning, he will cause deceit to prosper under his hand, and in his own opinion he will be great; without warning, he will destroy many, and will even stand up against the Prince of princes; but without hand will he be broken.

By his cunning: The word for "cunning" (root, *sakal*) normally means "to be wise," but here, used with "will cause deceit," clearly carries the idea of treacherous wisdom. *Will cause deceit to prosper:* The thought is that the king will employ deceit as a planned, often-used way of achieving goals. He will be willing to use it not only in an emergency, but as a way of rule. Antiochus was known for his deceiving tactics, and the Antichrist will be also (cf. 2 Thess. 2:9, 10; Rev. 13:12-14). *In his own opinion:* Literally, this reads, "in his heart." Antiochus was a proud, self-exalting ruler; and the Antichrist is continuously so characterized (cf. 7:8, 25; 2 Thess. 2:4; Rev. 13:

5, 6). *Without warning:* These words may be translated literally, "in security." That is, when men think themselves secure and safe from such attack, this one will bring destruction upon them. The thought fits well with the practice of deceit. He will endeavor to make men believe that he comes in peace, pretending friendship, and then will come instead to destroy them. A quotation from 1 Maccabees 1:29-32, given under verse ten above, illustrates this manner of tactic by Antiochus, and that the Antichrist will work in this manner fits all else that is stated concerning him. *Against the Prince of princes:* In verse eleven, Antiochus was seen magnifying himself against one called the "Prince of the host," who was then identified as God, being Prince of the Jewish host. The concept "Prince of princes," however, is quite different. It fits the pattern of such titles as "Lord of lords," or "King of kings" (cf. 1 Tim. 6:15; Rev. 1:5; 17:14; 19:16), which are regularly ascribed to Christ. This suggests that the One mainly in mind here is Christ, which means that the principal one opposing Him must be the Antichrist. In the pattern of Antiochus' disdain for God, then, the Antichrist will seek to stand against Christ when Christ comes in glory to bring vengeance upon him (cf. Rev. 19:19). *Without hand will he be broken:* The thought is that without human hand, this king will be broken. This came true in a sense regarding Antiochus, for, as stated in 1 Maccabees 6:8-16, he died of grief and remorse in Babylon. He had just been defeated in his siege of Elymais, and was not able to bear the shock. The hands of humans were involved in his death indirectly, however, in that they brought the defeat. But no man's hand will be involved in the breaking of the Antichrist. His army will be fully destroyed by Christ, through the "sharp sword" that goes "out of his mouth," and he will himself be cast alive "into the lake of fire burning with brimstone," also by Christ, as a mighty deliverance is brought to the oppressed Jews of the Tribulation period (cf. Dan. 7:26; 11:45; Rev. 19:20, 21).

8:26. The vision of the evening and the morning which has been related is true; and do thou preserve the vision, for it pertains to many days.

The vision of the evening and the morning: Since the only mention in the chapter of an evening and morning is in verse fourteen, it must be that reference is to the 2,300 evening-mornings there indicated as constituting Antiochus' period of Jewish oppression. The thought may be paraphrased: "The vision which concerns the period of time of 2,300 evening-mornings when Antiochus will oppress the Jews." This period, climaxing the history depicted in the first part of the vision, and foreshadowing the future time of oppression of the Antichrist, is the central feature of the vision. *Is true:* Though the words of Gabriel still continue, what he says constitutes comments regarding the vision rather than further explanation. His statement that the vision was "true" (*'emet*) was to reassure Daniel on this count. Such reassurance was helpful in view of Daniel's evident difficulty in understanding and emotionally accepting the information revealed. *Preserve the vision:* The word for "preserve" (*setom*) means literally "shut up." The thought is not, however, to shut the vision up in the sense of keeping it secret; but in the sense of preserving it. Daniel was to make sure that a record of the vision would be preserved and not lost. Some liberal commentators (who date the book to the time of Antiochus) find in this phrase a device employed by the writer to make the reader think falsely that Daniel had been the author. That is, the angel was made to command Daniel to shut it up (hide it away in secret, so that it would not be found) until the fulfillment time of Antiochus' day; and in this way satisfy the reader of that day (who would be thinking, erroneously, that Daniel had written the book) as to why the book had not been known to Jews before his time. This view must be fully rejected. Daniel himself did write the book over three and one-half centuries before Antiochus. *Pertains to many days:* This phrase gives the reason for preserving the vision well. The vision pertained to future events which would come only after many intervening days. Daniel was to realize that the events predicted would not occur in days soon to follow. The number that were to elapse has been discussed earlier, both as to the fulfillment with Antiochus and that with the Antichrist.

8:27. As a result, I, Daniel, was overcome and lay sick for days; then I arose and tended to the business of the king. But I was astonished by the vision and did not understand it.

I, Daniel, was overcome: The repetition, "I, Daniel," has the effect of bringing the reader's attention back to Daniel, who has been listening to Gabriel's lengthy explanation. The word for "was overcome" (*nihyêtî*) is the niphal (passive) form of the verb "to be" and means "to be over, ended" (cf. 2:1). The thought is that Daniel's conscious state ended, meaning that he fainted, similar to his experience in verses seventeen and eighteen. Further, he not only fainted again, but remained ill for several days. All of this indicates that Daniel suffered a most severe emotional reaction to the vision, apparently even greater than what he had experienced after the first vision (cf. 7:15, 28). *Tended to the business of the king:* As noted under 5:11, Daniel still worked for the king in this time of Belshazzar, though probably not as the head of the wise men, since the queen then had to tell Belshazzar concerning him. What the nature of his work was is not revealed. He was able to tend to it again after recovering from his illness. *I was astonished . . . did not understand:* Even after regaining his composure, Daniel remained astonished by what he had been told. The phrase "did not understand" *('ên mebîn)* means literally "not one who understood." It could refer to others not understanding, but it likely means Daniel himself. He had heard Gabriel's words, but all their significances were not clear. The implication is that he continued to run these matters over in his mind.

CHAPTER 9

Chapter nine is divided into two parts. The first nineteen verses set forth a prayer of Daniel—a prayer inspired particularly by Daniel's notice of Jeremiah's prediction that the captivity would last seventy years (v. 2). Daniel wanted these seventy years to be reckoned by God as soon to end. The last eight verses concern God's response to the prayer, given again through the angel Gabriel. The response centers in the prediction that seventy "weeks" of years (490 years) are planned for God's people, before certain important aspects of deliverance will be effected in their behalf. The appearance of Gabriel this time may well be in real, corporeal form, and not merely in vision, as in chapter eight. If so, this instance of revelation to Daniel should not be classed as a vision, but as an actual face-to-face communication (cf. v. 20). If the appearance is merely in vision, the occasion still is much different from those of the first two visions, for the only feature in it is Gabriel himself, communicating to Daniel.

The principal importance of the information given concerns the last "week" of the total seventy. An extended time lapse occurs just prior to this seventieth "week," in parallel with the time lapse implied in Nebuchadnezzar's first dream and Daniel's two earlier visions, so that, whereas the first sixty-nine "weeks" are completed at Christ's first coming, the seventieth transpires only just before His second appearance and constitutes the seven-year period called the Great Tribulation.[1]

A. THE GENERAL SETTING (vv. 1, 2)

As in chapters seven and eight, attention is given first to the setting of what transpires in the chapter.

9:1, 2. In the first year of Darius the son of Ahasuerus, from the seed of the Medes, who was made king over the realm of the Chaldeans; in the first year of his reign, I, Daniel, perceived in the books

---

[1] More accurately, only the last half of this period should be so designated, for it is then that the great suffering is experienced.

the number of the years which, according to the word of Yahweh to Jeremiah the prophet, should elapse in respect to the desolation of Jerusalem: even seventy years.

First year of Darius: This is the same Darius that was involved in chapter six. Another man of the same name, Darius Hystaspes, began to reign in 521 B.C., but Daniel was already past eighty years of age by the time of the first Darius. For a discussion of this man, cf. the introduction to chapter six. His first year was 538 B.C., which means that the events of this chapter transpired some thirteen years after Daniel's second vision, with Daniel being about eighty-two. The particular year is stressed by a reference to it in both verses one and two, probably because it marked the near completion of seventy years since Daniel's date of captivity (605 B.C.). Seventy years was the duration of time noted by Jeremiah as constituting the period of the Exile. *Son of Ahasuerus:* This Ahasuerus was not the same as the ruler who took Esther as his wife (Esth. 1:1), for that person is best identified with Xerxes (485-465 B.C.), who began to rule more than half a century after the time of this chapter. The Ahasuerus here is otherwise unknown. His lineage is given as Median, which contrasts with that of Cyrus, the head ruler of the time, who was Persian. *Who was made king:* The hophal (passive) form of the verb fits the history involved. Darius was made ruler by Cyrus. *Realm of the Chaldeans:* As noted under 2:2, the term Chaldean is used in two senses in Daniel: as a division of the wise men, and as an ethnic group. The latter is the use here. These people appear to have come south into Babylonia from the Kurdistan mountains, first notices regarding them showing in Assyrian inscriptions of Ashurnasirpal II (883-859 B.C.). They seem to have been the dominant race in Babylonia at the time of Nebuchadnezzar, and he was a Chaldean himself. The amount of territory to which reference was normally made by the designation "realm of the Chaldeans" covered the alluvial plain from above Hit to the Persian Gulf. The extent under Darius' authority, however, as known from numerous texts,[2] took in, not only this land of Chaldea proper, but also the "Region beyond the River" *(Abarnahara),* which totaled approximately the same area formerly constituting the Babylonian empire. Though this area was extensive, it was still far less than all Persia, over which Cyrus was chief in authority.

Perceived in the books: Daniel, well educated, could be expected to have read books of his day. The books here mentioned, however, were not just any books, because the article is used *(bass^eparîm);* they likely were a collection, recognized as sacred by the Judeans, which

---

[2] Cf. Whitcomb, *DM,* pp. 11f. These texts refer to Gubaru, who is best identified with Darius.

included the Book of Jeremiah. Because the article is employed, some expositors, who erroneously favor the idea of a later date for the writing of Daniel, assert that reference is to the official canon of the Old Testament, which was not yet recognized in Daniel's day. There is no reason for this conclusion, however. It is only to be expected that the Judeans, exiled for many years by this time in Babylonia, would have had with them a number of Old Testament writings which were generally recognized as sacred. *Number of the years:* This number is identified at the close of verse two as seventy. The book of Jeremiah, included in Daniel's reading, gives this number twice: 25:11, 12 and 29:10. *Word of Yahweh:* The name *Yahweh* is a transliteration of the Hebrew divine name (tetragrammaton). Because the name came to be considered too sacred to pronounce, the proper way of pronouncing it was lost to knowledge. Much later, when a vowel system was invented, the vowels for *'ᵃdonay* "my Lord," were used with the original four consonants, resulting in the name "Jehovah," a form first appearing at the beginning of the twelfth century. *Yahweh*, then, is the more nearly correct.

Should elapse: The word for "should elapse" is an infinitive construct *(lᵉmallo'ôt)*, meaning literally, "to fill, fulfill." The force of it is to say that God's assigned period for Judah's captivity called for a certain number of years to fill it, that number being seventy. The word for "desolation" *(harᵉbot)* is plural, no doubt to stress intensity. The significance of including this note is to give the occasion for Daniel's ensuing prayer. Daniel's reasoning appears to have been as follows: He longed for the cessation of Judah's captivity. The seventy years of which he had read in Jeremiah settled the duration; but not the beginning point, the *terminus a quo,* of the period. Thinking back to his own time of being taken captive, in 605 B.C., he realized that the seventy years would soon be completed if God should reckon that year as the starting time, but not if He selected either the second phase of the captivity (597 B.C.) or, worse, the third (586 B.C.). The burden of his prayer, accordingly, was that God would be gracious and consider the *terminus a quo* as 605 B.C. Some expositors have thought in terms of the intended *terminus a quo* being 586 B.C., taking, then, the close of the period, the *terminus ad quem,* as the date of the completion of the Temple, which came at 515 B.C., thus giving a period of about seventy-one years. This view, however, does not square with Daniel's reasoning here, because 515 B.C. was for him still well in the future. It is true that from 605 B.C., Daniel's time of captivity, to 538/37 B.C., the date of Judah's return, something less than a full seventy years elapsed, but apparently God was gracious in response to Daniel's prayer and saw fit to shorten the time by a few months. It should be recognized also that Jerusalem, the city, was not desolate all these seventy years, but only following

586 B.C. The phrase "desolation of Jerusalem," however, is not intended specifically, but only representatively for the whole captivity situation, it being a very important aspect of it.

B. DANIEL'S PRAYER (vv. 3-19)

Burdened for his countrymen, Daniel began to pray. Surprisingly, though his interest was in an early return of the people, he did not make this the stress of his prayer. In fact, he mentioned this request specifically only at the very last, with the words, "Defer not." His emphasis, rather, was on the sin of the people, making earnest confession of it before God. Daniel clearly was fearful lest the sin of the people should cause God to postpone the return, making him recognize that the greatest need was to seek God's forgiving grace rather than to present the request proper.

9:3. Then I set my face unto the Lord God to seek by prayer and supplication, with fasting and sackcloth and ashes.

I set my face: The word for "I set" means literally "I gave (root, *naṯan*), but it carries here the thought of deliberate action. Some expositors believe that the idea of Daniel setting his face toward Jerusalem, as in 6:10, is implied. This may be true, but the force of the verse is on his setting his face to God. *The Lord God:* The word for "Lord" is *'aḏonay,* meaning "Lord, master," rather than Yahweh, as in verse two. This shows that Daniel was coming to God in recognition of His Lordship and authority. This fits his manner of prayer; making confession and asking forgiveness. *To seek by prayer and supplication:* Attitude in prayer is more important than words. The stress of the verse is on Daniel's attitude. It is significant that no object is given to "to seek." The importance was not on what Daniel sought, but on his heart attitude in seeking. "By prayer and supplication" tells the manner. The word for "prayer" *(tᵉpillah)* means "intercession," and that for "supplication" *(taḥᵃnûnîm)* means "entreaty for mercy." *With fasting and sackcloth and ashes:* Further stress is laid on Daniel's humble attitude. That he came with "fasting" shows that he had been preparing himself before coming. The degree of his burden is indicated also by his dressing in sackcloth, with ashes sprinkled on his head. All three actions were customary for the day, when genuine contriteness of heart was felt (cf. Ezra 8:23; Neh. 9:1; Esth. 4:1, 3, 16; Job 2:12; Jonah 3:5, 6).

9:4. I prayed to Yahweh, my God, and I made confession, saying, O Lord, the great and awesome God, who keeps covenant and steadfast love with those who love Him and keep His commandments.

Yahweh, my God: Daniel addressed God by His personal name, Yahweh. In the book of Daniel, only in this chapter is this sacred name used. But here it is used seven times, including the mention in verse two, already noted. The name depicts God as the gracious, covenant-keeping God of Israel, who is willing to reveal to man and hear man when he prays. This name was the logical one for Daniel to use as he voiced the prayer. That he adds "my God" is significant for showing that he indeed believed in, and now prayed to, this God and not some false deity of the Babylonians. *I made confession:* Daniel states clearly the burden of the prayer: to make confession. The sins he confessed were mainly those of Israel, in which he himself had been little, if any, involved. But still he confessed as though he were as blameworthy as any. In this spirit, he was later followed by Ezra (9:5-15), both men demonstrating intercession of the truest kind. It should be noted that because Daniel's prayer carries this similarity to Ezra's and also to certain features of prayers in Nehemiah 1 and 9, some expositors assert that Daniel's prayer must have been composed later than those, showing dependence on them. This assertion is used as an argument for the late writing of Daniel. The view must be fully rejected. These prayers have similarities because burdens and needs of like kind were felt. If any dependence at all was experienced, it was Ezra and/or Nehemiah on Daniel, not vice versa. *O Lord:* Now begins the prayer proper, and it continues through verse nineteen. It is one of the longer prayers recorded in the Bible. Daniel began by citing some of God's glories, thus revealing still further his sense of humility. The word for "O" is *'anna',* a particle of entreaty, roughly equivalent to "please," or "ah, I pray." The word for "Lord" is again *"donay,* meaning "Lord, Master," *Awesome:* The Hebrew word is *nôra',* from the verb *yare',* "to fear," thus meaning "one to be feared."

Covenant and steadfast love: From God's greatness, Daniel turns to God's faithfulness. The two thoughts form a contrast, no doubt placed side by side intentionally. God's greatness exalts Him far above man, and His faithfulness brings Him near. Though God is indeed great, still He is willing to condescend in demonstrating faithfulness to unworthy man. The translation given does not show that both words "covenant" and "steadfast love" have the article. If this were true only of "covenant," one would think specifically of the Mosaic covenant. Since it is true also of "steadfast love," however, it is better to think of Daniel's using both words as appellative nouns, employed in a generic sense, which is the thought reflected in the translation. The idea is that God keeps *all* covenants He makes and then *always* extends steadfast love to man in his frailty and inability to live up to them. There is significance in the fact that Daniel puts the two thoughts together. God not only graciously makes covenant with man, but also extends necessary love toward man as man finds himself falling short of meeting his responsibilities in the covenant.

The word for "steadfast love" *(ḥesed)* is often translated "kindness," but it carries the additional thought of steadfastness on God's part in granting the kindness or love. *Who love Him and keep His commandments:* Daniel identifies those who can expect these gracious benefits; namely, those who love and obey God. These two thoughts also go together. Obedience is love demonstrated. The thought can be paraphrased: "with those who love Him and demonstrate it by obeying Him." Clearly implied is Daniel's recognition of why Israel was then in captivity: the people had not fulfilled God's requirement for blessing. It should be noted that Daniel employed, already in these opening lines, both the second and third person manner of reference to God, addressing Him directly at one time and then referring to Him by "Him" and "His." He continued this interchange throughout the prayer, speaking at one time to God and then about God. This is not unique to Daniel, however; cf. Ezra's prayer, for instance (Ezra 9:5-15).

9:5, 6.   We have sinned and committed iniquity and done wickedly and rebelled, turning aside from Thy commandments and judgments. We have not listened to Thy servants the prophets, who spoke in Thy name to our kings, our princes, and our fathers, and to all the people of the land.

We have sinned: Daniel began his confession forcefully, using four parallel verbs to stress the degree of Israel's sinfulness. The word for "have sinned" *(ḥaṭa'nû)* means "to miss the mark, wander from the way"; "committed iniquity" *('awînû),* "to distort, act perversely"; "done wickedly" *(hirsha'nû),* "to do known wrong"; "rebelled" *(maradnû),* "to defy authority." Israel was guilty in all respects. *Turning aside from:* The word for "turning aside" is an infinitive absolute, not parallel with the four verbs just noted. It gives the basic reason for them. Israel had sinned because the people had turned away from God's "commandments and judgments." The words for "commandments" and "judgments" are synonyms for God's Law, the first speaking of laws as authoritative demands of God and the second as products of His wise judgment. They do not in this instance seem to specify respective aspects of the Law, as they do in some contexts.

We have not listened: Not only had the Law not been obeyed, but the people had not listened to God's prophets, who had called this disobedience to their attention. The people were thus twice guilty. *Kings . . . princes . . . fathers . . . all the people:* Daniel listed, in a descending order of importance, those to whom the prophets had so spoken. Prophets spoke most frequently to people of greater influence, especially kings. However, they also contacted the common people, though mainly by sermon. It is this contact that called for their inclusion in the list.

9:7, 8. To Thee, O Lord, belongs righteousness, but to us shame of face as at this day, even to the men of Judah and to the inhabitants of Jerusalem and to all Israel, both near and far off, in all the lands whither Thou hast driven them, because of their treacherous sins which they committed against Thee. O Yahweh, to us is shame of face, to our kings, to our princes, and to our fathers, who have sinned against Thee.

To Thee, O Lord: Here Daniel set up another contrast: God's righteousness versus Israel's shame. The force is to say that God is in no way to be blamed for Israel's sinfulness. He had not been lax in warning, nor unclear in demands. The word for "Lord" is again *ᵃdonay,* a name indicating authority. *To us shame of face:* Since Daniel had already stressed the concept of sin, he then made the contrast with the result of that sin: Israel's shame of face. The word *boshet* is better translated "shame" than "confusion," as in KJV. The phrase "shame of face" is often used in the Old Testament (Ps. 44:15; Jer. 7:19), because shame felt in the heart is normally reflected on the face. "As at this day" is added to particularize and illustrate the shame in mind. The Judeans with Daniel knew this kind of shame, having been taken captive, their homeland being in ruin, and themselves experiencing the domination of a pagan people. *Men of Judah . . . inhabitants of Jerusalem . . . all Israel:* Daniel spelled out those who experienced this shame of face. He did so in this verse in terms of geographical distribution, and in verse eight in terms of station in life. He thus says forcefully that none have escaped this shame. "Men of Judah" refers to all citizens of Judah—the country, not merely the tribe. "Inhabitants of Jerusalem" picks the citizenry of the capital as being especially involved, their city having been extensively destroyed, and a greater percentage of their people likely having been taken captive. "All Israel" refers inclusively to all Israelites, whether in the homeland or dispersed throughout the world. *Whither Thou hast driven them:* The captives of the northern nation of Israel had been taken captive to Assyrian cities, those of Judah to Babylon, where Daniel was, and others had fled to Egypt after the assassination of Gedaliah (Jer. 43:1-7). Though the last group had gone contrary to God's will, as revealed through Jeremiah, they still were in Egypt as a general result of the conquest of Judah by Babylon, and Daniel apparently thought of them also as having been driven into exile as punishment for sin. *Their treacherous sins:* It is difficult to determine which effect Daniel had in mind as resulting from Israel's treacherous sins: whether Israel's shame of face or her being driven into pagan lands, both having just been mentioned. In a sense, the two were the same, the one leading to the other. That God had so driven them was what had resulted in the shame of face. The word for "treacherous sins" *(ma'al)* carries the connotations of stealth, treachery, unfaithfulness.

O Yahweh: Some textual doubt remains, but the favored reading shows Daniel reverting from *'ªdonay* to *Yahweh* in this verse as His term of address. Apparently Daniel wished to keep a fuller concept of God in mind as he wrote, the first name connoting authority, and the second, grace, as observed above. *Kings ... princes ... fathers:* Now Daniel depicts the extent of Israel's shame by noting the various gradations of people affected. Those who had suffered were not only the common people, but also kings, princes, and fathers. King Jehoiachin, taken captive in 597 B.C., had been kept in prison in Babylon for thirty-seven years (2 Kings 25:27); and Zedekiah, ruling in 586 B.C., had seen all his sons killed and then had been taken captive himself (2 Kings 25:7).

9:9, 10. To the Lord our God belong mercy and forgiveness; because we have rebelled against Him, and have not listened to the voice of Yahweh our God, to walk in His laws, which He set before us by His servants the prophets.

Mercy and forgiveness: In verse seven, as noted, Daniel spoke of God's righteousness; here, of His mercy and forgiveness. All three words carry the article, again as appellative nouns, used in a generic sense. The same is true of nouns so characterized in the discussion under verse four (which see). The word for "mercy" is *raḥªmîm,* meaning physiologically "the bowels," but then, figuratively, "pity, grace, mercy," which, it was thought, proceeded from the bowels. The word for "forgiveness" is *sᵉliḥôt,* used regularly of God's forgiveness or pardon. That both are plural signifies intensity in God's manifestation of them. *We have rebelled:* A paraphrase makes the thought clear: "To the Lord our God belong mercy and forgiveness; and we need these because we have rebelled against Him." Daniel thus further emphasized Israel's sinfulness.

Have not listened: This explains the way in which the people had demonstrated their rebellion; not having listened to God. Again the personal name, Yahweh, is employed; called for by the thought of condescension on God's part to voice words to finite man. *By His servants the prophets:* The Israelites had not listened to God in that they had not obeyed His laws. In noting that these laws had been set before the people by the prophets, Daniel spoke really of the reiteration of the laws. The thought is parallel to that of verse six. Literally, Daniel wrote, "By the hand of His servants the prophets," but this is merely a forceful way of depicting these men as God's instruments.

9:11, 12. Indeed, all Israel has transgressed Thy Law and turned

aside, refusing to hear Thy voice; and the curse and the oath, which are written in the Law of Moses, the servant of God, have been poured out upon us, because we have sinned against Him. So He has confirmed His words, which He spoke against us and against our judges who judged us, by bringing upon us a great calamity, so that there has not been done under all the heaven like that done in Jerusalem.

Transgressed Thy Law: The inclusiveness of Israelites who had sinned is again set forth. The interest this time is to show the propriety of God's curse and oath being effected. The word for "transgress" *('aḇar)* means first "to pass over" and then "to sin," probably in the sense of passing over or beyond the bounds of the Law. *Curse and the oath:* For an illustration of curses written in the Law, see Deuteronomy 28:15ff. Curses were solemnly threatened as a way of giving incentive for the people to obey God. The oath *(shᵉḇuʻah,* from *shabaʻ,* "to swear"), used in various forms, was added to statements, usually either promises or warnings, to lend a sense of authority or solemnity. The thought here is that God's punishing curse, backed by His solemn oath, had been poured out upon Israel. *Have been poured out:* The word used (root, *nataḵ)* may have as subject either water (Ex. 9:33) or metal (Ezek. 22:21, 22), and is highly expressive here in reference to the curse and oath. God had fulfilled His promised curse, not as a few drops sprinkled, but a volume poured out.

Confirmed His words: The word for "confirmed" (root, *qûm),* used here in the hiphil (causative), means "caused to stand." God had caused His word of curse to stand, by fulfilling it in this severe manner. God means what He says (cf. Deut. 9:5; Neh. 9:8; Jer. 35:17; 36:31). *Against us and against our judges:* The word for "against" both times is the preposition *'al.* God's curses are "against" a person when disobedience calls for their fulfillment. "Against" is the best translation here (and not "concerning," sometimes used), because Daniel views the curses as having had to be fulfilled. The word for "judges" refers to Israel's leaders generally, not merely those specifically called by the term prior to the monarchy. God's curses and oaths had concerned both the people at large and their leaders. *A great calamity:* Reference is to the captivity and its attendant suffering. Though Israelites were not greatly mistreated in Babylon (witnessed, among other factors, by many of them choosing to remain there even when given opportunity to return, in 538/37 B.C.), still their being away from home, Temple, country, and the freedom they enjoyed made the Exile an experience of real suffering. Daniel's phrase means literally "a great evil" *(raʻah gᵉdolah).* His added words, that the experience was worse than what had been meted out on any other nation, stresses the greatness of it. He may refer by this mainly to the destruction wrought in the land itself at the time the captivity was effected.

9:13, 14. Even as written in the Law of Moses, all this calamity has come upon us, for we have not entreated the favor of Yahweh, our God, by turning from our iniquities and giving heed to Thy truth. Accordingly, Yahweh has kept ready the calamity and has brought it upon us, because Yahweh, our God, is righteous in all His works which He has done; but we have not listened to His voice.

Even as written: Apparently Daniel felt the need of emphasizing that what was happening had been forewarned, even having been written down. The people should have taken heed. *We have not entreated the favor of Yahweh:* Literally, "we have not smoothed the face of Yahweh." The word for "entreated" (root, *halah*) means in the piel (intensive), here used, "to smooth," and the word for "favor" is "face" *(panîm)*. The figurative meaning is self-evident. *By turning . . . giving heed:* Daniel identifies what the people should have done to accomplish this entreatment; namely, turned from their sin and given heed to God's truth. "Giving heed to Thy truth" is literally "to act wisely in Thy truth." "To act wisely," means "to give heed." Both verbs are infinitive constructs. The "lᵉ" prefixed to each should be taken as "in respect to," a meaning approximated by the instrumental "by."

Has kept ready the calamity: The word for "kept ready" (root, *shaqad*) means "to watch over," especially when followed by *'al,* as here. The thought is that God had been watching over the warning curse of calamity (again *ra'ah,* "evil") through the centuries, that it might be kept in readiness to use at any time. *God is righteous:* The righteousness of God calls for justice in all His actions. It had called for justice here in the dispensing of the calamity due for the sin committed.

9:15, 16. And now, O Lord our God, who brought forth Thy people from the land of Egypt by a strong hand and hast made Thee a name, as at this day, we have sinned, we have done wickedly. O Lord, according to all Thy righteousness, let Thine anger and Thy wrath be turned away from Thy city Jerusalem, the mount of Thy holiness; because, due to our sins and the iniquities of our fathers, Jerusalem and Thy people have become a reproach to all round about us.

Who brought forth: This element continues the note of praise, and it is also preparatory for the important request of the prayer: that God return His people now from Babylon, in similar manner. *Hast made Thee a name:* God had made Himself a name at the time of the Egyptian deliverance, especially through the ten plagues (cf. Ex. 7:5; 9:16; 1 Sam. 4:7, 8; 6:6; Isa. 63:12; Jer. 32:20), and He had done the same in Babylon, particularly through Daniel (cf. Dan. 2:46, 47; 3:28, 29; 4:1-3, 37; 6:25-27). Daniel desired that God add to that "name" by showing His power in delivering His people again. *We have sinned, we have done wickedly:* Daniel's return to the theme of confession almost seems out of place now. One expects him rather to move on at this point to his request. That he did return to it shows further how deeply he felt its need. He could not yet presume on the grace of God until he had once more admitted sinfulness. He did so here more pointedly and succinctly than at any previous time, however, as if to move on as quickly as possible.

According to: At last Daniel began to state the request; and he did so, first, on the basis of God's own righteousness. Daniel did not claim that God owed Israel deliverance, for the Israelites deserved only the punishment they were experiencing. Rather, he asked on the basis of God's righteous acts of history, which had before been able to include gracious deliverance for His people, particularly from Egypt. One might paraphrase the thought in this way: "According to Thy righteous acts in history, which included gracious deliverance for Thy undeserving people, do Thou the same now." *Thine anger and Thy wrath:* The words for "anger" *('ap)* and "wrath" *(hamah)* are close synonyms, used together for emphasis. Daniel's first request was, then, that God turn away His displeasure, a turning away which would indicate that God considered that His justice had been satisfied by the punishment thus far experienced by His people. *From Thy city Jerusalem:* One would expect Daniel to have asked that God's anger be turned from the people, especially those in captivity. Instead, he substituted Jerusalem for the people, apparently as the place where the great sin occurred which called for the punishment. Perhaps, also, Daniel believed that a reference to Jerusalem as God's city, even the mount of His holiness, would provide a point that would incline God to extend mercy more quickly. Jerusalem was indeed the mount of God's holiness, because there the Temple had stood and would stand again. *Have become a reproach:* Daniel tied this thought with the former, both elements being designed to urge God's gracious response. Not only was Jerusalem God's own holy city, but, because of the captivity, it had become a cause for reproach among surrounding nations. God's name had been dishonored, for it seemed to Israel's neighbors that Babylon's gods were more powerful than Israel's Yahweh. It should be noted that Daniel assigned the reason for this reproach to "the sins and the iniquities of our fathers," and not to God's anger. He was careful not to imply any blame on God's part, recognizing that God's anger was necessary in view of the cause presented by the people.

9:17-19. Now therefore, O our God, hearken to the prayer of Thy servant and to his supplications; and, for the Lord's sake, cause Thy face to shine upon Thy sanctuary which is desolate. O my God, incline Thine ear and hear; open Thine eyes and see our desolations and the city which is called by Thy name; for not because of our righteousness do we lay our supplications before Thee but because of Thy great mercy. O Lord hear, O Lord forgive, O Lord give heed and act; defer not, for Thy sake, O my God, because Thy city and Thy people are called by Thy name.

For the Lord's sake: By this phrase, Daniel stated again the point of verse sixteen, just noted. For God to let the people return and rebuild the holy city and Temple would be for His own sake. It may be observed in passing that all prayer should be made for the Lord's sake. *Cause Thy face to shine:* At this point Daniel began a series of positive requests. In verse sixteen, the request was negative: let God put away His anger. Now, positively, let God cause His face to shine; meaning, let it radiate favor and good will (cf. Num. 6:25; Ps. 80:3). This is asked specifically in respect to the sanctuary (*miqdash,* meaning "holy place"). That Daniel should ask this for the Temple fits with the fact that the burden of his request was for the Lord's sake. God's house was more important than the people's houses. The Temple had been desolate, and therefore a reproach, since its destruction in 586 B.C., nearly fifty years before.

Incline Thine ear ... open Thine eyes: These are anthropomorphic expressions, serving to make the petition more concrete. The words for "incline Thine ear" mean literally "stretch out Thine ear." *Our desolations and the city:* Once more people and city are closely associated. "Desolations" *(shom^emôt)* refers to conditions resulting from being laid waste, with the plural form expressing intensity. The city was again tied to God's own interest. A literal translation is: "the city upon which Thy name is called." *For not because ... but because:* Daniel made clear that he asked only on the basis of God's great mercy, not on the basis of any claim of Israel, for none existed. Actually, all prayer must be asked on the basis of God's mercy, for no man deserves God's favor. Because Daniel knew that God's mercy is great, he believed he could ask God to incline His ear and open His eyes, thus accounting for the causal "for."

Hear ... forgive ... give heed and act ... defer not: These verbs bring the prayer, and especially the request, to a climax. The rest has been preparatory. The verbs come rapidly, like hammer blows of insistence. They still are reserved in tone, continuing to show Daniel's humble spirit, but his great earnestness shines through with clarity. He wanted God to "hear" his petition: "forgive" the people's sin, so that mercy could be extended; then "give heed" to the need and "act" to alleviate it, and so "defer not" in bringing the seventy-year captivity to a close. The last verb comes the nearest to expressing the precise request. As noted under verse two, Daniel wanted God to reckon the *terminus a quo* of the seventy-year period as 605 B.C., the date of his own captivity, rather than either 597 or 586 B.C., and accordingly asked that God "defer not." *For Thy sake:* This is one more indication that he had God's interest in mind as the basis for the request. In this connection, it should be noted that Daniel employed four direct addresses of God in this nineteenth verse, all serving further to indicate his interest in God's glory, and not the people's or his own. *Are called by Thy name:* This thought is repeated from verse eighteen; only this time the people as well as the city are included as being called by God's name. Because both carry His name, His deliverance of them would bring honor to Himself.

C. The Prediction of the Seventy "Weeks" (vv. 20-27)

God's response to Daniel, given through the angel Gabriel, came even before the prophet finished the prayer. The content of the response no doubt surprised him, because it does not refer to the seventy-year captivity at all. It speaks rather of a period of time called "seventy weeks (sevens)" as determined for the accomplishment of certain matters relative to God's people. Numerous interpretations have been suggested for the meaning of this expression and how the period it designates relates to Jewish history. The following are the principal types.

1. *View of many liberals* The view held mainly by liberal expositors, who date the book of Daniel late, depicts the period as running from Jerusalem's destruction to the time of Antiochus Epiphanes. Adherents of the view show differences among themselves as to how the specific divisions, designated as making up the period, are to be historically identified. Montgomery, a representative, holds that the first division of seven "weeks" runs from Jerusalem's destruction (586 B.C.) to Babylon's fall to Cyrus (539 B.C.); the next sixty-two "weeks," from then to the time of the high priest, Onias III (170 B.C.); and the last "week," through the rule of Antiochus.

2. *View of amillennialists* A view held by many amillennialists takes the seventy "weeks" as completed by the general time of Christ's first coming. Young, a representative of this view, sees the initial seven "weeks" as running from the first year of Cyrus (538 B.C.) to the completion of the work of Ezra and Nehemiah (about 440 B.C.); the next sixty-two "weeks," from then until Christ; and the last "week," as including the time of Christ's ministry and even, in some sense, Jerusalem's destruction forty years later. Young views the "weeks" as symbolizing indefinite periods of time, rather than durations of seven years specifically.

3. *View of Keil and others*   Keil and others also believe that the "weeks" are to be taken symbolically, but they see the first group of seven as extending until Christ's first coming; the next sixty-two, until the Antichrist; and the final "week," through the last-day events pertaining to Christ's second coming.

4. *View of premillennialists*   The premillennial view, followed in this exposition, takes the "weeks" as literal seven-year periods. It sees the relation between the response of God to Daniel's prayer as follows: that, whereas Daniel had been concerned regarding an early return of the Jews from their captivity to Babylon, God was interested in, first, their deliverance from a far more serious bondage to sin (which had caused their Babylonian captivity) through Christ's work at His first coming and, second, their final release from earthly oppression through the power of Christ at His second coming. Accordingly, God's answer was that seventy "weeks" of years (490 years) would be necessary to accomplish both aspects of deliverance; that after sixty-nine of these (483 years) the first would be effected through the death of Christ; and that, following an indefinite interval of time, the seventieth would ensue and the second deliverance would be carried out through a triumph of Christ over a great army led by the Antichrist. During the seventieth week, the Antichrist will have brought terrible suffering on Israel, which is the thought with which the chapter closes. The detail of Christ's victory is only implied here but is set forth clearly in Daniel's other visions (7:11, 26, 27; 8:25; 11:45).

In the commentary to follow, this last view will be presented, with corresponding argument in support. At the same time, some reference will be made to the other three positions, and mainly to that of the amillennialists, since many more conservative scholars hold to it than to the other two. Eight verses are devoted to this important message to Daniel through Gabriel, and of these the first four present the setting of that message.

9:20-22. **While I was yet speaking and praying and making confession of my sin and the sin of my people Israel, and laying my supplication before Yahweh, my God, for the holy hill of my God; indeed, while I was yet speaking in prayer, the man Gabriel, whom I had seen in the vision at the first, having been caused to fly swiftly, touched me about the time of the evening offering; and he instructed me and spoke with me and said, Daniel, now I have come to make you wise in understanding.**

While I was yet speaking: Daniel was interrupted in his prayer. Perhaps he had in mind to become still more specific in asking for the cessation of the captivity period, but he was not given the opportunity. Evidently God considered that he had said enough at this point and stopped him so that the answer might be given. The four verbs for "speaking," "praying," "making confession," and "laying my supplication," all used earlier in this chapter by Daniel, are repeated to give a full characterization of the prayer, as if to summarize all that Daniel had intended in it. The thought is also reiterated that Daniel had prayed for God's "holy hill," to note again that the interest in the prayer had been God-centered.

The man Gabriel: Gabriel, the chief angel of divine communication (cf. 8:16), is called "the man," likely as a way of identifying him with the one seen by Daniel in the second vision (8:15, 16). The word this time is different, however: *'îsh* instead of *gaḇer*. No doubt, he appeared in human form in both instances. *In the vision at the first:* This phrase serves further to identify Gabriel with the one seen before. "At the first" *(baṭṭᵉhillah)* does not refer to the very first vision, for Gabriel appeared only in the second. The propriety of the phrase exists in that the first two visions occurred close together in time (only two years apart), and thirteen years had elapsed since the second one. *Having been caused to fly swiftly:* The exact meaning of this phrase *(mu'aḇ bî'aḇ)* is difficult to ascertain. The first of the two words is a hophal (causative passive) participle, but whether from root, *'uḇ,* meaning "to fly," or *ya'aḇ,* meaning "to be weary," is not clear. The second word quite surely comes from the root *ya'aḇ,* but whether this root, which normally means "to be weary," can also mean "to go swiftly" (related in thought by weariness coming from swift movement) is disputed. The translation here given, taking the root of the first word as *'uḇ* and the meaning of the second as "to go swiftly," finds the following support. First, though *ya'aḇ* normally means "to be weary," a rather good case for its meaning also "to go swiftly" can be made (as does Gesenius, for instance) on the basis of its derivative *tô'apah* meaning "swiftness" as well as "weariness." Second, the principal versions—Greek, Latin, and Syriac—use translations having to do with the idea of "flying," a concept in keeping with swiftness of movement. Third, the idea of rapid movement, rather than weariness, fits the context better. In verse twenty-two, Gabriel spoke of having "come" to Daniel, and verses twenty and twenty-one show that he was already present even before Daniel finished praying. On the other hand, the idea of weariness does not fit the nature of a heavenly messenger at all. To escape this difficulty, Keil, who favors this idea, refers it back to Daniel's experience in the second vision, when Gabriel had first come to him. Daniel did faint at that time in Gabriel's presence, but one wonders at the sense and propriety of repeating that fact in this context. *Touched me:* The word for "touched" (root, *naga'*) can mean "reach, extend to" as well, and some expositors favor this translation here; especially since the verb is followed by the preposition *'el,* meaning "unto," rather than *bᵉ,* meaning "in, at, on." It is used elsewhere with *'el,* however, to mean "touch" (cf. Num. 4:15), and here the idea "touch" fits well because Daniel apparently was still praying when interrupted. A touch would likely have been needed to call his attention. The interruption came at the time of the evening sacrifice, a point in the day commonly used for prayer (cf. Ezra 9:5; Ps. 141:2).

He instructed me: "Me," the object of "instructed" (*yaben,* meaning "caused to understand"), is here supplied. The thought is: "he gave instructions as he spoke with me, saying. . . ." *Wise in understanding:* The word for "understanding" *(bînah)* is a noun and provides the area in which the angel desired to make Daniel wise. Gabriel's following words spell out the nature of that area.

9:23. At the beginning of your supplications, a word went out and I have come to make it known, for you are greatly beloved; so consider the word and understand the appearance.

At the beginning: This "beginning" may have been at the early part of the day in which the actual prayer was later offered, because, according to verse three, Daniel's preparations for this prayer started well beforehand, even including fasting. God did not need to wait until Daniel expressed his heart's intent in words to know what he desired. *A word went out:* The Hebrew speaks only of "word" *(dabar),* not "commandment," as in KJV. This "word" is no doubt the information contained in verses twenty-four to twenty-seven, calculated to give Daniel understanding as to Israel's future. God had conveyed this information to Gabriel at the time indicated. *I have come:* In turn, Gabriel had come to relay this information to Daniel. These words and those of the preceding verse, "having been caused to fly swiftly," favor the idea that Gabriel appeared to Daniel in an actual, corporeal body, rather than merely in vision, as in chapter eight. *For you are greatly beloved:* This notice gives the reason for the high favor bestowed on Daniel in being selected to receive this important information and for having it conveyed through an actual appearance of Gabriel. The word for "greatly beloved" *(ḥᵃmûḏôt)* means more literally "one desired, counted precious," with the qualifying "greatly" being taken from the plural form of the word. What a wonderful statement regarding a human mortal this is, and what a commentary on the kind of life Daniel had been leading while a captive in Babylon. *Consider the word and understand the appearance:* Before relating the information, Gabriel urged Daniel to give close attention. The same root verb *(bîn)* is used for both "consider" and "understand," but the first is in the qal form and the second in the hiphil, suggesting a desired increase in degree of understanding. The word for "appearance" *(mar'eh)* is often translated "vision" here, but "appearance" is better, for not only is this the basic meaning of the word (root, *ra'ah,* "to see"), but "vision" tends to confuse, implying that Gabriel's appearance was only in vision rather than actual. The overall thought might be paraphrased thus: "Consider the word I am about to give and understand all concerned in connection with my appearance to you."

9:24. Seventy weeks are determined concerning your people and concerning your holy city to restrain transgression, to make an end of sins, to atone for iniquity, to bring in everlasting righteousness, to seal up vision and prophet, and to anoint a holy of holies.

Seventy weeks: The word for "weeks" is simply "sevens" *(shabu'îm).* The word itself does not designate the units of time involved, whether days, weeks, months, or years. That they are to be understood as years, however, may be argued as follows. First the form of the word *(shabu'îm)* is a participle, meaning literally "besevened," i.e., made up of seven parts. For this reason it frequently means a "week," made up of seven days (Gen. 29:27-30; Dan. 10:2, 3); but it cannot mean this here, because a total of only 490 days (seventy such weeks) would be meaningless in the context. In contrast, a week of years does fit the context well, as the exposition will show. Second, it is clear that the Hebrew people were familiar with the idea of weeks of years as well as weeks of days, because the concept of the sabbatical year was based on this idea, providing the seventh year as a year of rest just as the seventh day was a day of rest (Lev. 25; Deut. 15). Third, since Daniel was here thinking in terms of the seventy-year captivity, he, as a Hebrew, could have easily moved from the idea of one week of years to seventy weeks of years. This follows because, according to 2 Chronicles 36:21, the people had been punished by this Exile so that their land might enjoy the sabbath rests which had not been observed in their prior history (cf. Lev. 26:33-35; Jer. 34:12-22). Knowing this, Daniel would have recognized that the seventy years of the Exile represented seventy sevens of years in which these violations had transpired; and he would have understood Gabriel to be saying, simply, that another period, similar in length to that which had made the Exile necessary, was coming in the experience of the people. Fourth, the only view which calls for rebuttal is that "weeks" is figurative of periods of indefinite lengths; as held, for instance, by both Young and Keil. This view makes the definite numbers, seven, sixty-two, and one, as applied to divisions within the total seventy weeks, hard to understand. Why should definite numbers be applied to periods of indefinite lengths? Moreover, even if for some reason this should be done, at least a length of time proportionate to these numbers should be shown by the historical divisions to which they are assigned, but this is not the case. In Keil's view, for instance, if the first division of seven weeks represents the more than 500 years from Daniel until Christ, then the second division of sixty-two weeks should represent nearly nine times as many years (sixty-two being almost nine times seven), or more than 4,500 years, running until Christ's second advent (which would mean that more than two and one-half millennia still remain today). Also, the third period of one week should then last more than seventy years, a length of time quite out of keeping with any realistic understanding of the last days.

Are determined concerning your people and . . . holy city: The word for "are determined" (root, *ḥatak*), used in the niphal (passive), appears only here in the Old Testament, and means basically (on the ground of comparison with the Aramaic) "to cut off," and from this "to decide, determine." The thought is that God had cut off these 490 years from the rest of history through which to accomplish the deliverances needed for Israel. Daniel had just prayed for both "people" and "holy city," and now the angel referred to both. Gabriel spoke of them as "his" (Daniel's) people and city, because Daniel was of both and had just shown great concern for both. It should be noted that Gabriel said the 490 years will be in reference to the Jewish people and the Jewish capital city, which would seem to exclude any direct concern with Gentiles. That this concern is to be with the city, as well as the people, militates against the idea that the 490 years carry reference only to Christ's first coming and not to His second. It is difficult to see how the physical city of Jerusalem was involved in the deliverance from sin which Christ then effected, but it will be in the deliverance from the destructive oppression which the Antichrist will bring prior to Christ's second coming.

To restrain transgression: This phrase is the first of six parallel phrases of the verse, which summarize what is to be acomplished during the seventy weeks of years. The verse constitutes a unit section as over against the last three verses, which also deal with events of the total period of time. The six items divide themselves into two groups. The first three are negative in force, speaking of undesirable matters to be removed; and the last three are positive, giving desirable factors to be effected. The word for "to restrain" (root, *kala'*) means "to close, shut, restrain." It appears in the piel here, giving the intensive sense, "to restrain firmly." Since this is the only occurrence of piel for this word, some expositors prefer to find its root in the word *kalah,* "to make an end, finish." This is possible, but not preferable, for there is no reason for changing from the more natural root. The strength of the piel actually fits well, as a way of giving emphasis. That which is restrained is "transgression," used with the article *(happesha').* Made thus definite, it probably refers to sin in an all-inclusive sense. *To make an end of sins:* There is a still greater question concerning the root of the verb in this element. The Kethib reading shows it from *ḥatam,* "to seal up," the same root as used in item five of the verse. But the Keri pointing shows that the

Masoretes believed it came from *tamam,* "to complete, make an end of." Numerous Hebrew manuscripts support the Masoretic view, as do the translations of the Syriac and Vulgate versions and the Greek rendition of Aquila. It is noteworthy, also, that when the verb *hatam* is used with the idea of "sin" in other passages, it normally means the sealing up of sin for the purpose of punishment (e.g., Deut. 32:34; Job 14:17), an idea foreign to this text. The word for "sins" *(hatta'ôt),* "to miss the mark" (cf. v. 5), is in the plural, probably in reference to the actual sins of daily life. *To atone for iniquity:* The verb here is *kapar,* "to cover." In the piel, when sin is involved, it means "to atone, expiate." This is the principal Old Testament word for the idea of "atonement." It can even mean "to pardon," when used in reference to God's acting as Judge. The preference must be for "to atone" here, however, for in the parallel section to follow, Christ is described as being "cut off" (v. 26), a clear reference to His crucifixion, when atonement for sin was made. The word for "iniquity," meaning *perverse action* (cf. v. 5), is used in a general sense again, much like "transgression."

Before moving on to the three positive items, a summary of these three negative ones is in order. All three refer to the riddance of sin—that which brought the Israelites into their state of captivity to Babylon. The first introduces the idea of riddance, saying that the coming 490-year period would see its *firm restraint.* In other words, God was about to do something to alleviate this basic, serious problem. The second speaks of the degree of this restraint: sin would be *put to an end.* The third indicates how this would be done: by *atonement.* Though Christ is not mentioned in the verse, the meaning is certain, especially in view of verse twenty-six, that He would be the One making this atonement, which would serve to restrain the sin by bringing it to an end. It is clear that reference in these first three items is mainly to Christ's first coming, when sin was brought to an end in principle. The actuality of sin coming to an end for people, however, comes only when a personal appropriation of the benefit has been made. Since Gabriel was speaking primarily in reference to Jews, rather than Gentiles (see above), this fact requires the interpretation to include also Christ's second coming, because only then does Israel as a nation turn to Christ (cf. Jer. 31:33, 34; Ezek. 37:23; Zech. 13:1; Rom. 11:25-27).

To bring in everlasting righteousness: This is the first of the three positive items. The word for "to bring in" (root, *bô'*) is used in the hiphil, meaning "to cause to come in." The word for "righteousness" *(tsedeq)* is the regular term for this idea in the Old Testament. The word for "everlasting" *('olamîm)* is in the plural, meaning literally "ages." Since "righteousness" is singular, a more literal rendition would be "to bring in righteousness of ages." "Righteousness" is the opposite of sin. In the first three items, sin was to be done away with; leaving the way open for its opposite to be introduced. When Christ died, He provided not only for sin to be removed, but also for righteousness to be granted. He made the provision of Himself, but again it should be noted that the actual becoming righteous by people occurs only when personal appropriation of the benefit is made. Israel as a nation is to make this appropriation at Christ's second coming in power. In this context, the term "everlasting" is significant. Israel had turned to God numerous times during pre-exilic history, and God had always brought blessing; but the turning had been followed regularly by renewed sinning, with consequent punishment. Israel's turning in the future day, however, will be permanent. *To seal up vision and prophet:* The word for "to seal up" *(ḥatam)* means to enclose something authoritatively, hiding it from view and showing that its functions are completed. The word for "vision" *(ḥazôn)* here carries the meaning of revelation (cf. Isa. 1:1; Obad. 1:1). "Prophet" *(nabî')* stands for the prophecy given by prophets. The words taken together refer to the final fulfillment of revelation and prophecy; i.e., when their functions are shown to be finished. The time in mind can only be the final day when Christ comes in power. Many prophecies still remain unfulfilled and require that such a day occur. Young argues against this conclusion, saying that the words "vision" and "prophet" are especially Old Testament words, requiring that the fulfillment in mind concern only Christ at His first coming. But much prophecy pertaining to last days is found in the Old Testament, as well as in the New, and was not fulfilled in Christ's first advent. It awaits the day yet future. *To anoint a holy of holies:* The word for "to anoint" (root, *mashaḥ*) means "to wipe with the hand, anoint." "To anoint" in this context means "to consecrate to religious service." The phrase "holy of holies" *(qodesh qadashîm)* occurs, either with or without the article, thirty-nine times in the Old Testament, always in reference to the Tabernacle or Temple or to the holy articles used in them.[3] When referring to the most holy place, where the Ark was kept, the article is regularly used (e.g., Ex. 26:33), but it is not when referring to the holy articles (e.g., Ex. 29:37) or to the whole Temple complex (e.g., Ezek. 43:12). In view of these matters, it is highly likely that the phrase refers to the Temple also here, which, in view of the context, must be a future Temple; and, since the phrase is used without the article, reference must be to the complex of that Temple, rather than its most holy place. Amillienialists, who reject the idea of a future Temple and who find the fulfillment of this overall passage in Christ's first coming, identify the phrase with Christ Himself, making Him the Holy of Holies. This, however, is

---

[3] Some find an exception in 1 Chron. 23:13, but this is based on forced exegesis.

contrary to the evidence cited. Christ's millennial rule will know a restored Temple,[4] and it is logical to find it as the point of reference of the phrase.

In summation, regarding the time of fulfillment of all six items, the first four are fulfilled in principle at Christ's first coming, when full atonement for sin was made, but fulfilled in respect to actual benefit for Israel as a nation only at Christ's second coming, when the nation will truly turn to God; and the last two items are fulfilled only in connection with the second coming, when prophecies of that time will be fulfilled and there will be a restored Temple to anoint.

9:25. Know therefore and understand that from the going forth of the word to restore and build Jerusalem until an Anointed One, a Prince, will be seven weeks and sixty-two weeks. Street and moat will be restored and rebuilt, but in troublous times.

Know therefore and understand: This begins the second division of the prophecy. It gives explanation regarding the way in which the six items set forth in the first division (v. 24) will be effected. The two verbs employed (roots: *yada'* "to know" and *sakal* "to be wise, understand") are imperfects, but are used in the jussive (indicating urgent obligation), which makes the translation given a proper one. *From the going forth of the word:* This is the indication regarding the beginning point, the *terminus a quo,* of the seventy-week period. The Hebrew means simply "from the time when a word of direction will be given for rebuilding Jerusalem." Since the issuance of this directive would mark the definite starting point of the seventy weeks, it follows that it should be an edict known generally, thus one set forth by an earthly monarch such as the Persian king. Three different edicts pertaining to the return of Judeans and the restoration of Jerusalem were issued by Perian monarchs, and the selection of the one best suiting all involved factors will be made in view of further evidence from the next two phrases. *Until an Anointed One, a Prince:* This is the indication as to the *terminus ad quem* of sixty-nine of these weeks. The word for "Anointed One" is *mashîah,* meaning "Messiah." The word for "Prince" is *nagîd,* meaning "leader, prince," from the idea of "one who goes before." Both terms are applied to various leaders of the Old Testament, but here they clearly refer to Christ. He is the supreme Messiah and Prince; no one else fits the chronology developed in the text; this One is said in the next verse to be "cut off," which fits for the crucifixion of Christ; and by far the majority of expositors agree on this point. Notice should be made that no indication is given as to the particular part of Christ's life, whether

---

[4] Cf. discussion under v. 27 following, pp. 378, 79; also Isa. 66:20, 21; Jer. 33:15-18; Ezek. 20:40, 41; 37:26, 27; 40-46; Zech. 14:16, 17.

birth, baptism, crucifixion, or death, with which the *terminus ad quem* is to be specifically identified.

Will be seven weeks and sixty-two weeks: The period of time between these two extremes is divided into two parts. The first is 7 weeks or 49 years long, and the second 62 weeks or 434 years long. It is logical to find the reason for the division in something of major significance happening 49 years after the beginning of the total period. Before determining the identity of that something, however, it will be helpful to establish the date of both termini, given now the total 69 weeks, or 483 years, separating them. The inquiry, then, concerns what two points of time are separated by 483 years and respectively fit the description of the *terminus a quo* and the *terminus ad quem*.

Almost all conservative expositors take for the *terminus a quo* one of the three times, mentioned above, when Persian rulers issued decrees relative to Jews returning to Jerusalem. They were, first, the decree of Cyrus (Ezra 1:2-4; 6:3-5), issued in 538/37 B.C., shortly after Gabriel's announcement here to Daniel; second, the decree of Artaxerxes (Ezra 7:11-26) given in 458 B.C., at the time of Ezra's return to Jerusalem; and third, the decree of the same Artaxerxes (Neh. 2:5-8, 17, 18) set forth in 445 B.C., at the time of Nehemiah's return. According to Gabriel's announcement here, the decree intended would be one which would deal with the restoration and rebuilding of Jerusalem, but actually none of these concerned this matter directly. The first stressed rebuilding the Temple; the second, the establishment and practice of the proper services at the Temple; and the third, the rebuilding of the walls, when, long before, most of the city had been rebuilt. It is easy to believe, however, that each instance did contribute to the rebuilding of the city; and, furthermore, it may be assumed that Gabriel's descriptive statement was intended in quite a representative way. The words "to restore and build Jerusalem" no doubt carry reference to all that was concerned with the reestablishment of Jerusalem as God's city, with God's people in it, doing the work of God. With these words so taken, any one of the three decrees would qualify.

As to the *terminus ad quem,* again most expositors choose from one of three possible times, all from the life of Christ: His birth (5/4 B.C.), His baptism at the beginning of His ministry (A.D. 26), and His Triumphal Entry (A.D. 30). Because Gabriel's indication here is simply that the sixty-nine weeks would run "until" Christ would come, and, in the following verse, only that it would be "after" these sixty-nine weeks when Christ would be "cut off," once more any one of the three possibilities meet the requirements. The question left, then, for making the precise determination for both termini is: which two of these sets of possible termini present an interval duration of 483 years?

Considering first Cyrus' decree of 538/37 B.C. as the *terminus a quo,* this occasion can now be discarded, because a period of 483 years simply runs out before Christ's birth. Those who hold to it, such as Young,[5] do so by taking the weeks as symbolic in length, finding the first group of seven to symbolize the period from 538/37 B.C. to the general time of Ezra and Nehemiah, and the next sixty-two to refer to the remaining years until Christ. The proportion of total times, however, does not correspond to the numbers, seven and sixty-two, even as with the interpretation of Keil, noted above. Unless the times symbolized are at least proportional to the definite figures used, there seems to be no adequate accounting for the definite figures being used (cf. under v. 24).

Numerous premillennial adherents hold to Artaxerxes' decree given to Nehemiah in 445 B.C. as best. They assert that this directive is nearest in kind to that for rebuilding the city and find evidence in some remarkable mathematical calculations by Sir Robert Anderson, as he seeks to fit the idea of 483 years to this date.[6] Anderson's figures show that between the dates March 14, 445 B.C. (Nisan, the twentieth year of Artaxerxes, Neh. 2:1) and April 6, A.D. 32 (date of the Triumphal Entry, according to Anderson) there are exactly 173,880 days, or 483 prophetic years (years of 360 days) to the very day. The idea of considering prophetic years (lunar years, of 30 days to the month) rather than solar in this context finds support in that the Scriptures, elsewhere in prophetic passages, speak of 42 months as equaling 1,260 days (cf. Rev. 11:2, 3; 12:6; 13:5). If the date of A.D. 32 could be substantiated as the correct year of Jesus' Triumphal Entry, this answer should be accepted as correct.

Since, however, most New Testament scholars do not favor this date for the Triumphal Entry, but believe that the biblical evidence, when tied with that of secular history, points rather to A.D. 30, the third possible *terminus a quo* may provide the best solution.[7] This terminus is the earlier decree of Artaxerxes, given to Ezra in 458 B.C. Figuring on the basis of solar years, the 483-year-period ends now at A.D. 26,[8] and this is the accepted date for Jesus' baptism. To this answer, the objection is sometimes made that actually the decree

---

[5] YPD, pp. 201-206.

[6] *The Coming Prince* (London: Hodder & Stoughton, 1895), pp. 51-129. Cf. also A. J. McClain, *Daniel's Prophecy of the Seventy Weeks,* for a condensed presentation.

[7] Some, such as Culver, *DLD,* p. 145, still favor the 445 B.C. date, and seek a solution to the difficulty by allowing a variance of a few months in the fulfillment. This, however, forfeits the precision of Anderson's dates. A recent article attempts to give credence to the date of A.D. 32; cf. R. E. Showers, *Grace Journal,* XI (Winter, 1970), pp. 30ff. The evidence presented is worthy of notice.

[8] It should be realized that only one year elapsed between 1 B.C. and A.D. 1.

relative to Ezra's return was, of the three possible, the furthest removed from the idea of rebuilding Jerusalem. In reply, however, it may be stated that both the decree and Ezra's resultant work did concern rebuilding Jerusalem in a moral and spiritual way; and there is reason to believe that considerable building operations, of a physical nature, occurred as well (cf. Ezra 9:9).

One question yet remains. What of the division of the 483 years into groups of 49 (seven weeks) and 434 (sixty-two weeks)? What occurred 49 years after the edict of Artaxerxes in 458 B.C., i.e. in 409 B.C., which was of sufficient importance to call for this grouping? The context suggests that it must have concerned the building of Jerusalem, because the very next phrase of the verse speaks of "street" and "moat" being constructed. Can the completion of rebuilding activity in Jerusalem be placed at 409 B.C.? Details are lacking for certainty, but some historical matters point in this direction. First, Ezra and Nehemiah were both assigned by God to rebuilding operations; Ezra mainly (though not exclusively, as noted) in regard to spiritual concerns and Nehemiah to physical. Second, though Nehemiah returned from Jerusalem to Babylon in 433 B.C. (Artaxerxes' thirty-second year, Neh. 13:6), he came again to Jerusalem after a short interval and stayed apparently for the rest of his life. During this second period in Jerusalem, he gave further attention, as had Ezra, to moral and spiritual rebuilding (Neh. 13:7-31), and it may be assumed that he continued physical rebuilding as well. Third, as to the year of completion of his work, Prideaux[9] states that his last action occurred in the fifteenth year of the Persian ruler, Darius Nothus (423-404 B.C.), which would be 409/408 B.C., the very year in view. The significance of the forty-nine-year grouping may have been, then, a setting off of the period of Ezra and Nehemiah and their efforts toward the reestablishment of the Judean capital.

Street and moat: The word for "street" *(r^ehôb)* means "a wide place," and could mean here "a market place" or "public square." The word for "moat" *(harûts)* means something *dug,* hence "ditch, moat," a possible aspect of Jerusalem's fortification. *In troublous times:* This phrase may be translated literally: "in the distress of the times." The thought is that this building activity would be carried on in the face of trouble and opposition. Ezra's difficulties in building spiritually are set forth in Ezra 9 and 10, and Nehemiah's problems in constructing physically are presented in Nehemiah 4:1ff.; 6:1ff.; 9:36, 37. Nehemiah experienced problems also in building spiritually, as indicated in Nehemiah 13.

---

[9] Prideaux (cf. *supra,* chap. 8, p. 218, n. 15) is quoted by Barnes, BD, II, p. 175. Prideaux was a fine historian, but Barnes gives no indication as to his source of information on this matter. What he says, however, is corroborated by Josephus (*Antiq.* XI, 5, 8), who states that Nehemiah "came to a great age, and then died."

9:26. Then after sixty-two weeks, the Anointed One shall be cut off, with nothing for Him. The people of a prince that shall come will destroy the city and the sanctuary; and its end shall be with a flood and until the end of the war desolations are determined.

After sixty-two weeks: Gabriel's words now describe what is to happen to this Anointed One, the Prince, at the close of the total sixty-nine weeks. He does so by referring only to the sixty-two weeks; apparently seeing no need to speak further of the first seven. The word "after" *('aḥ^{a}rê)* calls for notice. It is the only indication given regarding the chronological relation between these sixty-two weeks and the cutting off of the Anointed One. This event will occur "after" their close, but nothing is said as to how long after. The view just presented fits this manner of indication, for, in locating the *terminus ad quem* of the sixty-two weeks at the baptism of Jesus, the crucifixion is made to fall just a little more than three years after. *Shall be cut off:* The word used (root, *karat*) is the regular Old Testament word for the idea of *cutting off*. It is used sometimes to express the thought of the execution of a person deserving the death penalty (e.g., Lev. 7:20; Ps. 37:9; Prov. 2:22). Keil, who believes that the sixty-two weeks run symbolically from Christ's first advent to His second, has real difficulty in explaining this *cutting off* in terms of the second advent. He resorts to the idea that Christ will be "cut off" from "His place and function as the *Maschiach*,"[10] but this is an unsatisfactory meaning for "cut off," and it does not accord with the biblical picture of what Christ experiences when He comes again. The Scriptures depict Him as becoming King of the world, with nations doing obeisance to Him. The words of this verse can refer only to Christ's crucifixion. *With nothing for Him:* The word for "nothing" *('ayin)* is a noun, meaning literally, "nothingness." For this reason, the translation of KJV, "but not for Himself," is not likely, for one would then expect the adverb *lo',* meaning "not," to have been used. Since the phrase modifies the idea of Christ being "cut off," it is best to take it to mean that when Christ was crucified, He did so without apparent friends or honor. He was rejected by men, treated as a criminal, and even forsaken by the Father. In the realm of things attractive and desirable, His portion was equivalent to "nothingness."

People of a prince that shall come: Literally, "people of a prince the one coming." Notice should be made that the subject of the verb "shall destroy" is "people" not "prince." The word for "that shall come" *(habba')* is a participle modifying "prince," made distinctive by use of the article. Two matters of significance should be observed: first, this prince cannot be the same as the one similarly designated in verse twenty-five, who is Christ, for this prince is yet to come,

---

[10] KDC on Daniel, p. 362.

clearly after the death of Christ just mentioned; and, second, he will be important, when he comes, to warrant this sort of notice; this is especially indicated by the use of the article. The use of the article also suggests that this one has been noted in the book earlier (which indeed is the case, when he is identified with the "little horn" of 7:8, 24-26, something to be discussed soon). Also, because no relation exists here in verse twenty-six between the mention of this prince and other matters noted, the implication is strong that this reference to him is in anticipation of something to be said regarding him later, which, as will be observed, is true. *Shall destroy the city and the sanctuary:* The Hebrew word order is inverted, giving this element before the one just considered, thus placing stress on it. "City" and "sanctuary" can refer only to Jerusalem and the Temple, the subjects of the preceding verse, where the rebuilding of both was the matter in view. In this verse, then, there is presented the destruction of what has just been described as being constructed. The sense of the verse is that this destruction was to follow "after" the sixty-two weeks, just as Christ's crucifixion would; and history indicates that it did. It came forty-three years after, at the time when the Romans destroyed Jerusalem and the Temple utterly, in quelling the Jewish revolt of A.D. 70. The identity of the "people" of the prior verse is thus established: the Roman people. As to the identity of the "prince" that should be of this people, some expositors have taken him to be Titus Vespasian, who led the Roman legions in this destruction, but discussion under the following verse will show this to be incorrect. The rationale for mentioning this time of destruction here is best seen in a desire to present a full cycle respecting Jerusalem and the Temple, a cycle moving from the order to rebuild them to their destruction once again. That is, Gabriel's words were to set the beginning of the series of year-weeks in connection with the building of city and Temple, and then the conclusion in connection with not only the Messiah's appearance and death but also the destruction of both city and Temple. It should be noted, however, that not all seventy weeks are said to have elapsed in this cycle. Only sixty-nine have yet been mentioned, and the seventieth is discussed for the first in the following verse.

Its end shall be with a flood: This reads, literally, "its end in the overflowing." The antecedent of "it" is obviously Jerusalem. "Flood" or "overflowing" can refer only to the degree of destruction meted out. History records that the destruction of Jerusalem was very extensive. Titus, with four legions, brought an overflowing ruin on the city, including the Temple. *Until the end of the war desolations are determined:* The Hebrew is subject also to the following translation: "until the end will be war; desolations are determined." In either translation, "war" is best taken in reference to the Jews' struggle against Rome, and the "desolations" which are "determined" must be the desolate conditions which resulted. The two translations are close in meaning, the one laying stress on "war" and the other on "desolations." Either translation emphasizes the severity of the destruction concerned. It is difficult to choose which is best.

9:27. And he shall make a firm covenant with many for one week; and in the midst of the week he shall cause sacrifice and offering to cease; even unto the overspreading of abominations of desolation; and unto the end even what has been determined shall be poured out upon the desolate.

And he: The prior context presents two possible antecedents for this pronoun: the Messiah or the "prince that shall come." Amillenarians favor the former and premillenarians the latter. The following matters give evidence for the premillenarian view. First, the "prince that shall come" is the nearer of the two antecedents, making for a grammatical preference. Second, as noted above, the unusual manner of mention in verse twenty-six regarding that prince calls for just such a further reference as this. There is no reason for the earlier notice unless something further is to be said regarding him, for he does nothing nor plays any part in activities there described. Third, several matters show that what is now said regarding the one in reference does not suit if that reference is to Christ. (a) This person makes a "firm covenant" with people, but Christ made no covenant. God made a Covenant of Grace with people, and Christ fulfilled requirements under it, but this is quite different from Christ's making a covenant. (b) Even if Christ had made a covenant with people during His lifetime, the idea of mentioning it only here in the overall thought of the passage would be unusual, when the subjects of His death and even the destruction of Jerusalem have already been set forth. (c) The idea of the seventieth week, here closely associated with this one, does not fit the life or ministry of Christ, as will be shown presently. (d) The idea that this one causes "sacrifice and offering to cease" does not fit in reference to Christ in this context. The amillennial view holds that these words refer to Christ's supreme sacrifice in death, which made all other sacrifices and offerings of no further use, thus making them to cease in principle. But, if so, what would be the reason for such a statement (true as it is) in view of the purpose of the overall prediction? One could understand a direct statement concerning Christ's providing atonement for sin—though its placing at this point in the general thought order of the passage would be strange—because that would be important to sin-bondaged Israelites. But why, if that is the basic thought, should it be expressed so indirectly, in terms of sacrificing and offering being made to cease?

In contrast, several matters may be cited to show that what is here said regarding the one in reference does fit when that reference is taken to be to the "prince that shall come," identified with the Antichrist, the "little horn" of chapter seven. (1) He is said to be of the Roman people (v. 26), which, as noted under 7:8, 23, 24, is to be true of the "little horn" there described. (2) The use of the term "prince" for this one, the term used in reference to Christ in verse twenty-five, signifies him as one who would in some sense parallel Christ in the role he would play—something uniquely true of the Antichrist, who will be Satan's counterfeit for Christ. (3) As noted before, the use of the article with the participle, "the one coming" (v. 26), implies that this person has been mentioned in the book before; something again true in the figure of the "little horn" of chapter seven. (4) Since the Antichrist has been presented in Daniel's two earlier occasions of revelation (7:8, 23, 24; 8:23-25) and will be again in the last (11:36-45), one might expect that he would be brought into this third location as well. (5) As will be observed, the descriptions in the remainder of this verse fit all that is revealed elsewhere regarding the Antichrist. (6) Amillenarians frequently identify this one with Titus Vespasian, who led the Roman legions against Jerusalem, but Titus simply was not of sufficient importance to biblical history to warrant such a mention. Actually, since the interest of the text taken alone was only to tell of Jerusalem's destruction and not the identity of the destroyer, there was no reason to mention either "people" or "prince" unless both carried biblical significance, which one could expect to be shown elsewhere. Daniel's first vision presented this significance, using the figures of the "fourth beast" (people) and the "little horn" (prince). (7) A reply is called for in respect to an argument by Young, that the text speaks of "a people of a prince" (i.e., people who belong to the prince) and not "a prince of a people," which, he says, makes the thought of this prince living centuries later quite illogical.[11] The reply is that the thought relation intended between "people" and "prince" is not "who belong to," but "from whom will come"; something made clear immediately by the significant addition of "the one coming."

Shall make a firm covenant: Literally, "shall cause a covenant to be strong" (root, *gabar,* used here in the hiphil). A covenant is made strong by being made *firm, sure.* Young argues against this translation, using instead "shall cause to prevail a covenant," which he says means only that this person causes a covenant, already made, to accomplish its intended purpose. Because he believes that Christ is the subject of this activity, he sees this as having been done by Christ in His death, when He fulfilled the terms of God's Covenant of Grace.[12]

[11] YPD, pp. 211, 212.
[12] YPD, pp. 208-212.

In reply, it may be observed first that this would be a strange way to express such a thought. Certainly, "shall cause to prevail a covenant" is not the same as "shall fulfill the terms of a covenant." If the desire had been to say the latter, one would expect different words to have been used. Second, even if the words used could be assigned this meaning, one still confronts the difficulty of explaining the ensuing reference to "one week." Significantly, Young does not try to show how Christ fulfilled the terms of God's covenant for "one week" of years. Christ lived for a total of about thirty-three years, and He ministered for slightly more than three, neither of which periods corresponds to seven years. Third, evidence has already been presented that Christ cannot be the subject of this action, but that the Antichrist is. When he is so taken, the ideas stated in the verse fit together well. The meaning is that he, as king of the restored Roman confederacy (cf. discussions under 2:41-43 and 7:23, 24), will "make a firm covenant" with the Jewish people at the beginning of the seventieth week, setting it up, apparently, for a seven-year period. Since the word for "covenant" (*b*ᵉ*riṯ*) does not carry the article (contrary to the KJV translation), this covenant likely is made at this time for the first time (not a reaffirmation of an old one, then) and probably will concern some type of nonaggression treaty, recognizing mutual rights. Israel's interest in such a treaty is easy to understand in the light of her desire today for allies to help withstand foes such as Russia and the Arab bloc of nations. *With many:* Though no identification is made of these "many," the reference is clear; because Gabriel at the beginning indicated that the "seventy weeks" concerned Daniel's people and holy city. The "many" are the people of Israel. If others were in mind, further indication would have been necessary.

For one week: The seventieth week is now dealt with separately, suggesting special significance for it. Before noting the nature of this significance, however, it is well to take from this mention a further reason why Christ cannot be the subject of the verse. The idea of such a week does not fit the life or ministry of Christ in any respect. Some amillennialists have attempted to make it fit by saying that the first half of this week could be the period of Christ's ministry (nearly three and one-half years), at which time He made "sacrifice and offering to cease" in His crucifixion, and the last half could be the continuation of His ministry, only from heaven. But, if so, why stop after only another three and one-half years? Does not His heavenly ministry still continue? Nothing is known to have occurred three and one-half years after Christ's ascension which would in any way close the week. Some have pointed to the destruction of Jerusalem as being this closing occasion, since it is mentioned in verse twenty-six, but it happened much too late: A.D. 70 not A.D. 33.

This amillennial position proceeds on the assumption that the seventieth week must follow immediately after the sixty-ninth; but several matters in the text argue that actually an extensive time gap exists. (1) This seventieth week is treated in the text apart from the initial sixty-nine, which are presented as though they constituted a unit period of time. (2) The fact, as just noted, that there is serious difficulty with fitting the idea of a seven-year period into Christ's life and ministry calls for another occasion of fulfillment. (3) Both the crucifixion of Christ and the destruction of Jerusalem are mentioned in verse twenty-six, as coming "after" the conclusion of the sixty-nine weeks. The implication is that both also preceded the seventieth week, since this week is mentioned only after they are; and, since forty years intervened between them, at least this amount of time would have to be involved as a gap. (4) The idea of an extensive time gap should not be thought strange here, since the idea has already been set forth in Daniel's first two times of revelation,[13] and will be, as will be noticed, in his last.[14] The rationale for such a gap is simply that there was need to speak of times relative to both advents of ·Christ, and there was no need to speak of history between them, particularly when that history would concern primarily Gentiles, and Gabriel's message concerned Jews (v. 24). (5) This very message of Gabriel has already implied the existence of a gap, because in verse twenty-four the six items mentioned as being fulfilled in the seventy-week period call for the time of both advents to accomplish this, as noted. (6) In Matthew 24:15 (cf. Mark 13: 14) Jesus refers to the "abomination of desolation, spoken of by Daniel the prophet," as something yet future to His time, and, as will be shown presently, Jesus was referring to a feature of this seventieth week designated in this verse.

The special significance of the seventieth week may now be considered. It is treated separately from the first sixty-nine, and its content is examined in a manner different from them, because it is the one part of the total seventy weeks which deals with the time of Christ's second coming. This event still lies in the future today, and already some 1,900 years have elapsed; which means that the gap intended was to be very long. One should remember, however, that God's view of time is quite different from man's (2 Pet. 3:8). Events and conditions today suggest that it may not last much longer. Because the Antichrist is active during this seventieth week (cf. discussion under 2:41-43; 7:8, 23-25; 11:36-45), the time is to be identified with that commonly called the Tribulation period, descriptions of which appear frequently in Scripture (e.g., Ps. 2:5;

[13] Cf. *supra*, chap. 7, p. 187; chap. 8, pp. 222-24.
[14] Cf. *supra*, chap. 11, pp. 304, 305.

Jer. 30:3-11; Ezek. 20:33-44; Matt. 24:15-24; Rev. 6-18). The verse implies that the Antichrist's strong position in the world will continue for the duration of the seventieth week, and other passages indicate that it is at the climax of this period that Christ will come in power to defeat him (7:26, 27; 8:25; 11:45; Zech. 14:1-4; Rev. 19:11-21). The verse implies also that the first half of the week will be a comparatively pleasant time for the Jews, in view of the covenant made with them, but that a radical change will ensue at the middle of the week.

In the midst of the week: The word for "midst" *(hᵃtsî)* means "half" or "midst." Since the Hebrew gives no preposition before it, the phrase might be translated "for the half of the week." This thought too would fit, but it is likely that the beginning point of the action involved is in view rather than its duration. *He shall cause sacrifice and offering to cease:* The words for "sacrifice" *(zebah)* and "offering" *(minhah)* are the regular Old Testament words for these concepts. The thought is that three and one-half years after the Antichrist makes covenant with Israel, he will cause sacrifice and offering to cease. This means that Temple sacrifices will have had to be started sometime before this; and, since at this time the Antichrist will insist that they cease, it may be that a part of the treaty of three and one-half years earlier will have concerned permission to have them. At least a forcing of them to cease is out of keeping with the idea of a covenant still continuing, which means that the covenant, intended to last seven years, will be broken when only half its time has elapsed. That sacrifices will be made to cease by the person here involved provides further evidence for his identification with the Antichrist. The observation was made in chapter eight that Antiochus Epiphanes was typical of the Antichrist, and it was there stated that he also took away Jewish sacrifices in his time. This thought suggests a further rationale for the mention of the Jerusalem destruction in verse twenty-six, for, in the same pattern, Jewish sacrifices and offerings were made to cease at that time.

Even unto the overspreading of abominations of desolation: The word for "overspreading" *(kᵉnap)* is normally translated "wing," but it comes from the root *kanap,* "to cover over,"[15] and in Isaiah 8:8 definitely has the idea of "overspreading," in a destructive sense. The word for "abominations" *(shiqqûtsîm)* means "things detestable," particularly in the realm of false worship, referring often to false idols. The word for "desolation" is a participle (root, *shamam*), which can mean either "something desolated" or "something desolating." The overall thought of the phrase, though difficult and having widely divergent interpretations, must be in keeping with the following two

---

[15] Gesenius is preferred here over BDB; cf. Koehler and Baumgartner.

controlling matters. First, Jesus referred to this verse in Matthew 24:15 (Mark 13:14),[16] as just noted, and spoke of the "abomination of desolation" as something standing "in the holy place." In passing, it may be noted that His manner of reference makes likely the fact that "desolation," used by him in the genitive, is to be taken in the sense of "something desolating," rather than "something desolated." Second, the meaning here must be parallel in thought to an activity of Antiochus Epiphanes, because in 11:31 this same phrase "abomination of desolation" is used in reference to something established by him. Significantly, in both passages (this one and 11:31, cf. 12:11), the mention of this "abomination" immediately follows a statement regarding the taking away of daily sacrifices, thus implying that in some way it took their place. Since Antiochus was typical of the Antichrist (cf. discussion, chap. 8), the thought follows that Daniel's mention of this "abomination" in respect to the times of each was to show further parallel between them. In 1 Maccabees 1:45-54, an indication is given of the nature of the abomination in Antiochus' day. It states that what he did, following his order forbidding "burnt-offerings, and sacrifice, and drink-offerings in the temple," was to "set up the abomination of desolation upon the altar" and build "idol altars throughout the cities of Judah on every side." Then, in 2 Maccabees 6:2, it is indicated that in this way he polluted "the temple in Jerusalem and" called "it the temple of Jupiter Olympius." Whether this "abomination" was actually a statue of Jupiter (Zeus) Olympius or only a substitute altar on which to worship him is not sure, but it is quite clear that it was one or the other.

These two matters point to the overall thought as being that the Antichrist, like Antiochus, will set up in the holy place (the restored Temple) something detestable, like a false altar or a great statue, which will cause a desolate condition there, likely in the nature of worshipers refusing to come to the Temple under these conditions. To the possible objection that the expression "abomination of desolation" is not fully identical here and in 11:31, since here "abomination" is plural and there singular, it may be replied that this plurality could well be due to the greater importance placed on this abomination in the time of the Antichrist (plural of importance, often used in Hebrew).

The most difficult aspect in the overall phrase concerns the first two words *we'al kenap,* translated here "even unto the overspreading of." This translation takes the conjunction as "even," and the prep-

[16] Some have taken Jesus' reference to be to Daniel 12:11, where the phrase is again used, but the context there does not commend it as the intended one, for it implies that a mention of the same subject has been made earlier, like this in 9:27.

osition *'al* as "unto," both quite possible. It also takes *k^enap* as the KJV, "overspreading," similar to its use in Isaiah 8:8. Indeed, "over-spreading" would carry a thought quite parallel to that in Isaiah 8:8: the abominable idol of Antichrist causing an overspreading influence, desolating in nature, for the whole Temple complex and probably beyond. In paraphrase, the full thought would be: "The Antichrist will cause sacrifice and offering to cease and, in their place, erect, even unto the end of causing an overspreading influence, a detestable statue (or altar) in the Temple, desolating in effect."

Unto the end: The word for "end" *(kalah)* means something "finished, complete." Reference may be either to some activity or a length of time. Here the latter must be the case, for the following words indicate an activity to be carried out within it. The length of time in view, obviously, is the seventieth week, the period of the Antichrist's rule, or, more particularly, the last half of that rule when the destruction described will be effected. *Even what has been determined shall be poured out upon the desolate:* The word for "what has been determined" is a niphal (passive) participle (root, *harats,* "to cut" or "to determine"), signifying here "something determined." Reference is to what has been decreed or determined beforehand by God. The word for "desolate" *(shomem)* is another participle and is from the same root as the prior word translated "desolation" (but in the qal here, whereas before it was in the piel). It suits the context best this time if taken in the sense of "something desolated," referring to the ruin effected by the Antichrist. The thought is that, for the duration of the three-and-one-half-year period in view, all the desolating activity that God has determined beforehand would be poured out (the same word as in verse eleven [which see]) upon Jerusalem, making it desolate. The nature of this destructive activity is not described, but a general idea can be taken from what Antiochus did in his day (cf. chap. 8) and from the horrors wrought by the Romans in A.D. 70, an occasion intentionally mentioned for its parallel features in the preceding verse.

This chapter introduces the fourth and last of Daniel's predictive revelations. Taking a total of three chapters for its description, this time of revelation covers approximately the same periods of history as set forth in the vision of chapter eight (periods of Medo-Persia, Greece, and the Great Tribulation); but considerably more detail is given, especially concerning events after Alexander the Great and concerning the Great Tribulation still future. The information was presented, not in the symbolism of animals, as in the first two visions, but in direct word revelation through a heavenly messenger, who appeared to Daniel. This appearance seems again to have been in actual, corporeal form, as in the third revelatory time of chapter nine.

Chapter ten tells of the coming of this heavenly messenger to impart the information. The record of his coming is significant, because it involves his conflict with an emissary of Satan, and states or implies important facts relative to angels and demons and their respective interests in the people and work of God.

A. THE GENERAL SETTING (vv. 1-3)

The first three verses present the general setting for the messenger's appearance.

10:1. In the third year of Cyrus king of Persia, a word was revealed to Daniel, whose name was called Belteshazzar; and the word was true and involved a great conflict. He understood the word and achieved understanding by means of the appearance.

The third year of Cyrus: For the fourth time, Daniel began by giving the date of the revelation concerned. Clearly, he believed that the chronological relation of these instances to each other, and to other events, was significant. This present instance came in Cyrus' third year, which means two years after Gabriel's appearance to Daniel in chapter nine (the first years of Darius and Cyrus being the same). The four occasions came in two groups of two, then: in the first and third years of Belshazzar and the first and third years

264

of Cyrus, with thirteen years intervening. At the time of this fourth instance, Daniel was about eighty-three years of age. One significant thing to note relative to this fourth instance is that it followed about two years after the return of the Jews to Judah. Daniel had prayed in Cyrus' first year (9:1) that this return might soon be permitted, and God answered this prayer affirmatively, because it was in that same year that Cyrus issued the decree allowing it (2 Chron. 36:22; Ezra 1:1). The return may have been effected that very year, or at least no later than the next (538/37 B.C.). Since Daniel was still in Babylon in this third year of Cyrus, it is clear that he had not accompanied the group, probably for two reasons: his advanced years of life, and his high position in the government of Darius as one of three top presidents. Likely God saw best for him to continue in this significant place of influence, for the benefit he might there work in behalf of Jews, whether those who yet remained in the East or those who had already returned to Judah. Another significant matter relates to Daniel's episode in the lion's den. This, too, occurred in the early years of Darius, though after the king had instituted his government. Since there is no way to know how long after, it is impossible to say whether it happened later than the time of this fourth revelation or before, but it was probably near the same time.

King of Persia: Montgomery and others state that this title for Cyrus does not represent contemporary usage; which shows only such designations as, "the king," "the great king," "king of kings," "king of Babel," "king of lands," etc.[1] R. D. Wilson, however, has demonstrated that it was used in some instances,[2] and his conclusion is in keeping with its employment several other times in Scripture (2 Chron. 36:22; Ezra 1:1, 2, 8; 4:3, 5; *et al.*). One cannot use its employment here as an argument for the late writing of Daniel. *A word was revealed:* "Word" refers to the predictive information given through the heavenly messenger, recorded in chapters eleven and twelve. *Called Belteshazzar:* This was the name assigned to Daniel when he had first arrived in Babylon (1:7) and used by Nebuchadnezzar for him after this (4:8, 9, 18, 19). The reason for Daniel's mention of it here is likely to attest that, in spite of the overthrow of the Babylonian government, he was still the same person who had arrived as a captive seventy years before, when the name had been given. *The word was true and involved a great conflict:* The Hebrew word order has "true" coming before "word," thus giving emphasis to it. Daniel wished to reassure the reader on this count, for the information given by the messenger is remarkable (cf. Rev. 19:9; 21:5; 22:6). The word for "conflict" *(tsaba')* is often used to mean an *army*

[1] MICC, p. 405.
[2] "The Title, 'King of Persia' in the Scriptures," *Princeton Theological Review* XV (1917), pp. 90-145.

or *host* of angels and sometimes the *warfare* itself in which an army engages (cf. Job 10:17; Isa. 40:2). Though the word has been translated in a variety of ways here, the meaning most in keeping with the context is "warfare" or "conflict." The thought is that the information given by the messenger involved great conflicts in history to come, which made the overall message hard to believe, and this in turn called for Daniel's reassurance that it was true nevertheless. The conjunction "and" carries the thought of "even though." *He understood and achieved understanding:* The same root word *(bîn)* is used for "understood" (a verb) and "understanding" (a noun). The verb is best taken in reference to this fourth revelatory time, and the noun to the earlier ones, concerning which Daniel had remained puzzled at the times involved (cf. 7:15, 28; 8:27). The statement might be paraphrased: "He understood the word brought here by this messenger and achieved understanding covering all four revelatory times by means of this final appearance.

10:2, 3. In those days I, Daniel, was mourning three weeks of days. Delectable food I did not eat, nor did flesh or wine enter my mouth. I did not anoint myself at all until three weeks of days had elapsed.

In those days: According to verse one, the days in reference occurred sometime in Cyrus' third year; and, according to verse four, they came immediately preceding the twenty-fourth of the first month (Nisan). *I, Daniel, was mourning:* For the fifth time in the book, Daniel calls special attention to himself by the use of "I, Daniel"; his interest being to set himself off from others in the mind of the reader. Daniel's mourning took the form of fasting (v. 2). He thus set his "heart to understand" and to humble himself before God (v. 12). From verse one and the context of verse twelve, it is clear that the understanding he sought concerned the future of Israel. He wanted the best for his people. One may doubt that he thought in terms of this fasting leading to another time of revelation, but the fact that God did so employ it suggests that prophets could make a time conducive to revelation by a proper attitude of heart (cf. 2 Kings 3:15). It is significant also that Daniel, though a busy man in his important presidential post, still took as much as three weeks for this high spiritual purpose. *Three weeks of days:* The phrase "weeks of days" defines these weeks as over against those of chapter nine, which were weeks of years, the same word for "weeks" being used in each instance.

Delectable food . . . flesh or wine: The words for "delectable food" *(lehem h^amudôt)* mean literally, "food of delights." The plural form of "delights" lends emphasis to the idea. Daniel had access to the finest, most tasty food, as well as to the more standard meat and wine. He ate no food of either category, however, during his days of fasting.

Anoint myself: Daniel also abstained from self-anointment. He emphasized the completeness of this abstinence by the added use of the infinitive absolute, saying literally, "anointing myself, I did not anoint myself." The custom was to anoint oneself daily, the oil being applied to exposed skin that might be burned by the sun (Ps. 104:15). Anointing was a sign of joy (Prov. 27:9), and it was normally discontinued in the time of mourning, as here with Daniel (cf. 2 Sam. 12:20; 14:2). These acts of self-discipline were continued by Daniel for three full weeks. Such acts of themselves do not solicit the favor of God, but they constitute suitable exercises which, if sincere, encourage, and give demonstration of, the proper attitude of heart which does.

B. THE APPEARANCE OF THE HEAVENLY MESSENGER (vv. 4-8)

The messenger, who appeared to Daniel in this fourth time of revelation, now is vividly described.

10:4-6. Then on the twenty-fourth day of the first month, when I was beside the great river, that is the Tigris, I lifted up my eyes and looked and, lo, a man clothed in linen, his loins girded with gold of Uphaz, his body like the Tarshish stone, his face like the appearance of lightning, his eyes like lamps of fire, his arms and his feet like the gleam of polished brass, and the sound of his words like the voice of a multitude.

Twenty-fourth day of the first month: The overall passage makes clear that this day immediately followed the three weeks of mourning (cf. vv. 12-14), which means that the first day of mourning had been the third of this first month (Nisan). Since the fourteenth of Nisan was the day of Passover, followed by the seven days of the Feast of Unleavened Bread (15th to 21st, Ex. 12:14-18), both feasts had just nicely been completed by this twenty-fourth day. Probably the special time of the year had been a factor in bringing Daniel to choose it as the time for this fasting and prayer. *Beside . . . the Tigris:* Daniel was beside this river in bodily presence, not merely in vision, having companions with him (v. 7). The Hebrew name of the river is *Hiddakel,* after the ancient Babylonian *Idigla.* The Greeks gave it the modern name *Tigris,* though modern Arabs still call it *Diglah.* Because it is the Euphrates that flowed through ancient Babylon, and not the Tigris, Daniel was away from the capital at the time of this revelation.

A man: On this day, probably while continuing to reflect and pray, Daniel suddenly saw the person now described stand before him. The identity of this person is uncertain. He may have been Gabriel, who had appeared to Daniel for the revelations of chapters eight (v. 16) and nine (v. 21). If so, however, it is strange that he is not mentioned by name, as he was in those chapters. Also, he is described at length here, and was not before. Furthermore, as will be seen under verse twenty-one, the primary task of this person was not revelation, as was true of Gabriel, but waging warfare against particular emissaries of Satan. He may have been the second Person of the Godhead, because the description given is much like that set forth regarding Christ in John's vision on Patmos (Rev. 1:13-16). A difficulty rises here, however, since this one received assistance from the chief angel, Michael, in a conflict with one called "the prince of the kingdom of Persia" (v. 13). It is not likely that a mere angel could be, or would be called upon to be, of assistance to Christ. Some expositors have suggested that he was Michael, but this cannot be, since help is received by him from Michael, as just noted. Furthermore, according to verse twenty-one, Michael is assigned particularly as Israel's guardian prince, whereas this person fights generally against opposing princes sent by Satan. The most likely answer is that this one was another high angel, perhaps of parallel importance with Gabriel and Michael, who was sent with God's information to Daniel in this instance. The added qualifier in the Hebrew, *'ehad,* meaning "one," is indicative of singularity for this person, and is roughly equivalent to the English indefinite article. *Clothed in linen:* White linen symbolized purity; it was worn, for instance, by the priests (Ex. 28:42; Lev. 6:10; 16:4), by Jeremiah as prophet (Jer. 13:1), and by angels (Rev. 15:6). *Girded with gold of Uphaz:* A cloth girdle, varying from two to six inches in width, was customarily worn about the waist. The girdle here was of gold (*ketem,* a poetical word, meaning "precious"), likely signifying that it was woven with gold thread and perhaps covered with gold studding. "Uphaz," used one other time in Scripture (Jer. 10:9) remains unidentified. It may be the same as "Ophir" (1 Kings 9:28; Job 22:24; 28:16; Isa. 13:12).

His body like the Tarshish stone: From the clothing of the person, the description now turns to the person himself. The word for "tarshish stone" is *tarshish.* This is the name of a region at the south of Spain, the Tartessus of the Greeks and Romans, from which came the chrysolite, a gem often identified with the modern topaz. It is described as having a yellow and gold luster, quartzlike in structure, and exceedingly beautiful. The exposed parts of this person's body displayed such an appearance (cf. Ezek. 1:16; 10:9). *His face like the appearance of lightning:* Reference is likely to brilliance, like that of lightning. *His eyes like lamps of fire:* In the midst of the brilliant face glowed yet more brightly the eyes of this person, resembling burning lamps or torches (*lappid,* from a root meaning "to flame, shine"), signifying penetrating insight. *Arms . . . feet . . . gleam of polished brass:* The word for "gleam" (*'ēn*) is literally "eye," and "polished" *(qalal)* is "enlightened" (cf. Ezek. 1:7 for the same phrase). "Arms" and "feet" were those parts of the body which could be seen extending, respectively, below the sleeves and the bottom hem of the linen garments worn. These have already been described as being "like the Tarshish stone," but here additionally as gleaming (like the flash of the eye) in brightness. *Sound . . . voice of a multitude:* The word for "sound" and "voice" is the same, *qol,* meaning "voice." As this person began to speak, his voice carried the quality of a vast crowd speaking in unison: strong, deep, and authoritative.

Taken together, the full description shows this person, though human in form, to have been most awesome in appearance. The intention of this manner of appearance was likely to impress Daniel with the heavenly origin of this one and his full authority to say what soon follows. The ensuing verses show the high degree to which this impression was made.

10:7, 8. And I, Daniel, alone saw the appearance, for the men that were with me did not see the appearance; but a great trembling fell upon them and they fled to hide themselves. So I was left alone and I saw this great appearance, and there was no strength left in me; instead my comeliness was changed upon me to disfigurement, and I did not retain strength.

I, Daniel, alone saw: Though others accompanied Daniel, only he saw the awesome being. This statement by itself would suggest that the appearance was in vision only, not in actual corporeal form. In verses ten and sixteen following, however, this person is said to have touched Daniel for the purpose of strengthening him, and this indicates a real appearance. Perhaps God somehow "clouded" the vision of the companions, making the striking heavenly person invisible to them. Likely they were pagan in belief and, accordingly, were considered unfit subjects to view so glorious a person. *A great trembling:* These companions, however, were made aware that Daniel saw something unusual; in fact, to the extent that they were made to tremble, evidently in fright.[3] What so affected them, apparently, was Daniel's own fearful change of manner and appearance, as indicated by the following verses. *They fled to hide themselves:* This reads, literally, "they fled in hiding themselves," the word for "hiding" being a niphal (reflexive here) infinitive construct. The thought is that they wanted to hide, and fled for the purpose of doing so. Their actions provide a strong commentary on the degree of change they witnessed in Daniel.

I was left alone: The flight of the men left Daniel conveniently alone. This was to the good, that Daniel might concentrate more fully on

---

[3] A similar situation developed when Saul of Tarsus, years later, was on his way to Damascus, accompanied by companions (Acts 9:3-7).

what God was permitting him to experience. *Great appearance:* The word for "appearance" is *mar'eh,* properly used because what Daniel saw consisted only in the appearance of this grand person. It was "great" because of who the person was and the importance of what he was to say. *No strength:* Daniel experienced such a strong emotional reaction that his strength left him, apparently just as when he had seen Gabriel in the second vision (8:17, 18, 27). Loss of strength in the presence of the supernatural indicates a recognition of dependency, unworthiness, and the absence of a sense of self-sufficiency (cf. Judg. 6:22; Job 42:5, 6; Isa. 6:5). *My comeliness . . . to disfigurement:* The word for "comeliness" *(hôd)* means "majesty, splendor, beauty." Whatever lent such qualities to Daniel's normal expression now was changed. The word for "disfigurement" *(mashhît)* is from the root verb *shahat,* "to corrupt, destroy." The word suggests a death-like paleness, combined with a grotesque wrenching of facial features. Daniel's sense of unworthiness was great.

C. EXPLANATORY WORDS OF THE HEAVENLY MESSENGER (vv. 9-14)

The next verses tell of the heavenly messenger imparting strength to Daniel and then of stating the reason for not having come to Daniel sooner, that reason being that he had been hindered by one identified as the "prince of the kingdom of Persia."

10:9, 10. Then I heard the voice of his words, and when I heard the voice of his words, I fell upon my face in a faint, with my face to the ground. And, lo, a hand touched me and set me trembling upon my knees and the palms of my hands.

I heard the voice: In his state of emotional shock, with his companions now having fled, Daniel heard the majestic person begin to speak. The prior description, that the voice sounded "like the voice of a multitude," would have been in view of this time of speaking. The person's words, recorded in verse eleven and following, seem to have been given only after Daniel's recovery from the faint into which he had fallen, which means that they were not those mentioned at this initiating time. It may be that Daniel, in his condition of shock, did not even understand the first words, for which reason the reference here is only to the "voice" *(qol). I fell upon my face in a faint:* The sound of the messenger now speaking brought yet greater emotional disturbance to Daniel, causing him to fall in a faint. The same basic word *(nirdam)* is used here as in 8:18 and, like then, seems to refer to the unconscious state of a faint, because he fell upon his face, so that his face was touching the ground. The angel must somehow have protected him from injuring himself. *A hand touched me:* Further, as in the second vision, the angel touched Daniel to arouse him. Since such a touch would have had to be by an actual, corporeal hand, this appearance was that of an actual, corporeal person, not merely one of a vision. *Set me trembling:* The word used (root, *nûa‘*, "to move to and fro") is in the hiphil, meaning "to cause one to move to and fro." The thought is that as the angel brought Daniel back to consciousness, with ability to rise to a kneeling position, Daniel did so only to an unsteady condition, so that he tottered back and forth, trembling, on hands and knees. His strength was restored still only in part.

10:11. He said to me, O Daniel, a man greatly beloved, give heed to the words that I speak to you and stand straight, for now I have been sent to you. While he was speaking this word to me, I arose trembling.

He said to me: Having revived Daniel to this extent, the angel proceeded to speak, his words now being recorded, in contrast to the case prior to Daniel's fainting. *A man greatly beloved:* This is the same expression as in 9:23 (which see). Showing God's remarkable favor towards Daniel, the expression is used again as a way of reassuring this trembling servant, so that he might fully recover more quickly from his state of weakness. *Give heed:* The word used (root, *bîn,* "to perceive, understand") is a hiphil imperative. The thought pertains to becoming mentally alert. The admonition was needed to bring Daniel to the point of trying to throw off his dazed condition, so that he could properly understand the angel's words. *Stand upright:* Literally this reads, "stand upon your standing," the same expression as in 8:18 (which see). For Daniel to force himself to stand erect would help in bringing his mind to the necessary conscious attention. *I have been sent to you:* The thought is that Daniel should recognize the favor being extended by the sending of the heavenly messenger to him, and accordingly exert greater effort to bringing himself to a state of alertness. Thus far, Daniel's recognition of this had only resulted in his fainting, which to a point was commendable; but now he should go beyond this and rouse himself to hear all that the angel had to say. *I arose trembling:* The angel's words did penetrate Daniel's consciousness, and he attempted to obey. He rose to his feet, but was still unsteady. The degree of difficulty he experienced in regaining his composure shows the extent to which he had been emotionally distraught.

10:12, 13. Then he said to me, Fear not, Daniel, for from the first day that you set your heart to understand and to humble yourself before your God your words were heard, and I have come because of your words. But the prince of the kingdom of Persia withstood me twenty-one days; but, lo, Michael, one of the chief princes, came to help me, and I was left there beside the kings of Persia.

Fear not, Daniel: Seeing Daniel still trembling, the angel stated directly that he had no reason to fear. The logic of his following words is that Daniel did not need to fear, because God had already shown favor toward him in having heard his words of petition, as early as twenty-one days before. *Set your heart to understand and to humble yourself:* To set one's heart is to exercise strong willpower to a planned end. Daniel had been fasting and praying as the result of a fixed purpose. That purpose had been "to understand (root, *bîn*) and to humble" himself. The word for "to humble yourself" (root, *'anah,* "to be bowed down, afflicted") is in the hithpael (reflexive), giving the thought "to bow oneself down." It carries the thought of self-chastening. Daniel had wanted to understand all that God had previously revealed to him and had been willing to give himself in this way for that purpose. *Your words were heard:* These words imply, as one might guess, that Daniel had been praying during his period of mourning, from the first of the twenty-one days, no doubt asking God for the understanding he desired. The relation of God's response to the prayer and Daniel's own sincerity in praying should not be missed. *I have come:* God not only showed Himself willing to answer Daniel's prayer, but to do so by a personal appearance of this majestic angel. A personal representative had been sent, much as in chapter nine.

Prince of the kingdom of Persia: The angel explained why twenty-one days had elapsed between God's having sent him and his actual arrival in Daniel's presence. He had been hindered enroute by one identified as "the prince of the kingdom of Persia." Several matters must be kept in mind in determining the identity of this "prince." First, he held some relation to the kingdom of Persia. Second, though called a "prince" *(sar),* he must have been more than human to be able to resist this high angel and even to make necessary the assistance of the archangel Michael (v. 13). Third, since he resisted this messenger sent by God, he must have been opposed to God's will; therefore, he must have been an emissary of Satan, one of the numerous fallen angels called demons. Fourth, the relation which this "prince" held to the kingdom of Persia was a continuing one, for Daniel's visitor later stated that he must return to "fight" with him again (v. 20). These matters taken together show that this adversary was a demon, no doubt of high rank, assigned by the chief of demons, Satan, to Persia as his special area of activity. The nature of that activity may be conjectured as providing hindrance to God's will in whatever way Persia was concerned. More particularly, it would have involved God's people there, prompting the Persian king to show ill-will and disfavor toward them, refusing their requests and bringing hardship in general. Because Greece also would have a similar "prince" assigned to her in due time (cf. v. 20), and God's people would be under Greece's jurisdiction following Persia's fall to Greece, the suggestion seems reasonable that Satan often assigns special emissaries to influence governments against the people of God. Certainly this chapter has much to contribute regarding the nature of struggles between the higher powers in reference to God's program on earth (cf. Eph. 6:11, 12). *Withstood me:* Literally, "one standing before me." This phrase of itself need not mean an antagonistic withstanding, but, in view of the angel's further words of verse twenty, that he was soon to "return to wage war with the prince of Persia," it clearly means that here. This enemy "prince," then, had somehow been the cause of Daniel's visitor being detained in reaching Daniel for twenty-one days. The possible nature of this "withstanding" is suggested by the last phrase of the verse, to be discussed.

Michael, one of the chief princes: The chief angel Michael is mentioned three times in the Old Testament, all in Daniel (10:13, 21; 12:1), and twice in the New Testament (Jude 9; Rev: 12:7). Being called here "one of the chief *(ri'shonîm)* princes," and in Jude 9 the "archangel" *(archaggelos,* meaning "first angel"), it is clear that he was of the highest rank among angels. The relation of Daniel's visitor to him is open to question. He may have been of equal rank, or he may have been slightly lower. It may be that these two, along with Gabriel, shared an equality as three leaders of angels. The name "Michael" means "who is of God," and he was assigned by God particularly as Israel's prince (10:21; 12:1). That God should assign this chief angel to Israel shows the greatness of His interest in His chosen people. *Came to help me:* Daniel's visitor needed assistance in his encounter with Satan's emissary, and, accordingly, Michael, assigned to Israel's protection (no doubt to counteract just such opposition as now given by this demon of Persia), came to give it. Between the two of them, victory was achieved. The fact is noteworthy that, according to Jude 9, Michael at one time even fought with Satan himself, over the body of Moses. *I was left there:* The word for "was left" (root, *yathar)* is the niphal (passive) form, meaning "to be left over, remain." The word sometimes carries the thought of being left in a position of preeminence (as on a field of battle), and it is best so taken here. After the struggle with the demon, Daniel's visitor remained preeminent, as victor. That he was thus left "beside the kings of Persia" means that he remained in a position of influence with the Persian ruler, in place of Satan's representative. Apparently, then, the struggle between the two had been over this position of influence. Satan's emissary had held it, thus working to the detriment of God's program and people; and God's messenger to Daniel fought him for it, no doubt as a part of his assigned mission in coming to Daniel. A struggle of twenty-one days and the help of Michael had been necessary to win the position.

After it was won, the messenger had come on to meet Daniel, as here described. The word "kings" is in the plural, likely because the place of influence won would continue with future kings of Persia, as well as belonging to Cyrus then ruling—a total period, in fact, of more than two centuries, until Greece would take over world leadership.

10:14. Now I have come to make you understand what is to befall your people in the latter days, for the vision is yet for these days.

Now I have come: The angel had now arrived after the delay, with Daniel quite ignorant concerning the struggle that had ensued. Little do the people of God at any time realize what contention may go on concerning them among higher powers. *In the latter days:* The angel directly set forth the purpose of his coming; namely, to tell Daniel what would happen to Israel "in the latter days." The time reference *('aḥ⁰rît hayyamîm)* is the same as that used in 2:28 (which see). The identity of these "latter days" is evidenced by the ensuing message of the angel recorded in chapters eleven and twelve; namely, days coming after the time of Daniel, with stress on the days of Antiochus Epiphanes, and, following the established intervening time gap, on the days of the Antichrist. It should be noted that the weight of the angel's words would concern what would happen to Daniel's people, the Jews, not to the Gentiles. *Yet for these days:* "For these days" is literally "for the days"; but the article carries the force of the demonstrative pronoun, since it sets off the days in reference as the "latter days" just mentioned. Probably Daniel had been praying and thinking mainly about days in Israel's near future, but the angel was saying that his words would concern, not only near days, but those far ahead. Daniel thus was to learn and be made to understand far more than for what he had asked.

D. DANIEL STRENGTHENED TO UNDERSTAND (10:15-11:1)

At these initial words of the angel, Daniel was again overcome with emotion. The angel ceased to speak while once more he ministered to Daniel's need. Then the angel presented further words of explanation regarding his overall mission, and this set the scene for the detailed information of the two following chapters.

10:15. While he was speaking to me according to these words, I turned my face toward the ground and was dumb.

While he was speaking: Literally, the phrase is "and in his speaking." An infinitive construct is used, indicating continuedness of action. While the angel was continuing to speak, Daniel did what is now described, thus causing an interruption. *I turned my face toward the ground:* The word for "I turned" (root, *naṯan,* "to give") is in the perfect, indicating completed action. The thought is not, then, that Daniel kept his face turned downward all the while the angel was speaking (which would call for the imperfect, indicating incomplete action), but that he began to do this after first looking at the one addressing him. Clearly, a renewed sense of weakness flooded upon him at this point. *Was dumb:* The word used (root, *'alam,* "to bind") is in the niphal form (passive) and means literally "was bound," here in the sense of not being able to speak. Because Daniel had not spoken at all since the first appearance of the angel, it may be that he had been dumb from the time of that appearance. The renewed sense of weakness that came on him at this point, however, prompted the action, now to be described, which removed the condition.

10:16, 17. Then, lo, one like the sons of men touched my lips, and I opened my mouth and spoke. I said to him that stood before me, My lord, because of the vision my pains have come upon me and I retain no strength. And how can the servant of my lord here speak with this my lord, when now for me no strength remains in me and no breath is left in me?

One like the sons of men: Literally, "as the likeness of the sons of mankind." The thought is simply, "one who appeared like a human being." Though this manner of reference seems unusual, the designation is likely still of the same angel. The thought of another person being introduced merely to touch Daniel's lips seems improbable, especially when Daniel's visitor had previously touched him for a similar purpose (v. 10). The strangeness of the manner of reference may be attributed to the state of Daniel's troubled, cloudy mind. Looking down at the ground, he would not have been able to see the angel move to touch his lips; and the touch, being human in kind, could have prompted him to think of one so characterized as having done it. *Touched my lips:* This was to give Daniel the ability to speak again, imparting special strength (cf. Ex. 4:10-12; Isa. 6:6, 7). *I . . . spoke:* As soon as Daniel received this strength, he began to use it, stating why he was acting as he was. *My Lord, because of the vision:* "My lord" (*'adoni*) is a term of respect, but not here of divinity, which would call for *'adonay.* The same term is used three times in these two verses. "Because of" conveys the thought of the prefixed preposition, *b,* which is literally "my means of," used here in the instrumental sense. The word for "vision" is *mar'eh,* meaning literally "appearance, and refers to the grand angel's appearance. *My pains have come:* The word for "pains" (*tsîr*) carries the thought of *twisting* or *writhing,* and is used, for instance, in reference to the pangs of childbirth (1 Sam. 4:19; Isa. 13:8; 21:3). The word for "have come" (root, *hapak,* "to turn, overturn") is in the niphal (passive) and carries a similar connotation of *twisting or overturning.* Both together signify intense pain, brought upon Daniel by the extreme emotional disturbance he felt.

And how can: Racked by pain and drained of all strength, Daniel asked how he could possibly be a participant in the revelational experience proposed by the angel. His word "speak" (root, *dabar*) is not in reference primarily to his own ability to pronounce words, for which he had now received renewed capacity, but to his ability to be a proper conversational participant, both hearing and responding appropriately. The force of his question is twofold: to state the reason for his distraught condition (namely, the greatness of the person before him), and to indicate that he needed special strength if he was to fill the role in which he was now placed. The manner of address used was usual when the one addressed was of superior rank. *No strength . . . no breath:* The repetition of this thought emphasizes the extent to which Daniel sensed his inability. The idea of "no breath" being left in him suggests that he found it even hard to breathe.

10:18, 19. Again, one with the appearance of a man touched me and strengthened me. He said, O man, greatly beloved, fear not, peace be with you; be strong, yes, be strong. While he spoke with me, I did receive strength; and I said, Let my Lord speak, for you have strengthened me.

One with the appearance of a man: This expression differs slightly from that in verse sixteen, with "appearance" *(mar'eh)* being used in place of "likeness" *(d\u1ebfmût);* but the thought is the same, and reference is yet to the same angel. *Touched me:* This is the third touch of the majestic person. This time it was to give strength, whereas the second had enabled Daniel to speak, and the first had enabled him to rise from the ground. God, of course, was the One who imparted the strength, using the angel merely as an instrument.

O man, greatly beloved: This is the third use of the expression (9:23; 10:11) and carries the same thought as before, for the purpose of encouragement. *Fear not, peace be with you:* The angel now replied for the purpose of further strengthening the needy one before him. These first words were to remove his fear, so that emotional strength might replace it. Fear is the opposite of peace. The admonition not to fear had been given before (v. 12), but now was repeated with the addition of "peace be with you." *Be strong, yes, be strong:* The same word is used twice *(ḥᵃzaq)* in an identical imperative form. Daniel was commanded very emphatically to be strong. When fear is replaced by peace, one can be strong. *While he spoke:* The use of the infinitive construct *(kᵉdaḇᵉrô*, literally, "as his speaking"), shows that Daniel's strength returned while the angel's words were being formed. *I did receive strength:* The word used (root, *ḥᵃzaq* again) is in the hithpael (reflexive) and carries the sense of "I felt myself strengthened." Apparently, Daniel's strength returned by degrees, with the last impartation restoring him to the point where he could participate properly in the revelational experience. *Let my lord speak:* Daniel realized this renewed capacity and asked that the angel proceed. He recognized also who it was that had given the new strength.

10:20, 21. Then he said, Do you know why I have come to you? I must return at once to wage war with the prince of Persia; and, when I have gone forth, the prince of Greece will come. But I will tell you what is inscribed in the writing of truth. There is no one putting forth strength with me against these except Michael your prince.

Do you know: The force of this question was not to solicit an answer from Daniel, but, rhetorically, to bring Daniel to realize that the angel's coming had been for a larger reason than what was obvious. Prior to the break in his earlier words, the angel had stated the obvious: that his coming involved giving Daniel information in response to his prayers, but he had also indicated that there was a warfare among supernatural powers concerning these matters. Now he was about to continue to speak about this warfare and he wanted Daniel to know that this warfare was indeed involved in the full reason for his coming. *At once to wage war:* The meaning of "at once" (*'attah,* "now") here, in view of the angel's continuing immediately with his words of chapters eleven and twelve, must be: "directly after I have told you the following information." That the angel had to return to wage war with his demonic opponent, over whom he had already gained a victory, shows that this victory needed to be renewed. In other words, Satan's representative would be trying again and again to regain his place of influence with the Persian rulers, and Daniel's visitor was needed to resist these attempts. *When I have gone forth:* The angel did not state from where this going forth would be, but, in the light of the context, the meaning is clear: "when he had gone forth from maintaining his place of influence with the Persian kings." The expression "have gone forth" (*yôtse,'* literally, "one going forth") is used elsewhere of one *going forth to combat* (cf. 2 Kings 11:7), and it is so used also here. The foe in mind at this point was no longer the prince of Persia, but a new prince, one assigned to Greece. The thought is that the angel would continue contending for the place of influence with the Persian kings, until their period of world supremacy had ended, and then he would go forth from that area of warfare to the new one, involving influence with Grecian kings. *The prince of Greece:* This is not Alexander the Great, as held by some expositors, but another demon, one assigned, as just noted, to Grecian rulers. He is called "prince" *(sar),* in parallel with the prior Satanic emissary to Persia. The time when he would "come" would be when Greece had replaced Persia as the dominant world power, bringing Jews thereby under Grecian control (after 31 B.C., the time of Alexander's third and decisive victory over Persia). The angel's period of contending for Persian influence would last yet another two centuries (from 536 to 331 B.C.), then, before he would move to the Grecian area of warfare.

I will tell you . . . the writing of truth: The force of these words is only parenthetical, but they are necessary for two reasons: first, they let Daniel know that the angel intended to tell him God's message prior to going to renew the conflict with the demon and, second, they stated directly that this message would be one on which Daniel could fully rely, being "inscribed in the writing of truth." Daniel could be relieved of any possible renewed anxiety, then, which might arise in view of this continuing conflict just described. He could know, since the message was in God's own "writing of truth," that all would surely work out according to God's will and would be for good. *No one . . . except Michael:* Daniel's visitor made clear that he alone contended with Satan's emissaries, assigned first to Persia and later to Greece, except that he could call on Michael for help at any time. He had already done this, during the preceding twenty-one days. As noted under verse thirteen, Michael's main task was to oversee matters pertaining specifically to the Jews; but, since the Jewish welfare was vitally involved with the dominating empire of the day, it fell to him to assist at times in controlling matters regarding that empire as well. As for Daniel's visitor, these words show further that his primary task was waging warfare against Satan's high and trusted emissaries.

11:1. But in the first year of Darius the Mede, I for my part stood up to be a supporter and a stronghold for him.

The first year of Darius: Perhaps it was the insertion of this date which prompted a chapter division to be made prior to this verse, but it should not have been done. The thought continues directly from that of 10:21, with the break coming after this verse. Daniel's visitor continued to speak of his relation to Michael, referring to a past incident which occurred in the first year of Darius (two years prior to this third year, then). *I for my part:* This phrase was to call attention to Daniel's visitor as having gone also to Michael's aid at one time in the past. In other words, the two mighty beings held a mutual assistance arrangement, each helping the other as he had particular need. *Supporter and a stronghold:* The word for "supporter" (root, *hazaq* "to be strong") is a hiphil participle, meaning "one causing to be strong." The word for "stronghold" (*ma'ôn,* "a strong place") is a noun. Daniel's visitor had supplied the qualities of both concepts for Michael two years before, which means at the general time of the Jews' return to Judah under Sheshbazzar (cf. Ezra 1:1-11). Michael, wanting this return to be effected, had apparently encountered difficulty in influencing Darius and Cyrus to that end, and Daniel's visitor had come to his aid. Thus it comes to be known that Cyrus' decision to let the Jews go had been accomplished by God working through these two high angels; and it may be concluded that, whenever such decisions are made in high places relative to God's people, God's angels may well be involved in bringing about the desired result.

CHAPTER 11

With this chapter the predictive portion of Daniel's fourth time of revelation begins. Chapter ten has been important for its own purpose, but has not presented the message proper, which the grand angel was sent to give Daniel. This comes now, beginning with verse two.

The stress of the message is on Antiochus Epiphanes (vv. 21-35) and the Antichrist (vv. 36-45), the former typifying the latter. Again an implied time gap exists between the two. Neither is identified by name, but only by description of character and actions, something found true also in the previous contexts considered. Before either is mentioned, however, the angel's message tells of history preceding Antiochus. First, early Persian rulers are set forth and then Alexander the Great who defeated Persia for Greece. After this comes a remarkably detailed presentation of successive kings, who ruled two of the divisions of Alexander's empire: the Egyptian division, ruled by the Ptolemies, and the Syrian, ruled by the Seleucids. These two divisions call for this special consideration because the affairs of Palestine, lying between the two, were so often involved with their activities. The detail of this history as presented provides one of the most remarkable predictive portions of all Scripture.

A. HISTORY UNTIL THE DIVISION OF ALEXANDER'S EMPIRE (vv. 2-4)

The angel's message begins by telling of history starting with the time when Daniel lived. The angel spent little time, however, with either the Persian period or the meteoric rise of Alexander, a combined period of more than two centuries (539-323 B.C.), but moved on quickly to the era when Alexander's vast holdings had been divided into four regions.

11:2. Now shall I make known to you the truth. Lo, three kings are yet to stand in Persia, and a fourth shall accumulate greater wealth than the others; and, when he has grown strong through his riches, he shall stir up all against the kingdom of Greece.

I make known to you the truth: The angel indicated that he was about to begin the message proper. Designating the message as the "truth" *('ᵉmet)*, he identified it with the earlier "writing of truth" (10:21). He wished to stress that the remarkable message to be given was indeed true. *Three kings:* Because the fourth king of the following phrase must be Xerxes (486-465 B.C.), as will be seen, these three must be his predecessors. Actually four kings preceded him (Cyrus, 539-529 B.C.; Cambyses, 529-522; Smerdis, 522-521; Darius Hystaspes, 521-486), which means that one is omitted. It could be Cyrus, since he was already ruling when the angel spoke, and the angel did say "yet" *('ôd);* or it could be Smerdis, because he ruled less than one year and was probably an imposter in doing so. It should be realized that several other kings ruled Persia besides the four mentioned, namely, Artaxerxes Longimanus, 465-424 B.C.; Xerxes II 424-423; Darius II Nothus, 423-404; Artaxerxes II Mnemom, 404-359; Artaxerxes III Ochus, 359-338; Arses, 338-336; and Darius III Codomannus, 336-331. The thought here is that a total of three ruled before the one arose who attacked Greece, an attack which gave reason for the counterattack of Alexander, soon to be mentioned, years later. None of the Persian successors of Xerxes provided a similar reason.

A fourth shall accumulate greater wealth: This king is Xerxes (486-465 B.C.), identified clearly by the description given, especially regarding his expedition against Greece. His father, Darius Hystaspes, had also attacked Greece, in 490 B.C., but not with the same scope of operation. Xerxes also was very rich. His predecessors had amassed an enormous fortune, both through the lucrative conquests of Lydia, Babylonia, and Egypt, and a severe taxation program especially by Darius Hystaspes; and Xerxes added measurably to this wealth as a part of his preparation of four years for the Grecian strike. His feast of no fewer than 180 days (Esth. 1:1-12)[1] depicts something of the grandeur of this preparation. *Grown strong:* Reference is especially to his growing strong for the Grecian attack. *He shall stir up all against the kingdom of Greece:* Some translate this, "He shall stir up all the kingdom of Greece." It should be noted, however, that the word for "stir up" (root, *'ûr,* "to be hot, ardent") is used in the hiphil, indicating incitement to action. Those whom Xerxes incited to action were his own troops, not the enemy. The problematic *'et* may be explained either as meaning "with" or as what Keil calls the "accusative of the object of the movement" (cf. Ex. 9:29-33).[2] The thought is that this fourth king would put forth great effort to arouse

---

[1] The Ahasuerus of Esther is the same as Xerxes, the name Ahasuerus being a good Hebrew equivalent for his Persian name, Khshayarsha. Also the character of Xerxes fits the biblical picture of Ahasuerus.

[2] KDC on Daniel, p. 431.

his own country for attacking Greece with the largest force possible. History testifies that Xerxes did this, both as to army and navy, attempting to avenge the humiliating defeat of his father by Greece.

11:3, 4. Then shall a mighty king stand, who shall rule with great dominion and do according to his will. And when he has arisen, his kingdom shall be broken and divided to the four winds of heaven, but not to his posterity nor according to the dominion with which he ruled; because his kingdom shall be plucked up and be for others besides these.

A mighty king: This is Alexander the Great of Greece (336-323 B.C.), again unmistakable from the description. He retaliated against Persia and seized the entire empire for Greece. He is called "mighty" *(gibbôr)* because of the amazing strength and ability he displayed in conquering so much in one continuous extended campaign (cf. 8:5-8). *With great dominion:* Alexander demonstrated power of personality and strength of leadership scarcely paralleled in history, keeping his army intact for thousands of miles of travel and campaigning, and through years of continuous struggle and hardship. He forced his will on his army and on the people he conquered. The extent of his dominion finally reached from Greece and Egypt in the west to India in the east, an area still larger than Persia had controlled.

When he has arisen: The literal reading is "according to his standing," the form of the verb being an infinitive construct. The thought is that just as Alexander would nicely complete his conquest of all this territory, the kingdom would be broken, as mentioned next. *Broken and divided:* Alexander's kingdom was broken (root, *shabar,* used in niphal) after his early death at the age of thirty-two. It came to be divided among four of his generals, though only after several years of contention between them, as set forth under 8:8 (which see). *But not to his posterity:* Alexander had a half brother, Philip Arrhidaeus, who was mentally deficient; a son, Alexander, born to him posthumously by Roxana; and an illegitimate son, Hercules, by Barsine, daughter of Darius. At first a decision was made that the first two should rule as comonarchs, with other persons making decisions in their names for some time. Dissension broke out as to who those others should be, however, with bitter fighting taking place before long. In 317 B.C., the half brother, Philip, was murdered in the resulting turmoil; in 310 B.C. also the young Alexander, and in 309 B.C. finally the illegitimate Hercules. No posterity of Alexander then remained to inherit any part of the empire. *Nor according to the dominion with which he ruled:* Literally, this reads, "and not according to his ruling which he ruled." That is, none of the four successors would rule with his authority. Bitter fighting between several generals ensued at first, with the four continuing rulers emerging as such only after a prolonged struggle. These finally brought a measure of stability to the vast area, but none of them attained the dominance in his own area that Alexander had held. *Shall be plucked up:* The word (root, *natash,* in the niphal) has the basic meaning of plucking up plants by the roots, certainly a forceful thought in respect to the breaking of Alexander's kingdom. *Besides these:* The antecedent is "posterity." The kingdom would go to others besides members of Alexander's family.

B. THE PTOLEMIES AND SELEUCIDS UNTIL ANTIOCHUS EPIPHANES (vv. 5-20)

Having predicted that there would be four divisions to Alexander's empire, the angel continued to speak of only two: the Syrian division, lying just north of Palestine, over which the Seleucid line of kings would rule; and the Egyptian division, lying just south, over which the Ptolemaic line would be supreme. The significance of the angel's speaking further only of these two is that Palestine, where God's people dwelt, lay exactly between them and was continually involved in their later history. Especially important is the fact that the Syrian division would eventually see Antiochus Epiphanes, the "little horn" of chapter eight, come to power, as noted. The angel's message was to concern this one particularly, as he would foreshadow still another —the Antichrist of the far distant future. Before the rise of Antiochus, however, more than a century would elapse, and the angel first set forth this history. In doing so, he gave some of the most detailed prediction of a historical nature in all the Word of God. When subsequent history proves to fit it exactly, as pointed out below, it is no wonder that liberal expositors, who deny the supernatural in the Bible, insist that it must have been written after the history had transpired. Because it was indeed written before, it provides, conversely, an excellent demonstration of the fact that the Holy Scriptures are truly a product of supernatural revelation.

11:5. Then the king of the South shall be strong, but one of his princes shall be stronger than he and shall rule; his dominion shall be a great dominion.

King of the South: The word for "South" *(negeb)* usually means the desert area directly south of Palestine, but here it means Egypt, evidenced by the context and the specific mention of Egypt in verse eight. That the manner of reference to both Egypt and Syria throughout this passage is merely by mention of the two directions, south and north, fits the predictive character of the passage, in which one expects terms to be used that are more general in nature. Also, in respect to Syria, the country had no distinction as such in Daniel's time, which means that, had Daniel called it by that name, his readers would only have been confused. The king in reference is the first of the south division, Ptolemy Soter, son of Lagus and a highly capable general under Alexander. He was made satrap of Egypt in 323 B.C., directly after Alexander's death. He survived the time of struggle, and, following the deaths of all Alexander's posterity, he, along with other satraps, still surviving, proclaimed himself king of Egypt. He did this in 304 B.C. and continued to reign until 283. *One of his princes shall be stronger than he and shall rule:* Literally, "from his princes, even he shall be strong above him and shall rule." Reference is to Seleucus Nicator, a lesser general under Alexander, who was appointed satrap of Babylonia in 321 B.C. but was forced to flee when Babylonia was seized by Antigonus, another general. Seleucus then came to Ptolemy Soter in Egypt to serve under him. Later, when Antigonus was defeated in 312 B.C. at Gaza, Seleucus returned to his former satrapy, where he now greatly increased his strength. Finally he succeeded in controlling the largest of all the divisions, including Babylonia, Syria, and Media, and assumed the title of king the same year as did Ptolemy Soter, 304 B.C. *A great dominion:* This is the angel's indication as to how Seleucus would become stronger than Ptolemy; namely, in extent of dominion. As just noted, it did become much larger.

11:6. Then after some years, they shall make an alliance and the daughter of the king of the South shall come to the king of the North to make peace, but she shall not retain the strength of the arm, and neither shall he stand nor his arm. She shall be given up, and her attendants, and her child, and he that strengthened her in those times.

After some years: Literally, this may be translated, "to the end of years." History reveals that Egypt and Syria did make an alliance, as here described, about 250 B.C., some fifty-four years after both Ptolemy and Seleucus proclaimed themselves kings. In the interval, both kings had died (Ptolemy, in 283 B.C.; Seleucus, in 281) and the son of Ptolemy, Ptolemy II Philadelphus (283-246 B.C.) now ruled in Egypt, and the grandson of Seleucus, Antiochus II Theos (262-246 B.C.) in Syria. The latter had been preceded by his father, not mentioned in this history, Antiochus I Soter (281-262 B.C.). *An alliance:* Ptolemy II Philadelphus and Antiochus II Theos fought each other bitterly at first, but later they did make an alliance between the two countries. *Daughter of the king of the South:* The daughter in reference is well known in history. Her name was Berenice, daughter of Ptolemy II Philadelphus, and she married Antiochus II Theos, who was twenty-three years younger than Ptolemy. The marriage served to seal the alliance, a practice common for the day. The word for "peace" *(mêsharîm)* means literally "righteousness." The logic behind the use of the word is that, when Berenice went to marry

Antiochus, she fulfilled the terms of the agreement and made matters right. *Strength of the arm:* This phrase refers to the capacity to do what one wishes. *Neither shall he stand nor his arm:* The antecedent of "he" is clearly Antiochus, whom Berenice married. That he would not "stand nor his arm" means that he would not continue as king nor be able to exercise his capacity to act. History reveals that two years after the marriage, the father of Berenice, Ptolemy II, who had apparently forced the marriage, died. Antiochus II then took back a former wife, Laodice, whom he had been compelled to divorce, and put away Berenice instead, thus removing "the strength of the arm" (hers). Laodice, however, was not yet satisfied and, fearing continued fickleness on the part of her husband, had him poisoned, thus removing the strength also of "his arm." Then Laodice had Berenice killed, after which she proclaimed her own son, Seleucus II Callinicus (246-227 B.C.), as king. *Her attendants, her child, and he that strengthened her:* Not only was Berenice killed, but also her attendants (literally, "those who brought her") and her one infant son by Antiochus. The word for "child" is pointed in the Hebrew to give the meaning "begetter, father," but principal versions take it as "child," and it is known that her child did die at this time. Her father, as noted, also had died, but apparently not as a result of Laodice's wrath. The identity of the one "that strengthened her" is uncertain, but reference may be to her husband, Antiochus II. Whoever it was, he also died.

11:7, 8. One from the branch of her roots shall stand up in his place; and he shall come against the army and enter into the stronghold of the king of the North; and he shall deal with them and shall prevail. Also he shall carry captive to Egypt their gods, with their molten images and with their precious vessels of silver and gold; and then shall he stand some years against the king of the North.

One from the branch of her roots: The word for "branch" *(netser)* means something *growing green,* hence a "sprout, branch." Reference is to one who would come from her "roots," in other words, a brother. Berenice had a brother, and he did succeed their father, Ptolemy Philadelphus, taking the name Ptolemy III Euergetes (246-221 B.C.). He thus stood up "in his (Ptolemy Philadelphus') place." *He shall come against the army:* This new ruler immediately set out to avenge the turn of events in Syria, but arrived too late to save his sister. He easily overcame the Syrian army, however, and then had the vindictive Laodice put to death. After this he took his troops eastward into the heart ("stronghold") of the vast Syrian territory, penetrating even as far as the Tigris River. *Shall prevail:* Ptolemy III Euergetes was remarkably successful in the entire campaign. He moved where he wished, much of the time quite unopposed, and forced his will on people almost as he desired. The young Syrian ruler, Seleucus II Callinicus, maintained himself during this time by staying in the interior of Asia Minor. After Ptolemy returned to Egypt, Seleucus was able to recover much of the area that his rival had seized.

He shall carry captive ... gods ... images ... precious vessels: These words show the extent of Ptolemy's victory. If one can carry away the religious articles of a defeated people, he has truly humbled them. Egypt was significantly enriched by a great quantity of booty, including religious items. According to Jerome, Ptolemy brought home "40,000 talents of silver and 2,500 precious vessels and images of the gods, among them those which Cambyses had taken to Persia when he conquered Egypt."[3] The name, Euergetes, meaning "benefactor," was given to him as a result. *Against the king of the North:* The preposition translated "against" is *min,* normally meaning "from." Accordingly, some expositors take the thought to be that Ptolemy Euergetes would "stand from" the king of the North by living longer, and Ptolemy did live longer than Seleucus Callinicus by six years. The fact, however, is of little importance and hardly would acount for a mention of this kind. Others understand the meaning to be that Ptolemy would not attack Syria again for some years, but he did have to resist an attack brought against him later in retaliation by Seleucus Callinicus, which would seem to be out of keeping with this suggestion. The view of Keil seems best: that *min* carries the thought of *mipp^e nê,* meaning "from before" or "against," as in Psalm 43:1. Ptolemy did stand against Seleucus without defeat at any time.

11:9, 10. And one shall come against the kingdom of the king of the South, but he shall return to his own land. But his sons shall bestir themselves and assemble a multitude of great forces, and one shall surely come, overwhelm, and pass through; then he shall bestir himself again, even unto his stronghold.

One shall come: In view of the history, it is clear that reference is still to Seleucus Callinicus. As noted above, he succeeded in regaining his position in Syria, after Ptolemy's devasting campaign through his country. Then about 240 B.C. he attempted a return attack against Ptolemy in Egypt. *He shall return:* Seleucus was unsuccessful in the attempt and returned home without acomplishing his purpose.

His sons: Seleucus Callinicus had two sons: the older who became Seleucus III Ceraunus (227-223 B.C.) and the younger, Antiochus III the Great (223-187 B.C.). The former was killed while on campaign in Asia Minor, after an abbreviated rule. Antiochus the Great then became king, at the young age of about eighteen years. The word for

---

[3] Cf. Montgomery, MICC, p. 431.

"shall bestir themselves" (root, *garah*) is used in the hithpael (reflexive) and carries the thought of *becoming excited* or *angry*. *Assemble a multitude:* The prediction is that both sons would gather large armies, and both did. The father, after his unsuccessful campaign against Egypt, had left the country in a weakened condition. The sons reacted and attempted to restore the lost prestige. *One shall surely come:* The verb is singular, indicating that only one of the sons is now in view. The reason is that the older gave his attention to Asia Minor, where he was shortly killed, while the younger, Antiochus the Great, gave his to Egypt, which is more significant for the subject of this chapter. The Hebrew employs an infinitive absolute to lend emphasis ("surely") to the verb, suggesting unusual determination on Antiochus' part in this attention. *Overwhelm and pass through:* The word for "overwhelm" (root, *shatap*) is often used of a river overflowing its banks (cf. Isa. 28:17; 30:28). The two verbs together speak expressively of an overpowering army (cf. Isa. 8:8). Antiochus did move south in force against Egyptian territory. It should be realized that Egypt's control had included all of Palestine until this time; and, in fact, at the time of this move by Antiochus, due to the weakened condition of Syria, it extended even to the port of Antioch in Syria itself. Antiochus' design now was to push the boundary back to its previous limits at least, so that Coele-Syria might come within the Syrian domain again. This he did accomplish in 219 B.C. and was able even to push on into Palestine and across into Transjordan. The campaign was highly successful, and his army did overflow and pass through a large amount of land. *He shall bestir himself again:* The Hebrew employs two verbs in this phrase, which may be translated, "he shall return and bestir himself." The first verb (root, *shub,* "to turn, return"), however, as Montgomery points out, may in such a context mean only "again," indicating a repeated action of an accompanying verb.[4] The accompanying verb (root, *garah*) is the same as the one used earlier in the verse, which favors this suggestion. Antiochus desisted from the campaign of 219 B.C., but returned to the attack in 217 B.C. He was able this time to push all the way to the southern Palestinian frontier post of Raphia, where a major battle with the Egyptians took place. The word "stronghold" is probably a reference to Raphia.

11:11, 12. And the king of the South shall be enraged and move out to do battle with him, even with the king of the North; and he shall raise a great multitude, and the multitude shall be given into his hand. When the multitude has been carried away, his heart shall become proud; indeed, he shall cause myriads to fall, but he shall not be strong.

---

4 MICC, p. 437.

King of the South: The Egyptian king now in reference was Ptolemy IV Philopator (221-204 B.C.), son of Ptolemy Euergetes. He was the one against whom the two attacks of Antiochus the Great, just described, were directed. He was given to ease of life and luxury, and Montgomery describes him as a "dilettante voluptuary, ruled by vile ministers."[5] *Shall be enraged:* In spite of his natural reticence toward vigorous activity, this Ptolemy, acompanied by his sister-wife, Arsinoe, now came in force to meet Antiochus at Raphia. He had become enraged at the little success his Palestinian garrisons had experienced in 219 B.C. with the northern enemy and he determined to effect a different conclusion this time. *A great multitude:* Ptolemy is said to have gathered for this attempt 70,000 infantry, 5,000 cavalry, and 73 elephants.[6] *Into his hand:* The antecedent of "his" is not made clear in the text. History reveals, however, that it was Ptolemy and not Antiochus. Antiochus had a "multitude" with him also, consisting of 62,000 infantry, 6,000 cavalry, and 102 elephants.[6] It was his "multitude" that was given into Ptolemy's hand.

Shall become proud: The prediction is that this victory would make the man proud. It is easy to believe that this occurred, for the man was offensively proud anyway. *He shall cause myriads to fall:* This is repetitious of the closing phrase of verse eleven, giving stress to the thought. Ptolemy did win decisively over Antiochus, killing 10,000 infantry, 300 cavalry, and 5 elephants, and taking 4,000 prisoners.[6] The word for "myriads" *(ribo'ôt)* means "a very large number," sometimes translated "ten thousand." *He shall not be strong:* This phrase is added in criticism of the man, for, though he did achieve the victory, he did not follow it up and gain the position of strength that was now available. History reveals that directly after the battle he returned to Egypt and the life of luxury and indolence he so enjoyed. This in turn caused dissatisfaction on the part of his people, which left him really a weaker ruler after the victory than before.

11:13. Later the king of the North shall return and raise a multitude greater than the first; and at the end of some years he shall surely come with a great army and abundant supplies.

Shall return: The "king of the North" here and on through verse nineteen continues to be Antiochus the Great. Following the defeat at Raphia before Ptolemy, Antiochus did return in a renewal of the conflict as here indicated, but not for several years. During the intervening time, he put forth effort to recover the eastern areas of his country. The years 212-204 B.C. saw him campaigning successfully as far as the Caspian Sea and even the border of India.

---

[5] MICC, p. 433.
[6] These figures from Polybius, V: 86, given in Barnes, BD, II, p. 217 and Young, YPD, p. 238.

Then in 203 B.C., Ptolemy Philopater and his wife died in Egypt and they were succeeded by their four-year-old son, Ptolemy V Epiphanes (203-181 B.C.), which made the time ripe for Antiochus to move again toward Egypt. *At the end of some years:* That is, literally, "to the end of the times, years." All told, fourteen years intervened between the defeat before Ptolemy Philopator and this return engagement. One should not miss in these incidental mentions the degree of detail and exactness of the inspired record. *He shall surely come . . . army . . . supplies:* Stress ("surely") is placed on this coming of Antiochus by the use of an infinitive absolute, as in verse ten. As predicted twice in this verse, his army this time was larger than before, having been raised for, and used in, the victorious eastern campaigns. The word for "supplies" *(r°ḵush)* is from the root *raḵash,* "to acquire, gain," and refers to that which Antiochus had acquired as supplies of war.

11:14.   And in those times many shall stand against the king of the South; and men of violence among your own people shall lift themselves up to fulfill the vision, but they shall fail.

Many shall stand: Antiochus was not alone in his opposition to Egypt at this time. Philip V of Macedonia was also against Egypt, and he and Antiochus made a compact to divide Egyptian possessions overseas. Philip was thus encouraged to attack certain of these possessions. He succeeded in seizing several Aegean islands and localities in the regions of Caria and Thrace. In Egypt itself, one Agathocles excited a rebellion against the young ruler. *Men of violence among your own people:* The antecedent of "your" is obviously Daniel, to whom the angel was speaking. Reference, then is to Jews of Palestine. The words for "men of violence" mean literally "sons of breaking" (cf. Ezek. 18:10), and are best taken to refer to strong-willed men, given to revolutionary endeavors, who, history indicates, sought at this time to help Antiochus the Great against Ptolemy Epiphanes. It should be understood that Palestine had been under Ptolemaic control continuously since the division of Alexander's empire, except for the brief time when Antiochus the Great had held it fourteen years before. At that time, Ptolemy Philopator had won it back for Egypt at the battle of Raphia. Now these Jews sought to assist Antiochus in taking it from Egypt once again. *Shall lift themselves up:* Josephus wrote of Jews receiving Antiochus into Jerusalem at this time and giving him provisions for both army and elephants.[7] They had wearied under the ebb and flow of battle across their country, waged by Syria and Egypt, and now apparently thought their best interest lay in throwing their support to the side of the North. They had in mind

---

[7] *Antiq.* XII, 3, 3.

by this to "fulfill this vision," which likely means that they thus sought to bring to pass what had been predicted in this and other of Daniel's revelations. It is only to be expected that they would have known of these revelations—Daniel's book surely having been copied and circulated by this time, since it concerned these times of the Jews so significantly—and they could, then, have desired to fit themselves into the predictions as they saw what seemed to be opportunities to do so. *But they shall fail:* Literally, "but they shall stumble." The meaning is that these Jews would not accomplish what they intended, whether as to their own personal betterment or that of their country. The exact significance is not clear. History testifies, in any case, that peace for Palestine was not achieved.

11:15, 16. So the king of the North shall come and shall raise siegeworks and capture a fortified city; and the forces of the South shall not stand, neither his chosen people, for there shall be no strength to stand. But the one coming against him shall do as he pleases, with no one standing before him, and he shall stand in the glorious land, having destruction in his hand.

King of the North: The thought reverts back to verse thirteen and the return campaign of Antiochus against Egypt there in view. The intervening verse has been parenthetical in force. *Siegeworks . . . a fortified city:* The word for "siegeworks' *(sôl^elah)* means simply "mound," but here clearly in the sense of a device for capturing a "fortified city." History reveals Sidon to be the city in view. Antiochus' first onslaught into Palestine, in this campaign of 203 B.C., met with sufficient success that by the year 199 he held much of Palestine. In 198, however, he was driven back by one of Egypt's ablest generals, Scopas. Still the same year the tide changed once more and Antiochus defeated Scopas, first at Paneas, near the headwaters of the Jordan, and then at Sidon, the city here in view and to which Scopas had fled. The city was taken through siegeworks, as predicted, and this victory brought a final end to Ptolemaic rule in Palestine, with Syria being in control from this time on. *The forces of the South:* The word for "forces" *(z^ero'ôt)* means literally "arms," but here in the sense of sources of strength. Scopas' troops could not stand against those of Antiochus, neither at Paneas nor at Sidon. *Neither his chosen people:* Literally, this reads, "the people of his choices." It is known that Egypt sent three picked generals (Eropas, Menacles, and Damoyenus) to lift the siege of Sidon, but without success. So neither Scopas, who had been specially chosen in the first place, nor these three others could stand against the Syrians.

One coming against him: The "one coming" (root, *bô',* as a participle) is Antiochus. He was able to impose his will on the Egyptians, forcing Scopas to surrender at Sidon. *The glorious land:* This phrase is repeated in verse forty-one and is similar to the expression in 8:9 (which see). Reference is without dispute to Palestine. By reason of the significant victory at Sidon, Antiochus took lasting dominion of Palestine.[8] *Having destruction:* The word for "destruction" *(kalah)* means "finish, completion" and then "destruction." Because Antiochus is not known to have wrought extensive destruction in Palestine at this time, some expositors prefer the meaning "completeness," in the sense of the *completed land* having come into Antiochus' hand. This meaning is quite possible. If "destruction" is maintained, the thought must be taken principally in the sense of authority to bring destruction. Antiochus did gain this degree of authority over all the land at this time.

11:17. And he shall set his face to come in the power of all his kingdom, bringing equitable terms with him, and he shall fulfill them, for he shall give to him the daughter of women to destroy it, but this shall not stand nor be to his advantage.

Set his face: This phrase means "to purpose, determine." Having won Palestine, Antiochus purposed to gain control over Egypt itself, as well. *The power of all his kingdom:* Since Antiochus did not attempt to invade Egypt at this time with an army, the word "power" can hardly refer to military force. The thought concerns, rather, the power-position which Antiochus now held, having won control of Palestine, and other eastern territory also. He held a strong position for negotiating with Egypt. *Bringing equitable terms:* This clause is, literally, "bringing uprightnesses." The term "uprightnesses" *(y^esharîm)* is taken by some expositors to mean "upright ones" (cf Job 1:1, 18; Ps. 11:7). They take this as a reference to the Jews—God's upright ones—thinking of them as serving here as a military force. But, as noted, Antiochus did not invade Egypt at this time. What he did was make an agreement with Ptolemy Epiphanes, as the latter part of the verse indicates, and this makes the meaning "equitable terms" much more likely. *He shall fulfill them:* He shall carry out this plan of making an agreement with Egypt, fulfilling its terms. *The daughter of women:* Antiochus' agreement with Ptolemy Epiphanes involved the marriage of his daughter, Cleopatra, to Ptolemy. The agreement was made in 197 B.C., but the marriage did not take place until 193 B.C., because Ptolemy was still only ten years old in 197,

---

[8] Josephus, *Antiq.* XII, 3, 3, wrote of the suffering that Palestine had experienced during the prior years as the land had been a continually contested battleground: "The Jews, as well as the inhabitants of Colesyria, suffered greatly, and their land was sorely harassed; for while he [Antiochus the Great] was at war with Ptolemy Philopator, and with his son, who was called Epiphanes, it fell out that these nations were equally sufferers, both when he was beaten and when he beat the others, so that they were very like to a ship in a storm, which is tossed by the waves on both sides."

the arrangements all having been made by advisers. The unusual designation "daughter of women" is best taken as an appellation of eminence, Cleopatra being the first among women of the day, since she was the royal princess. The purpose of Antiochus in the marriage was to gain Ptolemy's favor, so that when Antiochus pursued warfare against Rome, which he intended shortly to do, he could have reason for a quiet frontier toward the south. *To destroy it:* Antiochus had also another purpose in mind: he wanted his daughter to be a member of the Ptolemaic family so that she could foster Syrian interests in Egypt. In fact, as noted above, he wanted to take control of Egypt, destroying Ptolemaic power there, and he believed that this marriage could play a key role to that end. *This shall not stand nor be to his advantage:* This clause may be translated literally: "she shall not stand nor be for him." The antecedent of "she" is the daughter. History reveals that she did not stand for her father, but rather became a proper wife to her husband. This is indicated by the fact that not only did Antiochus not succeed in his designs on Egypt, but Egypt did not remain quiet even in respect to his campaigns against Rome. Egypt actually aided the Romans by giving direct assistance against Antiochus. Antiochus' strategy did not work.

11:18, 19. Then he shall turn his face to the coastlands and shall take many of them; but a commander shall cause the reproach designed by him to cease and even turn his reproach back upon him. At this he shall turn his face to the fortresses of his own land, but he shall stumble and fall and not be found.

To the coastlands: The word for "coastlands" is *'îyyîm,* which refers to land near the water, whether of islands or mainland. Here it refers, as history indicates, to such lands in the general Aegean area. Antiochus undertook a vigorous campaign into Asia Minor and the Aegean region in 197 B.C., the year the treaty was concluded with Ptolemy. *Shall take many of them:* Antiochus was successful for some time, both on land and at sea. Numerous islands of the Aegean fell to him and also substantial portions of Asia Minor and Greece. In 196 B.C., he was able to seize even a part of Thrace. Not long after this, Rome withdrew from Greece, and Antiochus, having now been joined by the renowned, self-exiled Hannibal from Carthage,[9] was encouraged to invade Greece proper. Still he was successful, establishing a strong base at Thermopylae. *But a commander:* History identifies the commander in reference as the Roman general, Lucius Cornelius Scipio, called Scipio Asiaticus, brother of the more famed

---

[9] In preceding years, Hannibal had been the champion of Carthage in waging war with Rome. After a spectacular campaign into Italy itself, he had been defeated. But then he proved his ability as a statesman, becoming the political leader of Carthage. Rome finally demanded his surrender by Carthage, and he voluntarily fled to the East to Antiochus, who was now the principal Roman antagonist.

Scipio Africanus, who had earlier defeated Hannibal and the Carthaginians. When Antiochus was successful in Greece proper, this man was commissioned by Rome to bring a halt to his activity, and he did so. *Reproach:* This word *(ḥerpah)* refers to the humiliation which Antiochus had planned for all Greece, having done so openly and boastfully, in contempt for the power of Rome. *Even turn his reproach back upon him:* A literal translation is "except he shall return his reproach to him." The thought is that this Roman commander would reverse matters, so that the humiliation planned for Greece would be turned back on him who had planned it. This did happen. In 191 B.C., Antiochus was driven from his stronghold in Thermopylae, and then the following year was defeated at Magnesia in Lydia of Asia Minor. Finally, through the peace of Apamea, 188 B.C., which he was obliged to accept, he was forced to abandon all Asia Minor to the Romans. His reproach was truly turned back upon him.

The fortresses of his own land: Reference is to the strong cities of Antiochus' own land. Antiochus had no recourse but to return to these, having lost all he had gained. *Stumble and fall and not be found:* Little is known of Antiochus after his return, probably because he died only one year later, in 187 B.C. His grandiose plans had failed utterly.

11:20. Then shall arise in his place one who shall send a collector of tribute through the glory of the kingdom; but after a few days he shall be broken, though not in anger or in battle.

Then shall arise one: History again identifies without question the one in view: Seleucus IV Philopator (187-176 B.C.), son and successor of Antiochus the Great. Though the father had failed in his plan, the country inherited by the son was still sizable, consisting of Syria, Palestine, Mesopotamia, Babylonia, and Nearer Iran (Media and Persia). *A collector of tribute:* It is known that Seleucus Philopator inherited also an empty treasury and a great debt to the Romans (who demanded an annual payment of 1,000 talents) as a result of his father's abortive wars. Needing money badly, he took steps to get it. The word for "collector" *(nôges)* means basically one who *drives* or *impels* and then one who *collects* taxes (cf. Deut. 15:2, 3; 2 Kings 23:35). It seems clear that Seleucus sent out more than one such "collector" at this time, but a particular one is in view here, because he was sent into "the glory of the kingdom," meaning Palestine (cf. vv. 16, 41). This man is well known; he was the prime minister under Seleucus, named Heliodorus, who was sent to seize the funds of the Temple treasury in Jerusalem. According to 2 Maccabees 3, where the story is related, this attempt was thwarted by the appearance at the Temple of a divine apparition. *After a few days he shall be broken:* This is a reference to the death of Seleucus Philopator in 176 B.C., after a reign of eleven years. The propriety of speaking of this length of time as only "a few days" is to be understood in the light of the much longer thirty-seven-year reign of the father. *In anger or in battle:* Seleucus did not die in battle or in a popular tumult. He died quite mysteriously, almost surely by assassination, and probably through poisoning. His only son, Demetrius Soter, had been taken as hostage to Rome, when Heliodorus, his prime minister, evidently sought for the throne himself by committing the act.

C. ANTIOCHUS EPIPHANES (vv. 21-35)

Antiochus Epiphanes (175-164 B.C.), the "little horn" of chapter eight and type of the Antichrist, is now presented. He was the son and successor of Antiochus the Great. The text concerns him for the following fifteen verses. The reason for so much attention is that, as in chapter eight, he prefigured the Antichrist, and there was a need for telling more about him in this capacity. This is in anticipation of speaking of the Antichrist himself in the last portion of the chapter (vv. 36-45). The reason for the detailed history just considered is really to give background for the presentation now of this eighth Seleucid ruler. The first seven, as well as their Ptolemaic counterparts, were not of sufficient significance in themselves for mention—though their combined history has had the importance of showing the ravages of warfare that flowed back and forth over Palestine—but the record given of them, briefly stated, has prepared for the introduction now of this one who was indeed of major significance. The matter to keep in mind, as the text describes him, is that his life and activities are predictive of the life and activities of the Antichrist to come.

11:21. In his place shall arise a contemptible person, to whom royal honor has not been given; and he shall come without warning and seize the kingdom by intrigues.

A contemptible person: It is significant that Antiochus Epiphanes is introduced at the very first as a "contemptible" (*nibzeh,* root, *bazah,* "to despise") person. He was considered to be a schemer and untrustworthy. He came to call himself "Epiphanes," meaning "the manifest one" or "illustrious"; but others did not so think of him, giving instead the substitute nickname "Epimanes," meaning "madman." *Royal honor has not been given:* Antiochus was not given the throne, but he seized it, when it was not rightfully his. The throne belonged to Demetrius Soter, his young nephew and son of Seleucus Philopator. Demetrius was now hostage in Rome. Antiochus was in Athens at the time of his older brother's assassination by Heliodorus, and, on hearing of this event, came quickly to Antioch in Syria and had himself proclaimed king. The attempt of Heliodorus for the throne was apparently short-lived, for he was not heard from after that time. *Without warning:* The expression used *(beshalwah)* is the same as the one found in 8:25 (which see). It means basically "in security," and the thought is that when the leaders of Syria, probably including Heliodorus, would think themselves secure in their new government, Antiochus would come and make this play for power. This appears to be exactly what happened. *Seize the kingdom by intrigues:* The word for "intrigues" *(halaqlaqqôt)* means literally "slippery places" (cf. Ps. 35:6; Jer. 23:12), but here "slippery actions, intrigues." It is known that Antiochus accomplished his goal by first winning over the support of Eumenes, king of Pergamos, through flattery and then doing the same with key figures in Syria itself. There is reason to believe that he promised attractive gains for their assistance; and it is known that Rome, in an endeavor to keep a balance of power in the East, actually helped Antiochus at the time. Antiochus likely capitalized on Rome's help in making empty promises to those who gave the aid.

11:22, 23. And before him shall invading armies be overwhelmed and broken, and also the prince of the covenant. And from the time when an alliance is made with him, he shall practice deceit. He will go up and become strong with a small nation.

Shall invading armies be overwhelmed: A literal translation is "arms of the overflow shall be overflowed." That is, "armies of those who would invade Syria as an overflowing stream will in turn be over-flowed by Antiochus." Reference is particularly to the army of Egypt, the defeat of which is mentioned in greater detail in verse twenty-five and following. There is likely a general reference also to all enemy armies turned back by Antiochus. *Prince of the covenant:* The identity of this person, noted in particular as being "overwhelmed," is not clear. Reference may be to the king of Egypt at this time, Ptolemy Philometor (who had succeeded his father Ptolemy Epiphanes in 181 B.C.), whom Antiochus did defeat in the war with Egypt just mentioned. In support of this possibility is the propriety of calling him "prince of the covenant" because of the agreement, noted above, made between his father and the father of Antiochus. Perhaps more likely, however, is an identification with the high priest in Jerusalem, Onias III, making the designation "prince of the covenant," refer to him as one assigned to oversee matters concerning God's covenant with Israel. Onias was killed early in Antiochus' fourth year (171 B.C.) through treachery of his own brother Menelaus.[10]

From the time when an alliance is made with him: Literally, this clause reads, "from the joining together unto him." Since the follow-ing context deals with Egypt, the alliance in view must be one with

[10] Cf. discussion under 8:14.

this country. Because no formal alliance is known from history, reference must be to an informal one, in keeping with the friendly relation which is known now to have existed between the two countries. Antiochus' own sister, Cleopatra, was still active there, holding at that time the position of queen mother, since her husband's death in 181 B.C. *He shall practice deceit:* Deceit is now predicted on Antiochus' part in relation to Egypt. History shows that he offered friendship at first, as just noted, but that he later withdrew it when he became strong. Antiochus' father, Antiochus the Great, had promised the two states, Coele-Syria and Palestine, to Egypt as a dowry with Cleopatra, on her marriage to Ptolemy Epiphanes. It may be assumed that Antiochus reiterated the promise on first coming to the throne, in order to foster the friendship he then needed. It is known that he rescinded this promise in 170 B.C., however, five years after coming to power, by marching through both areas, asserting the control of Syria over them, and making the attack on Egypt set forth in verse twenty-five. *Become strong with a small nation:* This phrase has been referred by some expositors to Antiochus' going up to Egypt in this military campaign of 170 B.C., but this is incorrect, for the text still deals with Antiochus' activities generally. The thought is only that, as a result of defeating opposing armies and his practice of deceit, Antiochus did "go up" in power in the world of his day, and that he did this even though the size of his own nation had become small in comparison with what it had been before Rome's rise to power.

11:24.   Without warning he shall come into the richest parts of the province, and he shall do what neither his fathers nor the fathers of his fathers had done, scattering spoil, booty, and possessions among them. He shall devise plans against fortified places, but only for a time.

Without warning: This is the same expression as in verse twenty-one and 8:25, (which see). To come upon people and situations unexpectedly and without warning was clearly one of Antiochus' planned methods of operation. *Richest parts:* The word used *(mishmanîm)* means literally "fatnesses," here referring to the fertile areas of his own Syrian domain. The thought is that he would identify these, come upon them without advance notice, and seize their fine products for his own purposes. *Scattering spoil, booty, and possessions among them:* The antecedent of "them" cannot be these same "richest parts," for this "spoil, booty, and possessions" were taken away from the richest parts. The principal reference can hardly be to his political friends, either, for such a practice of distribution of booty to friends was very common in the world; and the indication here is that Antiochus' activities in this would be unique and different from that of his ancestors. The antecedent must be implied, namely, the poorer areas of his country. Apparently he would take good things from the rich districts and give them to the poor, thus building favor with the poorer people, who would have made up the majority of his populace (cf. 1 Macc. 3:29-31). It may be assumed, however, that he would not have omitted the interest of his political friends, either, desiring to gain every advantage where and as he could. *Devise plans against fortified places:* Reference is to another of Antiochus' planned methods, a procedure quite parallel with the former. He would "devise plans against" the strong, "fortified" communities in his kingdom for the purpose of weakening them. Understandably, he did not want to be opposed from within his own country by possible internal enemies when he would move out against foreign powers. *Only for a time:* This phrase is, literally, "until a time." The thought is that these various strategies of Antiochus would work for a while, but only so long as God permitted. Antiochus' untimely death came in 164 B.C., after a reign of only twelve years.

11:25. **He shall stir up his strength and his heart against the king of the South with a great army, and the king of the South shall bestir himself for battle with a great and exceedingly powerful army; but he shall not stand because they shall devise plans against him.**

Stir up his strength and his heart: The word for "stir up" (root, *'ûr*) means "to arouse from sleep, incite to action." "Heart" (*lebab*) stands for emotional response, particularly here in respect to courage. The proper emotional attitude is necessary if one's strength is to be used most effectively. After making the home base firm, Antiochus thus made ready to invade outside the country. *King of the South:* The country Antiochus planned to invade was Egypt, whose king at the time was Ptolemy Philometor (181-145 B.C.), one of two sons of Cleopatra, and also nephew to Antiochus (Cleopatra was the sister of Antiochus). As noted above, the battle came in 170 B.C. and concerned especially the control of Coele-Syria and Palestine. Apparently, Ptolemy Philometor had attempted to seize both when he realized that Antiochus did not intend to keep the promise of his father relative to them (cf. under v. 23); and Antiochus now moved to assert his mastery. The army with which he came was very large, as indicated. *A great and exceedingly powerful army:* This description is given of the army of Ptolemy Philometor, which was still larger, as these words indicate. *He shall not stand:* The main battle was fought at Pelusium, located just east of the Nile delta. This means that Antiochus was able to march the length of Coele-Syria and Palestine and approach to the very border of Egypt, before being stopped by the Egyptian force. Here Ptolemy was defeated, and a significant reason, indeed, was that treachery was worked against him by his own forces, a matter mentioned again in the next verse.

11:26, 27. Even those who eat his rich food shall break him; his army shall overflow but many shall fall down slain. In respect to both kings, their hearts shall be bent to do evil. They shall speak lies at the same table; but this shall not succeed, for the end of the appointed time is yet to come.

Who eat his rich food: Reference is to trusted counselors, those who ate at his own table. The word for "food" *(pat-bag)* is the same as the word used in 1:5, 8 (which see). Ptolemy would incur treachery on the part of his own court circles. *His army shall overflow but many shall fall down slain:* The Syriac and Vulgate versions show the passive voice here: "shall be overflown," giving the meaning: "his army shall be overflown by Antiochus' forces, and many shall therefore fall down slain." This meaning fits the context, but still the Hebrew reading, which is active, must be preferred. The Hebrew, which also fits the context, gives this meaning: "His army shall be overflowing in size, but still many of its numbers shall fall in death" as a result of the treachery. Young Ptolemy was even taken captive by Antiochus.
Both kings . . . shall be bent to do evil: The thought is that the two kings would harbor evil intention toward each other. After capturing his nephew Ptolemy, Antiochus professed friendship for him, apparently making much of their blood-tie relationship. He had a reason. At the time of this Egyptian defeat at Pelusium, the people of Alexandria put the brother of Ptolemy Philometor on the throne as Ptolemy VII Euergetes (later nicknamed Physkon, due to his bloated appearance), and Antiochus pretended friendship for his nephew to gain his assistance against the new ruler. He treated the young man royally, as though he were an equal, while actually holding him captive. *Speak lies at the same table:* There is indication that the two planned together how the nephew might take back his entire rule, Antiochus making promises that he had no intention of keeping and the nephew pretending to accept them while always distrusting his unscrupulous uncle. The figure of speaking lies at the same table is significant because, to the oriental, deception practiced at a table of hospitality was the very lowest in kind. *This shall not succeed:* The antecedent of "this" appears clearly to be the implied plan of the two, as respectively seen by each. Antiochus hoped to seize all Egypt, as he combined with the one brother against the other; and Ptolemy Philometor, it may be assumed, hoped to take back all Egypt for himelf. Antiochus did take the strategic center, Memphis, but was repulsed when he attempted to march on Alexandria itself, where the new king held forth. He settled for the installation of Ptolemy Philometor as king at Memphis. Ptolemy Philometor

did achieve renewed kingship at Memphis, then, but he did not succeed in gaining control again of all Egypt. On the departure of Antiochus for Syria shortly after the installation at Memphis, Ptolemy worked out a joint rule of the land with his brother and then married their common sister, Cleopatra (named after her mother), who thus became queen. *End of the appointed time:* The "appointed time" *(mo'ed)* in mind is God's time, in respect to the two kings and their countries. "End" appears to carry the thought of *goal,* rather than *close* of a period of time. The thought is that the goals of the two kings would not be realized because they did not coincide with the "end" God had in mind—an unidentified end which would come to fruition at a time still future.

11:28. Then shall he return to his land with great booty, and his heart shall be set against the holy covenant. He shall do his will and return to his own land.

Return to his land: The prediction is that Antiochus, after failing to take Egypt, would return home, taking with him much booty as a salve for his wounded pride. History verifies that this occurred (cf. 1 Macc. 1:19). *Against the holy covenant:* The term "holy covenant" appears to have the same basic meaning that it has in 1 Maccabees 1:15, where it is used in general terms to refer to all things religious in Israel. On his way home to Syria, Antiochus took time in Palestine to work great havoc against the Temple, the religious personnel, and the ceremonial system. The occasion of the action involved the Jewish reaction against the high priest Menelaus, who had catered to the favor of Antiochus in the past days.[11] Antiochus now sought to assist Menelaus and put down the minor revolt. Besides this, it is generally accepted that he was looking for a way to vent his anger after his disappointment in Egypt, and the Jews, whom he had come to despise, were handy as he made his way homeward. *Do his will and return:* The thought is that Antiochus would do as he wished in putting down the revolt and then return home. He did put down the revolt, for the Jews were incapable of resisting him effectively. Some of his despicable actions against them are set forth in 1 Maccabees 1:20-24, which is quoted under 8:11 (which see). With these matters effected, and Menelaus firmly established as high priest, the Syrian ruler continued his journey homeward.

11:29, 30. At the appointed time he shall return and come into the South, but this latter occasion shall not be as the former. For ships of Chittim shall come against him and he shall be dejected and return

[11] Cf. under 8:14 for details. Menelaus had now replaced Jason (in 172 B.C.) as high priest, having promised a higher bribe to Antiochus.

and rage against the holy covenant, and he shall do his will. He shall return and take note of those who forsake the holy covenant.

At the appointed time: Another time of campaign into Egypt was predicted, and this did occur in 168 B.C., two years after the first campaign. Antiochus had learned of the coalition formed by the two brothers and their sister, and he determined to break it. He had left the one brother, Ptolemy Philopator, in charge at Memphis, and he apparently felt that the young man had now betrayed him. The term "appointed time" is best taken as again referring to God's planned time. It would seem that God saw this return campaign against Egypt as a necessary part in the overall activity of Antiochus. *Latter occasion shall not be as the former:* Literally, this reads, "it shall not be as the former, so the latter." This campaign would be different from that of 170 B.C. The first time he had been successful for a time, but he would not be successful at all the second time.

Ships of Chittim shall come: The reason for the lack of success is indicated. "Ships of Chittim" (cf. Num. 24:24) stands here for the Romans, who had been persuaded to aid the Egyptians. "Chittim" properly meant "Cyprians," but it came to mean the islands and coastal regions of the northeast Mediterranean area, and even any territory to the west of Palestine along the northern coast of the Mediterranean, which included Rome. Romans, who had come to Egypt in ships, met Antiochus as he moved on Alexandria. *Dejected and return:* History indicates that Antiochus' army never fought in this campaign. Antiochus was met by the Roman emissary, Popilius Laenas, and handed a letter from the Roman Senate, forbidding him to make war against Egypt. When Antiochus did not acquiesce readily, the Roman, it is said, drew a circle on the sand around Antiochus and told him that he must respond before stepping from the circle. After a moment of further humiliating silence, Antiochus agreed to the demand. He apparently recognized that if he did not agree, he would be faced with an undesirable war with Rome. He was dejected as a result, of course, for this meant that he had brought his fine army the long distance from Syria for nothing; however, no course was left for him but to return home, which he did.[12] *Rage against the holy covenant:* Taking "holy covenant" to mean the same as before (v. 28), the prophecy states that Antiochus would stop en route home once again and vent anger against the Jews, the Temple, and the ceremonies. The word for "rage" *(za'am)* connotes excessive anger. *Shall do his will:* His formidable army with him, Antiochus would be able to effect all that he wished. The most offensive features of his actions are set forth in verses thirty-one to thirty-five.

---

[12] For further discussion, cf. Montgomery, MICC, p. 455; or Young, YPD, p. 244, who refers to Livy, ivv, 10 and Polybius xxix, 1.

He shall return: The repetition of "return" *(shûḇ)* may be merely to stress the thought of the coming back from Egypt, or it may refer to "turning hither and thither"[13] on arrival in Palestine in the anti-Jewish activities then conducted. *Take note of those who forsake the covenant:* The word for "take note" (root, *bîn*) means here "to bring one's attention to." The people of whom Antiochus would thus take note are called "forsakers" (participle) of God's covenant, meaning those who had already turned from God's law. The thought is that Antiochus would seek out such people for support in his attempt to stamp out observance of the Mosaic ceremonies. The leader among this group was the apostate high priest himself, Menelaus, who gave full cooperation (cf. 1 Macc. 1:43).

11:31, 32. Forces from him shall arise and pollute the Sanctuary, the Fortress, and remove the regular ceremonies and set up the abomination of desolation. Those who violate the covenant he will pervert by intrigue; but those who know their God shall be strong and take action.

Forces from him: The word for "forces" *(z°ro'îm)* is literally "arms," here in the sense of *sources of strength* or *troop forces. Pollute the Sanctuary, the Fortress:* The principal offensive actions of Antiochus are now set forth. First, he would pollute the Temple, which is referred to both as "Sanctuary" *(miqdash,* "holy place") and "Fortress" *(ma'ôz,* "place of strength"). The latter term is used frequently regarding a place of military strength. Here, however, its primary significance must be in respect to spiritual strength, though the Temple did afford also a place of resistance against physical attack (cf. 1 Macc. 6:7). This is witnessed, for example, by its holding out the longest against the attack of Titus on Jerusalem in A.D. 70. Antiochus' design in this, as set forth in 1 Maccabees 1:41-50 (quoted under 8:11 [which see]), was to force Grecian customs on the Jews. He had spent some time in Athens, prior to becoming king of Syria, and had apparently become enamored of the Grecian ways. *Regular ceremonies:* The word used *(tamîḏ)* is the same as that used in 8:11 (which see). The Mosaic ceremonies were declared illegal by Antiochus (cf. Josephus, *Antiq.* VII, 5, 4). People who sought still to follow them were made subject to death, and the lives of many were taken. *Abomination of desolation:* This expression *(shiqqûts m°shômem)* is the same as that found in 9:27 (which see), except that it is singular here. As indicated under 9:27, it refers to that which Antiochus erected in the Temple: a substitute altar and/or a statue of Jupiter (Zeus) Olympius (cf. 9:27 for general discussion). This offensive item apparently was put in the place of the brazen altar, indicating that the Jews were now to

---

[13] Suggestion of Montgomery, MICC, p. 457.

worship this chief Grecian god rather than the God of their fathers. It was in truth an abomination, which brought a desolate condition to the Temple, for now no one would come to worship at all.

Those who violate the covenant: A plural hiphil participle is used here (root, *rasha'*, "to be wicked") meaning "ones who act wickedly." This is a reference to those who are called "forsakers" of the covenant in verse thirty. *Pervert by intrigue:* The word for "pervert" (root, *ḥanap*, "to be defiled") is a hiphil form, meaning "to make one defiled." The word for "intrigue" (*ḥᵃlaqqôt*) is the same basic word as in verse twenty-one, meaning "slippery places" or "flatteries." The thought is that Antiochus, just as when he first came to power, would use flatteries in Judah to pervert still more those who already had abandoned the Mosaic rites, probably meaning that he would praise them and make promises of reward if they would aid him fully. *Shall be strong and take action:* Truly to know God is to stand firm for Him, no matter what the opposition may be. The prediction is that some at least would be of this kind. 1 Maccabees 1:61, 62 indicates that this proved to be so, stating: "Howbeit many in Israel were fully resolved and confirmed in themselves not to eat any unclean thing. Wherefore they chose rather to die, that they might not be defiled with meats, and that they might not profane the holy covenant." Many of them did die. Some, who lived at least for a time, took action to counter the efforts of Antiochus. Principal among those who resisted were the Maccabees.

11:33. Those who are wise among the people shall cause many to understand; yet they shall fall by sword and flame, by captivity and plunder, for many days.

Those who are wise: a hiphil participle is used, which may be translated "teachers." The thought, however, does not concern formal teaching, but rather informal instruction, by such as have greater insight than others. The areas of wisdom concerned are, no doubt, religion and theology. Those better informed would help others to know how to think and act under the great distress that would be inflicted (cf. 1 Macc. 2:42). *Yet they shall fall:* This imparted understanding would give peace and strength, but not deliverance from the enemy. Indeed, those who took the strong stand against the regulations of Antiochus proved to be those in the greatest danger. Mattathias Maccabeus, father of five sons, refused to offer sacrifice in the Grecian way; but instead he slew the king's representative, who would have compelled him. Then he and his sons, with others who chose to join them, fled to the mountains and began the famed Maccabean revolt. Many of them died, but the revolt was effective in resisting the heathen orders for some time. The word for "fall" (root, *kashal*) means literally "stumble," but here it should be understood clearly in the sense of "falling" in severe suffering and death. *By sword and flame, by captivity and plunder:* These are some of the ways in which this suffering and death would be inflicted. In one instance, when Antiochus' soldiers realized that the Maccabeans would not fight on the sabbath, they deliberately attacked on a sabbath and were able to slaughter many (1 Macc. 2:31-38). At other times, many were burned (2 Macc. 7:1-23). Other instances saw people taken captive and their possessions plundered. *For many days:* The Hebrew says only "days," but the thought of the qualifier "many" is clearly implied. These "days" in fact proved to be a few years.

11:34, 35. As they fall, they shall receive a little help; but many shall join themselves to them by intrigue. And some of the wise will fall, to refine among them and to cleanse and make white until the time of the end, for the appointed time is yet to come.

As they fall, they shall receive a little help: Literally, this reads, "In their being stumbled, they shall be helped with a little help." The thought is that some help would be given to those who stood against the enemy. Reference may be to help given by the Maccabees to people at large, or it may be to small groups of people who came to give help to the Maccabees. *Join themselves to them by intrigue:* The word for "intrigue" is the same as in verses twenty-one and thirty-two. The thought is that among those who would give him this help would be a number who would do so insincerely, by flattery or intrigue. This is more easily understood if the above reference is to the groups who wished to join the Maccabees, for intrigue did come to be used by some of them. As the protest movement grew, it became popular to join and some resorted to subterfuge to be accepted. Others did so out of fear when the Maccabees came to bring reprisal on those who aided Syria (cf. 1 Macc. 2:44; 3:5, 8; 2 Macc. 7:40; 13:21).

To refine . . . to cleanse . . . make white: Refining has always been necessary among the people of God, and the normal instrument used has been suffering. This is predicted for the people of this Maccabean time, including even those considered among the wise. The implication is clear that this refining would be accomplished through the afflictions of Antiochus. The word for "refine" (root, *tsarap*) is used for melting or refining metal; that for "cleanse" (root, *barar,* "to separate") is used in the piel, meaning "separate from impurity"; and that for "make white" (root, *laban,* "to be white") is also used in the piel, meaning "make white," employed here figuratively for *purity. The time of the end:* A double reference is likely intended for both this and the next element. As will be noted, the following main section, verses thirty-six to forty-five, concerns the Antichrist, who comes to rule only at the close of the present age, long after the time of Antiochus Epiphanes. This and the next element seem to provide a way of transition from the era of Antiochus Epiphanes to that of the Antichrist. The first reference of both elements is clearly to the time of Antiochus, the person of the preceding context, stating that refinement by suffering would continue until his demise. That a second reference, to the time of the Antichrist, is also intended follows from the fact that the phrase "time of the end" regularly signifies the final end-time (cf. vv. 40; 12:4, 9). Actually the time of Antiochus could not be called a "time of end" of itself, for it was not that. No "time" or age then ended. It could only prefigure such a "time." The meaning of the statement, in respect to the true end-time, is that refinement would continue among God's people until and through that climactic period, namely, the period of Great Tribulation (cf. 9:27). *The appointed time is yet to come:* The twofold reference continues. The same word is used here for "appointed time" as in verses twenty-seven and thirty (which see). The same meaning is intended—namely, that God controls time for His purpose—with the idea of control being taken in respect to both the oppressions of Antiochus and those much later of the Antichrist. The thought is that the duration of each would be under God's superintendence.

D. The Antichrist (vv. 36-45)

Bible expositors differ as to the identity of the king to whom reference is made in the remaining verses of the chapter. Some believe it to be Antiochus Epiphanes still; others, that it is the Antichrist of future time. Adherents of the first view point out that this continuing king should be assumed to be Antiochus, since no direct indication is given of a change in identity. There are several reasons, however, in favor of the second view—reasons which show that there is a change of identity as clearly as if the direct indication were given. (1) In the ensuing verses there are statements regarding the character of this king which were not true of Antiochus, but do agree with descriptions given elsewhere of the Antichrist, as the following commentary will show. (2) In verses thirty-six to thirty-nine, policies of this person are reviewed, as if to introduce him for the first time. This would be strange if reference were to Antiochus, whose policies and actual life-history have already been given. (3) Numerous historical matters from the life of this king are set forth in verses forty to forty-five; and these do not accord with historical events experienced by Antiochus, but do fit into the life-pattern of all that is stated elsewhere of the Antichrist. (4) Any further treatment regarding Antiochus should not be expected, for his story, as to his oppression of the Jews (the purpose for his mention) has been completed. (5) The form of reference used in verse thirty-six to introduce this person suggests a change of identity from Antiochus, because Antiochus has not been designated at any time as "the king" (the form used here, with the article) and Antiochus' predecessors have always been referred to by the designation "king of the North." (6) In verse forty this king is actually distinguished from another ruler called "king of the North," thus setting him quite apart from a line of kings so called. (7) Involved with this person's rule will be a time of trouble for Israel worse than any other period in history, as indicated in 12:1; and this corresponds to Matthew 24:21 (cf. Jer. 30:7) where the Great Tribulation is clearly in view, a time existing when the Antichrist rules. (8) Since the Antichrist has been presented in the three prior revelational times of Daniel, one should not be surprised to have him set forth in this fourth time as well.

11:36. And the king shall do according to his will, and shall exalt himself and magnify himself above every god, and shall speak astonishing things against the God of gods. He shall prosper until the indignation is ended, for that which has been determined shall be done.

And the king: As noted, neither Antiochus Epiphanes nor his predecessors are called by this term. In fact, Antiochus is not named by any definite term, being called a "king" only one time, and that jointly with Ptolemy (v. 27). Since his predecessors are called regularly by the designation "king of the North," the implication is that he could have been similarly identified had the context called for it. That this king, if he is the Antichrist, should be designated as "the king" (using the article) is reasonable, because the Antichrist has been clearly set forth in Daniel's previous times of revelation: first as "little horn" (7:8, 24), then as "a king fierce of countenance" (8:23), and further as "the prince that shall come" (9:26). *According to his will:* As has been seen, Antiochus was characterized by an insolent, self-centered manner, demanding that all be done as he wanted; and now it is stated that the Antichrist, as indicated also in prior texts considered (7:25; 8:24; cf. Rev. 13:7; 17:13), will be of the same kind. *Magnify himself above every god:* Antiochus was proud, but not to the point of magnifying himself above any god, for he worshiped the gods of Greece and demanded the same of the Jews. The Antichrist, however, will indeed try to set himself above every god (cf. 2 Thess. 2:4), blaspheming God's name (cf. Rev. 13:6) and attempting even to change God's natural laws (cf. Dan. 7:25). *Astonishing things:* The word used (root, *pala'*, "to separate") is a plural niphal participle, meaning literally "things done astonishingly, unbelievably." The thought of uniqueness is connoted. This person will speak things against God that will be unique to himself—different, apparently, from what any other would dare to speak, in degree of insolence and self-exaltation. *The indignation:* The word used (*za'am*) is the same word as in 8:19, a parallel context, where it was found to refer to the Tribulation period, when the Antichrist is the mighty

Roman king. The same time is in view here, the thought being that the Antichrist will succeed in his actions until the completion of that time (seven years, 9:27). *Which has been determined:* God is supremely in charge of history, even when the Antichrist rules. What the Antichrist will do will be only what God has beforehand determined. The reason why God permits his oppression of the Jews is to bring them to an attitude where they will receive Christ as their Messiah.

11:37, 38. He shall not regard the gods of his fathers, nor the desire of women, nor shall he regard any god; for he shall magnify himself above all. But in their place he shall honor the god of fortresses; a god whom his fathers did not know shall he honor, with gold and silver and precious stones and desirable things.

He shall not regard: An unnatural attitude on the part of this ruler is now presented—an attitude involving three matters on which men normally agree with approval. The Antichrist, however, "shall not regard" (root, *bîn,* "to understand" or "to regard with understanding") any of the three. *Gods of his fathers:* Men normally hold to, or at least respect, the god(s) of their ancestors, but this man would not do so. The particular gods in reference are best taken to be the gods worshiped by Romans (both the pagan deities and the true God worshiped by the Roman church) down through the centuries, since the Antichrist comes from Rome. Some expositors see here a reference to Yahweh,[14] as God of Israel (arguing from the characteristic "God of his fathers"), and take evidence from this that the Antichrist will be a Jew. There is evidence against this view, however, in the plurality of the word "gods" (*'elohîm*) as here used, which is truly indicative of plurality in this instance, since the singular form *'eloah* is used twice in the next few words. *The desire of women:* The thought intended may be the "desire" which men normally have for women, or the area of "desire" normally characteristic of women (such as mercy, gentleness, kindness). The first is not likely, because the Antichrist is prefigured in Antiochus Epiphanes, and he was known for his profligacy toward women. Moreover, it is very likely that the Antichrist will have little place for such graces as mercy, gentleness, and kindness. *Any god:* Not only will this man not regard the God of his fathers, but he will not regard any god at all. He will deny God, taking the place of God Himself, as he claims supreme power and authority (2 Thess. 2:4).

In their place: The Hebrew has "its place" rather than "their place," apparently taking as its antecedent specifically "any god" of the last phrase in verse thirty-seven. *God of fortresses:* The word for "for-

[14] Cf. under 9:2 for an explanation of this name of God.

tresses" *(ma'uzzîm)* is used six other times in this chapter (vv. 1, 7, 10, 19, 31, 39), either in the singular or plural, and each time to mean a *strong place,* which calls for the same meaning here. The thought is not, then, that the Antichrist will accept *force* or *power* as his god, as is sometimes held, for this would be contrary to the prior statement that he will accept no god at all; but rather the thought is that he will find his goal in fortresses, strongholds, and military programs, in place of such religious belief. *A god whom his fathers did not know:* From earliest days, Rome has been religious, but this future ruler will be different, denying all deity and pursuing warfare instead. Military activity will take the place of god for him. *Gold and silver and precious stones and desirable things:* Pagans have always honored their gods by making images of precious metals and stones, but the Antichrist will honor his by the expenditure of these valuables. Warfare has always been expensive, and this will be as true as ever for this ruler. The word for "desirable things" *(ḥᵃmudôt)* comes from the verb *ḥamad,* meaning "to desire." Being in parallel with "gold," "silver," and "precious stones," it may mean "jewels," or it may serve as a term of summation: "anything valuable."

11:39. He will act against the strongest fortresses by means of the strange god; those who recognize him he will highly honor and cause them to rule over many, allotting land as a reward.

Strongest fortresses: Literally translated, this reads, "strongholds of fortresses" *(mibtsᵉrê ma'uzzîm).* The Antichrist will not hold back from attacking any stronghold, as he puts his reliance in his war machine. *Those who recognize him he will highy honor:* That is, literally, "who recognizing he will multiply honor." Because "recognizing" *(hakkîr)* is an infinitive construct (not an imperfect), the subject must be "who" *(ᵃsher),* referring to those conquered and not the Antichrist, which makes the Antichrist the implied object. The thought, then, is that among those whom he conquers, he will honor those who readily give obeisance. *To rule over many:* They will be given positions of leadership, presumably either as officers in his own government or as subrulers over conquered provinces. *Allotting land as a reward:* Literally, this states that "he will allot land in connection with a reward." The thought is that the amount of land over which any subruler would be given authority would be granted as a reward, and that it would vary with the degree of obeisance rendered and the subruler's potential as an aid to the Antichrist.

11:40. In the time of the end, the king of the South shall push at him, and the king of the North shall storm against him, with chariot and horsemen and many ships; but he shall come in the lands and overflow and pass through.

The time of the end: Thus far, the information given regarding this final Roman ruler has concerned his general policies and practices. Now significant activities (those pertaining to the Jews) are set forth. These are introduced by the same time notice ("the time of the end") as employed in introducing his policies and practices (v. 35). The earlier notice concerned matters "until" *('ad)* the time of the end, and here it is "in" *(b^e)* that time. As observed then, this "time of the end" is a reference to the Tribulation period, when the Antichrist rules. *King of the South shall push:* The designations "king of the South" and "king of the North" have not appeared in this section concerning the Antichrist. Clearly, however, their meanings here cannot be divorced from those in the earlier part of the chapter, where reference was to the Ptolemaic and Seleucid rulers, respectively. Because the political situation in the world could well be different when the Antichrist rules, however, it stands to reason that the terms should be adapted to whatever that difference may prove to be. Judging from what exists today, it is noteworthy that Egypt (Ptolemaic power) is still strong and, indeed, the leader of an Arab bloc of nations. "King of the South," then, could well refer to Egypt's principal officer as leader of the Arab world. This ruler will "push" (root, *nagah,* "to push like a goat"; cf. 8:4) at the Antichrist, meaning that he will attack him, apparently in an effort to hinder him in his expansionist plans.

King of the North shall storm: The designation "king of the North" is not so easily adapted, for the present Syrian government hardly qualifies as a world contender of the stature of the Seleucids. This means that a replacement must be intended, and two views have been presented by expositors as to who this might be. One is that it is the Antichrist himself, and for this view two main arguments are presented. One argument is that since he has been the subject of the section, he is the most likely candidate; and the other that it is logical so to identify him, since he was typified by Antiochus Epiphanes, one of the former kings of the North. The other view is that this replacement is the leader of the present nation of Russia. This view must be preferred, in the light of several convincing arguments that show evidence either against the former view or in favor of the latter. First, this designation "king of the North" is not a likely reference to the Antichrist, since it is not used for him in the prior context, but rather he is there referred to by the more simple term "the king" and this shorter term appears in the verse (36) which introduces him, where one would expect the fuller term if applicable. Second, though Antiochus Epiphanes did typify the Antichrist, he did so as an individual person and not as a member of the Seleucid line called "kings of the North," and he is himself, significantly, not called by this term. Third, the designation "king of the North" is not an appropriate indication of the Antichrist, because his country, Rome, is not north of Palestine. A Russian ruler fits well, however, since Russia is directly north, with Moscow being almost on a direct north-south line with Jerusalem. Fourth, positive evidence in favor of a Russian ruler may be taken from a parallel passage, Ezekiel 38, 39, as follows: (1) A great battle is described in these two chapters, and it must transpire during the Tribulatioin period also (the period during which the war set forth in our present verse occurs [cf. under v. 36]), as several factors show: first, because it will occur after the Jews have returned to their land (38:8, 12); second, because it will be in "the latter years" *('ah^{a}rit hashshanîm)* (38:8) and in "the latter days *('ah^{a}rit hayyamîm)* (38:16), both phrases speaking of the Tribulation period; third, because it will be when the returned Jews are living in a sense of peace and safety (38:11), which could well be sometime during the three-and-one-half-year period of the peace-covenant with the Antichrist (cf. Dan. 9:27); and, fourth, because it must occur before Christ will have destroyed all Israel's enemies (Zech. 14:1-3; Rev. 19:11-21), for such an attack as here set forth could hadly take place after that. (2) But this means that this battle must be closely related to, if not identical with, the conflict described in this verse (11:40), because this conflict too must be near the midpoint of the Tribulation week, since the following verses in Daniel 11 tell of the Antichrist moving on into Palestine after this battle; and two battles, totally different, could hardly transpire in so short a time in the same general area (the Ezekiel 38, 39 battle also involving the Jews, as noted). (3) A close relation or identity between the two battles is argued also by the fact that a conflict, in which a large nation like Russia would come against Israel when the Antichrist had a covenant with her (cf. Dan. 9:27), is hard to imagine, unless the Antichrist would become involved, at least to protect his own interests. (4) The king involved in the battle of Ezekiel 38, 39 can be properly identified with the ruler of Russia, because his domain is said to be Magog, Rosh, Meshech, and Tubal (38:2, 3)—names of peoples in Old Testament time living in northern Mesopotamia and the Caucasus region of present-day Russia, who, it is commonly accepted, migrated north into Russia to make up much of its populace.[15] This identification is likely also because the country of this king of Ezekiel 38, 39 is described as being in the "uttermost parts of the north" (38:6, 15; 39:2), identifying him with the north (even far north, in view of "uttermost parts, *yark^{e}tê)* where Russia is. This stress on the "north," it should be noticed, accords well with the thought in the designation of our

---

[15] For documented evidence cf. Pentecost, *TTC,* pp. 326-31, and Walvoord, *NIP,* pp. 105-108.

verse, "king of the North." (5) A factor which argues for an identification of this northern king of Russia with the "king of the North" of our verse is that this northern king allies himself with Persia, Ethiopia, and Libya (*paras, kush, put*—Ezek. 38:5; cf. 30:5; Nah. 3:9) in this battle, and these countries could represent the same Arab bloc of nations as possibly led by the "king of the South" of our text, as noted.

To these arguments, two others of a different type may still be added. One is that on the basis of grammar, it is to be expected that the "him" of the phrases "at him" *('immô)* and "against him" *('alayw)* of our verse should refer to the same person, which is true if both are taken in reference to the Antichrist. If they are, however, the sense of the verse forbids that he be identified with the "king of the North." The other is that an identification of this "king of the North" with a Russian ruler makes good sense and fits contemporary history. When the Antichrist makes a covenant with Israel at the beginning of the Tribulation week (Dan. 9:27), the Arab bloc of nations could be expected to seek Russia's help to intervene, lest all hope of ever obtaining the land be lost. Russia could be expected in turn to respond favorably, in an attempt to offset the rising challenge of the Antichrist. The Antichrist, with his ambitious plans, would of course retaliate against such a rival alliance, and the three-pronged struggle depicted here could indeed occur. As for the verb "shall storm" (root, *sa'ar,* "to quiver"), which tells the action of this "king of the North," it is used here in the hithpael and means "to rush like a tempest." The significance is that this person will come against the Antichrist in great fury.

Chariot and horsemen and many ships: The weapons of this king are mentioned, whereas those of the "king of the South" are not, suggesting that the former will have more of them, as is true today of Russia in comparison with the Arab nations. The weapons listed are of a kind used in the Old Testament time, as are also those of the invading ruler of Ezekiel 38, 39. They are best taken as representative of their counterparts of modern warfare, however, for modern weapons could not have been listed in the day of Daniel if the reader then was to understand the writing. *He will come in the lands:* It is logical to take the antecedent of "he" to be the same as that of "him" in the two prepositional phrases earlier in the verse, each not needing clearer identification, because the Antichrist, the common antecedent, is the general subject of the passage. "Lands" is plural, likely referring not only to Palestine but to Egypt, Libya, and Ethiopia (vv. 42, 43). The phrase, along with the two following verbs, indicates clearly that the Antichrist will emerge victorious in the battle with the two opposing kings. *Overflow and pass through:* The word for "overflow" *(shatap)* is used commonly of a river overflowing land (cf. v. 10). The Antichrist will "pass through" *('abar)* Palestine, after overflowing it, on his way farther south to Egypt.

11:41. Then he shall enter the glorious land and many shall fall, though these countries will escape from his hand: Edom, Moab, and the chief of the Ammonites.

The glorious land: The thought is that the Antichrist, having triumphed over the two allied kings, will move on into "the glorious land," meaning Palestine (cf. the same phrase in vv. 16 and 8:9 [which see]). No indication is given as to where the battle proper will have been fought. From Ezekiel 38, 39, (38:8, 11, 16; 39:2, 4, 11), however, it is quite clear that it will have been somewhere in Palestine, probably toward the north, since an Arab-Russian alliance would want to keep such an enemy as far removed from Jerusalem, the capital, as possible. The suggestion carries merit that it may transpire near Megiddo, an ancient site of great battles, and from which the name of the climactic battle of Armageddon (Rev. 16:16) is taken. It is possible, in fact, that the three-pronged battle will be the opening aspect of this battle of Armageddon, the continuation of which would last, then, throughout the remaining half of the Tribulation week, reaching its climax at the fall of Jerusalem (Zech. 14:2). This is one way of accounting for the name of the battle being taken from Megiddo; there is otherwise a problem, since the climax of the struggle certainly occurs at Jerusalem. *Many shall fall:* These "many" must be Jews, since, with the three-pronged battle being over by this time, they would not be Russians or Arabs. If so, the Antichrist must break his covenant with the Jews (Dan. 9:27) at the conclusion of this struggle, marking the victory, then, at a point in time no later than the exact middle of the Tribulation week. The fact that he will want to break it is not difficult to understand. He will at that time be the supreme master of that part of the world and be in a position to force his will wherever he may desire. The Jews, with their restored worship of God at Jerusalem, will be a source of irritation to him, in his atheistic devotion to materialism; and their land, a long-standing prize of nations for its strategic geographical location and Dead Sea wealth, will be a tempting addition to his domain. Further, since he will have been controlled to a unique degree by Satan (2 Thess. 2:9; Rev. 13:4), Satan can be expected to motivate him to break the covenant and then inflict severe suffering on the people of God. Consequently, he may be thought of here as moving on into the land; forcing the cessation of religious ceremonies on the Jews; erecting his "abomination of desolation" in the Temple (Dan. 9:27), just as Antiochus Epiphanes did; and killing all who resist. *Edom, Moab, and the chief of the Ammonites:* These three countries were all to the southeast of Palestine. The thought is that their counterpart(s) at the time of the Tribulation period (today, Jordan), would not be invaded. "Chief· *(re'shît)* of the Ammonites" means their leaders. Just what this means in terms of the political situation today is not clear. Perhaps the common people (in distinction from these leaders), living especially in the portion of present-day Jordan held in old time by the Ammonites, will be taken by the Antichrist, whereas the leaders will somehow escape.

11:42, 43. He shall stretch out his hand against countries, and the land of Egypt shall not escape. He shall gain control of the treasures of gold and silver and all the desirable things of Egypt; and the Libyans and the Ethiopians shall be in his train.

Against countries: The word for "countries" *(ªratsôt)* is the same as for "lands" in verse forty. Further information is now given, then, concerning the identity of these "lands." Not content merely with Palestine, the Antichrist will look farther. *Land of Egypt:* Apparently one reason why countries to the southeast of Palestine will escape destruction is that the path taken by the Antichrist will lead southwest. That the Antichrist should be interested primarily in Egypt fits the interpretation of verse forty given above, for if the "king of the South" is the Egyptian ruler, then his country will have already been defeated in the earlier battle, leaving only the matter of actually occupying the country.[16] The words for "shall not escape" mean literally "shall not be for an escape," that is, "shall not be among those who have escaped." Reference is to those lands that will have escaped, as indicated in verse forty-one; but Egypt will not be so fortunate.

He shall gain control: This statement reads literally, "He shall rule." The Antichrist will be able to achieve complete domination of the land and its valuables. The word for "desirable things" is the same as in verse thirty-eight (which see). *Libyans and the Ethiopians:* The two countries here represented will also be occupied. Since Ezekiel 38:5 lists both as allied with Russia in the earlier conflict, it is likely that the kings of both will have been defeated at that time, even as the ruler of Egypt, making the occupation of their countries just as natural and easy. *In his train:* The word used *(bªmits'adyw)* is literally "in his steps." The thought is that the Antichrist will so make conquest of these countries that they will follow "in his steps," that is, they will be a part of his vast domain and obey his demands.

11:44. But rumors from the east and the north shall alarm him, and he shall go forth in great fury to destroy and annihilate many.

[16] It may be noted that the contemporary Israeli-Arab problem would be solved by the Antichrist's actions here, if not before; though it would be replaced by the more serious one involving the Antichrist.

Rumors from the east and the north: While in this section of Africa, the Antichrist will hear of trouble from the east and north, which will give him cause for alarm. The nature of the rumors or whom they concern is not indicated. Some expositors[17] believe they concern the invasion of a vast horde of 200,000,000 warriors from the far east (Rev. 9:16) under the leadership of "kings of the east" (Rev. 16:12), who will have heard of the Antichrist's victory over the earlier north-south confederacy and will then wish to challenge him for world leadership. Others see here only tidings from Palestine that will indicate that the troops left there by the Antichrist have suffered some serious reverses, presumably at the hands of the Jews. Which view is best is not easily determined, but it may be observed that Revelation 9:16 and 16:12 are subject to other interpretations than the one the first of these two views projects; and the figure of 200,000,000 for an army is almost beyond comprehension. Whatever the correct view, the Antichrist does hear disturbing news and returns to Palestine to bring remedy. *In great fury to destroy and annihilate many:* The rumors heard bring very strong reaction on the part of the Antichrist. The phrase "in great fury" shows this in the use of the adjective "great" *(g^edolah).* Two forceful words are employed to depict his treatment of the enemy: "destroy" (root, *shamad*) and "annihilate" (root, *haram*). The Antichrist clearly is able to bring complete defeat on those causing the rumors. This provides a further argument against the view which sees this enemy as a host of 200,000,000. One wonders if he could possibly be so successful against an army so large. It is reasonable to believe that he could put down an uprising of the Jews in this manner.

11:45. Then he shall place his palatial tents between the seas, at the glorious holy mountain. But he shall come to his end with none to help him.

He shall place his palatial tents: The clause is, literally translated, "he shall plant the tents of his palace." Ancient conquerors took tents with them for their official dwelling places, when on campaign. At the center of the encampment a large main tent was pitched and around it small ones for personal attendants. The thought here is that the Antichrist would be able to place his official tent where he wanted in Palestine, indicating complete subjugation of the land. The tent would serve both as a symbol of his domination and a base from which to continue his oppression of the Jews. *Between the seas, at the glorious holy mountain:* The mountain in reference must be Mount Zion, where the Temple was located (making it "glorious" and "holy"); this means that the seas must be the Mediterranean Sea

---

[17] For instance, Pentecost, *TTC,* p. 356, and Walvoord, *NIP,* p. 131.

and the Dead Sea. According to Zechariah 14:2, the Antichrist will bring complete destruction on Jerusalem, and this destruction would make possible the erection of his residence there in this manner. According to Zechariah 13:8, 9, he will by this time have brought either death or captivity to two-thirds of the inhabitants of the land, indicating an appalling destruction. *He shall come to his end:* Having reached his zenith of power and with Israel prostrate at his feet, the Antichrist will come to his end, both as to power and life. Before this, he will have brought Israel to a state of complete humiliation, with both army and government fully crushed, which will make the Jews of a mind to receive their great Deliverer when He comes to save them. At this time, the Antichrist will experience his doom. Only the fact is here stated, but the matter is portrayed elsewhere, especially in Revelation 19:11-21. Christ will come in power against the Antichrist and his army, as his forces are spread through the valley of Jehoshaphat (Joel 3:2, 12), east of Jerusalem. The Antichrist, along with his chief helper, the False Prophet, will be cast directly into the Lake of Fire, and then his army will be slain by the "sword" that proceeds from Christ's "mouth." No one will help the Antichrist, for none will exist who can help him. He, Satan's counterfeit world ruler, who will have been so self-sufficient until this moment, will suddenly find himself totally incapable to help himself, as he meets God's true King.

CHAPTER **12**

There is no change in subject matter in moving from chapter eleven to chapter twelve. In fact, the message of the grand angel to Daniel continues without break through verse four of this chapter, making his uninterrupted message to extend totally from 10:20 through 12:4. In verses six and eight, questions were asked by another heavenly messenger and by Daniel; and these prompted the grand angel to speak further in verse seven and then continuously in verses nine to twelve, which closes the chapter.

A. The Great Tribulation (vv. 1-3)

The grand angel continued to speak of the period when the Antichrist will rule, but he did so now more from the point of view of the people ruled, rather than that of the ruler. From their perspective, it is properly called the time of Great Tribulation.

12:1. During that time shall Michael stand up, the great prince who stands guard over your people; and there shall be a time of distress such as has not been since there was a nation until that time; and in that time your people shall be delivered, everyone that is found written in the book.

During that time: Three matters give evidence that the "time" in view is that commonly called the Great Tribulation: first, the continuance of thought, without break, in this verse from that of the closing verses of chapter eleven, where the subject concerns the rule of the Antichrist, which occurs during the Great Tribulation; second, the logic of identifying it with the reference to the "time of the end" in 11:40, where the period in view, as noted, is the Great Tribulation; and, third, Jesus' quotation of the verse in Matthew 24:21, 22, where the context identifies the period in mind as the Great Tribulation. It should be realized, then, that the period in view will not follow the demise of the Antichrist, mentioned in 11:45, but will be the same as that in which he is active in bringing his oppressions. For this reason, the translation "during" for the b^e prefix here used is preferable over "at," which is sometimes employed. *Shall Michael stand up:* This is the same Michael to whom the grand angel made reference in 10:13 and 10:21, as having helped him against the demon of Persia and as the angel assigned especially to the care of Israel. Here Michael is said to "stand up," and, in the light of these prior indications, the purpose of this act is likely that he may again come to Israel's defense. The one against whom such defense is to be made is quite obviously the Antichrist, the one oppressing Israel during the time in view. *Who stands guard over your people:* Literally, this reads "the one standing over the sons of your people." This is another way of saying "your prince," as in 10:21 (which see). *Time of distress such as has not been:* Cf. Exodus 9:18, 24 for parallel idiomatic expressions. This time of distress will be one which Daniel's people, the Jews, will experience, and it will be the worst ever. Since only one period can be so characterized, it must be the same as that indicated in Jeremiah 30:7 and Joel 2:2, as well as Matthew 24:21 (Mark 13:19) where the present verse is quoted. Each of these mentions is commonly and correctly taken in reference to the Great Tribulation. It is logical to relate the intense suffering in view to the oppression brought by the Antichrist, as just set forth. When one remembers former times of suffering, experienced down through history by the Jews, this way of describing the climactic time yet future takes on enormous significance.

Your people shall be delivered: Now is stated the benefit effected by Michael's activity. Israel will be delivered. The thought is expressed similarly in the parallel passage: Jeremiah 30:7, 11. Information set forth in Revelation 12:6-17 is pertinent to be related at this point, because it enlarges on this time of deliverance. The passage begins by speaking of Satan, in the figure of a "dragon," as cast from heaven[1] to earth, where, as a consequence, he concentrates on persecuting the "woman," who represents Israel. He continues to do this for 1,260 days (12:6), or three and one-half years (12:14), a period correctly identified with the last half of the Tribulation week. The same time period indeed is in view here, then as in our passage, and the same occasion of persecution. Apparently, Satan works through the Antichrist as his manner of effecting the persecution of Israel. It is interesting to note that it is Michael who casts Satan from heaven, just prior to these endeavors of persecution (12:7); and it is he again (as our verse indicates) who acts to deliver Israel from the persecution which Satan then masterminds, as a result of his being cast out. The ways in which this deliverance is effected

---

[1] This time cast out completely, so that he can no longer accuse saints there (12:10) as he could still following the occasion described in Isaiah 14:12-17; cf. Job 1:6-12; 2:1-7; Zechariah 3:1-5.

are described as "nourishing" Israel for the 1,260 days (12:6) and causing the earth to "swallow" a river of destruction which the dragon casts from his mouth (12:15, 16). This deliverance does not include all the people of Israel of that time, however. Another passage, Zechariah 13:8, 9, sets forth the startling figure of only one-third of the populace being spared, indicating extreme suffering and loss of life at the hand of Satan's agent, the Antichrist. Israel's identity as a nation survives through the one-third, however; and this is the same deliverance as indicated in Daniel 7:26, 27. *Everyone that is found written in the book:* This identifies the kind of people who will make up this one-third of the nation delivered. The "book" here in reference is best taken to be the "book of life," God's record of those who are justified in His sight (cf. Ex. 32:32; Ps. 69:28; Luke 10:20; Rev. 20:12). Other books are in view in a prior reference to "books" in Daniel 7:10 (which see). In view of two "witnesses" having proclaimed God's message in Jerusalem for forty-two months, during the Tribulation week (Rev. 11:3-13), and also the fact that 144,000 will have been "sealed" by God during this time (Rev. 7:1-8; 14:1-5), it is clear that by the close of the seven-year period many Jews will have become true believers in God. Besides this, the rest, who are spared from the Antichrist's oppression, will give their full allegiance at the time of Christ's second coming in power to destroy the great army of the Antichrist, effecting the final deliverance for Israel. The names of those in both groups will be found written down in God's book of life (cf. Matt. 24:22).

12:2, 3. And many that sleep in the dusty ground shall awake; these to everlasting life and others to everlasting shame and contempt. And those who are wise shall shine like the brightness of the expanse, and those who turn many to righteousness like the stars forever and ever.

That sleep in the dusty ground shall awake: The phrase "dusty ground" (*'admat-'apar*) means literally "ground of dust." The word for "shall awake" (root, *qûts*) means "to be aroused," as from sleep. Some expositors take the reference to an awakening from spiritual death, paralleling the thought with that of verse one: "everyone that is found written in the book"; but this cannot be correct because a part of those so awakened find themselves consigned to "everlasting shame and contempt." Gaebelein[2] sees the reference to an awakening of Jews from their sleep among the nations of the world, so that they return to Palestine, some of them being righteous in so doing and some wicked. Against this explanation, however, is the fact that the idea of a return to the land is not otherwise in the context, and must be inferred from other passages of Scripture. Both the words used

[2] GD, pp. 200, 201. He links this reference to Ezekiel's vision of the dry bones coming to life (Ezek. 37:1-14).

and the general context point rather to the idea of a physical resurrection, that which is literally from the "ground of dust." The preceding verse, in speaking of the deliverance of those still alive at the close of the Tribulation week, has left the question open as to the status of righteous Jews, who will have died under the crushing hand of the Antichrist. Will they be omitted from all benefit resulting when Christ comes to bring this deliverance and to set up the millennial reign? This verse answers that question by saying that they will not be omitted but will be raised again and made to share in all blessings with the living. The thought is parallel to that in Revelation 20:4-6, where, at the beginning of the millennial reign (which ensues immediately after the defeat of the Antichrist), those who have been "beheaded for the witness of Jesus," because of resisting the Antichrist, are pictured as now resurrected and participating in this glorious time. *These to everlasting life:* This is the first use of the phrase "everlasting life" *(ḥayyê 'ôlam)* in the Old Testament. Its meaning is the same as in the New Testament. Some liberal expositors assert that this is the first reference, also, to resurrection in the Old Testament, but this is not so (cf. Job 14:11-14; 19:25-27; Ps. 16:10; 49:15; Isa. 25:8; 26;19; Hosea 13:14; Heb. 11:17, 18). In fact, there probably was no time when the faith of God's people did not include belief in immortality and resurrection. The significance of the phrase here is that those who are raised following the Tribulation week will live to enjoy not only millennial blessing, but blessings of eternal salvation with Christ as well.

Others to everlasting shame and contempt: The word for "shame" *(hᵃrapoṯ)* means literally "reproaches," and the word for "contempt" *(dir'ôn),* from the root, *dara',* "to repel from oneself," means "something abhorrent." "Everlasting" *('ôlam)* is best taken as modifying both. Reference, clearly, is to the eternal state of the wicked in unending punishment. Some expositors take the meaning of the repeated use of the demonstrative pronoun "these" *('eleh)* to be that each refers to a portion of the "many" who are raised from the dead, yielding the thought of a double resurrection at this time, involving both the righteous and wicked. This cannot be, however, because Revelation 20:4-6, 12-15 teaches that the resurrection of the righteous here in view immediately follows the Tribulation week, and that the resurrection of the wicked comes only after the 1,000-year Millennium has intervened. The thought is better taken to be, then, that the first "these" refers to all of the "many" raised immediately after the Tribulation week, and the second to "others," who will be raised following the Millennium, a time of resurrection to "everlasting shame and contempt." The specific time when this second aspect of the resurrection will be effected is not indicated in our verse, for the reason that the persons involved are not those concerned in the context. A paraphrase of the thought would be: "And many that sleep in the dusty ground shall awake (to have part with the living righteous in millennial benefits); these, indeed, shall be to everlasting life, but others (of the sleepers, who do not awake at this time, but only after the Millennium) shall be to everlasting shame and contempt." Three matters may be cited in support of this viewpoint. First, since the passage in Revelation 20 is more detailed and falls much later in the history of revelation, this Old Testament passage in Daniel must be interpreted in view of it, rather than vice versa. Second, the word "many" *(rabbîm)* is used, instead of "all," as the designation of those who would arise, which suggests that reference is not to all who have died, but only a part, such as the righteous among them. Expositors, who see a general, all-inclusive resurrection here, have difficulty in explaining this "many." Third, in verse three, the word "many" is used again and this time with the article, as though pointing back to a prior "many," which could only be the "many" of verse two; and the "many" of verse three are those who have been turned to righteousness, thus showing that the "many" of verse two must include only those similarly characterized.

The question is pertinent as to the total identity of the righteous dead who will experience the resurrection here in view. Does the group include more than merely righteous Jews who have died during the Tribulation and to whom, certainly, a primary reference is intended? The answer is that it must include righteous Gentiles as well, often called Tribulation saints (Rev. 7:9-17), for they will also have been killed by the Antichrist during this period. Certainly they, as well as Jews, are in view in Revelation 20:4-6. Besides this, it probably includes also all Old Testament saints, as numerous expositors believe.[3] The question involved, as to when Old Testament saints are raised, concerns a choice between this time of resurrection and that preceding the Tribulation week, when the righteous dead of the Church are resurrected. Though this passage does not settle the matter, it is logical to believe that Jews of Israel's national status (i.e., constituted their own nation) from Old Testament time will be resurrected at the same time as Jews of Israel's national status of this future time. Additional evidence is to be found in the closing verse of this chapter (which see).

Those who are wise: These words translate a plural hiphil participle, using the article *(hammaskilîm),* the same form as in verses thirty-three and thirty-five of chapter eleven, where it carries the same meaning. In the former instances, it refers to persons who were wise themselves and helped to make others wise, in opposition to the persecution of Antiochus Epiphanes; here it is to persons similarly

---

[3] For instance, Pentecost, *TTC,* pp. 407-11; Walvoord, WD, pp. 286-88.

characterized, in opposition to the Antichrist. Those of the earlier day were wise in knowledge of God and His will, and the same would logically be intended here; this means that reference is to the group who either are raised, as described in verse two, or else are numbered among those "written in the book," as mentioned in verse one. A special aspect of the wisdom they will have is set forth in the last half of the verse. *Shall shine like the brightness of the expanse:* The same basic word is used for "brightness" as for "shall shine" (root, *zahar,* "to shine forth, to be brilliant"). "Expanse" refers to the space occupied by the stars, mentioned specifically in the last half of the verse. The thought is that each of the "wise" would shine like a star in the vastness of space. *Those who turn many to righteousness:* Another plural hiphil participle is used (root, *tsadaq,* "to be righteous") in parallel with the former, only this time in construct with "the many" *(harabbîm),* meaning literally "ones causing the many to be righteous." This details the special area of wisdom in mind for the "wise." In their wisdom, they will have been active in persuading others, especially Jews, to turn and be faithful to God, in opposition to all for which the Antichrist stands. *Like the stars forever and ever:* The idea of *shining* like these stars is implied, carried over from the first member of the parallelism. The duration of this shining will be "forever and ever" *(le'ôlam we'ed,* literally, "to an age and yet"), a common Scriptural reference to eternity. Strong motivation is thus provided for faithfulness in witnessing for Christ in the world. Though the particular time in mind is the Tribulation week, the application is good for any day, as Jesus gave illustration, especially in Matthew 13:43.

B. TRIBULATION CHRONOLOGY (vv. 4-13)

The angel's uninterrupted message ends with verse three. He spoke further in following verses, but mainly in response to specific questions, expressed first by another heavenly messenger and later by Daniel. The general theme concerns the chronology of last-day events.

12:4. But you, Daniel, preserve the words and seal the book until the time of the end; many shall run to and fro, and knowledge shall be increased.

But you, Daniel: Having completed the message proper, the grand angel turns to instruct Daniel relative to preserving it. *Preserve the words and seal the book:* The word for "preserve" (root, *satam*) is the same as the word used in 8:26 (which see). The word for "seal" (root, *hatam*) means "to close securely," particularly with an authenticating stamp. The word for "book" *(seper)* refers to written material, usually of substantial length. This could refer merely to Daniel's record of the angel's message just completed, but it more likely refers to a collection of the records of all four revelational times, or even the entire book of Daniel. At what point in his closing years Daniel did write his book is not known, but if he was not bringing it to a completion by this time, it must have been soon after, for he was now over eighty years of age (cf. 10:1). Whatever the extent of the material the angel had in mind, Daniel was to preserve it carefully, much as he had been instructed to do relative to the second vision (8:26). *Until the time of the end:* This is the same phrase as the one used in 11:35, 40 (which see). Reference is again to the Tribulation period, the time in view for the entire context. Daniel is to take precaution that the words not be lost until that period should come, preserving the words as a continuing source of information regarding it. The sealing of the book does not mean that its message was to be hidden, but only maintained safely. The implied overall thought is, likely, that Daniel's original record should be kept securely, so that from it copies might be made for actual reading by people. *Many shall run to and fro:* The verb used (root, *shût*) is in the polel and means basically "to move quickly, run to and fro." Leupold takes it in reference to a reader's eye running to and fro in Daniel's book, reading it.[4] But every other polel use of the verb in the Old Testament refers to movement of one's body to and fro, in search of something, especially information (cf. 2 Chron. 16:9; Jer. 5:1; 49:3; Amos 8:12; Zech. 4:10), which makes that meaning likely here. The thought is that people would run about trying to find answers to important questions, especially in reference to future events. *Knowledge shall be increased:* Young[5] believes that this element gives the purpose of the running to and fro of people, namely, that their knowledge might be increased, implying fruitlessness of effort. The view departs entirely from the thought of the purpose for Daniel's preserving his book, however, and the two seem necessarily related. A better interpretation, therefore, is to take the "knowledge" here in view as that which is supplied by Daniel's book, thus preserved. This explanation would give the following paraphrase of the thought: "Many shall run to and fro in their desire for knowledge of the last things, and, finding it in Daniel's book, because it will have been preserved to this end, their knowledge shall be increased." As to time in mind, reference may be especially to last days, when perhaps a marked increase in such a search for knowledge will exist, but not exclusively. Daniel is to preserve his book so that people of all time, from his day until the end, may have it for reference as to last-day events.

12:5, 6. Then I, Daniel, looked, and lo, two others were standing,

4 *LED,* p. 534.
5 YPD, p. 258.

one on this bank of the stream and one on that bank of the stream; and one said to the man clothed in linen, who was above the waters of the stream, How long shall be the end of the wonders?

I, Daniel, looked: Daniel once more became an actor. The angel had finished speaking, and Daniel, looking about, saw what was now described. *Two others were standing:* He saw two figures in addition to the angel. They were apparently of heavenly origin also, since they were not related here in any way to earthly matters. Daniel saw each on an opposite side of the stream (still the Tigris River, cf. 10:4) from the other. Because the Tigris is a wide river, this means that they were at some distance from each other, with the one on the same side of the river as Daniel being much nearer to him. These two angels were evidently of inferior rank to the glorious speaker of the extended revelation, because they now addressed a question to him. The situation was quite parallel to that in Daniel's second vision, when two heavenly speakers were seen talking, and a third, who was "between the banks of the Ulai," gave an authoritative command (8:13-16). It may be that, though words of only one of these angels are recorded, the two had earlier been speaking to each other, as was the case with the two in the second vision. Actually, there is little reason for two being mentioned if both did not participate in some manner. The significance of noting the presence of the angels at all is, likely, to show the interest that angels have in the affairs of men (cf. 1 Pet. 1:12); these two seemingly having listened to the words of the grand angel, and now giving voice to a question, which may have been on Daniel's mind as well.

One said: Though this speaker is not specifically identified, he must have been one of the angels, and likely the one on the same side of the river as Daniel. *Man clothed in linen:* The one addressed can have been only the grand angel again, for he is described as clothed in "linen" (actually "the linen," using the article, thus referring back to the angel's "linen" in 10:5). *Above the waters:* The angel was now seen "above" (literally, "from upon to") the water of the Tigris, evidently between the two other angels. It is possible that he had spoken from this same location in giving his long discourse; but earlier he had been active on the bank of the river, at least when he had ministered to Daniel (10:10, 16, 18). Standing now over the water gave him a position connoting supernatural power and authority, for he was able to defy natural law. Since the other two angels stood on the land, their position of power was depicted at a lower plane. It may be worthy of note that the word used in the context for the Tigris is not the normal word for "river," *nahar,* but *ye'or;* and *ye'or* is otherwise used only in reference to the Nile.[6] The significance

---

[6] The term is actually an Egyptian loan-word. Outside of this context, the word

may be that the Tigris is seen here by Daniel in the character of the mighty Nile; hence, representative of the strength and vitality of Persia, as the Nile was of Egypt. This symbolism, in turn, stressed the authority of the grand angel in standing dominant over this mighty, representative river. *How long shall be the end of the wonders:* Literally, this may be translated "until when the end of the wonders?" The word for "wonders" *(p^ela'ôt)* refers to things unique to themselves (cf. 8:24; 11:36). Reference is to the unique, oppressive actions of the Antichrist, not to all the history related by the angel. This limitation is evidenced as follows: first, from the content of the answer which the angel now gives to the question in that it does not concern all the time from Daniel's day and following, but only that in respect to the Tribulation week; and, second, from the form of the question, which asks specifically regarding the length of the "end of the wonders," not of the time until that "end." As has been noted several times, "end" in this context refers regularly to the Tribulation week. The angel may be expected to answer, then, in respect to the duration of time in which the Antichrist will be permitted to bring his oppressive measures against the people of God during the Tribulation week.

12:7. Then I heard the man clothed in linen, who was above the waters of the stream, as he raised his right hand and his left hand toward heaven, swear by Him who lives forever that it would be for a time, times, and a half-time; and that when the shattering of the power of the holy people has come to an end, then should all these things cease.

I heard the man: Daniel heard the grand angel give answer to the question. The one to speak is again described as "clothed in linen" so that there is no question as to his identity. *Raised his right hand and his left hand:* The gesture of raising one's hand to heaven carried the purpose of showing solemnity and importance for an oath about to be spoken (cf. Gen. 14:22; Deut. 32:40). Normally only one hand was raised, which means that when this angel raised two, he was indicating special stress to this end. *Swear by Him who lives forever:* "Him" can refer only to God, who alone has absolute immortality (1 Tim. 6:16). Nebuchadnezzar used the same phrase "who lives forever" in reference to God (4:34). The words constitute a form of oath of the day, this one apparently taken from Deuteronomy 32:40, where God Himself says, "I live forever." The form is quoted in Revelation 10:6, probably from our text. That the angel here should begin his answer with the use of a solemn oath is indicative of the importance both of the question asked (giving further evi-

is used for other than the Nile only in Isaiah 33:21 and Job 28:10, where no specific river is in mind either time.

dence that it refers specifically to the time of the Antichrist, and not an earlier, less significant period) and of the answer about to be stated.

Time, times, and a half-time: The answer is of two parts: this, which refers to a definite duration of time, a chronological answer; and the words which immediately follow, that give the reason for the period lasting for this duration, a rational answer. The definite duration given is the same as set forth in the first vision (7:25, which see) in regard to the duration of the activities of the "little horn" (Antichrist); namely three and one-half years. Reasons given under 7:25 that this combination of words does mean this length of time should be noted. The Hebrew word for time *(mo'ed)* used here is the exact equivalent of the Aramaic *'idan* used in 7:25. The length of time during which the Antichrist will pursue his anti-Jewish activities, then, will be three and one-half years, the last half of the Tribulation week. *When the shattering of the power of the holy people has come to an end:* This clause reads, literally, "as completing shattering of hand of people of holiness." The words for "completing" (root, *kalah,* "to complete") and "shattering" (root, *napats,* "to dash in pieces") are both infinitive constructs. "People of holiness" designates the Jews as God's people, chosen to be holy, who will truly achieve this condition in the Millennium. With this element, the angel gave the other part of his answer to the question, the rational part. The force of the answer is to say that the duration of the "end of the wonders" will last as long as it takes for the power of the Jews to be broken. The angel thus revealed the reason for God's permitting the Antichrist to bring his persecution, namely, to break the power of the Jews. As parallel passages indicate, this power and resulting sense of self-sufficiency will need to be broken so that the Jews will be willing to accept Christ as their rightful King. The two parts of the total answer are to say, then, that it will take the Antichrist exactly three and one-half years to bring the Jews to the state of humiliation where this willingness will be evidenced.

12:8. I heard but I did not understand, and I said, My lord, what shall be the end of these things?

I heard but I did not understand: The use of the personal pronoun "I" *('ªnî)* is unusual and indicates a stress on Daniel, in distinction, apparently, from the two angels who had also been listening. The significance may be that Daniel thought of himself as alone in the lack of understanding of which he spoke. The first verb is in the perfect; but the second in the imperfect and more literally means "I was not understanding," depicting Daniel as continuing to try but not succeeding. *My lord:* This is an address of respect only, and does not connote the divinity of the one addressed, indicating that Daniel did not think of the grand angel before him as a representation of God

Himself. *What shall be the end of these things:* Literally, this reads, "what is latter end of these?" There are two differences between this question and that asked by the angel in verse six. First, the basic question is "what" and not "how long"; and, second, it concerns "latter end" *('aḥ^arît)* and not just "end" *(qets).* The term "latter end" refers to the very last features of the end-time events. Daniel wanted to know what the nature of these would be. It would seem that Daniel had understood the meaning of "time, times, and a half-time," and also the idea that the strength of the Jews would have to be broken; but he did not understand the character of the events which would bring this period to an end. He may have been puzzled as to the degree of severity of this time of persecution, especially at its climax, or he may have wondered as to how the deliverance from the Antichrist's power would be effected, having been told that it would happen (12:1; cf. 7:26, 27).

12:9. But he replied, Go your way, Daniel, for the words are preserved and sealed until the time of the end.

Go your way, Daniel: Literally, this is simply, "Go, Daniel." The word for "go" (root, *halak*) is an imperative. The thought is not, however, that Daniel was to move physically. Rather, he was to do so in mental attitude. He was to desist in his inquiry just made and not be concerned. *Words are preserved and sealed:* The words of this element were used in verse four, showing an intentional reference back to it. The thought is that because the information Daniel had received is securely preserved and sealed, Daniel did not need to be concerned regarding his inquiry. These are words of both comfort and rebuke. The comfort consists in the fact that Daniel did not need to worry, since the events involved were far in the future; and, further, he could know that, since the information he had would be faithfully preserved, those who would then live, whose welfare might otherwise have been a matter of anxiety for him, would have it and be able to profit accordingly. Implied is the fact also, that further information, such as that for which Daniel had just asked, would be available for them by that time, and in the book of Revelation this has been revealed, as we now know. The rebuke consists in the fact that Daniel should not have asked for this information, which really was only for the satisfaction of his curiosity. He did not need to know all these matters at the time he lived, and he should have rested content in what God Himself had seen appropriate to relate. So often today, too, Christians want to know more details regarding some doctrine, especially concerning the last things, than God has revealed in His Word; but they also should rest content with what God has chosen to make clear.

12:10. Many shall be cleansed and made white and refined, but the wicked shall do wickedly; and none of the wicked shall understand but the wise shall understand.

Be cleansed and made white and refined: These are the same three verbs as those used in a similar series, though in a different order, in 11:35 (which see). Here, however, the first two are used in the hithpael (normally reflexive, though they may be passive) and the third in the niphal (passive or reflexive). Taking all three as passives, the translation is as given; taking them as reflexives yields this version: "Many shall cleanse, make white, and refine themselves." Either translation fits the thought of the verse, as will be noted. The angel was still referring to events in the Tribulation week. Daniel had just asked regarding events which will close this period, and the angel, though having refused the specific request, did add something of a general nature concerning the time. What he said is that during the last half of the seven-year period, many Jews will experience being "cleansed," "made white," and "refined"; and, since he employed the same verbs as are used in 11:35, it is clear that he intentionally paralleled this development with that of Antiochus' day. As many Jews then were "cleansed," "made white," and "refined," for a new and more devoted walk before God, so will this be true of Jews in the last days to come (Zech. 13:8, 9). To relate this group to the immediately preceding context, they will be the same as those who will be turned to "righteousness" by the wise (12:3). Taking the passive meaning for the verbs, the thought is that God will be the One sovereignly effecting this change of cleansing; and, taking the reflexive meaning, it is that man himself will desire and work to the end of his own cleansing. Either thought is in keeping with scriptural truth set forth elsewhere (cf. Ps. 51:7; 1 John 3:3).

Wicked shall do wickedly: The wicked in reference are all other Jews of the period, those who do not experience this cleansing. They will continue in their wickedness, as the righteous turn to God. Nothing is said here concerning the relative proportion of each group. In Revelation 7:1-8 and 14:1-5, a group of 144,000 is said to be sealed by God during this time; and it is made clear, especially in 14:1-5, that all of this group do exercise true faith in God. The matter is not clear, however, whether the number 144,000 is to be taken literally or representatively, or whether, if literal, it designates only a special group out of the total number who turn. It seems safe to say that the total number will be at least 144,000, and probably more. Further, Zechariah 13:8, 9 speaks of one-third of the Jews then living as being refined. This would be far more than 144,000, for there are approximately two and two-thirds million Jews in Israel at the present time. This one-third proportion, however, includes all who survive the Tribulation week, and is made up of those who accept Christ when He actually comes at the climax of this time, as well as those who have turned during the prior months. Again, the proportion in number between the two groups is not known, and it is possible that those who turn during the week itself may be a minority. On the other hand, many of those who will have turned during the week will have been martyred (12:2; Rev. 20:4), and will not be among this surviving one-third, which suggests again that the number will be quite large. No certain figures can be given. *None of the wicked shall understand:* The word for "understand" is from the root, *bîn,* and is used again in the next phrase "but the wise shall understand." An intentional contrast is thus set up between the "wicked" and "wise" as to understanding, the former not understanding and the latter doing so. What these do or do not understand are obviously the words of the angel in his message—that concerning which Daniel had just asked. The matter of principal significance for Daniel was that although he did not himself understand various aspects of the prophecy, the "wise" of the future day (those who turn to God) will understand. Daniel, then, was expected to bring himself to rest content in this recognition.

12:11. And from the time that the regular ceremonies are taken away and the abomination of desolation is set up shall be a thousand two hundred and ninety days.

From the time: A period of 1,290 days is designated here, and the occasion which begins it is indicated; namely, the time when the regular ceremonies (same word, *tamîd,* as is used in 11:31 and 8:11 [which see]) of the restored Jewish Temple will be taken away by the Antichrist and the abomination of desolation (altar and/or image of Jupiter [Zeus] Olympius, cf. 9:27) will be set up. This means the middle of the Tribulation week, as noted under 9:27 (which see). *A thousand two hundred and ninety days:* This is the length of the period in view, but the termination occasion is not indicated. One might assume that the termination point would be the cessation of the last half of the week, but this number of days is thirty too many to fit; and, moreover, verse seven has already given the length of that period as three and one-half years, or 1,260 days (figuring thirty-day months, as sustained by a comparison of verses six and fourteen of Revelation 12 and verses two and three of Revelation 11). The question must be asked as to the significance of the thirty additional days. In answer, some expositors take this and other numbers of the context as symbolical, but this will not do because these numbers (1,260, 1,290, and 1,335 from v. 12) are so near in size that no symbolism would fit them. Moreover, numbers mentioned earlier in Daniel (e.g., 2,300 days, 8:14) have been found to be literal. Other expositors have referred the passage to the time of Antiochus (taking all of the angel's message in this way, then) and seek a literal significance for 1,290 days from his time, but without success. Furthermore, numerous reasons have already been cited which show that the angel's message following 11:35 must refer to the Antichrist, not to Antiochus. The right answer can only be in terms of literal days, which somehow concern the Tribulation week. A clue as to how they fit this week is found in Matthew 25:31-46, which describes a time of judgment by Christ immediately after He comes in power at the close of this period.[7] The purpose of the judgment is to determine those who will be permitted to enter into and enjoy the blessedness of the millennial period. The passage shows that those so honored will be only the people who have treated the Jews properly, and have thus demonstrated a true relation to Christ through personal salvation. But such an act of judgment will take a period of time for its accomplishment. The added thirty days in question would seem appropriate. The cessation point in view, then, for the full 1,290 days may be the completion of this time of judgment. Judging will begin, apparently, soon after the defeat of the Antichrist and could, indeed, continue for those thirty days.

12:12. Blessed is he who waits and attains to a thousand three hundred and thirty-five days.

Blessed is he who waits and attains to: The word for "waits" is a piel participle (root, *hakah,* "to wait"), meaning "one who waits earnestly." The word for "attains to" (root, *naga',* "to touch") is an imperfect form, meaning "he will touch." A paraphrase gives this thought: "The one who waits earnestly will be blessed in that he will touch (attain to) 1,335 days." *A thousand three hundred and thirty-five days:* This figure is forty-five days longer than the one just considered and seventy-five more than the duration of the last half of the Tribulation week. What is the significance of the additional days this time? The idea of the preceding phrase, speaking of being "blessed," shows that whatever occasion falls at the conclusion of these days is something good and desirable. There will be blessing for those who attain to it. The thought is thus suggested that it will be the actual starting point of the Millennium. Those who will have passed the judgment of Christ, during the preceding thirty days, would be those who will attain to it, after these forty-five additional days. What will be the need of these forty-five days? It may be the time necessary for setting up the governmental machinery for carrying on the rule of Christ. The true and full border of Israel (from the River of Egypt to the Euphrates, Genesis 15:18) will have to be established, and

[7] Gaebelein, GD, p. 207, also presents this view.

appointments made of those aiding in the government. A period of forty-five days would again seem to be reasonable in which to accomplish these matters.

12:13. And as for you, go your way until the end; and you shall rest and rise again to your lot at the end of the days.

As for you: The angel brought attention to Daniel again, indicated by the special use of the personal pronoun. He saw the need for a further personal note as a concluding word in this grand message. *Go your way until the end:* This clause is literally "go to the end," which Young[8] takes as meaning merely "keep on living until the time of your death." It seems more likely, however, that the thought ("go" being an imperative from the root, *halak,* "to go") is parallel with that of verse nine, giving the paraphrase "cease being anxious concerning these matters, Daniel, but be satisfied with what you do understand, for as long as you live." *Rest and rise again:* These verbs are parallel in form, both imperfects, the first from *nûah,* "to rest," and the second from *'amad,* "to stand." They indicate that following Daniel's demise, he would rest in death and in due time stand or rise again, a reference once more (as in v. 2) to resurrection. Daniel was promised a part in the resurrection. *Lot at the end of the days:* The word for "lot" *(goral)* means either a lot which is cast or that which may be selected by a cast lot. The use here is in the latter sense, as also in Judges 1:3. Its corresponding Greek equivalent *(merida)* is used in Colossians 1:12 for the inheritance lot of the saint, which is approximately the thought here. Daniel would rise again to receive his *inheritance lot.* This would be "at the end of the days," meaning at the end of the days dealt with in the context, the Tribulation days. Daniel could know, then, that he would live again, following the Tribulation days, in time to enjoy his *inheritance lot* in the blessedness of the millennial kingdom, along with the others mentioned in the preceding verses. If Daniel is to be resurrected at this time, it follows that other Old Testament saints will be resurrected then as well, thus giving evidence that the likely time of resurrection for all Old Testament saints will be at the close of the Tribulation.

8 YPD, p. 264.

DANIEL'S PROPHECIES AT A GLANCE

	Babylon (605-538 B.C.)	Medo-Persia (538-331 B.C.)	Greece (331-146 B.C.)	Rome (146 B.C.—A.D. 476)	(PRESENT-AGE GAP OF MANY CENTURIES)	Last Days (Still future)
Daniel 2:31-45 Dream image (603 B.C.)	Head of gold (2:32, 37, 38)	Breast, arms of silver (2:32, 39)	Belly, thighs of brass (2:32,39)	Legs of iron Feet of iron and clay (2:33, 40, 41)		Toes of iron and clay (2:33, 42, 43) Stone cut without hands (2:34, 35, 44, 45)
Daniel 7 First vision: Four Beasts (553 B.C.)	Lion (7:4)	Bear (7:5)	Leopard (7:6)	Strong Beast (7:7, 11, 19, 23)		Ten horns (7:7, 20, 24) Little horn (7:8, 20, 21, 24-26) Reign of Christ (7:13, 14, 18, 22, 27)
Daniel 8 Second vision: Ram and goat (551 B.C.)		Ram (8:3, 4, 20)	Goat with one horn (8:5-8, 21) Four horns (8:8, 22) Little horn (8:9-14)			Roman "Beast" prefigured by little horn (8:23-25)
Daniel 9:24-27 Third vision: 70 weeks (538 B.C.)		From commandment going forth — Ezra, 458 B.C. (9:25)	69 weeks continue (9:25)	Until Messiah be cut off — A.D. 26 (9:26)		70th week of Tribulation (9:27)
Daniel 10-12 Fourth vision: Tribulation period (536 B.C.)		Four kings (11:2)	Mighty King and kingdom divided (11:3, 4) Kings of north and south (11:5-20) Vile king, Antiochus Epiphanes (11:21-35)			Roman "Beast," Antichrist (11:36-45) Tribulation and its chronology (12:1-13)

CHRONOLOGY of DANIEL'S PROPHECIES

600	500	400	300	200	100			100	200	300	400	500	Last Days

Daniel lived
about 620-535 B.C.

Babylon (605-538 B.C.)

Head of gold
(2:32, 37, 38)
Lion (7:4)

Medo-Persia (538-331 B.C.)

Breast, arms of silver
(2:32, 39)
Bear (7:5)
Ram (8:3, 4, 20)

Greece (331-146 B.C.)

Belly, thighs of brass
(2:32, 39)
Leopard (7:6)
Goat (8:5-14, 21, 22)

Rome (146 B.C. - A.D. 476)

Legs of iron, feet of iron and clay
(2:33, 40, 41)
Strong beast
(7:7, 11, 19, 23)

69 weeks (458 B.C. - A.D. 26)
(9:25, 26)

(PRESENT-AGE GAP OF MANY CENTURIES)

70th Week
Tribulation
(9:27)
(11:36-12:13)

Millennial
Reign of
Christ
(2:34, 35, 44, 45)
(7:13, 14, 18, 22, 27)

BIBLIOGRAPHY

Aharoni, Yohanan, and Avi-Yonah, Michael. *The Macmillan Bible Atlas.* New York: Macmillan, 1968.

Albright, William F. *From the Stone Age to Christianity.* 2d ed. New York: Doubleday, Anchor Books, 1957.

———. "The Biblical Period," *The Jews, Their History, Culture, and Religion,* pp. 3-65. Edited by L. Finkelstein. New York: Harper & Bros., 1949. Reprinted, The Biblical Colloquium, 1950.

Anderson, Robert. *The Coming Prince.* London: Hodder & Stoughton, 1895.

Andrews, Samuel J. *Christianity and Anti-Christianity.* Chicago: The Moody Bible Institute Colportage Association, 1937.

Archer, Gleason L., Jr. *A Survey of Old Testament Introduction.* Chicago: Moody Press, 1964.

Barnes, Albert. "Daniel." 2 vols. *Notes on the Old Testament.* Edited by Robert Frew. Grand Rapids: Baker Book House, 1950.

Barton, George A. *Archaeology and the Bible.* 7th ed. Philadelphia: American Sunday School Union, 1937.

Bleach, Matthew and Rowley, H. H., eds. *Peake's Commentary on the Bible.* London: Nelson, 1961.

Boutflower, Charles. *In and Around the Book of Daniel.* Grand Rapids: Zondervan Publishing House, 1963.

Bright, John. *A History of Israel.* Philadelphia: The Westminster Press, 1959.

Brown, Francis; Driver. S. R.; and Briggs, Charles A., eds. *A Hebrew and English Lexicon of the Old Testament.* Oxford: Clarendon Press, 1955.

Bruce, F. F., ed. *Israel and the Nations.* London: The Paternoster Press, 1963.

Calvin, John. *Commentaries on the Book of the Prophet Daniel.* 2 vols. Translated by Thomas Myers. Grand Rapids: Wm. B. Eerdmans Publishing Co., 1948.

Charles, Robert H. *Apocrypha and Pseudipigrapha of the Old Testament in English.* Vol. 2. Oxford: Clarendon Press, 1913.

—————. *The Book of Daniel.* The New Century Bible, edited by W. F. Adeney. New York: H. Frowde, Oxford Univ., n.d.

Cross, Frank M. *The Ancient Library of Qumran and Modern Biblical Studies.* Garden City: Doubleday, 1958.

Culver, Robert D. *Daniel and the Latter Days.* Chicago: Moody Press, 1954.

—————. "Daniel." In *The Wycliffe Bible Commentary,* edited by C. F. Pfeiffer and E. F. Harrison. Chicago: Moody Press, 1962.

Deane, H. *The Book of Daniel.* A Bible Commentary for English Readers, edited by C. J. Ellicott, Vol. V. New York: E. P. Dutton & Co., n.d.

DeHaan, Martin R. *Daniel the Prophet.* Grand Rapids: Zondervan Publishing House, 1947.

DeVaux, Roland. *Ancient Israel, Its Life and Institutions.* Translated by J. McHugh. New York: McGraw Hill Book Co., 1961.

Dougherty, Raymond P. *Nabonidus and Belshazzar.* Yale Oriental Series, Vol. 15. New Haven: Yale University, 1929.

Driver, Samuel R. *The Book of Daniel.* The Cambridge Bible for Schools and Colleges. Cambridge: University Press, 1900.

Farrar, Frederic W. *The Book of Daniel.* The Expositors Bible, edited by W. Robertson Nicoll, Vol. IV. Grand Rapids: Wm. B. Eerdmans Publishing Co., 1940.

Fausset, A. R. *The Book of Daniel.* A Commentary Critical, Experimental and Practical, Vol. IV. Grand Rapids: Wm. B. Eerdmans Publishing Co., 1945.

Feinberg, Charles. *Premillennialism or Amillennialism?* Grand Rapids: Zondervan Publishing House, 1936.

Finegan, Jack. *Handbook of Biblical Chronology.* Princeton: Princeton University Press, 1964.

Gaebelein, Arno C. *The Prophet Daniel.* New York: Our Hope Publishers, 1911.

Gibbon, Edward. *The Decline and Fall of the Roman Empire.* 6 vols. Boston: Phillips, Sampson, and Co., 1856.

Harrison, R. K. *Introduction to the Old Testament.* Grand Rapids: Wm. B. Eerdmans Publishing Co., 1969.

—————. *Old Testament Times.* Grand Rapids: Wm. B. Eerdmans Publishing Co., 1970.

Heslop, W. G. *Diamonds from Daniel.* Olivet, Ill.: Nazarene Publishing House, 1937.

Ironside, Henry A. *Lectures on Daniel the Prophet.* New York: Loizeaux Bros., 1920.

—————. *The Great Parenthesis.* 2d ed. Grand Rapids: Zondervan Publishing House, 1943.

Jeffery, Arthur. *The Book of Daniel, Introduction and Exegesis.* The

Interpreter's Bible, edited by George A. Buttrick, Vol. VI. New York: Abingdon-Cokesbury Press, 1956.

Josephus, Flavius. *Against Apion*. Translated by H. St. J. Thackeray. Vol. I. Loeb Classical Library. London: Heinemann, 1926.

—. *The Work of Flavius Josephus*. Translated by William Whiston. Philadelphia: John C. Winston Co., n.d.

Keil, Carl F. *The Book of the Prophet Daniel*. Biblical Commentary on the Old Testament, translated by M. G. Easton. Edinburgh: T. & T. Clark, 1891.

Kelley, William. *Lectures on the Book of Daniel*. 2d ed., London: G. Morrish, 1881.

Kennedy, Gerald. *Daniel*. The Interpreter's Bible, edited by George A. Buttrick. Vol. VI. New York: Abingdon-Cokesbury Press, 1956.

King, Geoffrey R. *Daniel*. Grand Rapids: Wm. B. Eerdmans Publishing Co., 1966.

Kromminga, D. H. *The Millennium*. Grand Rapids: Wm. B. Eerdmans Publishing Co., 1948.

Larkin, Clarence. *The Book of Daniel*. Philadelphia: Clarence Larkin, 1929.

LaSor, William S. *Amazing Dead Sea Scrolls*. Chicago: Moody Press, 1956.

Leupold, Herbert C. *Exposition of Daniel*. Grand Rapids: Baker Book House, 1969.

Luck, G. Coleman. *Daniel*. Chicago: Moody Press, 1958.

Mauro, Philip. *The Seventy Weeks and the Great Tribulation*. Boston: Scripture Truth Depot, 1923.

McClain, Alva J. *Daniel's Prophecy of the Seventy Weeks*. Grand Rapids: Zondervan Publishing House, 1940.

—. *The Greatness of the Kingdom*. Grand Rapids: Zondervan Publishing House, 1959.

Mendenhall, G. E. *Law and Covenant in Israel and the Ancient Near East*. The Biblical Colloquium, 1955.

Merrill, Eugene H. *An Historical Survey of the Old Testament*. Nutley, N.J.: The Craig Press, 1966.

Montgomery, James A. *A Critical and Exegetical Commentary on the Book of Daniel*. The International Critical Commentary. New York: Charles Scribner's Sons, 1927.

Newell, Philip R. *Daniel: the Man Greatly Beloved and His Prophecies*. Chicago: Moody Press, 1962.

Parker, R. A. and Duberstein, Waldo H. *Babylonian Chronology 626 B.C.-A.D. 45*. Chicago: University of Chicago Press, 1942.

Payne, J. Barton. *An Outline of Hebrew History*. Grand Rapids: Baker Book House, 1954.

—. *The Theology of the Older Testament*. Grand Rapids: Zondervan Publishing House, 1962.

Pentecost, J. Dwight. *Prophecy for Today*. Grand Rapids: Zondervan Publishing House, 1961.

————. *Things To Come*. Findlay, Ohio: Dunham Publishing Co., 1958.

Peters, George N. H. *The Theocratic Kingdom*. 3 vols. Grand Rapids: Kregel, 1952.

Pfeffer, Charles F., ed. *The Biblical World*. Grand Rapids: Baker Book House, 1966.

Porteous, Norman W. *Daniel: A Commentary*. Philadelphia: The Westminster Press, 1965.

Pritchard, James B., ed. *Ancient Near Eastern Texts Relating to the Old Testament*. Princeton: Princeton University Press, 1950.

Pusey, Edward B. *Daniel the Prophet*. New York: Funk & Wagnalls, 1891.

Rowley, Harold H. *Darius the Mede and the Four World Empires in the Book of Daniel*. Cardiff, Wales: University of Wales Press, 1935.

Schultz, Samuel J. *The Old Testament Speaks*. New York: Harper & Row, 1970.

Scofield, Cyrus I., ed. *Scofield Reference Bible*. New York: Oxford University Press, 1917.

Steen, J. Charleton. *God's Prophetic Programme as Revealed in the Book of Daniel*. London: Pickering & Inglis, n.d.

Strauss, Lehman. *The Prophecies of Daniel*. Neptune, N.J.: Loizeaux Bros., 1965.

Stuart, Moses. *A Commentary on the Book of Daniel*. Boston: Crocker & Brewster, 1850.

Talbot, Louis T. *The Prophecies of Daniel*. 3d ed. Wheaton, Ill.: Van Kampen Press, 1954.

Thiele, E. R. *The Mysterious Numbers of the Hebrew Kings*. rev. ed. Grand Rapids: Wm. B. Eerdmans Publishing Co., 1965.

Thomas, D. Winton, ed. *Archaeology and Old Testament Study*. New York: Oxford University Press, 1967.

————, ed. *Documents from Old Testament Times*. New York: Harper & Row, 1958.

Unger, Merrill F. *Introductory Guide to the Old Testament*. Grand Rapids: Zondervan Publishing House, 1952.

Walvoord, John F. *Daniel the Key to Prophetic Revelation*. Chicago: Moody Press, 1971.

————. *The Millennial Kingdom*. Grand Rapids: Zondervan Publishing House, 1959.

————. *The Nations in Prophecy*. Grand Rapids: Zondervan Publishing House, 1967.

————. *Israel in Prophecy*. Grand Rapids: Zondervan Publishing House, 1962.

————. *The Revelation of Jesus Christ*. Chicago: Moody Press, 1966.

Whitcomb, John C., Jr. *Darius the Mede.* Grand Rapids: Wm. B. Eerdmans Publishing Co., 1959.

Whitley, Charles H. H. *Daniel and His Prophecies.* London: Williams & Norgate, 1906.

Wilson, Robert Dick. "The Aramaic of Daniel." In *Biblical and Theological Studies.* New York: Charles Scribner's Sons, 1912.

———. *Studies in the Book of Daniel.* New York: G. P. Putnam's Sons, 1917.

———. "The Title 'King of Persia' in the Scriptures." *Princeton Theological Review* XV (1917), 90-145.

Wiseman, Donald J. *The Chronicles of the Chaldean Kings (626-556 B.C.).* London: Trustees of the British Museum, 1956.

———. "Nebuchadnezzar and the Last Days of Babylon." *Christianity Today,* II (Nov. 25, 1957), 7-10.

Wright, Charles H. H. *Daniel and His Prophecies.* London: Williams & Norgate, 1906.

Yamauchi, Edwin M. *Greece and Babylon.* Grand Rapids: Baker Book House, 1967.

Young, Edward J. *The Prophecy of Daniel.* Grand Rapids: Wm. B. Eerdmans Publishing Co., 1949.

Zockler, Otto. *The Book of the Prophet Daniel.* A Commentary on the Holy Scriptures, edited by John P. Lange, Vol. 13. New York: Charles Scribner's Sons, 1915.